"YOUR ISADORA"

The love story of
Isadora Duncan & Gordon Craig

DEC. 16 . 1904
Twovillins

"YOUR ISADORA"

The love story of Isadora Duncan & Gordon Craig

Edited,
with a connecting text,
by

Francis Steegmuller

Random House
& The New York Public Library
New York

Material owned by The New York Public Library:
Copyright © 1974
by The New York Public Library
Astor, Lenox and Tilden Foundations
Text and translations: Copyright © 1974
by Francis Steegmuller
All rights reserved under International and Pan-
American Copyright Conventions. Published in the
United States by Random House, Inc., New York,
and simultaneously in Canada by Random House
of Canada Limited, Toronto.

Library of Congress Cataloging in Publication Data
Duncan, Isadora, 1878-1927.
"Your Isadora": The love story of Isadora Duncan and Gordon Craig.
I.   Craig, Edward Gordon, 1872-1966.
II.   Steegmuller, Francis, 1906-   ed.
III.   Title.
GV1785.D8A43   793.3'2'0924   74-5178
ISBN 0-394-48698-6

Manufactured in the United States of America
First Edition
98765432

Designed by J. K. Lambert

FRONTISPIECE: *Isadora and Craig, December 1904.*
Inscribed by Craig: "Two Villains." Photograph probably by
Elise de Brouckère. (The Craig-Duncan Collection)

Editor's Foreword

THE CHIEF CONTENT OF THE PRESENT VOLUME IS THE MAJOR PORTION of the more than two hundred letters from the dancer Isadora Duncan to the artist and stage designer Edward Gordon Craig, written in Europe during the years of an association that began late in 1904. These letters deal with their meeting, their love, the birth of their daughter, and with their reading, thought and work: the dancing for which Isadora traveled throughout Europe, as far as the provinces of Russia; Craig's designing (and refusing to design) for European producers—Max Reinhardt, Eleonora Duse, Konstantin Stanislavski. Gradually Craig and Isadora became estranged, though never totally; their daughter died by drowning, and this later part of the story is told also in drafts of letters from Craig to Isadora. All these letters and drafts are published here for the first time.

Edward Gordon Craig, often called Gordon Craig, lived until 1966, when he died at the age of ninety-four. He preserved for many years a great mass of papers: letters both personal and professional, his stage designs and a celebrated library. The bulk of these he sold in 1957 to the Bibliothèque Nationale in Paris, where they remain. (A portion had been sold to Germany during the Second World War but was later restored to him.) His letters from Isadora, however, and his drafts of letters to her, he retained, along with much other relative material. In a series of manuscript notes, he has chronicled the task of rereading the letters:

Sept. 1944, Paris. Since 1904–8 I have not re-read her letters of that period—now I intend to read them once more. There will be pain in doing this perhaps—pain close to joy—remembering things that were most precious to us both.

Oct. 11, 1944. Now reading them—glancing at all to get the dates right & laying them in blue folders—a folder per year—though 1907 may take 2 folders. I find this work absorbingly interesting.

Oct. 24, 1944. [*Addressing himself*] But it proved such an emotional experience that you were pretty well prostrated after a week or ten days of reading & arranging & searching for the dates when written—and you had to send to Dr. Salomonov to come & put you right.

Oct. 25, 1944. The work is not yet over because although *more or less* in good order, flattened & in 2 good boxes, they can be still better ordered after I have gone through some Diaries & other papers—a longish work & a strain on the emotions assuredly but it has to be done.

When in 1962 Craig finally decided to sell, friends of The Dance Collection of The New York Public Library at Lincoln Center bought for the collection the letters and other documents pertaining to Isadora, forming what is now known as The Craig-Duncan Collection.[1] According to Craig's daughter Ellen, Craig had burned about ten letters that he thought "too personal."

Meanwhile, in 1956, Irma Duncan, who as Irma Erich-Grimme had become a child pupil of Isadora's in 1905 and subsequently, along with a few fellow pupils, had legally taken the name Duncan, presented documents and other items relating to Isadora to The Dance Collection. These, together with additional, later gifts, are known as The Irma Duncan Collection. Other collections of Craig-Duncan material also exist, some in private hands, others in the libraries of institutions—in particular The University of California (Los Angeles) and The Humanities Research Center at The Univer-

---

[1] Contributing to the purchase were: The Committee for The Dance Collection, The Cia Fornaroli Fund, Capezio Foundation, Mrs. Eugenia Delarova Doll, Charles Osborne, Mr. and Mrs. John D. Gordan, Jerome Robbins, Mr. and Mrs. Donald Hyde.

sity of Texas (Austin), which acquired from Craig's son Edward A. Craig papers known as The Craig Archives.

I have written a connecting text and notes making use of all these materials, as well as others, and have added some pages concerning Isadora's 1904 debut in St. Petersburg (now Leningrad) and her performances there and in Moscow early in 1905, with contemporary Russian comment on those recitals and their influence on the Russian ballet. None of this has hitherto been properly documented, and the narrative has been made possible chiefly by the letters themselves and by the kindness of Mme. Natalia Roslavleva, the historian of Russian ballet, in sending me articles from the Russian press.

In addition to the acknowledgments expressed elsewhere in this volume, I wish to thank the staff of The Dance Collection for its assistance in connection with the present work, and most particularly Nicki Nowlin Ostrom, a former member of the staff and compiler of the Register of The Craig-Duncan Collection, for her excellent arrangement and transcription of the letters, her suggested corrections of Craig's notes and chronology, and her constant cooperation. I am grateful for the unfailing generosity of Craig's son and biographer, Edward A. Craig. All material, published and unpublished, written by Edward Gordon Craig is quoted with the kind permission of The H. E. Gordon Craig, C.H., Estate, H. E. Robert Craig, Administrator. Anne Freedgood, of Random House, and David V. Erdman and William Coakley, of The New York Public Library, have been very helpful. The participation of my wife, Shirley Hazzard, has been my greatest joy in the work.

The idiosyncratic spelling and punctuation used by Isadora and by Gordon Craig have been in part retained, in order to convey a feeling of the original documents. Italics in the letters and other documents reflect some of Isadora and Craig's underlinings, which are frequent and often multiple. Isadora's innumerable capitalizations have not always been reproduced when they seem merely capricious or reflections of German usage. The letters are numbered as in The Craig-Duncan Collection, identified, as in the catalog, by the letters "CD."

F.S.

EDWARD GORDON CRAIG
ON ISADORA DUNCAN:

—— *1905* ——

"Inspiration is given out by the thousand volt per second from Miss D.
And I am alive again (as artist) through her."

—— *1943* ——

"She & I were two artists—I suppose I can state that as something certain."

—— *1952* ——

"She was something quite different from anyone and anything else."

Contents

"YOUR ISADORA"

The love story of
Isadora Duncan & Gordon Craig

Two Artists

THE LOVE STORY THAT WILL BE TOLD HERE IN THE LETTERS OF ISADORA Duncan to Edward Gordon Craig and supplemented by passages from Craig's own writings and other sources—a story that is now published in detail for the first time—is that of an attachment between two artists, extending over a period of several years. Isadora Duncan had a loveliness of face, figure, movement, mind and spirit; Craig was so handsome that Oscar Wilde once sent him a mash note (confiscated by his mother, the actress Ellen Terry). When they met in Berlin in 1904, Isadora was twenty-six, an American dancer in her artistic prime and full fame, with, according to her memoirs, only one earlier physical love affair; Craig was thirty-two, English, a great amorist who had been a prominent actor and was now setting out to revolutionize the art of stage design and production.

Isadora, whose dancing was watched by millions during her generation-long career, who in the last year or so of her life (she died in 1927) wrote, or wrote parts of, a sensational volume of memoirs, who is the subject of a shelf of books and the heroine of two films (in neither of which is she portrayed by a dancer), is by far the more widely known of the two. Craig, although he is impersonated in one of the Isadora films, is the hero of no film of his own; he is, however, a hero in the world into which he was born, and which

he continued to make his own—the world of the theater. There are
several books about Craig, as there are many books about Isadora,
but their readers are for the most part students or practitioners or
amateurs of the arts of the stage; his own writings, too, are familiar
chiefly to latter-day citizens of his own world. But to them he is
distinctly a hero, one of the heroes of the modernization of stage
design and production, along with the predecessors and contemporaries whom he himself admired: the Duke of Saxe-Meiningen,
Appia, Stanislavski, Antoine—and to a certain extent Max Reinhardt,
less intransigent than the rest and therefore better known, who
was Craig's great admirer and who sought in vain for his collaboration. There has long been this special cult of Craig and his genius
of the theater, as there has long been the very much wider cult of
Isadora and her genius of the dance.

IN 1904 IN GERMANY THE ISADORA CULT WAS FERVENT, AND WAS
extending far beyond that country's borders. Martin Shaw, for a
time her conductor, was soon to write almost casually of one of her
performances in Berlin: "Emerging from the stage door, we encountered the usual crowd of admirers lining the way to her carriage . . .
In St. Petersburg, Berlin, Paris, Vienna, Munich, Copenhagen, Stockholm, Amsterdam, her name was a household word even among the
ordinary public." Her friend Kathleen Bruce wrote of "the wild
enthusiasts who surged around the stage door and yelled their delight." And Craig writes of "[Germany,] that pleasant land, where
crowds of people ran to 'see her plain' as she passed in her carriage—
& crowded into the theatre to see her dance."

Isadora had come, literally, a long way—and by the hard way.
From the books (her own and others) something is known of her
childhood: her father's early disappearance, her mother's piano-
teaching in a small house in San Francisco[1] to support the four
children, Isadora, Elizabeth, Augustin and Raymond; Isadora's remembrance of herself "as a child in California, beside the sea, endeav-
oring to follow in rhythmic movements the rhythm of the waves."
Many of her letters in the present volume speak of this feeling of

---

[1] See notes for this page.

harmony with nature—a sense which, as she practiced and matured, she was increasingly able to express in dance and communicate in an extraordinary degree to her audiences. Though she claimed to have been completely self-taught as a dancer (when an interviewer asked who had taught her to dance, she replied, "Terpsichore"), some, including Craig, believed her to have been influenced by the theories of François Delsarte, whose *System of Expression*, stressing flexibility and body grace rather than formal gesture and position, was published in English translation in New York in 1885; certainly she was dancing to music in an unusually graceful and imaginative free-form manner as a very young girl.

Especially in her interviews addressed to a large public, Isadora encouraged the popular notion of art, including her own art, as being purely "spontaneous," "natural," and "effortless"; at other times, in some of her essays, she emphasized her research. The letters to Craig reveal both these elements: the indubitable natural gift, and yet the dedication with which she studied, practiced and prepared for her performances as well as her reflections on the nature of dance—in particular its relation to music and poetry. Isadora possessed in large measure the essential spontaneity of the artist which wells up mysteriously; she also achieved that apparent effortlessness which is the result of great discipline.

Perhaps Isadora's sense of having "just growed" into her art and personality was at the root of the nickname she and Craig shared for herself: Topsy. Though she founded a school and exerted a lasting influence on the dance, a Topsy-Terpsichore element was at the basis of her own presence and rendering—what Alexandre Benois called, in her, motivation "not by logic, but by elemental inspiration."

Starting out in her teens to earn her living, she found small roles in Chicago and New York revues and worked for a time in England; back in New York there were dance lessons, a pair of solo performances—one to music by Ethelbert Nevin, the other to illustrate a lecture on Omar Khayyám—and engagements in the homes of the rich. Then all five of the nearly penniless, semi-bohemian Duncans transferred themselves to England by cattle boat and for a time lived hand-to-mouth in London. Thanks to her talents and beauty, to her winning American ways, and to meetings with Mrs. Patrick Campbell and the painter Charles Hallé (son of the conductor), Isadora began to be applauded in the city's artistic circles. In Paris, where the family next moved, she danced in fashionable salons, including those of the Prince de Polignac and Comtesse Greffulhe, and was admired, painted, drawn and sculpted by artists such as Carrière and Rodin. Meanwhile she read poetry and philosophy and listened to music of all kinds: in music she found inspiration and accompaniment to her own art, which she was constantly refining and intensifying. And she was watching: she had opportunity to watch, among others, two great actresses, Ellen Terry and Eleonora Duse, with both of whom she was later to become involved—in different ways, and in each case through Gordon Craig.

Her first popular success came when, after dancing for a time on the Continent with Loie Fuller and her troupe, she was "discovered" by the impresario Alexandre Grosz; thirty solo performances which he arranged for her in Budapest were all sold out, and with that triumph fresh she moved on to Germany. In Berlin she was introduced to fashionable and artistic society by Frau von Parmentier, sister of one of the ladies-in-waiting to the Kaiserin, and became the rage. After another visit to Paris she and her family made a pilgrimage of several months to Greece. She had long had romantic feelings about classical Greece—ancient vase-paintings and sculpture had already inspired her style of dress and some of her dance movements—but about Greece she was no mere humorless sentimentalist: "We could not have the feelings of the ancient Greeks," she later said. ". . . I was, after all, but a Scotch-Irish-American. Perhaps, through some affinity, nearer allied to the Red Indians than to the Greeks."

In Berlin she had given a lecture, "The Dance of the Future," which was translated and published as an illustrated pamphlet, *Der Tanz der Zukunft*, and on her return from Greece in the summer of 1904, at the invitation of Wagner's widow, Frau Cosima Wagner, she danced—barefoot among the other, more conventionally clad Graces—in the Bacchanale of *Tannhäuser* at Bayreuth. By the time she met Craig the following December she had recently been dancing again in Budapest, and in Warsaw, and had just signed a contract to appear for the first time in St. Petersburg, then the capital of Russia. And, with her older sister Elizabeth, she had announced the opening of a school "for the regeneration of the art of the dance" in the Berlin suburb of Grünewald.

Craig later wrote of Isadora's dancing, "It's a great, a rare gift brought to perfection by 18 years of persistent labour," and her life had, in fact, been dedicated almost entirely to her work. It was only in Budapest that she had had her "first" sexual awakening—a brief affair with a handsome and sensual Hungarian actor.

Her dance programs at this time were of several kinds. One was against a background of waltzes, with orchestra and piano accompaniment: Brahms, Chopin, Schubert, and ending with Strauss's "Blue Danube"—always a tremendously popular finale, for which Isadora herself soon became somewhat apologetic. There were also all-Chopin programs. One of the most frequent offerings was called *Dance Idylls*, which usually included "Primavera, from the painting by Botticelli,"[1] "Musette" (Couperin), "Tambourin" (Rameau), "Angel with Violin" (Péri), "Narcissus" (Ethelbert Nevin), "Pan and Echo, Idyll by Moschos" (Ferrari) and, after the intermission, selections from Gluck's *Orfeo ed Euridice*. There was also a program consisting almost entirely of music from Gluck's *Iphigénie en Aulide*. It should be kept in mind that during these years, except for a few appearances with her pupils, Isadora always danced alone; there was no relief by assistants or a company. Craig wrote later of her magnetism onstage: "Isadora had such a powerful influence on the public that I would not even have risked placing a Shakespearian play before or after her performance, acted by fine actors. Fine acting beside a magnetic personality is swamped by the personality."

EDWARD GORDON CRAIG NEEDS MORE INTRODUCTION. ONE OF THE great figures of the twentieth-century theater, he is also one of the least explored of modern geniuses. His relative obscurity outside professional circles results partly from his own unresolved, protean personality.

---

[1] Isadora's "Primavera" costume, with its wreath of artificial flowers (though she wore fresh flowers whenever possible), is in The Irma Duncan Collection, The Dance Collection, The New York Public Library.

His mother, Ellen Terry, for half a century both "stage sweetheart" of all England and the nation's greatest actress, had surpassing
charm, and a will and generosity to match the charm. The daughter
of strolling players, she began her acting career in childhood. As a
girl of sixteen she married the eminent forty-six-year-old painter
George Frederick Watts, who prized her as a model, but after ten
months they separated. Four years later she fell in love with the
architect and designer Edward Godwin, abandoned the stage, and
went to live with him in a country house of his own design. Godwin's
work was "modern," in the idiom of the day: he was the designer of
Whistler's "White House" in Chelsea, and examples of his furniture
are on permanent exhibition in The Victoria and Albert Museum.
He and Ellen Terry were together six years, and she bore him two
children, Edith and Edward, who were, of course, without proper
family name. To support them—Godwin having shown himself
financially irresponsible—she returned to the stage; Godwin left her,
and she went on to achieve legendary fame in a career that ended
only with her death in 1928.

It was extraordinary, in 1874, for a woman known to have two
illegitimate children to confront and conquer the English public.
Ellen Terry's stage personality was bewitching, her character phe-
nomenally rich and full, and of this fullness motherhood was no less
a part than the rest. Her children were loved; with her when she was
acting in London, with governesses or at school during her inevitable
absences on tour, they were at all times the object of her constant
attention. Her care for them was continuous—before, during and
after her brief second unsatisfactory marriage (Watts divorced her
for adultery with Godwin) to an actor, Charles Kelly. The two
separated in 1880 and Kelly died five years later. In 1878 she had
begun her celebrated stage partnership with Henry Irving at the
Lyceum Theatre, and it was in 1885—when they were on tour in
Chicago and Teddy, the Gordon Craig of this volume, had been
sent for during his Christmas holidays because his mother was lonely
for him—that the boy played his first stage part: that of "Joey the
gardener's boy" in a melodrama called *The Fate of Eugene Aram*.
This was two days before his thirteenth birthday; at seventeen he
was expelled from his school in Heidelberg, because of his "very

ill-disciplined nature, with an impulsive temper," and Irving took him into the Lyceum. His mother had him trained in fencing and French and sent him to drill three times a week at the Knightsbridge Barracks. For eight years he acted with the Lyceum company, playing countless roles in Shakespearean repertory and modern drama, and toured summers with other troupes. He had been christened at sixteen and taken the name Edward Henry Gordon Craig. His son and biographer, Edward A. Craig, tells us that the name Craig derived from Ailsa Craig, the island off the Firth of Clyde, which had fascinated Edith and Edward as children, and that he had taken the names "Edward after his father, Henry after his godfather, Irving, and Gordon after his godmother, Lady Gordon." On the stage he was Gordon Craig; to his family and friends he was Teddy or Ted.

Ellen Terry always said that her son was "consummate" as an actor and considered his Hamlet one of the best she had seen. Craig was very well received, but the acting profession was uncongenial to him. He appears to have felt growing distaste for the company of other actors, finding them all too often dishearteningly unworthy of the great lines they spoke; his son suggests that Craig also was oppressed by the fugitive nature of an actor's fame and that, rightly or wrongly, he came to suspect Henry Irving—who had inevitably become something of a father figure—of having lost interest in him. Though he always wrote with near-reverence of his mother and Irving, he was to speak contemptuously of actors in general and would even propose replacing them, in an ideal production, with puppets. What he turned to quite early—drawing, stage design and production—brought him closer to the profession that had been his father's. Craig had not seen him after infancy and had no memory of him (he died when his son was fourteen), but Ellen Terry never spoke except with respect of Godwin—whose family name Craig could not bear but whose first name he had taken as his own, and with the modernity of whose artistic work he was always to say he felt a kinship.

At twenty-five Craig was designing posters and bookplates in London, launching a short-lived magazine of the arts called *The Page* and publishing a children's book, *Gordon Craig's Book of Penny Toys*. At twenty-seven he formed with his friend Martin Shaw the Purcell Operatic Society, which during the next few years staged

Dido and Aeneas[1] in a production of Craig's own design that attracted much attention and remains celebrated in theater annals, then followed it with an entertainment called *A Masque of Love* (arranged from a play by Phineas Fletcher with Purcell's music) and highly distinguished productions of Handel's *Acis and Galatea*, Laurence Housman's *Bethlehem, a Nativity Play*, Ibsen's *The Vikings*, and *Much Ado About Nothing*. Craig's drawings for these productions of the *fin de siècle* and earliest 1900's reveal his immediately revolutionary style: instead of a clutter of furnishings posed against a background of realistic interior architecture, or realistic exterior architecture against realistic foliage, his stage was a near-abstraction of spaces and planes, with elevations disposed in curves and angles in a way that evoked, with the aid of lighting, the essence of the work being played and all the necessary settings, from intimate corners and mysterious recesses to deep vistas and heights of simple grandeur. Today, when many of Craig's inventions have become part and parcel of stagecraft, the drawings and photographs seem to have been done but recently—or even to be visions of the future.

All of these productions were *succès d'estime*, and most of them were financed to the best of her ability by Ellen Terry;[2] they brought Craig both financial debts and the admiration and companionship of poets, artists and critics—W. B. Yeats, Augustus John, Arthur Symons, William Rothenstein, Max Beerbohm, and many more. Beerbohm noted of young Craig at this time: "Playing piano—leaping up —throwing back hair—flowing cloak. German student—Heidelberg —one expected sabre cuts—Unearthly—The Young Bacchus—His amours, almost mythological . . . pure type of artist—*Genius*."

[1] Martin Fallas Shaw (1875-1959) was an organist and composer of songs and other music. At the present writing, 1973, the Kensington Borough Council is trying to save from demolition the Coronet Theatre in Notting Hill, where the Craig *Dido and Aeneas* was staged.

[2] "Ted caught socialism long ago," Ellen Terry wrote to George Bernard Shaw in 1896, when Craig was twenty-four. "He is susceptible and catches most things. Against the advice of my friends, I allow him £500 each year so that he may be laid hold on by his whims and fancies whilst he is very young (he's a baby) and get it over very soon." £500 in those days had approximately the purchasing power of $12,000 in 1973—plenty for a young bachelor to get along on but not adequate to such costly artistic "whims and fancies" as Craig's stage productions.

BY THE TIME THE THIRTY-TWO-YEAR-OLD CRAIG LEFT LONDON FOR Berlin, where he had been invited to design avant-garde stage productions, the known results of his amours were seven children he had already fathered on three different mothers: his wife May Gibson, whom he had married at twenty-one and had left during her fourth pregnancy, and who was now divorcing him; his mistress Jess Dorynne, whom he had also left during her pregnancy; and Elena Meo, a charming young Italo-English violinist, who was then expecting her third child by him and who was to remain faithful to him, despite his countless infidelities, throughout her life.

In addition to his sexual magnetism, his beauty, and the capacity for tenderness sporadically evident in his writings, Craig was endowed with a galaxy of other attractions and talents. Not only was there his genius for theatrical innovation and invention, his "consummate" acting, his skill at drawing; he had a driving enthusiasm and a love of both simple and intellectual conviviality—with the distinguished friends he had left in London, and with those he was later to make, and sometimes retain, in Europe, among them Count Kessler, Max Reinhardt, Eleonora Duse. At the Moscow Art Theatre members of the company sat around him and made notes as he supervised what was to be his most famous success: a production of *Hamlet* that remained in the repertory for many years. He had an eye for the authentic wherever it might be found, from the brush strokes in a painting by Van Eyck to a *festa* in a Tuscan farmyard; commenting on Isadora, he once said that before meeting her he had met dancers only "in a street in Genoa and . . . in a barn near York." As he grew older his conversation seems to have become ever more pungent, ever more abundant in original observation, and his memory stayed firm. Those who knew him in his nineties describe his company as the most enjoyable imaginable. His spoken and written expression was rich and dramatic, due in part to his Shakespearean training; his vocabulary was unique—poetic, inspired. The charm and originality of the man leap out from the series of enchanting talks, later put on records, that he delivered on BBC radio in 1952 when he was eighty —among them electrifying commentaries on Ellen Terry, Henry Irving and Isadora.[1] His delivery, as the distinguished American Craig

[1] See pp. 359–363.

scholar Arnold Rood has said, is that of "a nineteenth-century actor at no remove whatever."

Indeed, Craig himself, in life, is an entire repertory of Shakespearean roles. It is impossible to speak of *duality* in his nature: the volatility of his temperament, as many-faceted as the diversity of his talents, nevertheless amalgamated, incredibly, as the reader of the present correspondence will discover, into one extraordinary being.

In this convivial friend and irresistible lover, this theatrical genius who influenced a revolution in twentieth-century stage design, one self-destructive flaw predominates, permeating his relations with the world and constricting his professional life. Throughout his career he was inhibited from working with others to a degree that continually impelled him to impose impossible conditions and thus deliberately abort most of the productions he was invited to design. Time after time his would-be collaborators were left exasperated and disappointed. He obsessively insisted on his "independence"—and always he was independent in his artistry—but much of what he called independence suggests a fear of the world, and it thwarted his own fulfillment as a *metteur en scène*. The number of his actual productions, during the sixty-two years following his departure from London, was less than half a dozen. He was at times the most arrogant of men, his arrogance often recognizable as a shield. Edward A. Craig links his father's fear and the defensive arrogance to the pall of illegitimate birth.

The fears that prevented Craig from working with others were reproduced in his private associations. "Be firm," he would tell himself at moments of crisis: "firm" meaning something close to "cautious" or "cowardly"—or "terrified." He passed through spasms of self-abasement, even self-disgust, when he could write to Isadora, "I was nothing, and you were you," and, commenting on harsh words he had sent her, "EGC, beastly hurt, disgustingly cruel"; pathos, in his story, runs parallel to his talents and his intractability. His unfailing admiration and praise of Isadora's art did not prevent him from exploiting her or from writing scurrilously of her in notes and notebooks whose preservation he took pains to assure. His fears were related to his own capacity to exploit the affections of others: the phenomenal nonagenarian had thrived not only on the devotion of artistic admirers but on the indulgence, indeed the self-immolation, of Elena Meo and their daughter Ellen, whose servitude he took for granted. "He could see a vision in a cloud of smoke," his son has written of him, "but he was too short-sighted to see a tear in a loved one's eye. Confronted by emotion, he 'just did not know what to do.' " In later years the fears rose to paranoia: Edward A. Craig tells of his father locking himself in a darkened room for days, convinced that "people were trying to destroy him with spells," and of his sometimes rushing suddenly, in the midst of a conversation, to open a door, lest someone be listening outside to "steal his ideas." In fact, because of his own failure, or refusal, to put his ideas into practice, many of them *were* appropriated by others, and Craig of course fulminated. Along with the paranoia he had the paranoid's preternatural insight into human behavior, including his own. "I should say that I had a touch of madness in me," he wrote of himself at eighty-four.

It is hard to realize, despite the breath-taking modernity of his theatrical art, that Craig died only a few years ago, for he had little in common with the "celebrities" of our day. His was the great force of genius that was bred by the Victorian age. Both his impetus and his staying power were tremendous: for all his fears and near-madness he ripened to the end. His demands for indulgence and his unsparing egocentricity were not, in fact, simple offerings to the Great God Self: as he himself said, it was "all for Hecuba." Born in an age of suffocating convention, he—and Isadora too—were nevertheless capable of living as total originals outside society and without giving undue weight to their social unconventionality.

Victorian society could stifle, but it was not yet—for those of independent means, professions and character—the mass society. Unlike modern "celebrities," Craig did not consider it his right to be rich, nor did he find it imperative to be publicly acclaimed by his contemporaries. What money he had went not for ostentation, but for his art: with the only large sum that ever came to him he founded a school—as, indeed, did Isadora. Much about him, we shall see, was monstrous; yet he had the *feu sacré*, and the term "sacred monster" might well have been invented to describe Edward Gordon Craig.

IT WAS TOWARD THE END OF 1903 THAT THERE APPEARED, ON ONE OF his frequent visits to London, the man who was to be responsible for Craig's arrival in Berlin. This was Count Harry Kessler, Anglophile, Francophile, half-Irish German diplomat and amateur of the arts. He lived in Weimar, where there was a theater financed by the Court.

"Kessler had seen *Acis and Galatea* and *The Masque of Love*," Edward A. Craig writes in his biography of his father, "and he had appreciated the beauty and simplicity of Craig's work, as well as its particularly English quality. But when he saw *The Vikings* he was even more enthusiastic, for this time there seemed to be a Wagnerian tone in the whole conception of the production which he knew would appeal to a German audience. He wanted to meet Craig in order to tell him how much he admired his work and to see if he would contemplate visiting Weimar and producing something in the theatre there." Craig told Kessler, his son says, that "he would certainly not accept the invitation unless he was given full power to carry out his ideas: when he had been in control, *Dido* and *Acis* and *The Masque of Love* had been good . . . but *The Vikings* had been a battle for artistic control all the time and the results had suffered. He had learned a lesson that he would not forget."

In January 1904, Kessler wrote Craig suggesting that "he send over some of his 'delightful drawings' for an exhibition in his private gallery in Weimar; he was convinced that if he could show some of Craig's work to Dr. Otto Brahm, the new director of the Lessing Theatre in Berlin, he could persuade him to give Craig a contract, especially as Brahm had a production of Thomas Otway's *Venice Preserved* in mind, obviously a play for an Englishman to design. [The play had been translated into German by the poet Hugo von Hofmannsthal, whom Kessler had also introduced to Brahm.] . . . On June 13 a letter arrived from the Lessing Theatre in Berlin; it was signed by Dr. Otto Brahm . . . It began as follows: 'I have heard your artistic capabilities very well spoken of, which you have put to use on the London stage so that you may now lend us artistic support . . .' Brahm went on to suggest that Ted should go to Berlin for a *'trial period'* from September to October, and after that make a contract for a yearly salary, to be paid monthly. The reference to a 'trial period' infuriated Ted: 'It suggests doubt in your mind as to my work,' he wrote. After much further correspondence . . . it was agreed that Ted should go to Berlin for a period of four months, during which time they would design the production of *Venice Preserved* and he could prepare the designs for the scenes and costumes. For this he would receive £200, some of which would be paid in advance. If they found they worked well together a contract would be prepared, with a starting fee of £500 a year." Craig set out for Germany on August 23, 1904, leaving considerable debts behind him; his mother had not been able to pay for everything, and his sense of financial responsibility was proving to be as undeveloped as his father's.[1]

From the moment of arrival, the story of his life in Berlin is one of artistic friendships—he was introduced to "everyone" by Kessler—and of the first appearance of the work pattern that recurred throughout his life: the ever-repeated refusal of what he called "compromise" and what actually involved on many occasions no more than co-operation. In the case of *Venice Preserved*, it must be said that he was given considerable provocation.

Otto Brahm was the quintessence of Teutonic arrogance; one has the impression that he was not overjoyed by the arrival of the young Englishman, who, he may have felt, had been imposed on him by Count Kessler. In arrogance, however, Brahm had this time met his match. Edward A. Craig tells of how, when Brahm sent word to Craig through an assistant that he was to "get in touch with the stage-manager, the scene-painters and mechanics, and to discuss all technical points with them," Craig replied: "I am doing the scenes, costumes, properties, and lighting scheme for 'Venice Preserved.' I hope to deliver them soon—Then Dr. Brahm's mechanics can tell him how they propose to manipulate the production. If they then find it an impossible riddle, I shall have much pleasure in showing Dr. Brahm how it is to be done."

All Brahm really wanted was drawings, and when Craig sent him only two, refusing all others pending assurance that he would be given a free hand in the production rather than be considered "a mere designer of scenery," Brahm terminated the agreement. "Craig wrote to Brahm insisting that his name should only be associated with the two settings he had designed and asking for printer's

---

[1] "My disgusting habit," he wrote Martin Shaw about this time, "is only to borrow from mama & call it no borrowing."

proof of the programme in order to make sure that his request was carried out." Controversy followed, with a letter from Craig printed in a newspaper and a subsequent interview with Brahm; ". . . and gradually the argument was lost in the winter snows. Craig had been in Berlin for five months and had seen Brahm only briefly two or three times, all communications having been second hand . . . It seemed a pity that Kessler had ever brought them together."

In December, after the break with Brahm and apparently an offer from another Berlin director, Craig wrote to Martin Shaw:

Martin dear Martin . . . As crazy & untamed as ever I have just returned a direktor a bran new contract to produce a play here . . . Say nothing of it to anyone— unless I do— they would not understand— but you understand how we return continents unaccepted when wrongly offered— how much more so mere contracts. Such long stories I have to tell you for your ear only (the whole truth) of strivings against untold odds— of outside failure & interior triumph— of slowly building-up of unshakeable foundations which will not let the world itself some day destroy them.

. . . Do you know— you can't quite— of the joy I have had for one moment looking forward to produce a play here, & now the *beyond joy* that I have refused— but the first joy was so young and looked so pretty— the old feeling— so strong in one, to be *doing*. Still my idea grows down and down spreading out roots as firm as steel or granite— soon a little bit of shoot may appear above ground—

The episode of Craig and Brahm, along with the letter to Martin Shaw, sketch, in brief, Craig's loftiness as artist and his intractability as practical man of the theater. In the pages that follow one will see him often irritated by lack of artistic understanding or frustrated by lack of financial means, and, on a few great occasions, fulfilled in success; yet there is always that *"beyond joy"* of "outside failure" when proposals are "wrongly offered." Joy in "outside failure" was to be so striking a characteristic of this immensely gifted man that one cannot help sensing a link between that particular satisfaction and certain other, more outright forms of irresponsibility and self-destructiveness that were also parts of his nature.

To continue to have faith and pride in one's work in the face of professional or popular indifference or scorn can, of course, be a supreme virtue—as Yeats said, ". . . . of all things known that is most difficult"; still, on the other hand, there is excess and disequilibrium in Craig's arrogance and in his perpetual prizing, glorifying and even inducing of practical failure.

IN THIS HE DIFFERED GREATLY FROM ISADORA DUNCAN, WHOSE POPULAR and artistic success left her remarkably free of vainglory of any kind. They met—two young English-speaking foreigners in Berlin's artistic society—in December 1904, shortly after Craig's break with Brahm.

Appointments in Berlin:
Book Topsy

W<small>E WERE BOTH IN THE 30'S,"</small> C<small>RAIG WROTE, NOT QUITE ACCURATELY,</small>
about his first having heard of Isadora, "which is not so very young
—but it is youth at its best I suppose . . . I was a producer of plays,
operas and ballets— not the usual kind of producer— in fact friends
in London who had seen her in Germany said to me that she was
the person for me— meaning that she as dancer would be the person
who would best understand what it was I was doing and who could
enter into the work better than anyone else. It was a fact— but talk
means little to a young artist of my experience in the theatre and
the name I.D. meant nothing to me and I forgot it almost as soon as
it was spoken."

And then in Germany her name came up again:

I had heard that there was a sort of governess who had taken to dancing
in an artistic manner— at whom some people laughed, while others
crowded in thousands to see her dance— the name Isadora Duncan. It was
chiefly in Weimar that the laughter was to be heard. Weimar at that time
was a center of culture and Graf Kessler welcomed (as a rule) the best
artists from other cities of Germany and from other lands too— France,
England, Holland, Russia. But America and dancing were not as yet
thought about in Weimar. The whole group surrounding the Graf were

at that time very critical of this dancer, and as I went to Weimar *before* seeing her dance and *before* speaking with her, the notion of a heavy-footed American who pranced was conveyed to me.

Nothing screamingly funny about a governess from America taking off her boots (she wore none) or sandals (she had some) and dancing nicely on her bare feet . . . but here came the trouble, here was the true reason for the laughter. She didn't dance nicely— she danced "artistically," said the Weimar group. But Munich, Berlin, Dresden and Vienna added "with genius."

. . . That explains why Weimar laughed. Dance from an American was a strange thought— GENIUS too! ! !

ISADORA'S AUTOBIOGRAPHY, *My Life*, CONTAINS THE FOLLOWING FLORID account of her first meeting with Craig:

One night in 1905 I was dancing in Berlin. Although as a rule I never notice the audience when I am dancing—they always seem to me like some great god representing Humanity—this evening I was aware of some personality sitting in the front row. Not that I looked, or saw, who it was, but I was psychically aware of its presence, and when the performance was over, there came into my loge a beautiful being. But he was very angry.

"You are marvellous!" he exclaimed. "You are wonderful! But why have you stolen my ideas? Where did you get my scenery?"

"What are you talking about? These are my own blue curtains. I invented them when I was five years old, and I have danced before them ever since!"

"No! They are my *décors* and my ideas! But you are the being I imagined in them. You are the living realisation of all my dreams."

"But who are you?"

Then came from his mouth these wonderful words:

"I am the son of Ellen Terry."

Ellen Terry, my most perfect ideal of woman! Ellen Terry. . . !

"Why, you must come home and have supper with us," said my unsuspecting mother. "Since you take such an interest in Isadora's art, you must come home to supper with us."

And Craig came home to supper.

So much of that is wrong, including the date, that in his copy of *My Life*, now in the Bibliothèque Nationale in Paris, Craig has festooned the page with corrections and written in the margin, "This cannot have been written by I.D." The mistakes on that page are not the only inaccuracies that have caused many to suspect that Isadora's manuscript of *My Life* was tampered with after her death by "friends" or editors or both (it was published posthumously); one writer on Isadora has suggested of this particular passage that she may have written it that way deliberately: "Isadora sometimes invented[1] anecdotes to make a point, and here the point seems to be the unexpected kinship between her ideas and Gordon Craig's."

Whatever the case may be, there exists a notebook entitled *Book Topsy* in Craig's hand (or rather hands: his chirography varied enormously). *Book Topsy*, which Craig augmented and emended throughout his long life, was chiefly written at the time of his meeting with Isadora in 1904, and describes the event quite precisely in Craig's original and vivid way. Confirming one of his corrections in his copy of *My Life, Book Topsy* shows that Craig and Isadora met before he ever saw her dance. The following is a transcription of parts of the hitherto unpublished *Book Topsy*, with the 1904 and later entries melded, and interspersed here and there with other remarks which Craig wrote elsewhere about the meeting and its sequel.

Book Topsy

It was in Berlin in 1904 that I first saw her— I am not quite certain of the date but it was a day or so before December 16.

ISADORA. A woman of brains & beauty— not a little woman, nor a huge one— but the right size—

The expression of her face changes & seems to me to be at times the faces of very many women I have known . . . Each day I suddenly recognize a familiar face in hers— or a familiar voice— It's queer.

I think she is really Aphrodite—which accounts for it.[2]

---

[1] However, see Craig's angry draft letter about the "blue curtains," and accompanying notes, on pp. 302 and 305.

[2] "I will give you the reason for my writing that line," Craig says later in *Book Topsy*, addressing Isadora herself. "I think you never defied the Gods. I once did go so far as to say 'If Venus herself should come down to earth I

She is the calmest thing I have ever seen in a woman.[1]

I met her one afternoon at her flat in Hardenburgstrasse, Berlin— taken there by Elise de Brouckere.[2] I entered the room with my eyeglasses off— so I could not see very well— I was introduced first to her sister Elizabeth— then to her— & her mother & so on— then to Sarah her sister-in-law. And Sarah's daughter, Temple, & Sarah's ~~husband~~ lover Augustin Duncan.

A nice group these 3 make. Why aren't they happy.

Owing to my short sight (when without glasses) at first I took Elizabeth for the famous dancer I had heard about & was struck by her strangely harsh accent—I felt puzzled but told myself at once that often it is the small & insignificant women who are remarkable. "What sort of dance can she put up" thought I [Elizabeth Duncan was lame]— & then I came to Isadora. Augustin Duncan I took to at once as most people did owing to his personal charm—

Isadora talks a lot of nonsense the 1st day— shows me gods— & pictures & all . . . A book with dancing figures— She was in fine spun robes— simple & lovely. (All this time I have not seen her dance, & I find she is a nice Greekish lady by art & a fine American girl by nature, and I am sure I shall be bored by her dancing.) She then talks on & on about the way she likes her theatre to be shaped— curving her arms to describe something. (This curving the arms was a movement of embracing an immense ball.) She at once suggests the amateur-hypnotic lady & I should distrust her if she were not beautiful & Beauty is the only thing we can entirely trust. This reference to her beauty is rather strange, for in features she was not beautiful, but in *movement* she made up for the lack of Mary Anderson or Lily Langtry features—

At this point the chronicle of *Book Topsy* is interrupted by the absence of two pages. "Someone seems to have got at this book

---

would not ———.' And then a very few days later— you. Venus is kind— but she punished all the same in this strange way. How? No, no . . . only a poet or a musician could tell it."

[1] Elsewhere Craig wrote [CD *339*]: "Never is Miss Duncan in a hurry. It is one of her most marked characteristics that she does nothing hurriedly— in speech, action, in her work, or, when giving directions about it. Perfect natural ease acquired by very few."

[2] In London, Craig had known Elise de Broukère's sister Jean, who had been one of the many enthusiastic amateur members of the Purcell Operatic Society.

though locked up— it seems to be torn out— a pity," Craig wrote on the next surviving page. "The loss of these 2 pages is a big loss to me today (1944). They described my going to see her dance a Chopin programme (to piano not orchestra), my astonishment & happiness, & my visit to her dressing room after the performance." Later, in his BBC radio talk about Isadora, he recounted the content of the lost pages:

I shall never forget the first time I saw her come on to an empty plat-form to dance. It was in Berlin, the year 1904—please make a note of that, somebody says it was 1905—the month December. Not on a theatre stage was this performance, but in a concert-hall, and you know what the plat-forms of concert-halls were like in 1904.

She came through some small curtains which were not much taller than she was herself; she came through them and walked down to where a musician, his back turned to us, was seated at a grand piano; he had just finished playing a short prelude by Chopin when in she came, and in some five or six steps was standing by the piano, quite still and, as it were, listening to the hum of the last notes. Quite still . . . You might have counted five, or even eight, and then there sounded the voice of Chopin again, in a second prelude or etude; it was played through gently and came to an end and she had not moved at all. Then one step back or side-ways, and the music began again as she went moving on before or after it. Only just moving—not pirouetting or doing any of those things which we expect to see, and which a Taglioni or a Fanny Elssler would have certainly done. She was speaking in her own language—do you under-stand? her own language: have you got it?—not echoing any ballet master, and so she came to move as no one had ever seen anyone move before. The dance ended, and again she stood quite still. No bowing, no smiling—nothing at all. Then again the music is off, and she runs from it —it runs after her then, for she has gone ahead of it.

How is it that we know she is speaking her own language? We know it, for we see her head, her hands, gently active, as are her feet, her whole person. And if she is speaking, what is it she is saying? No one would ever be able to report truly—or exactly—extraordinary, isn't it?—yet no one present had a moment's doubt. Only this can we say—that she was telling to the air the very things we longed to hear and until she came we had never dreamed we should hear; and now we heard them, and this sent us all into an unusual state of joy, and I . . . I sat still and speechless.

I remember that when it was over I went rapidly round to her dressing-room to see her, and there too I sat still and speechless in front of her for

a while. She understood my silence very well; all talk being quite unnecessary. She was tired after her dancing, and was resting. No one else
came to see her. Far, far off we heard applause going on . . . still going on,
still going on. After a while she stirs, she puts on a cloak and shoes,
and out we went into the streets of Berlin, where the snow looked friendly
and the shops still lighted up, the Christmas trees all spangled and lighted,
and we walked and talked of the shops. The shops, the Christmas trees,
the crowd—no one heeded us. Time passed, time went on.

And in his copy of *My Life* he drew a sketch of the scene with
a few words of description.

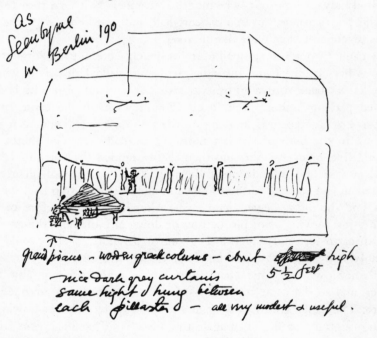

Book Topsy resumes:

After the dancing I return to her house with other friends & have supper with her. I sit next to her & an old friend, a writer (Karl Federn)[1]
on her other side.

The next thing she does is to ——— no, I will not write it— but I
remember it, and how she discovers (bless her) that I am just an ordinary
gentleman.— for her anyhow! ! !

[1] A German with whom Isadora had read Nietzsche. His introduction to his
German translation of her lecture-essay, *The Dance of the Future*, contains an
evocative description of her dancing.

All the [other] people at table are good souls & poor bodied persons (except for Augustin)— she has a good soul & a good body— is young in both, fresh in both, & while everyone talks a lot of lies we 2 go on talking either frank rubbish or all sorts of truth. She had the blessed sense of humor.

Anyhow we know that we know each other. She does not deceive me— much: & she can read me with ease. I flatter her— I say "It is flattering the Greeks of 2000 years ago to say she is like a Greek dancer." She says "now that *is* nice—" yet knows it's only a nice speech & yet feels & knows that I mean it.

And what is more I *do* & I *did* mean it. Because she is genius, & better than her it would be impossible to be.

Then after supper they all dance waltzes— she sits & won't dance except alone— the waist business not appearing to fit her.

So she sits with me & her old literary friend & we talk.

Near the time when I go she gives me a picture of herself & writes on it "with Love Isadora."

A regular hussy of a girl, one would say if one thought about it— but that only proves that to think is often a mistake— and leads to error. She can write so because she knows I read it well. No— put it differently— say she always signs her photographs so— & by the manner in which the "with love" is taken, she judges the man: perhaps so: but all the same here she knew what she was writing.

Next day she comes to my exhibition. (I had my designs for Theatre scenes & costumes on exhibition at Friedman & Weber's new establishment No. 9 Königgrätzerstrasse— December. For the Catalogue Count Kessler had written a foreword introducing me to the German public.— 60 drawings were shown on the walls, 13 of them sketches of English Landscapes. Some 31 were scenes & costume designs—)[1]

All in white she walks round with me & looks at each drawing— curi-

[1] "There was a whole room for me—" Craig wrote later about this exhibition, "even two, empty— to be done up luxuriously. It was far more luxurious than the bedroom I was sleeping in up at Siegmundshof 6, and had more furniture than my studio at No. 11 Siegmundshof. The gallery had lovely thick grey carpets, and lamps enough for light— gay but quiet. A very comfortable place for my sixty designs to rest in for a few weeks.

"And each day I would arrive early and hang around in case anyone should come who cared for these things."

The Siegmundshof buildings where Craig slept and had his studio were destroyed during the Second World War.

ously interested or bored, I don't know which— nor do I care but I guess she is feeling things— that is something— the rest feel nothing & talk a lot. She goes away— I took her to the door & I can still see her look as the large door closed slowly she with her eyes on me to the last, I my eyes on her— this moment has often returned to me . . . this farewell after meeting in our particular land— and I go to write her a letter in the café. (This café was called . . . . It was a large corner place with a very large glass corridor around it in which one was warm in winter & had plenty of light. It was Isadora's favorite Berlin café.) I tell her I must write a line— Just to speak— not because I have anything to say— I tell her I am just amazed! I ask her to come *once* more & see my *studio* drawings. She is *white* before my drawings which are so black. It was I remember a letter of love if ever a letter held love in it. I cannot post it, it is too late: I go round to her house— rush upstairs, leave it & tear off again.

Next morning (as agreed) 4 of us (Augustin, Sarah, Isadora & I) (we are 2) are to meet to drive out.

The 3 others call for me in carriage & 2 jolly horses. I join them— everyone is in such good spirits & they laugh so much they almost drown my spirits. I am stupidly thinking often of my letter which seems so foolish now these others are near us . . & now that she & I are so near.

She had rec'd a wire from Duse this morning asking her to join her, but she will not— goes out with us (me) to the Grünewald.

We visit her new school. The lilies (painted) on the walls revolt me— The others approve of it *all*. I find it all ugly except her. We lunch & laugh. Then we dance along by the trees & generally behave like 6 & 7 year old children. We salute passing strangers who seem quite happy to see us happy— Then we return— we have tea— & she tells me the fairy tale of Psyche— it breaks off like all fairy tales & as all the others go I have to go too.

Some days pass.
No answer to my letter.
I feel I've made a mistake & she is [odd?] or silly—

Wrong. When next I go to see her dance I am asked round to supper. Then she tells me she had come round to my studio & missed it, looked & looked & had to go away.

Then I find she is the she I thought she was.

We have supper— we sit together— she is just simple, lovely & we seem to be just about *one*.

After supper a Mrs. Maddison plays some music by the Frenchman Fauré!!

The rest (except for Sarah) walk up & down & talk a lot of rubbish.

We talk sense.

Saying something with our lips which cannot be written.

Then Mrs. Maddison goes & we slip down with her & jump into her cab & are going off when Isadora's brother (Augustin) descends like a thunderbolt & begs us to desist—

We do—

We return & later we go out with a pair of friends Dr. F[edern] & his sister— Away & away we speed—

Walking— Free—

We hire a motor car[1] & order him to go *on*.

He is an idiot & brings us in a circle back to our starting place. We take another motor car & order him to go to Potsdam.

It is about 1 o'clock in the morning.

On we rush— 4 of us.

A long journey. F. & sister in front— backs to us. The car fails at about 4 o'clock— we have a few minutes rest sleep & coffee at about 5 or 6 in a caffé-haus near Potsdam.

We travel on & on & at last are obliged to stop— motor given out entirely— We return at about 7 to Berlin. (All this time Topsy & I close together in the back seat selfishly egotistically lost to the world in our joy—)

We go to breakfast with Miss de B[rouckère] and stay there the whole day— it's the only thing to do— for to go back to H:strasse with Mama Duncan waiting to spring doesn't appeal to her.

In the afternoon Miss de B issues out to pay Isadora's family a visit & to see how things are going. They receive her in a chilling way[2]— glad Isadora is away & hope she will keep away!!! She does for that night— staying with Miss de B—

We are photographed (December 16) & all of us have a good time. In the evening Dr. F unfortunately laughs somewhat too loudly. Isadora says she will come & see me next day "to tea" at my studio at 4.

---

[1] "Carriage, horses, surely," Craig inserted in 1960.

[2] See note for this page.

(December 17, 1904)

At 4 she arrives— away we drive for an hour in her carriage. Then tea. Then carriage dismissed— Then supper— then we sleep together on our balcony. *17 December— our marriage night on the floor of the dear studio.* I tell her I am going to marry in about 4 months time— she does not believe in marriage—

We talk a lot before we make our bed on the wooden floor. All good or silly talk— all unnecessary, as is proved.

Our bed was 2 carpets on which a fur cloak (hers) with my overcoat as pillow & 2 blankets and a sheet as covering—

We do not sleep much all night, it is too lovely to have her there—

18th Dec. In the morning— we sit in the sun . . sit there . . talk a little . . but look . . . sit still— kiss & rest contentish.

In the evening at 5 we walk to her house— she dressed in the bed & I'm the pillow.

We walk along happy & as she says "It's wonderful how independent & free virtue can be & feel" & we laugh for that's *just it.*

Since we were born to lie holding each other, the scriptures of nature are only being fulfilled.

At her house is a reception. About 50 to 80 people.[1] We enter: she slips in and bathes.

The Reception happens. She like a queen— cold— cool— lovely— everyone else excited & struggling to have 2 minutes conversation with her—

By 6.30 everyone is gone & we dance into each other's arms.

Everyone very chilly towards us in the house. Mothers, sisters, cousins & aunts. Only Sarah is alive. The rest dead.

Then she goes out in the evening to another Reception. (Frau Begas.) I was going— but can't stand the fussy people all around us.

She goes alone— writes to me in evening after she gets back.

". . . writes to me in evening after she gets back": in the morning, rather, for such is Isadora's heading on this, the first of her letters to Craig.

[1] "Only Sarah (& I think Augustin) there & maybe Elizabeth to help her out with the receiving," Craig added later. "Quite uninteresting but very enthusiastic persons are there. One was a *Naturmensch*, dressed in almost nothing— I recall he had been at her performance & had stalked up the centre aisle of the stalls to lay flowers on the stage— looking stiff & agonized & *ernst!*"

——— *CD 1* ———

[Berlin] December 19, '04
morning

Dear—

You were quite right— it was a sort of Blasphemy to go among a lot of people— only dear Frau Begas[1] gave the party in my house or I couldn't have gone— it was Horrid.

Are you free today from 12 to 2— if so Sara & I will come at 12 to see you— if not when?

I have been sleeping like— like a very tired person— just awoke.

Isadora

———

Book Topsy continues:

[December 19] She comes at 12 with Sarah as chaperone, her mother being in a frantic way & her sister & brother having to try to look grave about nothing. She, Sarah & I stand inside my studio by the door— & there after hearing their talk, I— to appease the spirit of her mama who was not there— said "Well anyhow this is not serious" . . . took her hands— "no not *really* serious" . . . & we kissed. Sarah quite pleased & ordinary— we kissed again— 2 voices saying "not serious" but one had an upward inflection.

December 19, 20, 21, 22, 1904.— Our perfect time . . . we do not separate for 4 days & 4 nights until she goes to St. Petersburg.

In those nights she gives herself to me & reserves nothing.

[1] The wife of Reinhold Begas, designer of the Siegesallee, the academic and semiofficial perpetrator of numbers of Germany's most pretentious sculptures. A slightly earlier article in the San Francisco *Chronicle* (February 28, 1903), speaking of Isadora's celebrity in Berlin, says: "Bergos [*sic*], the sculptor, is to make a life-size statue of the danseuse, which is to be placed in the grand entrance of the theatre to be erected for Miss Duncan by public subscription." Publicity talk, probably: the theater was never built, and the statue is not known to exist.

One letter survives from those "4 days & 4 nights"—a letter from each of them to the other, apparently written in bed around a sketch of Isadora's dancing figure by Craig. She began it: "Isadora loves you." He crossed out the "Isadora," substituting his own name (adding a "Washington" in her honor), and added to her night and morning love messages.

And then on December 23 Isadora had to leave Berlin for a week, to dance in St. Petersburg for the first time. That day she wrote him twice.

——— *CD 5* ———

[Berlin] Dec. 23, 1904

Thank you Thank you Thank you for making me Happy— whole Complete I love you love you love you & I Hope we'll have a dear sweet lovely Baby— & I'm Happy forever

>   *Your*
>   Isadora

——— *CD 6* ———

[Berlin, 23 December 1904]

Dearest Sweetest Spirit

You will never know how beautiful you are. Only I know that. You will never know what an immense Joy *Giver* you are. All that joy is with me. You have given joy & love unspeakable. What shall I give you in return— All all that I have in my power to give & that is not enough— but perhaps you will find a cold empty corner for it.
I am packing my trunk.
Every one is calling me to Hurry.
Darling until we meet again— until I return to the Heart in which I was born— *Your*

>   Isadora

address me Hotel d'Europe, St. Petersburg

You have the most beautiful eyes in the world— & the dearest hands. You contain the sweetness of all the flowers & soft winds & sun— & I love

you— as the essence of all that is good & sweet in creation— & I am above every thing else Grateful— Grateful— Grateful— to you— & will always be grateful to you. We were born in the same star and we came in its rays to earth, & for a little I was in your heart & then I wandered far away & now I am back. That is our History.
No one could understand it— but us.

     Good night.

               I am your love if you will have me— if not—
               but I am
                   Your
                     Isadora

Craig returned to his studio—perhaps from her train—to find a note.

——— *CD 249* ———

Isadora
    loves
       you
         loves
            you
Signed
  Isadora

"Studio, 11 Siegmundshof, Berlin— Home here at 5 o'clock—" Craig wrote on that note, "good God— & find myself saying 'if only she were here.' She is not here— she is rushing through space, away from me."

She wrote him twice in the train while crossing Pomerania, West Prussia, East Prussia.

——— *CD 7* ———

Dear— I am passing a river. I don't know the name but the flowing waters
are quite *black* & the banks covered with snow make the most amazing
contrast— stretching off in great desolate fields with here & there a black
forest patch— It might be the river Styx— and my poor soul ready to
cross to the land of shadows. Dear you would like to see it— what a
picture for you— I'm being borne away away away— The clouds are
flying past— Am I transformed to a grey bird flying always North— I
think so— or am I just

    Your Isadora who loves you   Yes you

——— *CD 8* ———

Darling

    Great flat countries covered with snow, funny forlorn little towns—
This morning *Blue* sky & the sun shining on the whiteness. The train
stopped for 45 minutes. I walked up & down looking out over the waste
& felt just like Napoleon—

My Army—
    a Maid
    " Kapelmeister
    " Pianist
    " Secretary
Isn't it funny

Darling I love you forever— Your Isadora

She wrote him a letter and two picture post cards while she was
waiting at the customs station at Wirballen (Werzhbolovo) on the
Russian border to have her passport and luggage examined and to

change to the wider-gauged Russian train. The next day this letter, the two post cards and the two notes from the train were all post-marked, in Russian, "Postwagen" ("Post-Office Car"), with the "old-style" Russian date December 11 (thirteen days behind the Western calendar), and carried off toward "Herr Gordon Craig, 11 Siegmundshof, Berlin, Deutschland."

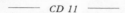

——— *CD 11* ———

Dearest— They have put us in a great room 1 2 3 class all together to examine passports & trunks— There is a good deal of wrangling going on in ten languages— a poor little dark yellow lady next me has *six* tiny children & two have the whooping cough!— I feel as if I were travelling steerage to America. Another woman has a baby wrapped in a big red quilt— & its cries penetrate through the quilting— A large band of amiable fiends are busy throwing boxes & trunks & bags about— & shrieking. The poor 1 class passengers stand about like frightened oxen— The 3 class sit on the floor & make themselves Comfy— It all smells Horrid. I don't see why this should be a part of travelling to Petersburg— but it's interesting after all— I wish you were here you could make pictures of it. Last night I cried real tears. We won't arrive until *tomorrow morning* at 8. Think of it. Another night in a sleeping car going *pum a de dum*! *How* I love you— *How* I love you *How* I love you— That's how the train goes— and I cried *real* tears— old fashioned idiotic old kinds of tears & *felt*— No— I'm rather glad to know that it's possible to feel so bad. Things inside hurt me in a most incredible way— I was rather glad— By aid of timely tips they've released me to the Buffet. They make as much noise here— I don't feel like Napoleon any more— I feel like a travelling Menagaree—the least & most Harmless animal of the show— Good bye sweet—

> Your Poor Isadora
> loves you.

———————

Of the two picture post cards, one shows the busy interior of the "Revisionssaal": "This is the dreadful waiting saal where all the lost souls summed up their earthly goods & chattels," she wrote, and drew an arrow pointing to a group of porters, "The gentle fiends." The other, "Grüss aus Wirballen," shows the exterior of the railroad station, with another arrow—this one pointing westward toward the word "You"— and a message below: "Off on the Broomstick. Why?"

Reaching her St. Petersburg hotel on Sunday, Christmas Day (by the Western calendar, though not yet in Russia), she sent him a telegram [CD *14*], HAPPY CHRISTMAS HEARTS LOVE, and two letters.

-------- CD 12 --------
GRAND HOTEL D'EUROPE
ST. PÉTERSBOURG
RUE MICHEL

Just arrived this morning—
Christmas morning
    Here its
    the *12* of December

My Darling—

   I don't like it at *all*. All the Chairs are staring at me in the most frightful way— And there is a Lady on the Mantel piece who has taken a Great objection to me— & I'm awfully scared—
This is no place for a person with a nice cheerful disposition like me— it looks like those parlors in the Novels where they plot things—
All night long the train has been not flying over but going pim de pim over Great fields of snow— vast plains of snow— Great bare Countries covered with snow (Walt [Whitman] could have written 'em up fine) and over all this the Moon shining— & across the window always a Golden shower of sparks— from the locomotive— it was quite worth seeing and I lay there looking out on it all & thinking of you— of you you dearest sweetest best darling—
The City is covered in snow & little sleighs rushing madly about— All things go in sliders of course. I sent you many little missives along the way— Hope they arrived!—
I must go now & wash the soot off & have my Breakfast.
I say this is a fine way to spend one's Christmas— They brought me first into the Great Bridal Suite here but I stoutly refused to stay in it— These rooms are hung in Dark Dark Green. It would be an awfully good sort

of place to indulge any disposition to suicide[1] lingering in an odd corner of one's disposition.

Give my love to Dear Dear No. 11— and to that nice musty little dear Home No. 6 and for your dear self my heart is overflowing with just the most unoriginal old fashionedest sort of love.

Write to me—
& tell me—
I go now to splash

     Your
       Isadora

——— *CD 13* ———
GRAND HOTEL D'EUROPE
ST. PÉTERSBOURG
RUE MICHEL

Dec. 25 [1904] 2 PM

Dear   I have been asleep ever since— dreadful lots of People came but I was quite savage & frightened my little maid out of her Wits— telling her to make 'em go away at once— Then I closed my eyes— & such a Wonderful thing happened— I could *feel you breathing.* You sweet You dear— it's almost too nice to write about but I could. After that they woke me up and I had to come & see awful people who talked at me. They've all gone thank the Gods— only the lady on the Mantel piece is left. She glares at me but she's preferable to the others.

O *you* you darling— I've just got your telegram— You Sweetheart— I love you I adore you— I am nothing without you— I kissed the telegram which is silly because it didn't come from your dear hands— You dear— dearest sweetest & Best. I think the best thing to do with St. Petersburg is to forget it— and pretend I'm not here. I'll not see it— I swear I won't— Darling— Sweetest Love— I shut my eyes think of it and I heard you Breathing— but when I awoke when I awoke I was alone— alone alone—

It's Horrible. It's Ghastly. If I could only sleep until the 30—

     Your
       Isadora

You Darling— I love you— Know what that means— Am I Yours—

———————————

[1] Isadora's husband, Sergei Esenin, was to commit suicide in this hotel—some say in this very room—in 1925.

It was probably during Isadora's week in St. Petersburg—that last week of the year 1904—that Craig wrote the 1904 portions of *Book Topsy* quoted above. To what had gone before he now added the following:

. . . there has been no panic & fighting [or] struggling about it all. All has been easy & without regrets & silly things. All has been as it should be between a woman and a man who attract each other as we do.

Do I love her?
Does she love me?

I do not know or want to know. We love to be together. We love to hear each other, see each other, & to kiss & to lie arms round each other.

Is that love? I do not know.

She says she loves me. What does that mean from her? I do not know. She tells me about her life & whom she has loved (?) before. Laughs & laughs & laughs— we always laugh (courage & fear is in this laughter) but always seem to know what a laugh means—

St. Petersburg

Iɴ *My Life*, Iꜱᴀᴅᴏʀᴀ ꜱᴀʏꜱ ᴍɪꜱᴛᴀᴋᴇɴʟʏ ᴛʜᴀᴛ ꜱʜᴇ ᴀʀʀɪᴠᴇᴅ ɪɴ Sᴛ. Petersburg for the first time in January 1905, during the early morning hours of the day following the infamous "Bloody Sunday" (January 9, old-style)—that day of horror when large and peaceable crowds, bearing the Csar's portrait and holy images in a procession to petition him for improved conditions, were hemmed in and shot down by army troops in the squares and main streets of the capital. Isadora calls this Sunday "January 5," thus misdating the event itself as well as her own first arival in the city. She tells of seeing the long procession of the victims' coffins "in the indistinct dawn," and says that if she had not seen it all her life would have been different. That erroneously dated account (later we shall see some of the possible reasons for Isadora's mistake) has been perpetuated by her various biographers. Her actual St. Petersburg debut in December 1904, though fully documented in Russian journals and now precisely dated also by the letters to Craig, has heretofore been lost sight of. Its history is of interest, not least because of its immediate impact and lasting influence on ballet.

For some time preceding her arrival in the city, St. Petersburg newspapers and musical and theatrical journals had been carrying advertisements for two forthcoming performances by "the famous

dancer Isadora Duncan"[1] for the benefit of the Society for the Pre-
vention of Cruelty to Children, to be given in the Hall of the Nobles
(Dvoryanskoye Sobranye), one of the city's principal auditoriums.
The single evening originally scheduled, December 13 (December 26,
Western calendar), had been quickly announced as sold out, and a
"second and last" performance on the sixteenth had been added.

Isadora's fame had reached St. Petersburg—the capital of Russian
classical ballet as well of the Russian Empire—by way of Russians
who had seen her dance in the West, particularly in Germany; it
was there, in November, that she had received her invitation:

Society for the Prevention of Cruelty to Children
in St. Petersburg and its environs

Fräulein Isadora Duncan
Berlin

St. Petersburg
28 October ⎫
10 November ⎰ 1904

Very esteemed Fräulein,

At the request of the Russian Society for the Prevention of Cruelty to
Children, of which I am a member of the Board of Directors, I take the
liberty of asking whether you would be willing to put your Art at the
service of our cause for one evening.

Our Society, which is under the exalted protection of Her Imperial
Highness, Grand Duchess Olga (sister of the Czar), organizes annually a
single important spectacle or concert, which is always an event of the
season and takes place either at the Imperial Opera or in the Hall of the
Nobles (a counterpart of the concert hall of the Berlin Philharmonic).
This annual affair earns a major part of the funds which the Society
needs for achieving its humane purpose—namely, to rescue unfortunate
children from the hands of their tormentors, of whom there are alas so
many; to educate them, to house and feed them, etc. It is our ardent hope
that you will sympathize with the purpose of our Society, and if only
for that reason will not refuse our request.

---

[1] Because of a misunderstanding of the pronunciation of the vowels *I* and *U*,
Isadora's name was rendered into Russian as Айседора Дункан, pronounced
"Eyesedora Dooncàn," and such remains the general pronunciation in Russia
today. (See note for this page.)

I believe, however, that you will have nothing to regret, even in your own interest, should you accept; for it is difficult to imagine a more favorable milieu for a debut in the Russian capital: the most prestigious concert hall, the most select audience of Petersburg, the virtually certain presence of the Imperial Family, etc. So far as the artistic circles and the press are concerned, they always appear *in corpore* at our events.

The charitable purpose does not in the least exclude a financial consideration, and we therefore ask you to be so kind as to state your conditions. We are sure that there will be no difficulty in agreeing on the terms.

If it is at all possible, we beg you to brighten our month of December with your guest appearance; and that with your answer—which we trust will be affirmative—you will send us some of the existing printed material concerning your new Art. Thus we should be able, at the proper time, to familiarize the Russian public with its main features.

Awaiting your prompt reply,
Yours most respectfully
For the Board of Directors of the "Society for
the Prevention of Cruelty to Children"
A. Gabrilovna

Please address your
answer to
St. Petersburg, Russia
Kuznechny 15   Mr. Arthur Gabrilowitsch

Probably in response to the request for "printed material concerning your new Art," the *St. Petersburg Theatre Journal (Peterburgski Dnevnik Teatrala)* published in its November 14 (27) issue an interview with Isadora—the first ever to appear in Russia—by its Berlin correspondent, Maurice Girschman. It began:

Duncan, the celebrated American barefoot dancer, has settled permanently in Berlin, where she will seek to publicize her ideas and dreams concerning what she calls the renaissance of ancient classical tragedy. In Berlin she wishes to found a school for fifty to a hundred children, to instill them with her own exalted conception of the dance. For her, she has said, dancing is the very purpose of her life, her dream, her ideal. Anyone who has seen her a single time will never forget her, but since she is little known in Petersburg I thought it would be interesting to tell you of the impressions I took away with me from my conversation with the "little American."

There followed descriptions of Isadora's entrance hall, where "wreaths, some of them of laurel, with ribbons of various colors, immediately proclaim that you are in the home of a famous person," and of Isadora herself, in her "simple white classical toga, her hair bound with a narrow fillet, like the women of ancient Greece." Then:

"What I show the public," she told me, "was already known many centuries ago. I am trying to revive that beauty, which—alas!—is at present forgotten and buried. As you know, I illustrate, in my dances, the thoughts of the composers. Newspapers often ridicule me when at the end of my performance I address the public in an attempt to recruit talented dancers.

". . . I have danced in various countries. When I was in Russia, in Warsaw,[1] I was invited to Kiev by an operetta producer, A. A. Levitzky, but I could not accept, being fully engaged for November.

"I want to be like a gardener, who sows in spring and harvests his fruit in autumn. I have not yet arrived at what I want, but I am sure that I shall find artists who will bring perfection to the dance, and then we shall no longer see in Opera so many bad dancers as we find today . . . Here in Berlin I have decided to portray in dance the music of Beethoven, and I try constantly to make my dancing purer and more noble. How can dance attain the supreme heights if we do not use the music of the best composers? I am sure that if the great Beethoven were still living he would not be angry with me; he might even applaud me," the celebrated Duncan said with a smile as she ended our conversation.

Isadora's two performances in St. Petersburg a fortnight later—an all-Chopin program and *Dance Idylls*—were tremendous successes, recognized by dancers and amateurs of the dance as sensational, epoch-making events. Diaghilev has paid them tribute: "I knew Isadora well in St. Petersburg, and I went with [Michel] Fokine to her first performances. Fokine was crazy about her, and Duncan's influence on him was the initial basis of his entire creation . . . Isadora gave the classical ballet of Imperial Russia a shock from which it could never recover." The memoirs of dancers—Fokine and Kchessinska—and of Alexandre Benois, the painter and designer of ballet sets and costumes, all speak of those momentous evenings. (The Society for the Prevention of Cruelty to Children had kept its word, and the first performance was "graced by the presence of their

---

[1] Poland was then a Russian province.

Imperial Highnesses Grand Duke Vladimir Alexandrovitch with Grand Duchess Maria Pavlovna and Grand Duke Boris Vladimirovitch.") Most of the immediate reviews were ecstatic. During the weeks and months that followed, Isadora's dancing was to be the subject of considerable controversy in "serious" Russian theatrical and musical journals, but the press had been nearly unanimous in hailing her. In fact, one critic wrote that readers might well be led to suspect him and his colleagues of "conspiring" to show that Russians could be as appreciative of a modern innovative artist as their counterparts in the West. From a reading of the notices[1] it is evident that the Berlin interview with Isadora had touched on aspects of her art that were of particular Russian interest.

The fact that "barefoot" is one of the interviewer's opening words underlines the great novelty, indeed the sensationalism, of Isadora's stage appearance: in those days her bare feet, bare legs, and scanty garments produced a shock similar to that felt by English and American audiences in the late 1960s when total nudity began to be seen on stage and screen.[2] There were "Nature" movements in all countries (we have already seen Craig's mention of the *"Naturmensch,* dressed in almost nothing" who appeared at one of Isadora's performances and at her party, and Russian familiarity with Naturists will soon be referred to), and it was with cults like these that Isadora was often quite mistakenly associated in the minds of the conventional. To others, especially self-styled "men about town," her "nudity" was salacious.

This aspect of Isadora's art was immediately dealt with, and put in proper perspective, by the very first reviewer of her initial St. Petersburg performance. The following is the body of the serious and appreciative notice by "N. Georgievich," the pseudonym sometimes used by the well-known St. Petersburg theater critic Nicolai Georgievich Shebuyev, which appeared in the *Peterburgskaya Gazeta* on December 14, 1904. It is a fair sample of the enthusiastic response Isadora's debut elicited in the city.

---

[1] See note for this page.
[2] In the early years of the century Chaliapin caused sensation and scandal when he sang the title role in Boito's *Mefistofele* bare-chested.

Yesterday all fashionable Petersburg assembled in the Hall of the Nobles, prepared to see La Duncan dance some kind of virginal cancan. There was indeed something to see, and much of it was indeed virginal; but much of it was also thoroughly feminine, and some of it expressed sorrow, even tragedy.

. . . On the stage, a thick rug, a sky-blue backdrop. At the sides, cigar-like poplars and fragments of classical columns, to take one to Rome or to Greece, to the days of ancient Attica . . . A grand piano . . .

[After an introductory rendering of Chopin's Nocturne in F-flat major by the mediocre pianist who is Miss Duncan's accompanist] a rosy light shone out at the rear of the stage on the left, and pale violet tones began to gleam on the blue backdrop. The sound of Chopin's Mazurka (B-major, op. 7, no. 1) made one's nerves tingle, and onto the stage there entered a sylph. A bit of pink-blue gauze mistily enveloped her slender waist, and veiled yet revealed her bare feet. She is not at all beautiful, but her face is as exotic as Baroness d'Alheim's,[1] and on it, with equal expressiveness, joy, sorrow, a tear, a smile, are fleetingly born and quickly die.

She emerged and swam like an Undine, swaying in time with the beat, waving her hands with the beat, smiling, diving with the beat—and suddenly she flew up like a bird and soared carefree, joyful, chirping soundlessly—no: tunefully, rather—for her dancing merged into a single chord with Chopin's Mazurka. And then she floated down again from the sky—touched the cold surface of the river—shuddered—and swam again, green and graceful, proud of her cold, nymphlike beauty. And dived again—and once again froze, her arms stretched forward at the finale.

That was all.

But on analyzing what at first glimpse seems little, one finds much.

First, the marvelous plastic sensibility. Her body is as though bewitched by the music. It is as though you yourself were bathing in the music. Then, the expressive hands. Have you ever heard of mimicry by hands? . . . And yet Duncan's hands are expressive as her face. And the legs? For after all, it was the legs, the bare feet, that were supposed to be the sensation of the evening. It was considered very dull not to make witty remarks about the "Kneippist"[2] ballerina, and one lost count of how often

---

[1] The concert singer Marya Olenin.

[2] Sebastian Kneipp (1821–1897), a German priest, had developed a system of hydrotherapy known as "Kneippism." A Russian translation of his work *My Water Cure* was very popular in Russia at this time. Kneipp also recommended walking barefoot on grass, as well as other natural methods of conditioning the body.

one overheard Briusov's line: *"O, cover thy pale legs!"* Actually, the legs play the least important role in these dances. Here *everything* dances: waist, arms, neck, head—*and* legs. Duncan's bare legs and bare feet are like those of a rustic vagabond: they are innocent: this is not a *nudité* that arouses sinful thoughts, but rather a kind of incorporeal nudity.

For the Mazurka in A-flat (op. 17, no. 4) there came onstage a figure severe and sorrowful, looking intently upward, all her being yearning for heaven while her hands seemed to beg, trying to seize something. Then suddenly her eyes flashed with Bacchic ecstasy—the flame died—there was another flash—then once again a look of severity and prayer.

With the Mazurka in D-sharp (op. 33, no. 2) everything changed. Now she is a Bacchante—she leaps wildly—calls and entices someone, and suddenly runs off in a torrid whirlwind.

The Mazurka in C-sharp (op. 33, no. 3), short and clear, brought almost no dancing—just poses. And you felt yourself an ancient Greek as you watched this dancer who seemed to have stepped out of a painting by Semiradsky[1] . . . Such expression!

With the Mazurka in A-flat (op. 33, no. 4) she danced an entire tragedy. As she entered, consternation was on her face—the face of a bewitched Trilby; in her dancing, fear, tears, horror alternated with a morbid, decadent, convulsive *Presto*. And when, with this tragic look in her eyes, she approached the footlights and rose on her toes, she seemed to grow taller —majestic, fateful. This number moved the audience more than any of those preceding it.

The last of the Mazurkas was that in A-sharp major (op. 24, no. 3), lacelike, woven of soft, catlike, stealthy leaps; and there was a sort of caressing languor in her swaying movements that was at once feminine and maidenly.

Even more interesting are the four Preludes (op. 28, nos. 4, 7, 20, 6.) To the first of them she listens, standing at the piano. Almost motionless, she mimes the entire melody from beginning to end. Then, when it began to repeat, she moved to the back of the stage and illustrated it with poses. How much unsatisfied languor and lassitude, how many questions, could be heard in her gestures! To the second Prelude she stretched with the utmost grace, and thawed. The third was a funeral dance: the wailing woman, shattered by grief, now seeks forgetfulness in dancing, now is tormented by memories, and, at the end, falls to the ground exhausted.

---

[1] Genrikh Ippolitovich Semiradski (1843–1902). A Russian painter of Polish origin, member of the Petersburg Academy of Arts, known for his paintings on themes drawn from antiquity.

There is no dance for the fourth Prelude—only a mood, the mood of autumnal leaves and autumnal tears, autumnal beauty and sadness.

The best number of all, however, was the Polonaise in A-sharp major, op. 53. This was the dance of Diana. In a short red gauze tunic, her legs bare, she leaps, gambols in a round, shoots from a bow; there are occasional flashes of something animal . . .

Duncan has thin, pale feet, not at all beautiful . . . But they are expressive, like all else about her, and sometimes they are even eloquent. Being bare, they touch the ground lightly, soundlessly.

Duncan has no ballet technique; she does not aim at *fouettés* and *cabrioles*. But there is so much sculpture in her, so much color and simplicity, that she fully deserves the capacity audience which she is already assured for next Thursday . . .

Extracts from two reviews that appeared the following day, equally serious and complimentary, and containing excellent descriptions of Isadora's style, show that they, too, mentioned her bare feet and her "nudity" almost as though her greatest triumph were to have distracted the concentration of public attention from them:

Well, here it is: a fairy tale for you, a fable about a barefoot girl . . . Miss Duncan's bare feet might have provoked laughter and her improvised dancing caused disillusionment. But neither the one nor the other was the case . . . By the end of the program the barefoot dancer had many admirers, who gathered at the footlights in the dimmed hall endlessly demanding encores.

I have almost forgotten to say something about Duncan's bare legs. Indeed it was these legs that everyone had been waiting for. And—what do you think? A complete disappointment they were. Just imagine: ordinary women's legs, strong and graceful, but devoid of any alluring perfections. And yet it is these very legs that have made the *artiste* known the world over, and effected a complete revolution in choreographic art. The barefoot girl shocked nobody, and her nudity was pure and imperceptible. Indeed, it would be ridiculous to force a pair of boots on Terpsichore . . .

It would, of course, have been not only strange but also utterly absurd, if, having set out to restore classical choreography, Miss Duncan had embodied its soul in the form of today's ballet. This is why she found it absolutely necessary to preserve also the costume of the ancient dancers;

i.e., to cover her body only with a light, transparent fabric. Elimination of corset, bodice, ballet tutu and slippers results in a special flexibility and freedom of motion, a special charm and softness of the human body as a vehicle of plastic expression. There is nothing here to shock the moral sense, just as nothing can shock us when we look at Tanagra statuettes—this nudity is ancient, and, as such, natural. Nudity is repulsive when it is hypocritical, incomplete or deliberately stressed, but when it is dictated by historical or artistic necessity it is not repulsive but positively attractive. More generally, the entire question is pointless in this case: only a thoroughly corrupted member of our present bourgeois society will see this nudity of the revived classical statue as a violation of the laws of decency or morality.

Miss Duncan's dances are fascinating . . . Each one is a mobile sculpture, a piece of music in its imagery, a poem in its rhythm . . .

In a few veiled words in the Berlin interview—those about the many bad dancers seen "in Opera"—Isadora had touched on the issue of greatest pertinence to members of the St. Petersburg dance world. For dancers in opera appear in opera ballets; and the phrase was Isadora's first salvo—a gentle one—against the classical ballet that was St. Peterburg's tradition, particularly illustrated by the long existence in the city of the Imperial School of the Ballet, a state institution under the patronage of the Csar himself. But if the ballet was St. Petersburg's tradition, it was not at that moment its glory—any more than it was a glory elsewhere in Europe until revived by Diaghilev. (Degas gave ballet in France its greatest glorification in painting at a time when it was in fact in the doldrums on the stage.) Alexandre Benois, who a few weeks later was to be Isadora's defender against a series of printed attacks on her art, and who was to be one of the chief scenic and costume designers for some of Diaghilev's most celebrated ballets (*Le Pavillon d'Armide, Giselle, Petrouchka*), writes in his memoirs that even in Russia ballet had lately fallen into a state of "dreamy lassitude," with most of its repertory the work of Marius Petipa, the great choreographer from Marseilles, long resident in Russia and now grown elderly and repetitious. Many dance enthusiasts, including critics and even a few of Petipas's younger pupils, particularly Gorsky and Fokine, were becoming bored with the old repertory and experimenting with new forms. Two leading Russian historians of the ballet are in accord as to the perfect timing of Isadora's arrival in St. Petersburg: Natalia Roslavleva says that just before Isadora's irruption Fokine, "when visualizing the unachieved ballet *Daphnis and Chloe*, studied sculptures and bas-reliefs of ancient Greece and was ready to use this style of *plastique* in his production"; in Lydia Krasovskaya's words, "The soil was prepared." The interest of the St. Petersburg dance world was intense. All the immediate reviews of the first performance, including those already quoted, testify to the realization that Isadora brought a great stimulus to the ballet at a time when it was intensely needed.

The music of Chopin . . . lends itself particularly well to choreographic interpretation, and this, one of Miss Duncan's most interesting discoveries, may induce our routine choreography to take a new direction . . . Her performance was attended by many ballerinas, representatives of our School of Ballet, ballet critics, and *balletomanes*.

Rejecting the dead formalism of the so-called ballet, she strives to create a dance not severed from nature and life, but flowing from life . . . Miss Duncan has taken the art of the dance, which had found itself in a blind alley, on to the true road.

Isadora tells, in *My Life*, of the welcome quickly extended to her, the day following that first performance, by the Imperial Ballet. She was visited by the ballerina Kchessinska (former mistress of the Csar and now living with the Grand Duke Mikhail—"a most charming little lady, wrapped in sables"), who had already seen Isadora dance in the West and who now, as the Ballet's representative, came bearing invitations. Isadora, wearing her "little white tunic and sandals," attended a gala performance at the Opera and a glittering supper party at the Grand Duke's afterwards; Pavlova visited her, she watched Pavlova dance in *Giselle*, there was another supper party, this time in Pavlova's house, where "I sat between the painters Bakst and Benois, and met, for the first time, Serge Diaghileff, with whom I engaged in ardent discussion on the art of the dance as I conceived it, as against the Ballet."

Alexandre Benois has written about that second supper party:

I became acquainted with Miss Duncan's views on the ballet at the supper given by a few of her admirers after her second concert. On that festive occasion, Duncan, in the true American way, managed to make a long and effective speech, in which she clearly and articulately expounded her ideas about dance in general and, in particular, about dance as spectacle. I must note at once that it is pointless to look for philosophical principles in her ideas; as a genuine artist, she is motivated not by logic, but by elemental inspiration.

In her opinion, the only thing that matters is beauty, the pursuit of beauty in order to make all life beautiful. In the presence of beauty even suffering has no terrors, even death does not frighten, beauty illumines everything, it is mankind's best comforter. In answer to a question asked by a writer who was present, "But what are we to do about ugliness, since it exists in the world?" Miss Duncan, still aglow after her impassioned speech, replied without hesitation, "*Il faut la tuer, la laideur! Il faut la tuer!*"

"The ballet in its present form is incontestably an 18th century legacy," [Miss Duncan said.] "With a few exceptions, the ballet, viewed as a whole, represents an overcoming of difficulties, an acrobatism, some sort of complicated and excruciating mechanism. There is no human dignity in the ballet. The dancers are mere puppets in motion, not people. Even the costume contributes to this result: the incompatibility of the decolleté with the improbably tight waist, the improbable pink tricot on the legs, the blunt ballet shoes. Nor is there any beauty in the dancer's motions. Except for various character dances and a few beautiful *pas*, today's dances consist of bewildering turns, unnatural leaps and twists. The most horrible thing in ballet is this total disregard of rhythm in the movements, the jerkiness of the gestures (*des gestes saccadés.*) The dancers perform their number, begin and end it, but there is no transition from one number to another, no harmony. The indispensible smoothness, symmetry, consistency, are absent."

It is impossible to ignore all this, if we recall the horrible foreign ballets, but I believe Miss Duncan would somewhat modify her opinion if she were more closely acquainted with our ballet, the ultimate pride of the Russian scene. However, the days of our own ballet, too, are numbered. After rising high under the patronage and loving care of I. A. Vsevolozhsky, it has already taken several steps downwards. The "fairylike" style, a certain foolishness in staging, tasteless innovations in the dances have begun to sneak into our own ballet. Under the existing direction, in ten, at most fifteen years, our ballet will deteriorate, as everywhere else; it will sink to the café-chantant level and eventually vanish. This decline will be inevitable because, no matter how good are its traditions, one cannot live on them alone. What is needed is creative renewal, walking in step with the time . . . an infusion of new life.

Fokine's experiments with innovations in the ballet were to culminate, less than two years later, in his choreography for *Les Sylphides* (originally called *Chopiniana*)—to music by Chopin and with classical costumes reminiscent of Isadora's. And with Nijinsky soon to explode onto the scene under the aegis of Diaghilev, another of Isadora's ideas expressed that evening to Benois was prophetic:

Today Duncan keeps dreaming about her school, about the "new" ballet. For the time being, she takes only girls, because she realizes that she, a woman alone, could not cope with rambunctious boys; but she hopes that in seven or eight years male dancers, too, will be found, and then she will be in a position to come forward as a new ballet mistress. In this connection she made the following remark concerning male dancers in her awkward French: "*Si un homme pouvait danser bien, cet homme serait un dieu!*"

And, true enough, only with the inclusion of male parts in the ballet does it preserve its dignity and virtually the first place on the boards; in the contrary case, the ballet turns into an "exhibition of pretty women," which has nothing in common with the tasks of scenic art.

SUCH WAS ISADORA'S INITIAL, TRIUMPHANT APPEARANCE ON THE Russian scene.

This first visit to Russia [she tells in *My Life*] was cut short by previous engagements which recalled me to Berlin. Before I left I . . . signed a contract to return in the spring. In spite of the shortness of my visit, I had left a considerable impression. There were many quarrels for and against my ideals; and one duel was actually fought between a fanatic *balletomane* and a Duncan enthusiast. It was from that epoch that the Russian ballet began to annex the music of Chopin and Schumann and wear Greek costumes; some ballet dancers even going so far as to take off their shoes and stockings.

The heroine of this momentous chapter in the story of the dance returned, that December night of 1904, to her hotel room and, fresh from applause and acclaim in the Hall of the Nobles, wrote the following to her lover.

—— *CD 15* ——

Monday night.
[St. Petersburg, 26 or early 27
December 1904 (Western calendar)]

Darling Love

The Lady what dances came back & danced all over the place— The
yellow dog & the gas man liked it and so apparently did all the Kings
& Queens in the audience— (It was full of Imperial Loges and Kings
and things like that)— The Lady what dances was in an awful rage &
danced horrid at all the people— then she went in the dressing room &
fought with the other lady— 'You're a nice sort of person, she said &
your *muscles* are all Capoot!!' 'I'm in *love love love* said the other Lady
and I want to go *home* to No 6— and kiss my Darling & kiss & kiss & kiss
my Love and I don't like dancing any more'— but sweetheart it's true
my *muscles* are quite *Capoot*— & I can't dance worth a Cent!!!!!!
And now I've come back to the Hotel & it's Midnight— & I'm going into
a Great Big Hotel Bed All By Myself— And I Don't Like Things!!! The
House is sold out for the two nights and they want to give a *third* but
I tell them that it's very nice of them but I've got to go Home. Darling
no letter from you— write me— I'm so tired— Oh if I only had your
Arms about me now— Your dear dear dear dear Arms— you sweetest
best dearest. Love You

> Your Isadora
> This is how I feel after a "great success"
> These is tears

————————————

A few hours later she wrote him again.

—— *CD 16* ——

Tuesday
[St. Petersburg, 27 December 1904]

Dear— Your letter came this morning— I put it in my heart & the hurt
went away— You Darling— What can I say— it was getting past endurance but your letter helped a good deal—

There is no train on the eve of the 29— so I must take the one early Friday morning— I will be in Berlin at 7 on Saturday eve, & then I will come to you. I *must*— I will be very dirty & sooty & tired— will you mind that? You dear— I have written you about 3 letters a day since I left Berlin— did they all come safe? I danced *awfully* last night— half the time I was quite unconscious that I was there— I was always running up the stairs at No 6— I think that as an inspiration for a Dancer *you* are not a Success. How do you find *me* as inspiration? You give me only one inspiration and that is to run away from all Publics and the like and rush to you— & then *die* or what ever— Darling I love you.

I will come Back *Soon Soon* and then— Then we may grow *gradually* to some Inspiration— It's too cruel at present. Your dear sweet eyes— your hands— you— your feet— all I love
& your letter—
I love your letter—
I simply refuse to see St. Petersburg— and when people come to see me they think I'm a unique idiot!! I'm not fit for Society— & I don't want to dance for 'em any more—

I want *you*— my love

Your
Isadora

And again the next day.

——— *CD 17* ———

[St. Petersburg, probably 28 December 1904]

Dear— I have been out riding in a funny little sleigh elbow to elbow with hundreds of other funny little sleighs and horses that go like mad. St. Petersburg is very fine covered with snow & the air like Champagne— I write you only a word today. Good night to you dear dear spirit— dear heart— dear Friend, you to whom I owe so much joy— How did it Come— it was like a sudden Thunderclap & then all was changed— & now———— Now dear I am grateful to you Grateful Grateful Grateful & will always be— because you are *what* you are— you are *Beautiful*.

Good night
Isadora

She was impatient for her Russian stay to be over.

———— *CD 18* ————

[Telegram,
Wednesday, 28 December 1904]

SOON SATURDAY NIGHT

———— *CD 19* ————

[Telegram,
Friday, 30 December 1904]

TOMORROW LOVE

————————————

There is a picture post card [CD *20*] which she did not send but brought with her; once again it is from Wirballen, this time showing the railway bridge at the Russo-German border, with "To You To You To You I'm Coming—*Dearest*" written along the tracks.
And she wrote a letter on New Year's Eve, from the train that was already close to Berlin.

———— *CD 21* ————

Darling— This darned old train is 3 hours 3 centuries 3 eternities late late late— We will arrive about ten and the secretary & the maid will *yank* me up to Hardenburg Strasse— but I will slip away as soon as I can & come to No. 11— I *won't* come to No. 6 because I haven't the outside key— Darling I've come back Back Back from the Land of Snow & Ice— I think I discovered the North Pole— Will you wait for me at No. 11. Oh Sweet— I am almost crazy & half dead— you Darling in two little hours I will see you— Will you be glad— Will We ———— Will

we ———— The only thing that has kept me from . . . Kept me half alive is
your sweet picture— and now I will see you you You— Imagine since
yesterday Early morning in this train— Years & Centuries *coming to you.*

Your Isadora.

———————————

Craig's answer to Isadora's "Will We ————? Will We ————?"
was a little double sketch of two heads, a man's and a girl's—are they
peering out over a blanket?—which he dated January 1.

———— *CD 22* ————

The Year 1905

"AND THEN," CRAIG WRITES AT THE END OF THE 1904 PART OF *Book Topsy*, "for the next few months we are together nearly all the time. We go to St. Petersburg, Moscow, Hamburg, Dresden, Cologne, Breslau, Frankfurt— together— she dancing and I doing little— resting and being happy with her."

There was plenty of love and laughter and kissing—they often used that last word in the French sense—as Isadora and Craig moved about Germany for her dancing engagements during that January of 1905.

On the fifth they went to Cologne, where Isadora danced her *Chopin Abend* in the Alte Stadt-Theatre and where they stayed on a day or two at the Dom-Hotel.

—— CD 22 ——

DOM-HOTEL

KÖLN.

№ *Mo. 55*

Januar 04

M. DuMont Schauberg, Köln. 4.48™.

		Omnibus o. Bagage	
6.	Logis *Nachtrag*		14 —
	Déjeuner (obligat.)		
	Hors d'oeuvres		4 —
	1 pom. frites 2 Beefsteak		4.00
	1 Pfirsich Compot		1.50
	2 Apfelkrapfen		1.50
	1/2 Pommery		1.50
	4 Eier		1. —
7.	*2 Thé spl. 2 Kuchen*		2.50
	1 Apoll		1. —
	1/2 Poularde 1 Salat		5.50
	2 Birnencompot 1 Sahne		3.50
	2 Stangen Spargel Hr. Zoll.		4 —
	1/2 Pommery		7.50
	1 Biscuit		50

M 57.60

Mr 61.10

taken to Station or Boat by Omnibus only.

All Luggage

Gepäck-Beförderung

geschieht nur durch Omnibus.

se fait settlement par l'Omnibus.

Le transport de bagages

Any incivilities on the part of staff of the hotel to be reported to the management.	Unzulässigkeiten des Personals bittet man zur Kenntnis der Verwaltung zu bringen.	Prière de faire connaître à la direction les employés dont on aurait à se plaindre.

Note: Restaurant bill misdated, a New Year mistake for 1905.

Their Pommery (an excellent brand of champagne) and steak in the restaurant there inspired a dialogue in their respective handwritings on hotel stationery—a dialogue perhaps written while still at table:

(*He*): Champagne she cried
And steak she cried
And all the other things
Which make a banschee
Nice & Dancie
And give my darling wings.

The guilty couple took to drink
Because they had not time.
The rest I cannot here relate
I cannot find a rhyme.

(*She*): I've drunk enough here God knows.

(*He*): But God will never tell.

(*She*): Isadora has decided that the father of her child shall be the man she loves.

(*He*): A world of thought can be given to this

(*She*): Don't worry about Isadora's child. It's *all right* in Heaven, waiting for the appointed time. Being a child of great intelligence decides its parents better grow to something before it makes its appearance.

(*He*): The guilty couple took to drugs
Because they had not time
To think of other tricks & bugs
Which the Gods used as lime.

On January 15 they took an express from Berlin to Dresden, where Isadora had already danced the nights of the tenth and eleventh. There were other people in the compartment, and once again they "talked" by writing—this time on pages of Craig's sketchbook which they passed back and forth between them. The sheets have become disarranged over the years, but their "conversation" went somewhat as follows:

———— *CD 23* ————

(*She*): I am called Isadora.
That means Child of Isis— or *Gift* of Isis.
Isis is the Goddess of Birth—
Isis will always protect me because I have her name.
This is the 15 of January 1905.
                    Isis Protect Me.

(*He*): (with drawing of an Egyptian deity)
To Art, imagination is almost a necessity.
With nature— it is best to wait for fac's.
Fac's *is*— really *is*— Damned stubborn things
& Don't forget it Mrs. MacCarthy.

(*She*): Yellow Tulips white Hyacinths Great Wondrous Spaces of Sky
Black Steps leading to a Balcony four red pillows
Dearest Baby if you come remember these things & always love
    Them

(*He*): Mein antwort.[1] If company were not present I should drop here
things which come from the eyes & are wet & hot. Only that
way could I speak & I won't write.

(*She*): O you— *You Darling! You*—

(*He*): The most Beautiful thing in the world— what is it.
It is that thing which is most complete.
A perfect sphere is complete in form.
What is then the most beautiful of beautiful things— a perfect
woman. Than a woman no more imperfect thing exists. Now
we are getting to it— For imperfection is one of the requisites
for a perfect thing—
I cannot finish my thoughts— they are swept away by a name—
Isadora—

(*She*): (immediately following the word "Isadora")

is
a looking
glass.

———

[1] G., "My answer."

You
are
Beautiful.

(*He*): Mother has only 2 weak points. One is her handwriting— t'other is her vows. Her nails it is true taper more exquisitely than do mine. What of that— I make no vows & so I do not need nails. Mother's poetry, too, is a bit shaky. For instance, she always imagines Joy rhymes with sleep & Tanagra with Love.— And 1905 with 1906. Now even to a child such reasoning is absurd. Still mother is so perfect that we argue about this to no purpose for we ADORE her!?

(*She*): 1905 rhymes with Eternity, for Eternal joy love & desire were this year inspired by you.
Love rhymes with You for you are *Love*. Joy rhymes with *You* for you are joy.

O Baby What you *think* of yer *Par*!?
Baby answers— "Who's me Par"?

(*He*): It's an old saying & a
sometimes true one
             that
Its a wise child that
knows its own father.

This is wrong—
Its nothing to do with
             wisdom
Its a matter of instinct
& proves that its a mighty
thick son that cant
choose his own pa.

Mother has what is in the vernacular called "dried up"— for the moment.
But as you know, Babe, mother *can* speak when she likes.
Only wait— spring returneth—
I firmly believe that mother is the better man of the three.

(*She*): When I lay— back alone— I opened my two arms and 2 hands with Palms upwards— That meant I was lonely—
And I slept.
When I woke I was still alone—
So it was many many nights—

There was a little ache in my Heart,
a larger ache in my breast—
Broken glass in my Heart
and much ash further down.
Now it is some what different
It's so different—
That I have registered
  a Vow
    &
will
Never Sleep
  alone
  again
    x
    x
    x
    !

(*He*): Threats ill become the wife of an Irish nobleman![1]
         sure—
  But if its *persuadin* you'd be at I'm
  Your man my darlin.

(*She*): You don't quite catch the deeper meaning of me *allegorical*
          phrases—

  My darling is Beautiful & *good*. Almost *too* good (for me) to
  be true. My sweetheart is lovely.

(*He*): She is so beautiful that she sees beauty in all things— even in the
         sun— sky— water, tears, wind & me.

(*She*): Who am I? I who contain possibilities.
  Some attain Greatness & some have
  Greatness thrust upon them— Ye Gods!

  Mrs. Maddison sat at the Piano & played tum de tum— de tumdy
  tum & then My Darling Kissed me. After that we runned away.
  But me Brother cummed after us— & we walked up four flights.

(*He*): What perfect taste— that was to be expected—
  How *perfectly* she mistakes my mask for me.

---

[1] They both joked a good deal about their Irish ancestry. One of Craig's
grandfathers was Irish, and Isadora claimed that her Irish-born grandmother
crossed the North American continent to San Francisco in a wagon.

What beauty is in her blunder.
Isis!! did no god love you—
tell him to come to me—
Only your lover can be my protector.
Artists call them patrons I believe.
Anyhow— schicken.[1]

(*She*): My Love has beautiful eyes & a dear kind smile. He is very beautiful by Moonlight but especially Beautiful by daylight. His hands are filled with tenderness and his Being radiates Love— His force is irresistable and his face is like the Heavens. Dearest Baby— If you Come perhaps you would like to know that you were *WANTED*.

(*He*): And you Babe will know with me what all that word means.
She your mother is wanted.
She my darling is wanted.
If your name is Jack or Jill it don't matter.
You will want *her* right on to the *end*.[2]

"Mother has only 2 weak points. One is her handwriting— t'other is her vows . . . I make no vows . . ." Was it a warning? The kind of warning that Craig claims, in later entries in *Book Topsy*, he gave her from the beginning?

In the first days I used to laugh gaily whenever she grew deadly serious about "mein liebe mann" & "Hochzeit"[3] & all the rest of it for I used to say to her, "we are *not serious*" "we cannot be *serious*"— & she would take up the refrain "no, not serious" & then her arms round my neck & mine round her we would kiss lightly or youthfully— never once can I recall her teeth meeting mine— or the tip of her tongue— never once— she kissed as much with the eyes as with the lips.

[1] G., "send."

[2] On another train journey they entertained themselves by listing, each of them on the same sheet of large paper, the addresses of the various places where they had lived in London. They discovered that at different times they had both lived in Pembroke Studios.

[3] G., "marriage."

"no, no"— week after week, "not serious, Topsy," "It can't last Topsy— love never lasts does it Topsy—" & then she would be apt to turn the talk or take a rather offended tone— She could not admit then that love never lasts & could she have really seen into my heart & head she would have seen there the same refusal to believe that our love could die. *Only I had already begun to provide for the future catastrophe so that when it came up I should be able to stand up to it.* This she did not know— how could she . . .

Certainly there was no warning in the little morning-notes they passed between them when they awoke in Dresden.

——— *CD 24* ———

Nor in Isadora's note and drawings from the Hotel Hamburger Hof in Hamburg, where she went with Craig for a week's engagement on the twenty-fourth (after having danced in Leipzig on the seventeenth)—

———— *CD 25* ————

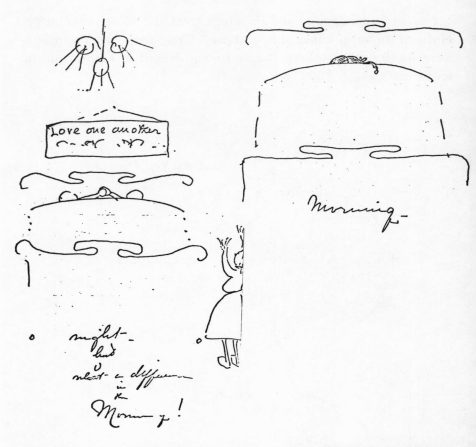

Note: During this visit to Hamburg, where she danced in the Thalia Theatre, Isadora announced in the press that she would "audition" girls between six and ten as candidates for free board, lodging and education in her dance school at Grünewald. One little seven-year-old Hamburger, Irma Erich-Grimme, who was brought by her mother to Isadora's hotel suite and who passed the tests, and who grew up to be Isadora's most famous pupil and one of several who took the name Duncan, has described the interview, Craig's presence in the room, and how it was Craig who persuaded Isadora to accept her after first saying no. Irma subsequently wrote to Craig: "Many, many years later, when I once asked Isadora what exactly had persuaded her to choose me for a pupil, she replied: 'Why, don't you know? It was Gordon Craig! he said to me: "take her . . . she has the eyes!"' Do you remember saying that about me?" Craig's comment: "Yes, I remember— she was being led away— I saw her look back . . ."

Irma tells also of the train journey back to Berlin, with Isadora and Craig and the other accepted children. Craig's two drawings of Isadora in the train returning from this visit to Hamburg are among the illustrations.

Martin Shaw, Craig's friend and associate in London, was the recipient of several letters that January, telling about the happiness and the enchantment: "I have been to Dresden, Leipzig, Cologne in last 3 weeks & had a glorious time . . . I am in magnificent company . . ." Shaw had apparently questioned whether Isadora could be called an "artist," and Craig replied: "My dear lad, artist or not — this is a marvelous being— beauty— nature & *brain*. I don't like brainy women but brains intelligence is a rare and lovely thing. If you could see *one* dance you would understand how wonderful it is. Beauty & Poetry is art when it is *created* no matter how by a living being. I have seldom been so moved by anything. It's a great, a rare rare gift brought to perfection by 18 years of persistent labour— & we may all agree to worship such things." Craig was excited by what he considered Isadora's Americanism: "A lot of Americans live in Berlin & *one* or two especially typical Americans. Now for the first time do I *see* (& I watch with breathless interest) [what] the young American Walt[1] sang for and loved to see growing to a god. The Daring!!! Martin, our 2 years at those operas was near this kind of daring— but these darned Americans make their attempts succeed." And from Hamburg, whence they left directly for St. Petersburg on January 31: "I am leading a queer life— Restlessly roaming all over Germany & presently all over Europe. But there is a good deal of reason in this wandering. Brahm was a failure, but Brahm is not Europe or Germany or Berlin for that matter. Reinhardt who promised me *Hamlet* is a 1st class man for the work whether he let me do it or not. However he has not spoken to me since. He's 'tip top'— a favourite foreign phrase supposed to be English . . . My address in St. Petersburg is Hotel de l'Europe. I may be in Russia for a month."

[1] Both Craig and Isadora were readers of Walt Whitman. Craig had loved him since childhood. Ellen Terry had brought back for him from one of her American tours some original manuscript poems of Whitman's (one of which will be mentioned later) and a first edition of *Leaves of Grass*. Later Craig wrote about Isadora: "Whitman she spoke of & read because she liked his 'barbaric yawp.' I loved Whitman for his music & hated his 'yawp.'" Isadora's own Americanism sometimes grated on Craig, especially in retrospect. He wrote later: "We both spoke the same language— hers the American brand, mine the English . . . The Star Spangles were all over her, & her speech was modelled on Daniel Webster."

THEY ARRIVED IN ST. PETERSBURG—"BY TRAIN DE LUXE," AS CRAIG wrote Martin Shaw—on February 2 (January 20, old-style). Only eleven days after the infamous "Bloody Sunday" of January 9, the horror of the massacre was still vivid in the city and throughout Russia. The St. Petersburg newspaper *Rus*, in its issue dated January 22, along with other Russian newspapers, printed a long list of the victims: one hundred nineteen named and eleven unidentified. That was an official police report and probably minimized the total: it states that the one hundred thirty included those who died of wounds in hospitals. Given that some of the latter could quite possibly have been buried as long as eleven days after the event; that interment of all victims took place, by official order, at night; and that Isadora's train was probably late (unrest and protest were rife), she may well have seen one of the funeral processions "in the indistinct dawn" of her arrival—which in *My Life* she mistakenly calls her first in the city. It is unlikely that this vivid memory was an invention. By the time *My Life* was written, in 1927, Isadora had for some time been a passionate supporter of the pre-Stalin Soviet regime, and one of her dances to Russian revolutionary songs was dedicated to the memory of the victims of "Bloody Sunday." Partisanship and compassion may have played their role in her misrecollection of her first arrival; or, her editors may have altered the narrative to make it more dramatic.

Craig, who all his life was to be indifferent to matters of great public interest, made a single passing reference to the recent massacre in a letter to Martin Shaw: "Petersburg sleeps as calmly as a child. Revolution seems the last idea Petersburg could take into its head." Of more interest to him was that "It took 2 whole nights and one whole day to get here— my Gooorrd!!" and "Nearly lost my ears today, driving for ¼ of an hour in the air— Oh Looorrd!!" This same letter contains another of his tributes to Isadora: "Personality is a wonderful force. It is that which so many of us lack— & I. has it. The electric personality which sweeps out in a torrent and takes everything prisoner."

The evening of the day following their arrival, Isadora gave a recital in which—to use her own words as reported in the Berlin interview—she "portrayed in dance the music of Beethoven." It was an unlucky event. During the first half of her program, in which she danced to the "Pathétique" and "Quasi una Fantasia" sonatas (very poorly played, the critics said, by her pianist-accompanist), there was a feeling in the hall that things were not going well; the second half—the Seventh Symphony—was a disaster. The orchestra was the St. Petersburg Philharmonic, whose conductor, Leopold Auer, considered the occasion demeaning to his musicians and to himself and an insult to Beethoven (he later claimed to have conducted unwillingly and with his eyes fixed on the score, refusing to look at the "profanation"). The orchestra performed lethargically, and Isadora, feeling the hostile atmosphere, was not at her best. Some thought Auer had been influenced by the hostile criticism of Isadora in the "serious" musical journals following her earlier welcome by the daily press, and that a cabal might have been organized against her; yet even from her greatest defenders almost the kindest words to be printed about the Beethoven evening were that "there was no spiritual link between Miss Duncan's dancing and the music" or "between the spectators and the dancer," and that "The dancer was not in the mood. Perhaps because of the conductor's hostility, perhaps because of trouble with the administration, perhaps something else, but she was not in the mood—inspiration failed her, and her dancing lost its brilliance, faded, wilted." Contrary to Isadora's words in the Berlin interview, the spirit of Beethoven did not applaud her that night.

After that single performance Isadora and Craig went on immediately to Moscow, where three performances were scheduled and a fourth was added.

In Moscow, at that time the "second" capital, the general public was artistically more conservative than in St. Petersburg. Konstantin Stanislavski, director of the Moscow Art Theatre, tells in his memoirs of Isadora's debut in the city:

I appeared at Isadora Duncan's concert by accident, having heard nothing about her until that time, and having read none of the advertisements that heralded her coming to Moscow. Therefore I was very much surprised that in the rather small audience that came to see her[1] there

---

[1] Craig's copy of Stanislavski's *My Life in Art*, annotated by him, is in the Bibliothèque Nationale. At this point he has noted: "??? What can he mean—the theatre was packed tight." Neither Isadora nor Craig met Stanislavski during this visit to Moscow; their association would come later.

was a tremendous percentage of artists and sculptors with Mamontov[1] at their head, many artists of the ballet, and many first-nighters and lovers of the unusual in the theatre. The first appearance of Duncan on the stage did not make a very big impression. Unaccustomed to see an almost naked body on the stage,[2] I could hardly notice and understand the art of the dancer. The first number on the program was met with tepid applause and timid attempts at whistling. But after a few of the succeeding numbers, one of which was especially persuasive, I could no longer remain indifferent to the protests of the general public and began to applaud demonstratively.

When the intermission came, I, a newly baptized disciple of the great artist, ran to the footlights to applaud. To my joy I found myself side by side with Mamontov, who was doing exactly what I was doing, and near Mamontov were a famous artist, a sculptor, and a writer. When the general run of the audience saw that among those who applauded were well-known Moscow artists and actors, there was a great deal of confusion. The hissing stopped, and when the public saw that it could applaud, the applause became general, and was followed by curtain calls, and at the end of the performance by an ovation.

From that time on I never missed a single one of the Duncan concerts.

At that first Moscow performance attended by Stanislavski, Isadora danced her all-Chopin program. The review the next day in *Novosti Dnia* (the Moscow *Daily News*) was headlined AN EVENING OF DELIGHT AND BEWILDERMENT and expressed the ambivalence of its title in the conclusion:

En somme?
Interesting two hours of music, of expressive miming, exquisite plasticity, strange leaps, knotty knees and beautiful hands.
Nightmarishly devoid of ideas, but stirring and interesting.
"Is this art or cheap clowning?" someone asked at the end of the recital.
Without doubt, it is not cheap clowning. But is it art? *Que sais-je?* What *is* art?

[1] Savva Mamontov, the Moscow Maecenas of the arts.
[2] Another note by Craig in his copy of Stanislavski's book: "Not exactly the way to put it."

That same newspaper and others preferred the *Dance Idylls* program to the Chopin; nevertheless, during the last *Dance Idylls* performance there was an unpleasantness—Natalia Roslavleva thinks probably a provincial reaction to Isadora's "scanty garments." The following note appeared in the "Moscow Chronicle" of the St. Petersburg *Musical World*:

At her last soirée in the Moscow Solodovnikov Theatre, when one part of the public began to boo, the famous "Greek" dancer Miss Isadora Duncan, taken aback by such a reception, addressed the audience with reproaches. In broken French she declared: "This is impolite and unkind. This offends me as a woman. Those who do not like it may leave."

Controversy continued, but the elemental quality that was so strong in Isadora's art made its usual impression. The magazine *Iskusstvo* (*Art*) paid it tribute:

To dance, in the case of Isadora Duncan, means to express that concept of aesthetic intuition which is alotted to the whole mystery of the body, not located exclusively in the cognitive faculty . . . We had never imagined that what is deepest and most active in the life of the mind could be expressed by the hands, the fingers, the soles of the feet—not merely by the face.

It was as well that Isadora's Moscow performances took place when they did, for the day after the last of them the city was the scene of a political assassination that brought on a week of official mourning. On February 17, 1905 (February 4, old-style), Grand Duke Sergei Alexandrovitch, son of Csar Alexander II and uncle of Nicholas I, and commander of the Moscow military district, was killed outside the Kremlin by a bomb thrown by Ivan Kalyaev. Craig, who was fascinated by the Kremlin (in a letter to Martin Shaw he described it as being "like the palace of the Arabian nights . . . so feathery & light although so huge") appears to have witnessed the event: "By the way," he wrote Shaw when he was back in Berlin, "I was present at the bombardment of the Dook Sergie in Moscow!! My boy!!!"

FOLLOWING THEIR RETURN TO BERLIN FROM RUSSIA, WELL BEFORE
the end of February, certain aspects of the relationship between
Isadora and Craig become rather striking: not only is Isadora paying
for everything, but the lovers have "gone into business." That latter
element is first indicated by a few phrases in a series of three undated
letters sent from Isadora to Craig while both were in Berlin. The
first is in an envelope not sent through the post, inscribed to "Gordon
Craig— Living above the heads of mortal men— but shining his light
down among them to illuminate Beauty."

———— *CD 26* ————

The girl says she knows the bank is *not* open. I wasn't able to send her
before as she was out shopping.—
I am just reading however.
Before Kant we were in Time— Now Time is in us.—
O, Divine Philosophy—
Isn't this nice of Spinoza & Bruno. "Their miserable existence and death
in this western world is like that of a Tropical plant in Europe. The banks
of the *Sacred Ganges* were their true spiritual home. There they would
have led a peaceful & honored life among men of their own mind. In the
lines in which Bruno begins his book for which he was brought to the
Stake he expresses clearly & beautifully how lonely he felt himself in his
age and he also shows a presentiment of his fate which led him to delay
the publication of his views— till the inclination to communicate what
one Knows to be true which is so strong in noble minds prevailed."[1]
We eat about 1.30— don't be late.
Love— Isadora.

———————————

The next is on letter paper stamped "I.D." (which Isadora has
extended to read "I.D.id— and do— & always will").

———— *CD 28* ————

Dear Heart

We waited lunch so sorry you didn't come— I will come to tea with
you about 6. If you aren't in put a piece of paper on the gate as before.

[1] This passage has not been attributed.

Spring is coming—
Spring is almost here.
　　Dear Love—

　　　Your
　　　　Isadora.

————————

And the third—

———— CD 27 ————

Dearest

I enclose the check 3,600 marks.
Telephone me what time I can meet you at Siegmundshof or where you
like.

　　Love
　　Isadora

All here is well only they keep up a constant Bogie man fright.

————————

Craig has scribbled a note on the last of these missives: " 'They,' "
he says, "is Isadora's family—Ma, Eliza & (a little bit) Gus. Bogie
means me." But he offers no explanation of the bank and the 3,600
marks (purchasing power, approximately $16,800 in 1973).
　　The fact is that almost from the moment the brilliant "Bogie man"
entered her life, Isadora had been supporting him. His letters to
Martin Shaw are full of talk of his English debts and of stratagems
for outwitting the long-unpaid landlord of his London studio, who
was threatening to seize the furniture and pictures he had left behind.
"I'm not making a penny but living like a Duke," he had written
before leaving for Russia with Isadora. "It's fearfully exciting, but
wish to God I could rake in a bit more." And from Moscow: "As
you may guess, I am not paying my own hotel bills & haven't a sou
in the world—but am damned if I'll starve or sit on a stool & wait
for things." From her dancing Isadora was earning good sums, which
went to the maintenance of herself, her mother, her manager (her
brother Augustin), her accompanists, her school (managed by her

sister Elizabeth[1])—and now Craig as well, while he, in his own words in *Book Topsy*, was "doing little— resting, & being happy with her."

Craig was capable of all kinds of enjoyment, and in some of his letters to Shaw he reveled in his present lack of work. "I sometimes guess I am born here not to do anything but just to live. I see people doing mighty poor things & for mighty poor reasons— whereas to dance, laugh & sing & run through the snow & the green grass, that *is* something." But he missed being busy: "I am not working, I may tell you privately. You would laugh to see me, though it is no laughing matter, this idleness." "All work seems to hang fire at present," he wrote before returning to Berlin from Russia.

That was the trouble. Reinhardt had promised that Craig would be commissioned to design a production of *Hamlet*—but so far there was only the promise. And Count Kessler had come through with a suggestion concerning his friend the great Italian actress Eleonora Duse, and a production of *Elektra*: "Just heard from Kessler that he has entire control of Duse & *Elektra* & I am to do the d——d play in *Florence*— April 30. We shall see! Florence, my boy!"[2] The artistic distinction of those people who were his best "possibilities" did not stifle Craig's arrogance: "Reinhardt, Kessler, Duse, all of them monkeys and I delighted even at the least show of cordiality from them. But for the future? trust none of it— I demand my theatre & my rights from the whole pack."

Meanwhile his drawings were being exhibited in various German cities (there were at this time no sales), and he was "discussing plans" for his own theater as well as for an international theater magazine (later to be born as *The Mask*) with Kessler, Reinhardt, von Hofmannsthal, architect Henry van de Velde and Gerhart Hauptmann —all of whom admired him. He was also designing a "portable

---

[1] Elizabeth had power of attorney for Isadora, and signed many of her contracts. In that capacity she had signed one, "per Isadora Duncan," with Augustin on September 1, 1904, appointing him Isadora's "business manager" until January 1, 1905, agreeing to pay his "railroad expenses, board and lodging while on tour, and 5% of Miss Duncan's share or guarantee of performances."

[2] This *Elektra* was an adaptation by von Hofmannsthal, and as it turned out Craig did make designs for it but Duse withdrew; she and Craig did not meet at this time.

wooden theatre" and puppets to act in it, making drawings for
hoped-for productions of *The Tempest* and Shaw's *Caesar and Cleopatra* (both of which had been "suggested" by Reinhardt), illus-
trating a volume of von Hofmannsthal's poems and, for a series of
posters, drawing Isadora as she danced. Still, except for the Duse
designs and the von Hofmannsthal illustrations, he was earning no
money.

It was, as Edward A. Craig says in his biography of his father,
"a period of a hundred schemes"—and one of the schemes returns
us to Isadora's three Berlin notes. Craig had told Shaw in a recent
note: "I've written MacFall[1] who writes me a sad letter, saying he
better come over & be my business man. I need a man with push
& address. I can't pay him till he draws the 1st blood— then he can
be paid. Here's a darned fine country & I'm a darned fine bit of
goods just now & no one to sell me!! That's the situation. With
proper management I ought to visit town after town doing a new
play at each and so get around again to London. And it's a job
worth about 5000 [pounds] to me & 2000 to my manager." Such
Craigian bombast was doubtless familiar to MacFall (it certainly was
to Shaw) and probably raised whatever self-protective hackles they
both may have had, but now in Berlin Craig met someone quite willing to fall in with his scheme. This was a picturesque, picaresque,
American-born adventurer named Maurice Magnus,[2] decidedly
shabby in more ways than one, utterly unendowed with the capacity
for securing the solid financial backing Craig needed, yet with a way
of making himself appealing. Almost overnight Craig "hired" Magnus as his "manager," to receive a small salary plus earnings from
commissions. They took an office (a room in Craig's studio building),
employed a secretary and invented a firm name—Direktion Vereinigter Künste (United Arts Management)—with the telegraphic
address FOOTLIGHTS BERLIN.

Isadora was immediately involved. In Edward A. Craig's words:

[1] Haldane MacFall, a London critic of arts and letters and mutual friend,
who had written appreciatively of the Purcell Operatic Society productions.
[2] Magnus, who in desperate straits later joined the French Foreign Legion,
is best known for his *Memoirs of the Foreign Legion*—or, rather, from his
portrait by D. H. Lawrence in the latter's celebrated introduction thereto.

[Magnus] suggested that they might conduct all Miss Duncan's business from their office as well; they would probably make better bookings for her, and could look after her publicity properly. At the time her bookings were being handled by her brother, Augustin, who was a lovable person but hardly a businessman.

Isadora liked Magnus, and his idea. She also felt that Craig's experience of production could be used to her advantage. It was agreed that "Vereinigter Künste" would take ten percent from her receipts. Gordon Craig and Isadora Duncan then opened a joint account at the National Bank für Deutschland.

Such is the explanation of Isadora's "I enclose the check 3,600 marks," and her earlier mention of "the girl" and "the bank." The account may have been joint, but deposits cannot have been. One can well understand that for the rest of the Duncans the young Englishman who was being supported by Isadora, who with an unknown stranger had taken over as Isadora's manager (and who didn't even show up for lunch), should have been the "Bogie man."

JUST AS CRAIG FELT THAT ISADORA HAD GIVEN HIM RENEWED LIFE AS an artist,[1] she felt her dancing affected by him: sometimes for the better, sometimes—when she missed him too acutely and felt he was more important than her audiences—the opposite. They spent much of that year together, and she wrote him at least once a day whenever they were separated. Late in February she went off with her maid Anna on a tour of German cities.

[1] Despite the fact that his work was "hanging fire," Craig was constantly writing to Shaw these days in the highest spirits, full of the certainty of "winning this time"—feelings that he attributed to Isadora's company. "I could jump over St. Peter's or the Pyramids . . . She's a genius— & more. A *sun* genius— horribly like me— only I'm not a genius & the sun knows me only sometimes. If I succeed now it will be due to *myself*— dammé— I am drinking in 'American *push*'— Walt in a book is alive— but Walt walking, dancing, is LIFE."

———— *CD 29* ————
PALAST-HOTEL FÜRSTENHOF
FRANKFURT-A.-M.

[24 February 1905]

Darling—

6.30— dark as pitch— raining— pim-e-de-pim all night. Pillow soaked with tears— no sleep. Why aren't you here? Great Big Beds— *2* of them— Hélas!— Poor little me— *alone*. You are asleep now— you darling dearest sweetest Best. You are asleep up in the little balcony— and I not there— only your wonderful work surrounds you, and you live for that— only for a little while you lived for me— Those [blots] is tears. I kiss your dear hands, and your feet, and I love you— but you know— you must know. Anna is rather awed by my general gloomy mien, & trembles with fear at my frown. She says *es war viel netter wenn Herr Craig war mit*[1]— *Netter*— My Gods I should think it *war netter. This* is rather gashly— I have no heart to get into the Big Beds— I will draw until daylight—[2] No— I will read Walt—[3]

The first page I opened said "Think of Womanhood & you to be a Woman"— how can I? With you I had some faint hints of it— what it

---

[1] G., "it was much nicer when Mr. Craig was with [us]."

[2] Much later Craig wrote: "In 1905 Isadora took a sudden fancy to teach herself to draw— So she drove out (always drove in a carriage and pair if possible!) and bought some photographic reproductions of some of Raphael's drawings— mainly babies and saints. Back in the hotel in her sitting room she set up the photos and began a series of fearsome copies. I helped her a little, though not being a trained draughtsman I could be of very little use to her here. She never persevered, so she never learned to draw— even later in life so far as I know."

[3] Isadora apparently traveled with Whitman's complete works, as the poem she quotes from here, "Think of the Soul," appears only in the most inclusive editions. Its last stanza reads:

> Think of womanhood, and you to be a woman;
> The creation is womanhood;
> Have I not said that womanhood involves all?
> Have I not told how the universe has nothing
>   better than the best womanhood?

Isadora's love for Craig was beginning to make her think increasingly about her own femininity and about womanhood in general.

might be. Darling, you don't know— I think I have died & passed among
the shades. I guess I won't read Walt— he makes me feel like a tissue
paper fool— I'm afraid I am one— He says so on about every page— but
if *this* is tissue paper it hurts fearful. Well, I'll try to stand it— (if I can't
be a woman) at least like a man—

Darling, I will give you ten minutes of peace now—

> Your
> Isadora

——— *CD 30* ———

PALAST-HOTEL FÜRSTENHOF
FRANKFURT-A.-M.

[Probably 25 February 1905]

Darling—

I am just woke up in one big Bed & look over to see the other empty.
Not to see you when I wake in the morning— your sweet eyes— that
is dreadful— I feel as if I were dead & living only as a shadow—

What you are to me— if I could only imagine I was *that* to *you*—

Dearest Love that sticky man is very dangerous[1] and *must* be *stopped*
at *once*. You have no idea what they are in Berlin. They have no laws or
decency and he must be *stopped* at *once*. Telegraph me *immediately* how
much he wants and I will telegraph it. This is no matter to fool about—
so please do what I say. If you go to a lawyer go to Justizrat Nelson &
tell him you come from *me*— he will be nice & friendly & speaks English
perfectly. I believe it is against the law to stick things on an artist's pic-

---

[1] Here Craig has written "Furniture" in the margin of the letter. As we shall
see, his Berlin studio was several times visited by bailiffs. One such visit is
recorded by Martin Shaw, who was to arrive in Berlin the following January
and stay with him: "Craig owed a tradesman some small amount and had let
a few weeks pass without attending to the matter. We were both thunderstruck
when one morning there came a self-important individual who, without so
much as a by-your-leave, went round the studio with an appraising stare and
calmly started sticking little labels on pictures and furniture. Slackness in paying
bills in Germany, it appears, is strongly deprecated. If you did not settle within
a very short period of grace your goods were attached without further notice."
Edward A. Craig says that the first time Isadora came to Craig's studio the
gas had been turned off.

tures or anything that one makes a living from— a musician's piano etc.—
but I am not sure. It is in America, but the laws in Germany are terrific.

Here is my route.

25 Frankfurt
26 I will remain here as it is only an hour to
27 Wiesbaden
28 travel

1
2 } Breslau

on the 3rd I will be in Berlin.

If you go to Italy[1] in April & *want* me I will go with you. If you *Want* me— do you?

I am going out for a little walk because the Sun is shining— I have on me Spring Clothes.[2]

Au revoir Love

> *Your xx*   *xx* That means if you *want* me—
> Isadora

———— *CD 31* ————
PALAST-HOTEL FÜRSTENHOF
FRANKFURT-A.-M.

[Probably 25 February 1905]

My Darling—

It just struck me as a Blooming Farce your not being here & I sent a telegram asking you to come. I wonder if you Will?[3] You could go from here to Weimar. It is Beautiful here & *such rooms*— 2 Wonderful B*xx*s[4]— made of real olive wood, & a marvellous Bedroom in *rose satin* à la Marie Antoinette. Heavens why aren't you here— I feel as if I hadn't seen you

---

[1] Duse had not yet withdrawn entirely from the *Elecktra* project, and there was still a question of Craig's taking his designs to her in Florence.

[2] What Isadora's spring clothes were—so different from the fashions of the time—is shown in several of the illustrations. One of her winter costumes is described on p. 113. It was probably her unconventional clothes that accounted for the "incidents" while traveling, mentioned later.

The children in the school, Irma Duncan tells us, walking in Berlin in *their* spring clothes—brief tunics and sandals— with their governesses, were often accosted by adults who expressed everything from pity to threats of calling the police. Boys sometimes pelted them with stones and horse dung.

[3] Here Craig has written, "I did!"

[4] This is the burlesquely prudish way Isadora sometimes spells "Beds."

for 10 years. I went out for walk— Oh— Teddy you won't believe it I walked 2 miles— all by myself in *me Spring Clothes*.

Teddy Come along— I'm trying to Hexry you— & do you feel it? I Want You to Take The Train & Come—

come come come come come come come
come come come come come come come
come come come come come come come
This is Hexerei—

Darling Love, Sweetheart, Come Here— I've been 50 ages alone now, & I Want you right away. I wonder if you'll come— only 8 little hours away— 8 little hours—

I am here till the 27, when I part for Wiesbaden. Wiesbaden is only an hour from here so I think I'll go there from here, as this is such a Wonderful Hotel. If you took the train tonight you'd be here by 6 tomorrow morning. O Come along—

I'll Pose for you like an angel—

I'll stand on my head I'll do anything— only Come & put a stop to this dreadful Aching—

I'm not seeing any one but Anna—

I feel lovely— I feel you all over— And then *no you*—

O Come along—

How can you stay—

I love you—
Isadora

——— *CD 32* ———
PALAST-HOTEL FÜRSTENHOF
FRANKFURT-A.-M.

[Probably 25 February 1905]

Darling— I've read Walt
& I've drewed 2 hours
& I've danced 2 hours—
Aint I *Good*!

I feel like a Saint— I've sent every one away that called. Now I'm going out for a Walk—
All alone—

As its snowing I'm going to wear me Spring Clothes.

Dearest Sweetest— I love you
I Love You

but I'm standing it— although I feel dreful—
And You—?
        but Spring is Coming—
It will be warm & sunny—
And *We* ——— Shall We?
I will if you will ——— Will you?
I will be Home March 3.
      In the Meantime
        If you like
          Take the Train
            &
          Come to me
Sweetheart—
      I sent you a letter at 6 this morn—
Write me—

    Love
      Isadora

——— *CD 33* ———

[Frankfurt, probably 25 February 1905]

Darling— I have such a lovely feeling about you today— As if we would be together all our lives & after— It is beautiful & warm— Sunny— I guess it is the first Spring day—

The Coachman took me out in the woods and I walked quite a long way. Now I have left off that old Winter Cloak I will show you how I can *Walk!*— Sweetheart— I haven't spoken to a Soul but Anna & I feel peaceful & delightful & *you* all over.

You Dear— dearest— What shall I do for you—

I'm afraid you think me a little Brute do you— I sent you 3 letters and 2 telegrams yesterday and a letter & telegram this morning. Ring me on the Telephone— no. 4167.

I am here till Monday, when I leave for *Wiesbaden.* Will leave Monday night after the Performance for Breslau— where I dance 2 nights, 1 & 2nd— in Berlin on the 3—

I love you—

    Your (if you want her)
      Isadora

By that time, Craig was probably on his way to her. He wrote later:

February 25, 26: *With Topsy to Frankfurt-am-Main.*
On the 26th we drove in a carriage and pair to a fine old villa outside Frankfurt, on the other side of the river. There I saw round windows and tent-like rooms— of 1806–8? I forget their exact date.

March 1, 2: *To Breslau.*
I drew Topsy dancing, seen from the side wings of the stage; the drawing is one of those reproduced in the Insel-Verlag portfolio. (See illustration.)

And he wrote about Breslau, where Isadora danced her *Chopin Abend* and a second program in the Thalia Theatre:

At Breslau where she danced more perfectly than ever with more care more freedom more love there they sat still & stupid. How strange a slight. An ugly little theatre full of ugly & foolish people & on the darkened stage a figure growing at each movement more perfect— lavishing beauty on each side of her as a sower sows rich corn in a brown & ugly field— poems glitter and shimmer all round her, floating in the air with her waiting to be flung out into the air never to return— all there waiting.

———— *CD 56* ————
HOTEL ROYAL
HANNOVER

[N.d.][1]

Stop over for an hour here. Been reading Nietzsche all the way & feel the presence of his extraordinary ghost rather too strongly. If he pro-

[1] Isadora danced in the Residenz-Theater, Hanover, Tuesday, March 7. Craig wrote later (but perhaps inaccurately) that after returning to Berlin from Breslau, Isadora "went off to Hannover alone" on the sixth and thence again to Frankfurt on the eighth. Whatever the sequence of her dates, it is evident from the scattered positions of those cities and the distances between them that Isadora was nothing if not a trouper that winter and spring, and one well understands her imminent complaint about "Too much travelling." The reader might be reminded once again that her performances consisted entirely of her own solo dancing.

claims Wagner dangerous, what does he think of *himself*? He's *very* dangerous— at least to lone unprotected females like me. Does he think one could "dance to *his* measure"? Wagner is more of a dance tune in comparison.

Come along to Gottingen to enjoy some country air— do.

He says women are slaves or tyrants but never friends— I wonder what you're turning me into. I feel such extraordinary convolutions going on— one moment I feel I could live on bread & water on the highest mountain top & *think*, and the next as if I'd like to bask all my days in a valley with flowers & *kiss*— & the changes come so quick & unexpected that I feel a bit rattled. Battled— rather say.

We must go now—

So long— Come to Gottingen do come—

>   love
>   love
>   Isadora

——— *CD 57* ———

HOTEL ZUR KRONE
GÖTTINGEN

[N.d.]

Dear— We didn't arrive here till *8* o'clock. I don't think Nietzsche is the thing for Mother's child to read— any way, after perusing him for 7 hours I feel a profound gloom mingled with a sensation that my brain will go pop. Only Goethe's Conversations with Eckermann eased me up Considerably. They are in Goethe's old age, but filled with cheer. We poor mortals need cheering after all. By the way the Conversations are in *3* volumes— this is the *first*.

It seems a million years since this morning. I wonder if you went to Leipzig— I wish you'd telegraph. Knowing you is alternate Paradise and Torture— & there's no Poetry in saying I can't live without you— it's fact.

These 'Conversations' would please you— speaks a good deal over his color theory. Country around here looks Beautiful— Green & forests— *not* Pine forests. Come & walk kilometres—

O you you you— I am slipping away from myself and becoming nothing but a longing and reflection, and I tried to tell you the other day my *work* was the principal thing. *Work*— I haven't a thought or feeling left for it— that's the truth— it's this Infernal feminine Coming out at all places.

And yet— how far I am from wishing to be a Man!— but O how happy must the woman be who doesn't know what this tearing to pieces element means.

Come if you can—
Let's walk Kilometres—

Love—
Isadora

—— *CD 34* ——
PALAST-HOTEL FÜRSTENHOF
FRANKFURT-A.-M.

[Postmarked 8 March 1905]

Darling— When I arrived in Hanover I went to sleep and slept as if I were drugged until ½/5 in the afternoon. I woke feeling as if ⟨~~~~~~~⟩ razzle dazzle— I can't explain it. I managed to get to the Theatre somehow and get dressed— I don't know how I danced— I was sea sick between all the dances— got back to the hotel & fell asleep again until 2 when Anna woke me to get the train. I was awfully ill all night in the train & arrived here at 9 got to bed & went to sleep again. Went for a little drive this afternoon but I never felt quite so rum in my life. Seem to have gone generally capoot— Too much travelling— I guess I'll be all right in the morning but at present I can't even hold the pen straight.

I'll go through tomorrow night as well as I can and come home after the performance— so will arrive Friday at 8— I'll telegram you which station. Will you come & meet me? Gus & Sarah have gone I believe to Holland for a trip.

Good night darling Love I just sent you a telegram— I'll tell you in the morning if I'm better. Don't worry it is nothing but trains I s'pose— Life without you isn't worth anything— No it isn't.

I hope your work is going all right— Dearest heart— I have been looking all evening at the Acis & Galatea[1] programme— It is lovely—

---

[1] Craig was now undertaking to redesign Isadora's programs, and had probably shown her that of *Acis and Galatea* (1902) for that purpose. It is very handsome indeed: perhaps she had not previously seen an example of his book designing.

Be patient— a Chicken jumps out of the shell & begins picking up grain in two minutes but an Eagle remains long in the nest.
All my love Dear Heart

> Your Wery Wery Sick
> Isadora

THE FIRST OF THE TWO LETTERS THAT FOLLOW BEARS A SCRIBBLED note by Craig: "I wonder what this was? letter opening? jealousy?"

When Craig, in later life, assumes this particular tone of wonderment, the chances are, one comes to learn, that he is playing one of his favorite roles (and one should remember that his mother thought him "consummate" as an actor)—a role that might be called that of the Naïve Father, a bewildered Innocent asking the angels, or the stork, "Whence all these children?"

His "letter opening? jealousy?" probably is the explanation of Isadora's "awful kind of rage" for which she then apologizes, in her next letter, so humbly. One wonders how much of Craig's situation it was that she just now discovered. The letter she may have opened would doubtless have been one sent to Craig by (or, from Martin Shaw, about) Elena Meo, the adoring young half-Italian violinist in London whose first child by Craig, a daughter born in 1902, had died early in 1904 just after a second daughter had been born, and the birth of whose third child, Edward A. Craig, had occurred as recently as January 3, 1905, during the love-drenched week in Berlin following Isadora's return from St. Petersburg. Perhaps it was her discovery of that date that tore particularly at Isadora's heart. Craig's love-making since her return, the badinage, with its serious overtones, about "Isadora's child" in the restaurant and in the conversation in the train—all had taken place with Craig's awareness that a babe was about to be, and then had been, born to him in Kensington, and that the babe's mother and sister awaited him there, not to mention the existence of their five half-brothers and half-sisters here and there in England. Whether or not Isadora knew of his marriage to May Gibson, his liaison with Jess Dorynne, and his children by them, he had clearly not told her everything concerning

Elena, his "Nelly." When he told Isadora, on their "marriage night on the floor of the dear studio," that he "was going to marry in about four months' time" (actually, after his divorce from May, he never did marry again), how much more did he tell her? Not all, certainly, or there would scarcely have been Isadora's "awful kind of rage" later on. Nor, one suspects, can Isadora have known that in the letters Craig was writing to his confidant Martin Shaw—as he and she traveled and "kissed" and he "wasn't making a penny but was living like a Duke"—he was enclosing money for Shaw to send to Nelly, or asking Shaw to get funds from Ellen Terry for Nelly, or even saying, after describing his renewal as an artist thanks to Isadora: "I *will* win this time— absolutely must— & then I'll return with the spoils of war & lay them at the feet of my son & his mama." Nelly was sweet-tempered, worshipful and domestic; it was to Nelly and her children—not to anyone else; not to his earlier or later loves—that Craig would continually return, now and again, whenever he felt domestic and always at his own convenience. Nelly and her children were loved and supported by Ellen Terry, who, after Craig's divorce from May Gibson, also paid May's alimony for years.

Edward A. Craig, who has said that the arrogance which frequently characterized his father's behavior was often a mask worn to hide a fear of rebuff, a fear deeply rooted in his illegitimacy, says also that until he was in middle age this fear kept him from making the first overture to a woman. But Craig had learned early in life that for him to make an overture was seldom necessary. So great was his attractiveness that he had only to be still; the woman would advance, and eventually a child was born, with Craig acting the innocent, almost the victim, protesting that he hadn't asked for anything and that as for the woman—she had simply got what she wanted.

This picture of Craig does not particularly coincide with Craig's own description of his initial wooing of Isadora, and it coincides only partially with the Craig who emerges from some of the Isadora-Craig letters—especially the letters and notes written jointly by the two of them. But his own later scribbled notes on Isadora's letters, his drafts of letters to her, the later-written parts of *Book Topsy* and his letters to Martin Shaw do much to confirm it more generally. Fervor such as Isadora had already been showing, particularly in the letters from Hamburg, could only in the long run encourage the tendency to self-exoneration in such a man as Craig. That she already sensed it, and was trying to protect herself, is evident in her repeated "If you want me"; it is clear, too, that she was already realizing that he was at least as devoted to his art not only as she was to hers, but as he was to her. Isadora and Craig were two geniuses of illusion—one of the dance, the other of stagecraft: in the midst of the physical and spiritual involvement that had precipitately engulfed them, each was beginning to display his own degree of realization of the other's human qualities.

––––– CD 35 –––––

[Probably Berlin, March 10–15, 1905]

Dear— I feel awfully ashamed— ashamed is not the word.

I feel dust & ashes— it was an awful kind of rage that took possession of me—

Let my pain atone for it— I'm afraid you will never be able to think of me in the same way again.

And I didn't mean to tell you.

That is the worst of it—

You are so dear & kind

but I know what you must *think* of it.

I would give   I can't write about it— I hate myself— I am in despair over it—

forgive me—

but you can't make it *undone*[1] can you—

––––– CD 36 –––––

[Note by Craig: "March 16, 1905 at Magdeburg to me Berlin. She is in Berlin March 17."]

Dear— I received your letter this morning. "Be Calm Big Clear & Cool" instead of Crazy Small seeing red & purple & hot—

[1] Here Craig has written: "It is— for I forget what it was. (1944) Ted."

I'll try—

At any rate I will not "lie awake (any more) all night weeping over my sins." I'll put it down to Primitive Instincts, Inherited Tendencies— (Probably my Great Great Grand Mother was a shockingly wicked person—) and so shift the responsibility of it off my shoulders— for if I go on thinking that I did such a thing I will certainly go crazy. I never had a very good opinion of my virtues as far as that goes but there are some things that we *don't* do— however it was bad enough to have done it without worrying you out of your wits about it.

My windows look out on the Bahnhof. As far as I can see, Magdeburg is fearfully picturesque & ancient— but I'm awfully afraid it's another of those venerable towns in which the worthy citizens refuse to have dust thrown in their eyes—

and All the time my Brother my wise little Brother boy[1] is singing to his goats on the hill side while his little Greek girl plays on the flute— and beyond they see the glory of the Parthenon with the sunlight blazing down on it and the Blue Blue Sky— Ooooo— How I wish you would go with me there. I am sure it would be like a new life to you to see that. Other places may belong to different times— Greece is eternal— Beauty belongs to Eternity.

Speaking of Time and Eternity— I will be home tomorrow morning leaving here 8.20 [arriving] by about 10.20. I will telegraph you exact time. Don't meet me at the station but if you like I will come up to your studio for a cup of tea arriving there about 10.30.

You need not write "Never not love me"— I love all that is beautiful and I will always adore you because you are beautiful— (Is that Calm & Cool enough). Besides you have given me Everlasting Joy— I would say more but Joy is the highest— Joy includes Suffering— I suppose Suffering is a part of Joy— Well you have given me joy enough to last a life time if need be— (Is that Big and Clear enough). Yes you have given me unspeakable joy and made me Happy beyond my dreams of what happiness could be. You have taken me to the heights— the highest— and now, whatever comes— I will always be grateful & happy—

(See how Calm I am)

Wonderful isn't it?

As *Plato* says— "That soul which has Contemplated the highest Beauty is forever Blessed and Harmonious."

---

[1] When the rest of the family left Greece the year before, Raymond Duncan had stayed on, hoping to found a Duncan "commune." His "Greek girl" is perhaps Penelope Silelaneos, later his wife.

As *Marcus Aurelius* says— "Nothing can disturb the calm of the *reasoning* soul."

As Beatrice said to Dante— "Here live all in Peace and *Universal* Love."

As Christ said— "Love one another." Also he said some things about *little children*— and Isadora considered these things and prayed: "Save me from the *Green Demon Jealousy*! and the *Red Devil Desire for Complete Possessorship* and the ten & twenty thousand friends who accompany them."

"Glory Glory Haleughyer," sang the Salvation Army— "Kum 'n be saved!"

NOW ISADORA WENT OFF TO FILL ENGAGEMENTS IN BRUSSELS AND Amsterdam, with her maid Anna as usual and this time with Sarah, Augustin Duncan's wife, to guard her against importunates. The tone of the first letter from Brussels is strange, disquietingly ebullient; in the third letter Isadora provides the, or at least *her*, explanation: continuing repercussions from the "awful kind of rage" and its aftermath had left her not knowing how to write. In the subsequent letters one feels the atmosphere clearing on both sides, and toward the end comes Isadora's generous prayer that "you and All you love may be well." Had Craig perhaps even felt his ardor for Isadora *confirmed* by her "awful kind of rage"? Certainly in this Brussels-Amsterdam sequence he is so intensely present as almost to supply his missing side of the correspondence.

——— *CD 37* ———

[Brussels, 22 or 23 March 1905]

My Dear Ted—

(You Brute—)
You Darling
(Beast)
Most Wonderful Man
in
Creation

I have been afraid— ⌒⌒⌒⌒⌒⌒⌒
    Yes afeared ⌒⌒⌒⌒⌒⌒⌒
        To write you—
Because you'll call it
      Hysteria
        or
it feels a cross between that and
      perhaps the D-T's—
            That is
If you weren't such a
         Sweet
         Sympathetic
         dear Soul—
         (Heartless
         Misunderstanding
         Wretch
You mightn't altogether
         Comprehend
            So
            I
         Cant
          Write
             it—
So thats why I can't write at all.
Thats why theys so much Blank
                Space—
    Space   Space   Space
Nothing but Space
    Two Beds & nothing but
d —   =   =   =   =   Space
D—— it all. Woman's ought[n't] to swear— They ought to
      no no no   be
I wish I were a Man no   meek
      no no no   &
With very long legs   gentle
         Berlin   &
            that   patient
       Köln like   I
        step   aint—
Brussels one
    take
I'd

but
You know I can't write—
Brussels is lovely place—
Sort of Miniature Paris
Darling Love— put out your hands—
(That's Hysteria?- ? ?
I'm dying for you
(Thats nerves ? ? ?
I can't eat or drink or sleep.
(Whats that ? ? ?—
You see I can't write—
Duse plays *this* week in Paris—
We are *4* hours from Paris here.
Come along Sunday night and we'll go hear Duse—
                                        or
Will you?   see
Come along quick— *quick as you can*—
I'm half dead for you—
                    flying
        Strikes me this isn't *persuing*— I can't manage that
persuit & fly arrangement somehow—
I feel I'm like an Amazon
Amazon persued & brought the stalwart Warriors home—
                    'n Kissed 'em to death.
        They did—
I think I is an Amazon—
If you like the persuing idea you'll have to put up with me persuing at
the same time & Clash Bang Crash *Collision* in the Middle—
        So long—
        Come along—
    +   I love you—
        I am Your

                                    Whats that mean—
                                    Haven't you even guessed that?
            Isadora
    +   Whats that mean?
I'll look for the dollies—[1]

___

[1] Craig was making designs for marionettes—*wooden* marionettes, as will
become clear later.

Pictures lovely—[1]
    You—
Come Sunday night—
        Theres a dear darling
          do Come

    I mean
You must   Come along & *persue me*
    Please Persue Me—
I'll pretend to fly fine
If you'll only persue me—
I'll be More fun than a fox hunt
    Come persue me *do*   Whats
      You   that
    I love you— I love you   mean
                It means this— I love you.

CD 38

[Almost entirely obliterated
Brussels postmark, 26 March 1905]

Dearest— I have just woke up & Anna brought me your letter.

I feel so queer— so very queer without you— I wouldn't like to tell you just how queer— I'm afraid to write it.

I believe I wrote you one rather idiotic letter. It's a funny feeling— one couldn't call it unhappy because it's full of joy— one couldn't call it happy— so much pain and yet I guess its Happy. I guess it's Heaven, in a way. I never feel my hands without feeling yours too & every other part of me the same— and this dual feeling is so wonderful it's like being a whole Creation, a God.

All the Green is Coming on the trees in the Park. The Spring is much further advanced here and lovely little white flowers & violets to be picked at one's feet— also the Chestnut Trees are in Blossom here— and I feel so much in touch with it all— the Birds too. I wonder if you are Coming tomorrow? Duse is acting Nouveau Theatre in Paris until about the 7— of April. Paris is only 4 hours from here— We could go & see her— I

---

[1] Probably Craig's six drawings of Isadora that were being reproduced for publication in a portfolio and for display as posters in theaters. One of them is among the illustrations in this volume.

telegraphed you that yesterday— It's a bait put along with the satin chairs[1] Because I want you to Come.

I feel these Spring days belong to me— to make all other Spring days Beautiful here after.

I had a splendid Audience here— rarely have had so much enthusiasm, from the very first dance on.

Every one here has a light tripping step and a pleased look— quite refreshing.

If you start from Berlin tonight this letter won't reach you but something infinitely sweet lovely happy will reach me. In either way I can hardly be parted from you— that's the Beautiful of it.

Had a letter from Ray. He says little lambs when they are born— *at once* begin to *dance!*— & jump *four* feet in the air—

You Darling— I *Love* you— You—

> Your
> Isadora

―――― *CD 39* ――――

[Brussels, March 1905]

Dear— I have just opened my eyes and received your card.

You know I didn't arrive here till Wednesday, and it takes two days for a letter— still I had written some and torn them before the one you received— which was sufficiently absurd, I believe. You see you rather paralyzed me Tues night. I came off wondering, wondering if— you didn't feel you needed a Complete vacation from all mention of ――――. I don't know— Any way it's difficult to write when one doesn't write what one feels— feels— feels—

Of course I might send you a description not how I feel but how Brussels looks. As far as I can see from the Post Cards it's a delightful little town. You better come & see for yourself— I feel like sending you a telegram every second saying Come— so that they would arrive like flock of birdies dancing dancing flying tumbling into your studio and burying up all your work and you to the Neck till you had to climb out and Come to save yourself. Herr Maas writes that he brought you the

――――――――

[1] Perhaps Isadora's mention of "satin chairs" was in one of the letters burnt by Craig as being "too personal."

Costume books *and* the patterns— save one of each kind for me & the others are yours.

You *Dear*—

You better Come 'n find out about the halabolooing— Perhaps you'll be awfully surprised!

You funny Boy—

Every one Spoils You—

until you're Unbearable—

or like a *Bear*

And no one *Manages* you

and I don't know how—

I guess Managing is a fine Art.

Perhaps if you'll tell me what way you prefer being managed I'll try—

The last two days it's been Constantly raining— I forgot to bring my Books— I'm going out now to get something to read & read me head off—

Sarah is delighted with every thing— I don't have to do any interviewing. I sleep and she receives all the people like an Angel, and gives them tea— I don't even have to appear.

I spend most of my time with my eyes shut— thinking of you— delicious occupation— lovely little pictures of you flitting by or long sweet picture books of you— or recalling this you said or that— or how you laughed or many dear things you did— I can spend hours that way and not know they've passed in a sort of intoxicating dreaminess— a sort of Hashish but lovelier than any Poppy-eating velvet dreams. At such times I feel you quite as if you were here— perhaps you are— but *of Course* you are—

Also at night I dream of you— Wonderful and sweet dreams, so I am living more in Dreamland than in Brussels. Yes! I'm having a "*Good* Time"— I think all times will be *good* to me from now hereafter. My longings go out to you in waves always flowing from me but I seem to by receiving something in return which flows to me in Waves— and I have times of such deep still perfect contentment as I had not supposed was possible this side of Paradise— but this is Paradise—

Love—

Your

Isadora

――――― *CD 40* ―――――

[Brussels, probably March 1905]

Darling— It is about 3 o'clock— I have been sitting up writing the *Marvellous Book!*[1] Had a wonderful torrent of ideas falling over each other— Don't know if they are of any worth.

Astounding what I feel when you are not here— become suddenly very severe— don't care for eating or sleeping but filled with lovely feelings and twice as sensitive to sounds lights colors etc. It's all a matter of magnetic forces— same things that keep the Earth circling about the sun in constant rhythmetical waves of attraction & repulsion making the Complete Harmony— Wonderful.

Aren't we wonderful—

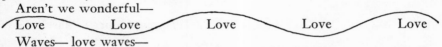
Love   Love   Love   Love   Love

Waves— love waves—

I've been writing about dance waves   sound waves   light waves— all the *same*—

How many thousand miles an hour do light & sound waves travel— so quick travel never-ceasing love waves from me to you— and from you to me— distance doesn't matter because the supply is never ceasing—

――――――――

[1] This is undoubtedly Isadora's essay "The Dance and Nature," which remained in her notebook until after her death. (It was printed in *The Art of the Dance*, 1928.) Addressed to women, it urges them to seek a greater "knowledge of their own bodies," and, as in this letter, there is much talk of waves: "Where are we to look for the great fountain-head of movement? . . . With the strengthening of the breeze over the seas, the waters form in long undulations. Of all movement which gives us delight and satisfies the soul's sense of movement, that of the waves of the sea seems to me the finest. This great wave movement runs through all nature, for when we look over the waters to the long line of hills on the shore, they seem also to have the great undulating movement of the sea; and all movements in Nature seem to me to have as their ground-plan the law of wave movement . . . I see waves rising through all things. Looking through the trees they seem also to be a pattern conforming to lines of waves. We might think of them from another standpoint: that all energy expresses itself through this wave movement. For does not sound travel in waves, and light also? And when we come to the movements of organic nature, it would seem that all free natural movements conform to the law of wave movement: the flight of birds, for instance, or the bounding of animals. It is the alternate attraction and resistance of the law of gravity that causes this wave movement."

Only the near touch is something too and I want that. Living with you
makes me feel so Strong I think I could easily own the Earth—
Isn't it beautiful.
The transfusion.
I am filled with *force*
It is *You*
>
> Good Night
> Love—
>
>> Your
>> Isa Dora

--------- *CD 41* ---------

[Brussels, 27 or 28 March 1905]

Dearest— Anna has just closed the doors and I am alone with a little red
light, and the other Big Bed stretching away in the distance and the rest
of the room looking mysterious. Silence within but without the noise of
the Boulevard. The people here are very gay and the students pass singing & crying out— also the noise & bells of the cars. All this Life— Wonderful and delightful life— Life is splendid— above all things to be *alive*.
Raining all day— I went out & bought some Books as there was nothing
else to do in such weather. The Contemplations of Victor Hugo— and
another about Jan Van Eyck— Splendid Beautiful People— Love fire
and endurance and Beauty burning always through them—

This afternoon we visited the studio of M. Rousseau[1] in whose work
I [am] interested— very Beautiful. His studio like a Temple and he a
slight small man with big black intense eyes in the midst like a High
Priest— all wrapt up in it—

A young man bending over a girl closing something in her hands— nude
figures—

A group of 3 women— reclining— one dreaming, one in thought and
one half risen—

Three men going forward hand in hand—

[1] Probably the Italian sculptor Medardo Rosso, who worked chiefly in
Paris and Milan. The studio in Brussels may not have been his own. In 1904 he
had had a one-man show at the Paris Salon d'Automne, of which he was one of
the founders. (See Margaret Scolari Barr, *Medardo Rosso*, Museum of Modern
Art, New York, 1963.)

I think after Rodin his things please me most of all the modern sculptors—

Anyway quite different from any of the present Berliners!—

He had a statuette— girl nude with a hat— Suddenly I thought of that delightful little person with the hat in the Musée of St. Petersburg—

Heavens— Miracle! The *Critics* here are *pleased*— I am enchanted— but it is true I *never* in all my life danced so well as Saturday night— I felt it— from the moment I began I had a feeling of extreme lightness and joy come over me— felt like wings— Have you given me wings— you took me to Heaven— it is possible—

You Dear—

I've done a great deal of Hexerizing— I've sung Hocus Pokus to the moon— I've danced wickedly in a Circle enough to bring you on the next train— I can only ascribe my defeat to the Baneful and Powerful influence of that Chief Lady Marionette, the Painted Jebezel [*sic*]—! who keeps you glued to her side! So you've decided you prefer 'em made of Wood!!!!——— and she's Hypnotizing you against my Hexerizing is she?— Whew——— !

I wonder why I'm not with you wicked as you are tonight instead of sitting up here big eyed and gazing out in the darkness— Gods what a rest it is— you are a thousand years pain stopped— and eased forever— Me tumbling round the old World pretending to feel Perky over it and feeling like ——— all the time— and then suddenly you—

Who gave me all.

You Dear— I love you—

Eyes to see with— Strength to feel— to live to fly—

    Come— Here

                             That's Hexerei

    To

                              more Hexerei

    Me

if you likes—

I have something to tell you—

    Your
     Isadora

—— *CD 46* ——

[Brussels, 28 or 29 March 1905]

Darling— I am just woke up— I wrote you last night and I thought I won't bore my dear— so I tried to write about different things— & keep the rest off the paper— Hope you appreciate the noble effort—

Anna has just brought me your letter— It was such joy to read it— pouring into my heart floods of joy & light. I can see outside also— the Sun is shining— you and Sunshine what a Beautiful World—

Here's the Coffee—

What's the fun of Coffee alone? On account of your dear letter I shall Arise & dance in the Sun— Arise and dance in the Sun.

Yes I feel like it—

Did I say you had no heart?— but I couldn't have said that— have I not often heard your heart beating— happy me—

happy happy me—

When I think—

When I guess—

You Darling

You are all the Beauty & best part of the World—

We'll fix everything—

Now I must arise and Dance in the Sun—

Love— it's written across the sky—

       Your
        Isadora

———————

The euphoria of this letter, and Isadora's "We'll fix every thing," must have meant that Craig had announced his coming; he did visit her in Brussels for several days. They photographed each other on the balcony of the hotel, in the park, and on an excursion they made to the ruined Cistercian abbey at Villiers-la-Ville. The climate of the reunion is suggested by lines in a letter from Craig to Martin Shaw: "I have been seeing all the Van Eycks at Antwerp— whew! how lovely— and the gallery at Brussels. It is all wonderful this *love* shown in the Van Eycks' work . . . no other thought is permissible in front of them except love. How they are stroked over and over by his hand— love strokes— "

―――― *CD 42* ――――

[Brussels, probably early April 1905]
You Compact Sweetness & Joy!—

Dear Heart—

Am just off for the Theatre. House is sold out to the *last* seat. Isn't that Jolly—

Have been awfully sick all day!! The Lord knows why— except I guess my entire system rebels at your absence. We leave tomorrow for Amsterdam— dam it all— She then *swooned* & recited these Cutlets—

In Amster*dam* by
Rotterdam
They dam the Dikes
O
Dam Dam Dam—

affinity— affinity— Elective Affinity— I have found my *Mate*—
You are he—
And you *can not Escape* me— Don't try—

Your *Dora*

―――― *CD 43* ――――

[Postmarked Amsterdam, 12 April 1905]

Dearest Heart— We have been travelling all afternoon & I am so sleepy & tired. Dutch Country so pretty— tulips & hyacinths— fields— and all like some one's back garden— but so *damp*— so very wet all interspersed with long canals and water— every where— and Amsterdam is really too wonderful with all the houses leaning side ways on one another or just falling forwards— but all rather somber grey & dreary—

The last evening in Brussels was packed— even turned people away, and here it is ausverkauft[1] for tomorrow eve—

[1] G., "sold out."

I am nodding asleep— Good Night—
You make me so happy thinking on you
   You dear one—

   Your
      Isadora

———— CD 44 ————

[Amsterdam, April 1905]

Dearest

   Just woke up.
   Have been lying thinking of you— Sunny today— Amsterdam is quite
transformed by sunshine— The waters of the canal that looked so gloomy
brighten to gold & silver & dance— and the black & white funny houses
take all sorts of tints—
   You would *like* it here—
   The Audiences have been splendid— I am going to try & get a Peek in
the Art Gallery today—
   There is no night train from the Hague for Sat night *after* the Theatre—
so we will either arrive Sunday night in Berlin or Monday morning ac-
cording to trains. Before this reaches you perhaps I will be with you—
with you— you and me.
   It is past what *I* can express in words— Words are not my medium—
I could perhaps dance a little of it.
   Without End
   Circles—
   Boundless—
   You see those words all mean the same thing—
   Perhaps there is only one thing to mean—
   Love— I You You I You Love   that means all the same too—
   & Work— That's the *same*. When I dance *well* then I am the same as
in your arms— or when I think *well*— or when I am filled with love then
I am filled with You—
   Of course if one was great enough just loving would be the *same* as
feeling seeing touching kissing— but oh oh oh oh I am not great enough—
until I *see* you— to kiss you again—

   Your
      Isa Dora

————— *CD 45* —————

[Amsterdam, April 1905]

Dear Loved One—

Just came home from the Theatre— Packed House & very enthusiastic. I received your dear letter just in time to make it easy to dance.

This town seems as if it hadn't changed since hundreds of years— so *quaint*— We drove to Rembrandt's house— I found a lovely engraving of his "Syndix" I will give to you if you like it, and I found that exquisite Madonna of Jan Van Eyck's— you know, before the Cathedral— quite a good Photo of it.[1] I have it at the foot of my Bed— by the way, it is Saint Barbara. Isn't it lovely! Also I found rather a nice book, Life of Whistler, with good reproductions of some of his things— Wonderful!— I have spent the afternoon reading it— It made me cry to think of him dead— *dead* is a *stupid word*— he's *living* enough—

Which reminds me— that I think you take Darwin[2] from the *wrong* end— Is the flower less beautiful for understanding about *roots*— but then I find roots rather beautiful & I find Darwin beautiful too— & fine— he is always fine— puts one on one's feet— & supplies the best Philosophy.

Divine Philosophy—

& if read aright his observations teach the living truth of universal life and Love—

And we *must* have Philosophy— Without that we would die of pain like dumb brutes. When they put on the torture then Philosophy is the thing— or call it what you will. Some people draw it from one source & some from another. A *Van Eyck* before me & a book of Darwin in my hands suits *me*— & Love in and over All— & now and then a Prayer to the Gods. Some people pray one way & some another— sometimes I *dance* mine & sometimes I think them and one of the ones I think deep down is that you and All you love may be well—

Good Night— Love—

[1] There are inkspots on the page here, and Isadora has written: "The ink is tumbling about the Bed— doesn't it make quaint pictures?"

[2] In her *Dance of the Future* Isadora had already spoken of "my most revered teachers, Mr. Charles Darwin and Mr. Ernest Haeckel." Haeckel, Darwin's apostle in Germany, was a respected scientist and an exponent of materialist philosophy. Isadora wrote to him of her admiration and offered to dance for him.

Next Day—

Lovely Sunshine— our rooms look out on the canal where we see the heavy barges & boats steamers tugs etc. go up & down.

I have been printing [?] your post cards some are *very* nice but I can take much better of you.[1]

I will be home Sunday morning if possible train— if not Sunday evening.

Your sweet letter just received—

All I can say is

    Darling— *you.*

Here is the yellow Pollen of Lillies mixed with red rose leaves[2]— it creates *undying love* in him who receives it—

Wonderful critics this morning. I've been so much roasted that I confess good critics are soothing.

O hast thou seen the Jaba wark? Love Love Love— *3 days more*— & I will be with you—

    Your Isa Dora

IN A LETTER TO SHAW WRITTEN SOME TIME AFTER HIS RETURN TO Berlin from the reunion in Brussels, Craig pays Isadora the strongest of all his tributes: "Miss Duncan has ended her season, or rather ends tomorrow, in Amsterdam . . . Inspiration is given out by the thousand volt per second from Miss D. And I am alive again (as artist) through her. You know how life-giving or -taking one artist can be to another." For the mercurial Craig it was a moment of high optimism: "The Duse scene & costumes leave for Italy tomorrow! Whoopla— something accomplished!" He had been paid for the

[1] These words are difficult to decipher and understand. Just possibly some of the photographs she had recently taken of Craig in Belgium had been made into post cards and she was printing something on them, perhaps in connection with his exhibitions.

[2] The pollen and rose leaves may have come from flowers presented to Isadora onstage the night before by some of the "very enthusiastic" public.

Elektra drawings (£300, through Kessler) and felt rich,[1] and it was at this same time that he accomplished something else. "I'm off to the fields with my manager to dictate the 1st chapter of my BOOK," he had written Shaw a little earlier; now he recorded: "On May 4, Berlin, finished writing my book (i.e. in Seven days) and read it to Topsy." The book—which he elsewhere indicates took him about double seven days; in any case it was written in a quick creative spurt—was his brief but important and well-known treatise *The Art of the Theatre*, the first major written expression of his theatrical ideas, his intransigence and his sense of mission. As he wrote it in 1905 (later editions, under a slightly altered title, include added material), it consisted entirely of a sharp dialogue between the "Stage-Director" and the "Playgoer." Realism in scenery and costume is roundly condemned. "The artist of the theatre of the future," the Stage-Director says, will create his masterpieces out of "Action, Scene and Voice"—or, on another page, out of "Action, words, line, color, rhythm." This "artist of the theatre" is the stage-director himself. "The relation of the stage-director to the actor [and to all the other technicians] is precisely the same as that of the conductor to his orchestra, or of the publisher to his printer." He must be the captain of his ship; his orders must be unquestioningly obeyed; he must be in absolute control of all aspects of a theatrical production. (Preferably he should be a man "of peculiar accomplishments" and the actors should be "men of refinement," willing to be controlled by him.)

Stage-Director

. . . The East still boasts a theatre. Ours here in the West is on its last legs. But I look for a Renaissance.

Playgoer

How will that come?

Stage-Director

Through the advent of a man who shall contain in him all the qualities which go to make up a master of the theatre, and through the reform of the theatre as an instrument.

---

[1] Even so he refused to pay any of his English debts, explaining to Shaw: "It would be insulting England to pay [them] with German gold!"

There are no two guesses as to who, in Craig's mind, was that "master of the theatre" whose advent he proclaimed, and ever since the publication of his dialogue Craig has been the hero of stage directors; his spirited 1905 insistence on the director's supremacy looms behind many pre- and post-opening-night stage battles of today. He was not the first to advocate this autocracy (among older directors the Duke of Saxe-Meiningen and Adolphe Appia had done it before him), but nowhere had the message been given in such attractive and concentrated form. The book, which appeared first in German, translated by Magnus and with a foreword by Count Kessler, was soon published in English and Dutch, and later in French, Russian, Japanese, Hungarian and Danish.

Craig's contempt for most of the contemporary acting profession has already been mentioned. "The dear old theatre was never meant for actors to play games in" and "Actors and actresses I think are exceptionally foolish all the world over"—both remarks made in letters to Shaw—are but two examples of his often expressed disdain.[1]

In one of Isadora's notebooks there exists, in her handwriting, a sketch for an enthusiastic article about Craig and his book—a sketch that one suspects may have been dictated, in part, by Craig himself. If this is so, then it is a case of the artist dictating to his Muse, rather than the usual opposite. Craig often paid Isadora the tribute of saying that much of what he wrote in *The Art of the Theatre* and else-

[1] In a letter to Shaw written about this time, Craig further remarked: "I do not *advocate* the supercession of the playwright by the director. I say that as a fact the stage director is the master of the theatre and the poet does not belong to the theatre at all. This is not a *historical* but a *natural* fact.

"It's the Chinese, Indian, Egyptian— besides the Greek— theatre I point to. Egyptian Theatre? Is there was there any?? Yes— Their ceremonies & religious rites were invented by the men who had that peculiar talent which I say is the talent of the master stage director. It's not the Poet's talent, is it? Obviously no.

" 'Every reader knows that in book form *Hamlet* is incomplete,' says the *Times* man. Then can it ever be complete, and do wanton and extravagant wavings of arms, mispronunciations, ugly scenes, and correct costumes make it more complete or less complete? Less, far less complete by EACH ADDITION."

where about action and movement, including what he called "still action" (pose and gesture), was inspired by her dancing.[1]

It is because of the intransigence expressed in *The Art of the Theatre*—the same intransigence that he displayed with considerable justification in his dealings with Otto Brahm, and which will be seen in frequent, later, less justified eruption—that Craig's genius for the theater has impressed itself principally through his writings, drawings and personality rather than in actual productions directed by him. *The Art of the Theatre* was to be followed a few years later by a volume called *Towards a New Theatre*, containing "40 designs for stage scenes with critical notes by the inventor Gordon Craig"— soaring, nonrealistic designs that have never ceased to inspire subsequent scenic artists; of similar impact have been the polemical articles he wrote under various names for the magazine he was to start in Florence, *The Mask*, some of which were republished in another volume, *The Theatre Advancing*. It is chiefly to these and other drawings and writings, and to two productions, his *Rosmersholm* for Eleonora Duse and his *Hamlet* for the Moscow Art Theatre, that Craig owes his reputation. Many think he might have achieved more. His famous intractability brought him harsh words from George Bernard Shaw: "Gordon Craig has made himself the most famous producer in Europe by dint of never producing anything," Shaw once said. And further: "If ever there was a spoilt child in artistic Europe, that child was Teddy Craig. The doors of the theatre were wider open to him than anyone else. He had only to come in as others did, and do his job, and know his place, and accept the theatre with all its desperate vicissitudes and inadequacies and impossibilities, as the rest of us did, and the way would have been clear for all the talent he possessed." This criticism by Shaw, who had his own brand of intractability, is certainly on the whole well justified, despite the crude inappropriateness of admonishing an artist to "know his place." But Shaw said also: "[Craig's] polemics have influenced stage directors wherever there is an artistic theatre in the world."

[1] See note for this page.

SOMETIME THAT SUMMER CRAIG, DURING A PERIOD OF DISCONTENT about his work (*The Art of the Theatre* was not yet published, and Duse's expected summons to Florence for the production of *Elektra* had not come), traveled to England for what seems to have been his first view of the son who had been born to him and Elena Meo in January, and who was apparently ailing. It was perhaps before he decided to go that Isadora wrote him about money for Elena and the children.

—— *CD 263* ——

[Probably Berlin, summer 1905]

Dear— Forgive me if I mistake but it strikes me you may be worrying about telegraphing money to England— Are you?— I meant to go to the Bank today & get some but it was closed— perhaps till then the enclosed will lift the strain? In admiration comradeship & love—

    Isadora

—— *CD 47* ——

[Probably Berlin, summer 1905]

My Dearest—

    God be with you— all the Gods watch over you & yours— I am so anxious to hear if everything is all right with the Baby.[1] Please telegraph me— You don't think I'm an indestructable doll without any feelings do you? or a wound up jumping jack? On the contrary I have so much sympathy that it makes me feel like h—— & I can't express it— but I *feel* it and when you are worried so am I— and how— My Being seems to have taken possession of yours & become rooted in your love— It is always growing and will never cease growing— growing & growing— an eternal Life. It is so Beautiful living with you I feel myself changing & Changing— I think if I have a chance I may turn into some thing quite nice—

[1] Note by Craig in margin: "What Baby— Teddy?"

Being with you does it—

But for you— have Patience

Sometimes the Greatest things are just on the way when we least expect it— It will all come to you— I am sure of it—

Your intense work will meet its fulfillment— I am sure of it— That is what the world is composed of for *us*— Work— and Love— If we could by some miracle make the two one— I suppose they are one— and all Contention will turn to Harmonie—

Work & Love, Love & Work—

Love—
Your Isadora.

———————

One of Isadora's notebooks contains several indications of another kind of activity she was engaged in that summer: raising funds for her school. The notebook lists many titled and untitled ladies in Berlin society—beginning with the Kaiserin—to whom Isadora wrote letters, and there are several drafts for the letters themselves. She wrote as follows to Princess Henry VII of Reuss, who was close to the Imperial court:

Dear Princess:

For the last eight months twenty little girls have been living together in my school in Grunewald creating much joy to themselves, a delight to all who have seen them, and a radiant hope for the future of the Art of the Dance.

I wish to take twenty-five more next winter. This will necessitate a new building erected on the vacant plot next door. As you know, I have given my entire earnings to the maintenance of the school and am most pleased to do so in the future. But they are not enough for the new ground and erection of the second building to be connected by a passageway with the old one. So I am giving a benefit at Kroll's Opera House on July 20th, as a means of raising money for it.

Of course we do not expect people who are out of town to be present but that they may subscribe and give their tickets to artists, etc. All the artists who have visited the school have been enthusiastic in their praises for the lovely dancing of the little girls and are unanimous in their belief in the value of the school to art and the state.

I myself am delighted with the progress of my pupils and am convinced that almost every child has more or less talent for the dance if directed along natural channels; and that the dancing of these little girls will be a source of much joy to the public in the years to come. For this reason I do not hesitate to ask for help in the advancing of my idea and feel sure my request will meet with your sympathy.

Isadora Duncan.

"The subscription list mounted daily," says Irma Duncan, "with Princess Reuss contributing a thousand goldmarks; Princess von Meiningen, a hundred; Frau von Mendelssohn of the banking family, also a thousand; Countess Harrach, a lady-in-waiting to the Kaiserin, five hundred; Siegfried Wagner, son of Richard Wagner of Bayreuth, a thousand . . . Isadora gave us new silk tunics in pastel shades of blue, pink, and yellow to wear for the occasion, making us discard the cheesecloth ones entirely. Also we had small wreaths of rosebuds for our hair." As the day approached, difficulties of some kind surged up: perhaps, as on a later occasion, the Berlin police, probably acting on orders from the puritanical Kaiserin, disapproved of the children's scanty tunics. Pleading telegrams were dispatched to various influential personages, and, though some good may have resulted, there exist telegraphic replies from at least two noble ladies—an unidentified Royal Highness in Bonn and the Hereditary Princess of Meiningen—regretting their inability to help "in this instance."

In any case, the performance took place on schedule and delighted the invited public;[1] Irma, who was one of the children, says that she and her little companions greatly enjoyed themselves. Only the Kaiserin is said to have been displeased—by the sight of "bare limbs." As we shall see, however, that single subscription performance did not suffice to put the school on its feet. Despite Isadora's brave words in her letter, the immediate goal was not enlargement but survival, and even for survival other means had to be sought.

MOST OF THE SUMMER OF 1905—SUMMER WAS A SPARSE SEASON FOR bookings—Isadora and Craig were together. In August they spent

[1] See Craig's description of the occasion in his BBC radio talk (pp. 361–362).

a week at Tützing, a resort on the Starnbergersee in the Bavarian
Alps; on the twenty-ninth Isadora danced in Zurich, where they
stayed at the Baur au Lac Hotel—"and what a very nice hotel it
was," Craig noted. When the new season began in September, there
were performances in Baden-Baden, Frankfurt am Main and Halle.
"Mr. Rumsmoke the stage carpenter," Craig wrote in relation to the
theater in one of those towns, "—was he from U.S.A. or England?
I forget . . . it felt like home hearing his name." In his letters to Martin
Shaw, Craig often shows himself homesick for England. Isadora,
American though she was, never expressed nostalgia for the U.S.A.;
as Craig said of her, "in her eye was California, and this eye looked
out over Europe and thought well of what it saw."

Beginning October 10, when they were both once again in Holland, Craig for the first time begins to list Isadora's box-office receipts:

October 10: In Amsterdam, Topsy's takings, 1893 florins
October 12: In Utrecht, 3200 florins
October 14: In Amsterdam. The news comes that [Henry] Irving is dead.
October 18: Leyden. 1110 florins.

Magnus had been eliminated—temporarily, as it turned out—from
the immediate scene. "I have taken control of all Miss Duncan's
business affairs," Craig announced to Shaw. (He also wrote, "I hope
to have all Duse's affairs to manage as well as Miss D's"—a hope
that fortunately for Duse remained unfulfilled and that one suspects
was but a Craigian dream.) According to Craig, Magnus was dis-
pensed with when his "borrowing" from the business account of the
Direktion Vereinigter Künste became so frequent as to make his
continuance uneconomic; Edward A. Craig, however, hints that the
chief objection to Magnus's "borrowing" was that it cut down on
Craig's own—which, because of his privileged situation, was no doubt
considered by him, and by Isadora too, something of a different
nature entirely. "Magnus (no more *with* me) but most friendly,"
Craig wrote to Shaw. "Is agent for about 6 American publishers."
Now Craig himself took over as manager, with a contract between
himself and Isadora dated Amsterdam, October 10, 1905, to extend
for seven months. According to its terms, Craig was to get 50 percent of Isadora's gross receipts, in return for paying for "theatres,

lighting, orchestra and orchestra direction, advertising, railway and carriage expenses" and arranging for "first-class theatres only" and "not less than twelve performances a month." Isadora, for her part, agreed to give at least twelve performances a month and to provide four different programs, including a new one by January 1906. The document was elaborately drawn up by one Hendrik Wertheim, an Amsterdam notary, signed by Isadora and Craig, witnessed by a clerk and porter of the Amstel Hotel, and registered with the American consul. It is difficult to know what its real significance was. Thereafter Craig sometimes did enter into direct negotiations for Isadora with impresarios in various cities, but there seems always to have been some other manager in the picture as well. A letter dated December 23, 1905, from one exasperated impresario, J. Stumpff of Amsterdam, to a certain Jul. H. Krotoschiner at Vereinigter Künste in Berlin, points out that on Miss Duncan's behalf, Stumpff had had to deal, successively, with "A. Duncan, Magnus, Lawertsky, Craig, *und nun wieder ein neuer*"[1]—presumably Jul. H. Krotoschiner himself, whoever he may have been. Magnus was soon to act as manager or agent again, from an office of his own, but he is always a shadowy figure and his sense of financial responsibility was apparently about equal to Craig's. For us the Amsterdam contract remains chiefly a curiosity—a business document between lovers, its stiff officialisms contrasting rather grotesquely with the language of the letters.

After Isadora's performance in Leyden on October 18, with its 1,110 florins to the box office (estimated as the equivalent of approximately $2,200 in purchasing power in 1973), they drove the ten miles back to The Hague through the Wassenaar Woods. The next day Craig returned to Berlin. Isadora continued to dance in Holland.

———— *CD 50* ————

[Probably The Hague, 19 October 1905]

Dear Heart

Now you're going Dum ti dum on the r.r.
Didn't we have a Wonderful Magic ride last night— and a Wonderful

[1] G., "and now yet a new one."

Magic walk by the Sea this morn— It will all fit in you'll find in your
work— all this fine little Holland Country. I received the telegram from
Magnus at nine— opened it as I thought it might be from Stumpff—

Sounds pretty nice—

I can imagine you're transforming Shaw's Anthony[1] & Cleo into something pretty fine—

I Love you— if you knew how flat the wine tastes without you— well
I'll work to keep up with you & live on Bread & water till we meet—

Me Comes to Berlin if you telegraphs—

    Your   10.30
        Isadora   *Thursday night*

Isadora's imagining that Craig was transforming George Bernard
Shaw's *Caesar and Cleopatra* "into something pretty fine" was based
on his having sent her the news that in Berlin Max Reinhardt and
Count Kessler had asked him to design a production of that play.
The resultant fiasco is a prime illustration of Craig's intransigence.
Negotiations were protracted. Craig insisted to Reinhardt that absolute control of the stage and everything on it must be given to him.
On November 29 Magnus wrote Craig that Reinhardt could not
accept the conditions as stated. On December 9 Craig reiterated them
—this time to Kessler. On the thirteenth Kessler replied: "I feel, that
if this scheme with Reinhardt comes to nought, my force in your
service is spent. I have given too much of my thought and nerve
power to it, to be capable of raising a similar loan on myself again,
if this is to be lost." Craig then declined a compromise offer of
autonomy plus an interpreter. (Since neither Reinhardt and his
helpers, nor Craig, spoke the other's language, an Anglo-German
interpreter seemed essential to everyone—except Craig, who claimed
that an interpreter's presence would "split the authority.") Next he
objected to the financial terms, then returned to the question of
autonomy. Finally he withdrew, saying that the continued delays
"by Reinhardt" had left insufficient time for preparation and rehearsals. Kessler wrote to Craig on January 10, 1906: "Reinhardt

[1] Isadora's error for "Caesar."

has written to me, saying he is sorry and amazed at your changing your mind. I much regret it too, as I cannot help thinking this decision of yours a great mistake. However, you must know best, and so I can only wish that you may soon find some other way of realizing your plans." None of this had prevented Craig from making beautiful drawings—the only surviving elements of the project, aside from the correspondence—which indicate that the production might well have been "something pretty fine." Nor did it prevent him from writing to Martin Shaw: "I am as it were cut off from the Theatre— I who possibly happen to *be* THE THEATRE— Queer."

———— *CD 48* ————

HOTEL DU VIEUX DOELEN

LA HAYE

[Postmarked Gravenhage (The Hague),
24 October 1905]

Dear Ted

Rec your dear letter
You funny man—
Am sending you a photograph you will like—
Spent the day between the Sea and the Museum— out from the Pictures came again all the words you said of them— I adore Jan Steen— all of his seemed warmer more tender & lovely than ever— What a man— lived in Leyden & kept a tavern— Wasn't he Happy & Nice— & did his work pretty well didn't he. Wish I could dance nearer that Steenish Breadth [of?] Nature. Ted when you are not here it is as if my Soul were not here— but I think of bits of you. Don't dare think of all of you— would die of Longing— & I find you in all Beauty. In the Sea today & in Rembrandt letter— especially in the one of which I send you the photo— O— by the way— Topsy were very ill— & very bad pain— & awful— & then wonderful magic things— so I guess Vereinig. Kunst can book that tour right along— till next summer.[1]
Helas! one can not have everything but still it made me pretty glum & glad & glum— Aren't I ever going to have any little Baby of my own but always go on dancing round Strange Foreign Countries & dancing & dancing & dancing & no more—

[1] A miscarriage, or a delay of what she called her "bad days"?

Answer me— but any way what *ever* happens you is the Wonderfullest
Man & I love you truly & am forever as much as you like

    Your
      Isadora—
        Your own—

Why should you ramp You *Have* it all
Tell Shaw[1] to stop on the way & see me.
Mustn't I come up for that Law Courts on the 29? Arnhem is the 28.
Mustn't I? Me come right along—

              CD 51

TRABENERSTRASSE 16   *GRUNEWALD BERLIN.*

                [Probably The Hague, October 1905]

Dearest Ted—

That little daisy 3. ID up there gives me infinite pleasure every time I
look at it— (A thing of Beauty is a Joy forever) & you are full of it—
your hands are so Wonderful & Strong & Beauty comes pouring out of
them. Did you know that Leyden where we took the magic ride is the
Birth place of Rembrandt— & he lived there till he was sixteen, and . . .
wandered about probably through those same woods we drove through at
night. At 16 he went to Amsterdam but returned & taught for 7 years at
Leyden. & Jan Steen was born there too— 20 years later & kept a Tavern
there— & had all that nice jolly family there— Why aren't people always
jolly like Jan Steens Family?

---

[1] Craig had often invited Martin Shaw to visit him in Germany, and had
lately proposed that he come as pianist for two months into Isadora's school.
But Shaw seems not to have arrived before January 1906, when, as we shall
see, he became Isadora's conductor for several months. At various times there
was a question of Shaw's writing dance music for Isadora, and on one of Craig's
letters to him she wrote her request: "Can you write music on Greek rhythms
— ᴗᴗ — ᴗᴗ. . . It must be a *Pastorale* with flutes and oboe. Something about
Pan & satyrs. *Long* rhythms." Shaw, who seems from Craig's letters to have
been somewhat torpid, apparently procrastinated over this piece, which he
and Craig refer to as *Pan*; in another letter Craig tells him: "Pan Dance. Apollo
Dance. Dionysus Dance. Write the Apollo now!!!! Fine long rhythms & as
noble as hell."

Your Badecker Information Bureau Guide to Lots of Places— I'm loving you all the time

    Your
       Topsy—

Note: For some of these letters Isadora was using stationery with a letterhead designed by Craig for her school (to which her arrow is pointing):

—— *CD 52* ——

[Probably The Hague, 30 or 31 October 1905]

Darling Ted—

Wonders will never cease. Here's Topsy me up at seven o'clock— Topsy me can't sleep very well any more— jus get up— no fun sleeping without Ted— Not a Bit—
Danced last night on a tea table in a Cunning Cracker Box called a Theatre at Haarlem— all sold out— only 800 gulden in House— rather silly place to dance. I wish you'd tell Mr. Stump not to book a theatre that only holds 800 gulden— he probably thinks I'm in my dotage & want to play Circus in the Barn. Wish you'd tell him not to book small towns that take all day to travel to them with nice little rustic audiences & Hotels that charge more than the receipts— Might as well dance in *Cities* while I'm about it— Don't you think so— Plenty of Cities in the world without going about to all the Villages. How can I make a new programme, Ted darling? when I spend all my spare time in Railway Carriages— or trying to rest from going tum de tum— I don't like this Touring Business. Don't you think the inhabitants of some large city some place might like to see Topsy me dance more than 3 times—
The wind is blowing all the autumn leaves around in a Swirl and the porter is feeding whole flocks of Birds before the door— one can't tell sometimes which are birds and which leaves—
Now a man has come with a great Basket load of fishes selling them to the Hotel man right on the side walk—
I am sorry you didn't see the Children dance—[1] Your wire came first & made me cry from Joy— but O you fraud perhaps they didn't have any

---

[1] This was a second performance by the children, without Isadora, at the Theater des Westens in Berlin, Sunday afternoon, October 29, 1905. See note for this page.

success at all— I have not yet heard definitely— However I had sent a long telegram to Elizabeth two days before to send you a loge— also wrote. Little Beasty she didn't do it—

Dear will you send me my Whitman— Anna will give it to you—

If there are no more dates after Nov 3 I will come back to Berlin—

Hurrah!

Yesterday I walked two hours on the beach. It is extraordinary the light effects here. People from quite a long distance were clearly outlined as if cut out of black paper— against the sea & sky— and one could see every little detail of hat & dress from long way off— just as one sees the minute details in the pictures. Lights certainly happen here that never happen any wheres else—

Well Topsy me go do a "Bit of Work" to Copycat Teddy— See Kunst der Toe Kunst![1]

Toololooolooolooooooooo

> I remain
> your darling (ain't I?)
> Isadora.

Why don't you send me Mr. Shaw's piece? I would dance it!—

——— *CD 60* ———

[Two post cards,
probably The Hague, early November 1905]

No letter from you today my only Sun Shine rays— Here all is Misty Misty— Kathleen[2] walked in on her way to Paris. Will stay till Tuesday.

---

[1] "Toe Kunst" is what might be called Duncan-Deutsch: "Toe Art." The German title of Craig's *The Art of the Theatre* is *Die Kunst die Theaters*.

[2] Kathleen, of whom more will be heard, was at this time Miss Kathleen Bruce, a twenty-seven-year-old English sculptress, who had a studio in Paris and had studied with Rodin. Later she married Captain Robert Falcon Scott, who perished in 1912 while trying to reach the South Pole; her second husband was Lieutenant Commander Edward Hilton Young, later Lord Kennet. She executed the Scott memorials in Waterloo Place, London, at Portsmouth, and in Christchurch, New Zealand, as well as likenesses of many other prominent Englishmen. She died in 1947. Her brief "Autobiography" and parts of her diary, arranged by the late Lord Kennet, were published in 1949 as *Self-Portrait of an Artist*. See note for this page.

I was so glad to see her, but would be gladder to rush into your dear arms— How goes it? Dear Dear Love— I long & long for you.

Poor Topsy me—

––––– *CD 59* –––––

Sunday
[Probably The Hague, 5 November 1905]

Dear Ted

I received your telegram first— I was so glad. I have been way up to the North of Holland— Awful wooly journey all day. I find it quite impossible to be alone— several incidents traveling, etc.— & so have asked Kathleen to come & stay with me a few days till I can find a suitable maid— She is a nice quiet English girl— I think you would like her to be with me—
I am getting pretty lonesome to see you—
When I get 3 days free I will just run up to Berlin— Topsy can't stay alone So long— Makes Topsy Very sad—
Topsy me come Berlin soon—
  Yes?—
Good Night Dear Love. I'm pretty tired from so much travelling, and Life 'thout you isn't the Dear old Jan Steen existence that it was—

      Your
        Isadora.

––––– *CD 61* –––––

[Probably The Hague, 5 November 1905]

Dearest Ted

I'm worried about your not feeling well— Isn't it *Neuralgia* of the nerves, just as I had? The powders Dr. Honan gave me stopped it at once. You mustn't ride in open Droskys or Autos, at least without a fur cap. Your letter was very clever and Beautiful too— You Dear—
I have just been having my lunch alone— awful good joke in a way.

Kathleen falls suddenly ill & Dr. says "overstrain." No one seems able to
stand this life but me. So she is in Bed sleeping—
If she is better will return to Paris tomorrow or day after. She is a very
sweet & gentle girl— rather wore herself out over Mama & Raimond I
fancy— So its only fair I should see to her—
Isn't it funny all my maids fell ill too—
I hear the Audience applauded frantically for the Kiddies. Wish I knew
what they did! I went to see Julio Caeser [*sic*] here. Insult to the Intelligence or rather they took it for granted that Audience had no intelligence to insult. It looked like one of those highly colored costume books
come to life— It was too funny to laugh at and too sad to weep for—
Marc Antonius addressed the crowd like a peddler selling goods at a
fair— & all we saw of the crowd was the back of twenty-five pair of
wrinkly wooly tights. Stout ladies regaling themselves in long veils of tulle
talked inanely about having *Hystreeks* over Poor Caesers death.
As for Caeser— he was a fat Irishman on a Bit of a Spree— Before the
evening was over I had almost decided never to put foot in a Theatre—
Either side of the curtain again— However I am composing that programme & I will do it in a theatre for my own edification once a month.
I wouldn't book it more than once a month for I'm sure no one would
come to see it. I do it early mornings— I can't sleep any more for some
reason or other— fall into a sleep about 3 o'clock and wake at 6. However
I take long walks and feel in the best of health. I would like to dance
in Paris— Kathleen tells me that the manager of the Trocadero told her
he wrote offering me a Guarantee. Did you get it? No I wasn't fooling
you bout them incidents. Several times, although I got expressly in 'Dame
Seule Coupée,' men got in & stared my head off the entire trip, and then
it wasn't nice on railway platforms either. O— I have the dearest little
dark green suit[1] made like my white gowns only with belt, & collar &
cuffs of fur and a kilted skirt & a dark green cape to match and a brown
fur cap & I look well simply Scrumptious. It just came today— had it
made to order. And *Black* shoes & gaiters & I look too neat for words.
You'll be awfully pleased I guess—
What a sweet picture you sent me—

---

[1] Even this new winter "suit" sounds like a variation of Isadora's usual
Greekish costumes. Irma records that from Holland at Christmas this year—
probably from the same dressmaker—Isadora sent the children at the school
"pretty new dresses and bonnets expecially designed by her and made in the
Hague. Both the dresses and velvet bonnets were blue and edged with swans-
down."

Going for a little air now. Til next time Good day Dear Dear Dear
Dearest Love—

>   Your
>   Isadora

Always Loving You
Night & day time too
        oo oo.
Toololoololoo oo! oo—!

——— *CD 62* ———

Monday
[Probably The Hague, 6 November 1905]
Thank You for the Lovely Picture—

Dearest Ted— I open one eye in the morning & shout Briefe[1] Briefe Briefe
and then the maid brings me your letters & I have a Wonderful Party
reading them. Certainly without a doubt You is the Most Wonderfullest
Man in the World—
I adore your letters— they are The Letters of the World— Never were
there any thing like them—
Kathleen had a High Fever for 3 days. I was afraid it would be very serious but she is all right now— she returns tomorrow— is very anxious
about some statue whose clay will crack if she doesn't get back—
Poor itty me I live in Raily way trains—
I was doing some wonderful Big Magic practicing but I became[2] some
big magic pains in my leggies so I stopped. I take a Cold Icey cold shiv-
erry iverry Bath each morning to try and make me sleep because although
in the Best of Health I don't sleep at all any more— although I religiously
walk an hour or two each day— generally by the sea— Ooo— the Sea is
Beautiful— I have nice red cheeks from the Salt Sea Air— but I can't
sleep—
No not a Bit—
I muse myself pretty well thinking of you all night. I have such a lovely
lot to remember— all of you.

[1] G., "letters."
[2] For G. *bekam*, "got."

I've been reading Motely[1] but he wasn't made for my comprehension & although "Most Iteresting" is somewhat a penance— However when one has no Sins one can amuse oneself with Penances—

O, but you would like the way I am dancing— really very nice if I do say it— & without the slightest effort I could easily dance every night at this rate— I am learning the more reserve the better— I refused the Donau[2] after Iphigenia the other night although the Audience *roared* for it— but I only bowed & bowed gravely nodding my sagacious head— I see & speak to no one but I feel brimming over with Love for the All of it— Thank you for the Whitman— I read him on the cars coming home. I am feeling so joyous after your letter today— you know you say very sweet things to your Topsy— Honey Comb things. You make me filled to the Brim with Happiness—

I remain always your obedient Topsy when with you— Turvey when away— forever adoring you

Topsy

Dear Ted all I write seems quite absurd when I think how you make the world one Perpetual Gladness to me, and stead of writing I could sing & chirrup like the little birds out side the window— Being with you I have sometimes been selfish jealous odious but away from you that you exist that you think of me a little makes me feather light with Joy—
You dearest Thing in the Universe— that's *You*—

---

[1] Probably J. L. Motley's *History of the United Netherlands.*

[2] Isadora was beginning to be apologetic about the tremendously popular "Donau"—Johann Strauss's "The Blue Danube" ("An der Schönen Blauen Donau") —and to recognize, perhaps under Craig's guidance, the inferiority of some other portions of her early programs.

——— CD 260 ———

[Picture post card of Japan,[1]
probably The Hague, November 1905]

Joy & Mirth! Let us make a little trip to the Land of Beauty some day—
What do you say?
How lovely it would be—
I want to come back to Berlin I do— I am hungry to hear your voice—
When you want to be you are Paradise enough— You are Heaven to me
with all the Gods in *one*—
I dance here a poor little body but my spirit is with you— is it and don't
you feel its arms about you—
or *dreful thoughts*— but No—

Love
    Your
        Topsy
        only

——— CD 58 ———
AMSTEL HOTEL
AMSTERDAM

[Probably November 1905]

Dear Ted

I came over here this afternoon as I thought it better than travelling at
night.
I guess all that Wonderful Magic Life came from *you* as I don't find it
any more so Magic—
Even the Black & White cows looked sad & I saw three ships on the

[1] On another Japanese picture post card [CD *259*], marked "2," there exists
the second half of another message from Isadora to Craig, perhaps written at
this time: ". . . have feminine insides. Above [an arrow points to the Japanese
scene] is the land where they know how to raise women & flowers. I must
stop as my temperature is high. Oh you love me— Why in Heaven Earth or
Hell should you?"

canal without feeling the least excited— and any number of lovely houses
without any one to Poke me proved insipid—

I guess *you* are the Magic.

I sent you telegram last night as it is just three [?]. I suppose you are
fixing up Mr R[einhardt] and C[ount] K[essler] in the way they
should be—

That's right—

You *are* you know & I always said you was the Wonderfullest Man in
the World.

I'm going to sleep now as I didn't get a *wink* last night. A feverish note
from Ray saying Pen would have to go to "Pauper Hospital"— & a
pathetic little note from Pen were the cause of my sending 400 francs—
Hope that will see 'em through—

Tonight I dance for you Very Careful & return to La Hague tomorrow
morning early & look at the Sea. I found *2* letters for you here & sent
'em on to you by Eile Brief.[1]

Me Come to Berlin whenever you telegraphs

Me *likes* to.

        Your TopsyIsadoraTopsy

        ——— *CD 54* ———

                        [Probably Amsterdam or Brussels,
                                November 1905]

Darling Ted

I am Bounding Dancing Jumping Bumping Mad to go to Berlin & I'm not
doing it—

Obedient Topsy me.

O I want to see you & all these telegrams

You Dear Sweetest Wretch Whats the matter with your Nerves?— I
think it's Neuralgia. Don't ride in Open Carriages or Autos— remember
the Head I had—

Lovely evening last night— Enthusiastic Public— House not large as it
was billed too quick— next time will be sold out. I've been trying to roast
chestnuts at the fire & burnt my fingers & my nose— awful good Chest-

---

[1] For G. *eilebrief*, "special delivery."

nuts. Wish you were here— Why don't you get my letters— I write 'em— For instance did you get a *long* one written Nov. 6. Say where's that Telegraph address? Please register it because 11 Sieg'hof makes 4 words address—

Darling I'm worried about you going to Dr. You're strong enough. What's the matter? Do you *walk* 2 hours a day? *I do*— am getting awful thin. You like nice thin Topsy?

Awfully good health me but can't sleep!!!— more than half hour at time— When do I come back? What date I see you?

Ooo please get well— you're too serious I fear—

That was an Interesting Article—

but as Walt says—

Beyond & Beyond and for Reasons—

They can't understand you—

I don't think dancing every night hurts me a bit— feel light as a feather!— only weigh 58 Kilo— last year I weighed 65. Look what an Artistic Improvement you've made in your Topsy!— 14 lbs!!!

The Bois where we walked in Spring is Glorious Red Brown Autumn Leaves— Vales of Fallen Leaves— I enjoy walking there—

O apropos— of Nothing— Ted I want to see you *right way*

I do—

Just compare me this time last year[1] & now— I was so restless then— I feel so secure now— Then I liked to talk to everyone— Now my Biggest Bliss is long thinks on you— Then I didn't know— Now I know— I love you love you love you—

Then I was alone— Now you're all about me in me every where with me— & your dear Hands I always feel them— & I don't want to see or speak to any one. Thank the Lord I don't— they only spoil the Beautiful atmosphere thought of you makes about me—

What shall I do for you?

What can I—

Love you

& Dance for you—

Your *most most* obedient
Loving TopsyIsadoring
     you—
       adoring

---

[1] I.e., before they met.

don't
spress it

7 o'clock—[1]

Ted Dear
I did come Berlin
Will wait for you at Studio 11 Siegmunds Hof
Hurrah nice me

   Topsy

———————————

ON NOVEMBER 16, ISADORA'S BERLIN MANAGER—IT ISN'T KNOWN
which one—sent a letter to the management of the Solodovnikov
Theatre in Moscow, asking on what dates in December the theater
might be free for "a possible guest appearance by Miss Isadora
Duncan." She danced in Leipzig and Dresden the last week of
November, but whatever the Moscow response may have been, by
the time it arrived she had doubtless decided that any tour that
would take her as far afield as Moscow had best be postponed. The
reason is given in a letter which contains the first reference to the
child that was to bring her great joy and terrible grief.

——— *CD 55* ———

[Probably Berlin, January 1906]

Dearest Heart

I am sorry I give you pain— you give me a heap but that doesn't matter—
I try to do the best I can— although you don't seem to think so—
Chiefly you expect too much—
The Dr was here this morning he says I must be careful but that I can
dance till end of May— I wish you would know that in all the hundreds
of times you have kissed me there hasn't been *one* that every thing in
me hasn't cried out— make me fruitful— give me a child— not once— I
have always had that constant longing impossible to control and I think
if it hadn't come I would have gone crazy from the struggle— as it is

———

[1] Here begins a separate note written on the last page of the letter.

I can't help feeling happy about it— I *can't help* it— I have the most exquisitely happy feelings at times—
but that's no good to you—
I wish you would send some one to Sweden— I am sure Sweden in the month of April would be as good as Holland— and cover the summer— Dr says I can probably dance again next Dec 1— Listen that isn't so bad— Love to you—

Your Isadora—

———————

Isadora and Craig had discussed the possibility of "Isadora's child" quite gaily at the beginning of the year, in the Cologne hotel and on the train. Now the reality was troubling them both. Had Craig expressed dismay at the actual advent of this, his ninth child?

All year Isadora had been dancing incessantly, supporting, so it would seem, almost everyone in any way connected with her. Could the last sentence of her letter—"Dr says I can probably dance again next Dec 1— Listen that isn't so bad"— be an answer to a chorus of "What's to become of us?" with Craig's voice among them?

One of his only two known comments on the immediate situation is a scribbled note on that last letter, beside Isadora's "Chiefly you expect too much": "*TRUE*— always that is my Folly" (although this is more probably a vaunting of his own excessively high artistic standards). And elsewhere he wrote: "December [1905] . . . Topsy's thoughts were all of baby-clothes. Mine were certainly not— mine were of *The Mask*."

The baby was due in September.

Pregnancy and Birth:
Villa Maria

In an effort to "cover the summer," as she had put it in that letter about her pregnancy (this summer there would of course be no bookings whatever), Isadora now proceeded to dance as often as she could during the months permitted. The list of her engagements from January through May, 1906, formidable for any dancer, is astonishing for a dancer with child: Berlin, Stettin, Leipzig, Halle, Magdeburg, Weimar, Erfurt, Görlitz, Lübeck, Hanover, Munich, the Dutch cities, Copenhagen, Stockholm, Göteborg, among others —with multiple engagements in some (nine in Stockholm alone) and return engagements in others. The last performance seems to have been on May 18 in Göteborg.

The absence of letters during this period, and a few notations by Craig himself in his memoirs, indicate that as her manager (one does not forget that Isadora was "covering" *his* summer, too), and perhaps out of some consideration for her condition, Craig accompanied her on most of this early 1906 tour. He records:

March 18, 19 [1906]: In Munich
March 21: In Augsburg
              What a band! Isadora danced, all the same.

April 13: Amsterdam. Bach's (St. John) Passion music was given at the Koepelkirk

Topsy and I went there, and in a fine old pew with tall wooden sides we sat and listened to it all. The thought came stealing into my mind, "What is this music to her?"

To me it was something very much greater than myself, and if we may speak of this music as a voice, there are commanding messages in that voice. She and I are what are called two artists: I wonder whether each is an artist? As a being, I should certainly place her in a much higher category than myself or most people I have come across. But there again, when I see the way she handled music in her own performances, I am brought to a full stop. I know very well I would not have done such a thing: I think probably I have more of the fear of God in me than she![1]

Isadora, in *My Life*, says little about those strenuous early months of 1906 except: "I had to take this tour because of the depleting expenses of the school. I had drawn upon my entire reserve funds, and had no more left." A detailed account is given in the memoirs of the third person who went along on the tour—Craig's old friend Martin Shaw, who arrived in Berlin in January or February.

As a sort of side-line [Shaw begins], Craig was doing décors[2] for Isadora Duncan, who was then touring Europe with a programme of dances to the music of Gluck, Schubert, and such early composers as Rameau and Couperin. She wanted a conductor, Craig said. Would I come? I jumped at the offer, and within three days was shaking hands with Craig at the Bahnhof in Berlin.

Without a moment's pause we drove straight off to the theatre—I forget which it was—where that evening the famous dancer was giving

[1] Irma Duncan has written of this passage: "Craig wondered at the time what she was thinking. Well, I for one know for sure that it was not dancing St. John's Passion and making money! I must say, he had some weird notions. He had the nervous habit of biting his nails furiously all the time, maybe even while listening to Bach! 'What is this music to her?' he queried. To her, also, 'Something very much greater' than herself. I, who actually knew the real Isadora, can vouch for the fact that she always listened to music with the greatest concentration, 'with my whole soul,' as she put it. She was invariably completely immersed, oblivious of her surroundings."

[2] Craig always denied that he did this for Isadora. See especially p. 227.

a performance. It was her Gluck programme. I had never seen her before and the simplicity and beauty of her movements gave me deep enjoyment. There were no leaps or pirouettes, only beautiful floating movements and gestures. The theatre was crowded and the audience in a state of ecstatic delight throughout. Isadora provided the whole programme. This in itself is remarkable. I doubt whether any other dancer has ever been able to carry through a whole evening's entertainment unaided. All the time I conducted for her she was the sole performer on the stage. Craig's *décors* were just right and seemed part of the dance. After the performance I was taken round to see the wonderful creature in her dressing-room. She looked at me with the untroubled gaze of a child and spoke a few simple words of welcome in an American accent which the extraordinary sweetness of her voice robbed of the least suspicion of harshness. All her movements were deliberate, reposeful, never for an instant hurried or nervous. One simply could not imagine her catching a train.

Emerging from the stage door, we encountered the usual crowd of admirers lining the way to her carriage, to which she walked with a kind of floating sway from the hips. She took us back to her house to supper, which, after Chelsea fare, seemed a banquet fit for the gods. Her serenity made me think of a still, deep lake over which no breeze made the faintest ripple.

. . . At the time of which I am writing Isadora had no children of her own [Shaw discreetly continues] . . . Craig had a sort of studio flat in Berlin at the top of a very high building, and there I took up my abode.

The portion of the tour in which Shaw participated was to begin at Nuremberg, where Isadora, after picking up necessary music in Berlin between engagements at the Residenz Theater in Hanover on March 10 and 22, joined her conductor and her manager. From Hanover she wrote the following unsigned note to Craig.

——— *CD 250* ———

Hannover, Wednesday night
[Probably 21 March 1906]

Just arrived very sleepy— found your letter. Thank you. Couldn't get here sooner because the music wasn't ready till today— rehearsal tomorrow. Day after I rush to Nuremburg. I will be just pretty glad to see *you*— Going to Bed now. I just like to be your Topsy*me*.

The translation[1] is sent all right to Insel Verlag—

The major portion of Martin Shaw's entertaining narrative of the tour, in which he speaks a good deal more about himself than about Isadora, and which is printed later on in this volume,[2] takes us as far as Stockholm, where he recounts his and Craig's meeting with playwright August Strindberg, and the detail that Strindberg (notorious for his antifeminism) refused to meet Isadora because "he was afraid of her." The terror that she inspired in this great woman-hater was reported to Isadora, who reacted with typical spirit. Strindberg wrote to his third wife, the actress Harriet Bosse (from whom he was soon to be separated, as he had been from her two predecessors), that Isadora wanted "to build a special box for me, on the stage, because I '*must* see her' . . . if you're not at home to save me, then I'll leave town. Schering writes that Craig is Isadora's lover and that he ruins her, for which reason he is poorly thought of." And the Swedish writer Albert Engström tells of his own attempt to persuade Strindberg to meet Isadora, as well as Craig:

"Duncan and I," Craig said to me, "have travelled to Sweden exclusively in order to get in touch with Strindberg, but he is behaving intolerably. We intend to stay here until he receives us. We only ask for five minutes." I promised to try, and went to Strindberg.

"No," he answered. "I am not going to run the risk of any attempt at seduction by that woman."

"Are you afraid you might succumb?"

"No: but hasn't she tried to seduce you?"

---

[1] Of a "poem" which Craig had written about Isadora and was about to publish in a portfolio of his drawings of her. See p. 129 and note for this page.

[2] See note for this page.

"No," I answered with the same emphasis. "Can't you go for five minutes and watch her dance from a closed box and 'look at her with a man's eye,' as she put it to me?"

"There—you see: it's almost rape, sex murder, everything. Never!"

And that was the end of it.

Shaw concludes his narrative:

Our tour ended at Gothenburg in an oppressively self-conscious *art nouveau* concert hall of which the good Gothenburgers were very proud. The hall was matched by a conceited, self-conscious orchestra, who, because they were a "concert" orchestra, thought they need take no trouble over a mere dancer's music. I told them that a concert orchestra even more famous than they, the Nuremburg Philharmonic Orchestra, conducted by Dr. Bruch, had not thought it a condescension to play for Isadora Duncan. This brought them down a little, but I disliked Gothenburg and was glad to leave it. I heard of a ship sailing for England, got a cabin, and after two days' continuous sea-sickness, arrived home feeling better than I had ever felt in my life. And yet I was sorry to say goodbye. I had enjoyed seeing a slice of Europe—but my chief pleasure had been to be in Craig's company again. Dear old Teddy! What a companion! We would be arm-in-arm in Munich and my name on the posters would be about as large as Isadora's. We would disagree in Nuremburg and my name would shrink to the size of the author's on an English theatre poster. But what did it matter?

As a still further attempt to put the school at Grünewald on a firmer financial footing, there had been inaugurated in Berlin on February 14, 1906, just before the tour with Shaw, the Verein zur Unterstützung und Erhaltung des Tanzschule von Isadora Duncan (the Society for the Support and Maintenance of the Isadora Duncan School of Dancing). This was the work of Elizabeth, who was increasingly in control of the school. Even by Craig, the "Bogie man," Elizabeth Duncan was admitted to be a clever woman, but this time her efforts were undone by the results of the Bogie man's "seduction" of Isadora. (So it was called, according to Isadora, by her mother, whose temper during Isadora's pregnancy "became most uneven" and who shortly returned to the United States.) What

happened is the subject for one of the more celebrated passages in
Isadora's *My Life*:

My sister Elizabeth had formed for the Grunewald school a committee
of very prominent and aristocratic women of Berlin. When they learned
of Craig, they sent me a long letter, couched in majestic terms of reproach, and said that they, members of the good bourgeois society, could
no longer be patronesses of a school where the leader had such loose ideas
of morals.

Frau Mendelssohn, wife of the great banker, was chosen by these ladies
to present to me this letter. When she came with this tremendous parch-
ment, she looked at me a bit unsteadily and, suddenly bursting into tears,
threw the letter on the floor, and, taking me in her arms, cried: "Don't
think I ever signed that wretched letter. As for the other ladies, there is
nothing to be done with them. They will no longer be patrons of this
school. Only they still believe in your sister, Elizabeth."[1]

Now Elizabeth had her own ideas, but she did not make them public,
so I saw the creed of these ladies was that anything is right if you don't
talk about it! These women so aroused my indignation that I took the
Philharmonic Saal and gave a special lecture[2] on the dance as an art of
liberation, and ended with a talk on the right of woman to love and bear
children as she pleased.

. . . This lecture caused considerable scandal. Half of the audience
sympathized with me, and the other half hissed and threw anything that
came to their hands onto the stage. In the end, the unconsenting half left
the hall, and I was left with the others, and we had an interesting debate
on the rights and wrongs of women, which was considerably in advance
of the Woman's Movement of the present day.

Among the press notices concerning the dance recitals in various
cities by the children of Isadora's school, there is one from the Leipzig
Abend-Zeitung, which begins:

[1] But then Frau Mendelssohn was Italian, a singer and pianist, and daughter
of a Florentine painter. Born Giulietta Gordigiani, she had been introduced to
her husband, Robert von Mendelssohn, banker and amateur cellist, by their
common friend Eleonora Duse.

A different story has it that at a meeting of the indignant ladies of the Verein
Isadora suddenly appeared in a doorway, calmly said, "May I come in? I am
with child," and won over some of them.

[2] Perhaps a version of the "Marvellous Book" ("The Dance and Nature"),
which was addressed particularly to women. See above, p. 91.

In the splendid rooms of the Villa Albertina at Gautzsch twelve children from the Duncan School of Dancing performed before a distinguished gathering of Leipzig Society . . .

What the Villa Albertina precisely was is not known to the present writer: it is of interest here chiefly in being associated with Gautzsch, a town in East Germany described by the West German consulate general in New York as now "a section of the city of Markkleeberg, near Leipzig." It was in Gautzsch, undoubtedly a quiet spot, that Isadora lived for a while during the spring and early summer of 1906, after she stopped dancing.

In a series of letters [CD 63–69] that she wrote from Gautzsch to Craig in Berlin we learn that she was staying with friends, a Dr. Felix Zehme and his wife, of whom little is known. They had a comfortable house; Frau Zehme "played" in public (what she played is not said); Dr. Zehme was perhaps a lawyer—Craig once sought his advice as to protection against theater people who copied his drawings—and was in some way interested in Craig's theatrical plans. Otherwise most of what we know about the doctor is what Isadora says in one of her letters [CD 63]: that he "dictates in the Library *3 hours* to a stenographer . . . He says a stenographer is much better to dictate to than a type writer." Craig sent Dr. Zehme a copy of his portfolio of drawings of Isadora, now about to be published. Most of the letters from Gautzsch are uncharacteristically subdued in tone—one senses that Isadora was lonely and uneasy, and the place ultimately uncongenial. She considered going to spend the summer in Como, near Milan ("I believe Duse is in Milano if so I will see her"), but in Gautzsch talk of what sounds like abortion, and of adoption, so disturbed her that she irrationally began to fear Italy as being even more threatening: "Every country has its customs and it seems here they hire those amiable old ladies with slaughterous intentions— even Dr. Z. offered to 'adopt' it— I'm really getting scared and *don't* feel like falling over myself to get to Como— if the honest German is such what would the wily Italian be— The future King of Ireland must be protected from these Conspiracies . . . In the meantime it is very comfy here— perhaps I better curl up and refuse to budge." [CD 66] Eventually she and Craig decided that Holland, a country with which she was by now somewhat acquainted, would be the best place, and, since she was now beginning to feel occasionally "dizzy and ill" when she made certain movements, she began to look for a nurse who would accompany her. [CD *67*] Meanwhile she practiced yoga exercises and took long walks: "Yesterday I walked to Cospuders[1] 4 Kilo away— all by myself— I saw a long many colored line moving slowly across the field— and when I came nearer found it to be women on their hands & knees with different colored shawls over their heads creeping forward in a line stretching right across the field— pulling up weeds from around the vegetables. I sat me down on a bank & reflected— in Yogi fashion— fifty mothers creeping on the back of old Mother Earth, and at home their babies are creeping on the floor . . . You might ring me on the telephone now & then & say Hello." [CD *66*]

The search for a nurse began to get "langweilich."[2] [CD *65*] Then one day a candidate presented herself: "The *Nurse* appeared. She had a Face like the red player queen— I sent her gently but firmly away. I think I can go to Holland alone all right & find some one there or it will be easy from there to send to London. Any way I feel so well & jolly"—the reader begins to sense Isadora's resolution to spare Craig any mention of discomfort or difficulties— "I don't know what I'd do with one of those silly old spooks . . . You are Beautiful— That's what you are, & I love you. Your *very* obedient Topsy*me*."[3] [CD *68*]

The doctor forbade her to travel by night, so she had planned to go "from here to Hannover, stay there the night and go by the Schnellzug[4] the next day" [CD *68*]; the last letter from Gautzsch, however, tells of a change of plan and presages what was to be one of the circumstances of the remainder of her pregnancy: infrequency of Craig's presence and occasional uncertainty as to even his whereabouts.

---

[1] Identified by the West German consulate general in New York as "a paper mill in the area of Markkleeberg," but at this time obviously rural.

[2] For G. *langweilig*, "boring."

[3] A note by Craig on this letter: "Why never date your letters to me."

[4] G., "express train."

—— *CD 69* ——

[Probably Gautzsch, June 1906]

Dearest Love—

Where are you?—
No letter since a century. Are you *vereist?*[1]— I vereise mich tomorrow
morning early at 7— as the way by Hannover was found impractical. As
I couldn't find *any* sort of nurse here, frl. Königen[2] will travel with me
and stay a week till I have found nurse, villa, arzt and all the other re-
quirements of my Royal Highness—
I will be tomorrow night at Vieux Doelen unless the journey proves too
tiresome when I will rest on the way— Will you bring or send my trunk
to Hague & don't forget to bring the watch & Kodak with you— I will
send you telegrams from along the route— but I wonder if you are in
Berlin?
Yours— loving You

  Isadora

Did you know Duse was at your Mommie's Matinee— saw an account in
Tribune— I am very proud that she receives the Book . . . "inspired"
by little me's dancing on one toe—[3]

[1] For G. *verreist,* "out of town, away"; same line, *verreise mich,* "set out";
below, *Arzt,* "physician."

[2] Irma Duncan mentions a "Fraülein Konegen" who was one of the children's
governesses at the school in Grünewald.

[3] Ellen Terry's jubilee matinée was held at the Theatre Royal, Drury Lane,
London, June 12, 1906.
The Book is the so-called "Isadora Mappe" (Isadora Portfolio), a portfolio
of reproductions of six of Craig's drawings of Isadora dancing: *Isadora Duncan,
Sechs Bewegungsstudien v. Edward Gordon Craig* (Insel-Verlag, Leipzig,
1906). The reproductions are splendid (see illustration). Craig introduced the
portfolio with several dozen lines of blank verse in English, but these were
translated into German for the Insel-Verlag publication. The original English
verses were printed separately, in a leaflet which was inserted in the copies of
the portfolio sold in England. See note for this page.

——— *CD 70* ———

[Probably Hôtel du Vieux Doelen,
The Hague, June 1906]

Dearest Love— I arrived here safe & well last night & sent you a telegram. Just before I started I rec. a *big box* from Paris & forwarded from Grunewald. Eliz didn't know what it was but said they looked like new patent bombs, to blow up Royalty. The Air Cushions! from the old gent we met coming from Sweden. Two enormous ones forming a large mattress and two for pillows— & they made the journey lovely & comfy, just like resting on a cloud. Started from Gautzsch at six morn. & arr here 9 at night but I felt very well all the way and ate a Big Bifsteak from the Spisen Wagen[1]—

I have here our *first* bedroom with the only two genuine Bxx's in the Hotel— I confess I was outrageously happy when I saw them— I am a Yogi of the Epicurean School—

I brought frl K. as I thought it not wise to travel alone and the *only* good nurse, the old stout lady, now says she is engaged till the 1st of November. The others were too awful for consideration.

Also I can send frl K. to look for the villa— as it is best for me not to be seen walking about.

She will go today to Nordyck and see what is there— In a day or two I can see whether there is one to be found on coast of Holland & if not I will try coast of Belgium near by—

Your letter add. Gautzsch just arrived forwarded.

When I get a villa fixed comfy perhaps you'd like to come & write a great Big Magic Book—

I am bursting with pride over the picture book from The Insel— I am rather puffed up with pride any way on all accounts—

I am longing to see the Sea— The Earth is beautiful but the sea— I would rather be near it than all the finest views of Earth. When I get my Egyptian pictures up and the sea in front of me— I will just be a very fine Yogi—

The Bxx is wonderful and the one next it looks just as wonderful— I wish you were here.

I need my trunk rather, as I only brought a few things to Gautzsch.

---

[1] For G. *Speiswagen*, "dining car."

Tell Reinhardt to walk into your pocket as it's the best & safest place for him. Perhaps you will be here before this reaches you—

Love,— Your Topsy—

———— CD 71 ————
Hotel du Vieux Doelen
la haye

[Probably June 1906]

Good Morning, Dearest

I am just woke up and sitting in Bed drinking tea & eating honey cake, but I have your letter which is sweeter far to me than honey on my tongue. Yesterday I looked all day for a Villa and after seeing many villainous places with fearful prices I found hidden behind a big sand dune a little white cottage with blue shutters and blue letters across the front— "Villa Maria"— and it is really very nice and I took it at once and will move there this evening. View of the sea from all the windows, and a little balcony upstairs— I can live there quite unobserved. The only thing is that everything in Holland seems fearfully dear— they reckon florins as we do marks. The villa costs 900 florins for the season till Nov. 1— but it is completely furnished— very tasteful— dinner, tea sets and all very complete. There are six rooms— 3 bedrooms with two beds each. All the others I saw were twice as dear. One pays half down in the beginning and the other half on leaving— so will you send me 1000 marks by post—

    Address: Villa Maria
             Noordwijk on Sea
             near Leyden
             Holland

One takes a steam train or a carriage from Leyden.
It is only 1 hour from Amsterdam. Holland is Beautiful— the country looks a dream, and I feel quite happy here. The lights on the sand dunes and over the sea are wonderful.
Bring with you some of your pictures to put up. I mean the *reprints*. The sun would hurt the others.
Now I pack & take the train to Leyden— off I go.

    Your
        Topsy—

———— *CD 72* ————
HOTEL DU VIEUX DOELEN
LA HAYE

[Probably June 1906]

Dearest— Many many thanks for the books— have been reading Plato all morning—
And for the Booful pictures— I laughed till I cried— and now I'm going off to live in a little white house with blue shutters and you better come quick— The view over the sand dunes has the Solemnity of looking over a great mountain range. I have enquired about a nurse & they promise to send me one in a few days—
Love Love Love to You— You have no idea how much happiness you give— I love the Gods & I love you—
I am glad to be alone again— living with the most beautiful has spoilt me for other society—

Your *Topsy*

———— *CD 73* ————

[Probably June 1906]
Just arrived— Villa Maria—
Noordwijk on Sea, bei Leyden

Here's Brer Rabbit got a fine Bunny house— big sand dune on the side— big sand dune on t'other— only me can see *out*— over the sea— The sun is just setting— it's pretty wonderful— & a garden full of white shells—
I went today and engaged an old lady to cook. An ancient sybil I guess— no one knows how old she is— & *thin* but she looked so *trusty*— & so like an old work of art— she protested she could *cook fine*.
Nothing heard here but the sound of the sea— you will make great magic pictures of these sand dunes— They are so mysterious—
I am so glad to be alone myself, and think of you. Just the difference between you and other people is that you are Beautiful & they are not. With you all is transformed to wonder & loveliness— with other people things suddenly lose their light & become commonplace— so if I'm not

with you I'd a thousand times rather be alone— when I am truly with you just the same. You just manipulate those little men in Berlin a while. They will all walk around and do what you like— it's only a matter of a little time.

Love to you, dearest heart. There is no joy in the world like loving you and now your kisses are imprisoned and living within me—

> Your truly obedient
> *Topsy*

I found these two little flowers— the *only* ones— growing among the white shells.

———— *CD 74* ————

Sunday morning
[Noordwijk, probably 24 June 1906]

Dearest— I am simply delighted with my old lady. She goes about smiling in the sweetest way— and whenever I carry a pitcher of water she rushes to take it, explaining in her three languages— "trop lourd pour[1] Madame— sehr schwer[2]— is it not so?" She was up this morn at peep of day, and will never stop working. She tells me she was housekeeper for many years for the American Minister, which accounts for her elegant air. I won't need any nurse anyway till the 1st of Aug. There is a good doctor near by, in case of need— so— Anyway I never felt better. This morning I took another two hour walk on the sands. This place is Paradise— *one doesn't meet a soul*. The old dame's name is *Cornelia* if you please. She is now cooking me a fine dinner— yum, yum. There is a special apart room for you to write in with a big square table— your thoughts will come here with the rhythm of the waves— it is also a wonderful place to read. I'd like to have a 1st little girl's wonderbook of sea animals— there are such queer shells & jelly fishes on the beach— I'd like to know more about 'em—

[Letter incomplete]

[1] F., "too heavy for."
[2] G., "very heavy."

——— *CD 75* ———

[Postmarked Noordwijk, 25 June 1906]

Dearest Love— How have you spent your Sunday? I spent mine reading
over your Plato again. That is wonderful—
I love you

    Your
      Topsy

The sun is going down behind the sea all red just as Socrates must have
seen it the eve he took the potion. Life, Death— and Love— all the same—
Beautiful— *You* are Beautiful and every thing that comes from you is
Beautiful— my heart is full of you

——— *CD 76* ———

[Noordwijk, probably July 1906]

Dearest— I am anxious to hear how all the different conferences[1] came
off— I wish I was there I do. This being a Yogi is Beautiful, but I'm
always spoiling a little to be in the thick o' the fight—
The sea today was just the color of the Plato you sent me— so I perched
myself high on a sand dune & read it through—
Your letter just came—
You are dear to write me so often—
My old sybil is fine & *cooks* just right— and looks as if she just came
from one of the frames in the Rijks museum— doesn't speak any language

---

[1] Reinhardt so admired Craig's designs and ideas that despite the latter's behavior concerning *Caesar and Cleopatra* he continued to seek him out. On
June 26, 1906, he offered him a choice of contracts: one for a single play, apparently *Macbeth* or *King Lear*, to be produced by June 1907; the other for
three productions—one of the Shakespeare plays, *Everyman*, and a play by
Maeterlinck—to be done between November 1906 and February 1907. Craig
replied the same day: "I enclose my conditions, and all you have to do is to
accept or refuse." His conditions could not be met. Still later, Reinhardt proposed an *Orestes*, with the same result. It was this holding out by Craig for a
theater he could call his "own" that was soon to take him to Florence. (For
these last Reinhardt offers, see pp. 295-296.)

particular but understands me quite well when I talk a little of all mixed at her—

This little house is awfully nice— a *trifle* dear perhaps— but I thought it cheaper than staying at the Hotel & always paying so many carriages to look for another— it is quite new & the plumbing etc. in excellent order.

I'm so glad you took Miss de B[rouckère] out— she is really quite nice, I like her exceedingly.

They say I can find a good nurse at Hague— I enquired there, and will hear in a day or two.

I'm fearfully proud about the article[1]— I guess I'll write some more. This is a wonderful place to write— The vague neutral tints of the dunes, & then no muskitoes no bugs or slugs like in the country— it is really beautiful—

As for my health, I never felt so well in my life— I walked *two* hours along the beach today without meeting a soul—

I think one really might grow wise here— (note, after reading Plato I feel awfully superior).

If you bring the trunk with you it is enough— now that I am away from people I don't need clothes. It is splendid to go out and be sure of not meeting a soul—

But be sure bring the camera— fine light for pictures. It is just growing dusk— The ancient one is singing a dutch song—

I will run put this in the post. The box is about 15 min. from here. Good-night dear— I am your

      Topsy

——— *CD 77* ———

[Noordwijk, probably early July 1906]

Dearest

I am on the sands—

Beautiful— Also to escape the racket of my peaceful little house. The auld one has suddenly the deil in her. I don't know whether she's

---

[1] An article (in German) entitled "Gordon Craig" and signed "Isadora Duncan" appeared in the Berlin magazine *Die Schaubühne* (*The Stage*) for July 19, 1906. Obviously put together by Craig himself, it discusses his theatrical ideas.

drunk my spiritus zu einreiben[1] or what! For the last week a mysterious individual has seated himself opposite our house and stared for hours at the windows, causing us much uneasiness which came to a climax when the old one said he had a gun which he pointed at our dog. She barred all the doors & windows & refused even to put her nose outside. Finally she sent for the Police. Today the mysterious individual called in high dudgeon— said the Police were following him on the beach and everyone calling him a roiber.[2] He explained in a lengthy letter that he was a *reporter*[3] & wanted an interview. I tried to appease his wrath by telling him the old lady was "nervous."

Although it is true, he had made us all *nervous*— said he shot rabbits! The old one is in a fearful tantrum & we can't tell why. She abused me like a pick pocket. We will get another from Hague as soon as possible. It isn't so easy to have a Peaceful Existence!

Other reporters came from Leyden & Amsterdam, but the nurse with soft words sent them away. She has just translated me the notices. Lovely.

[1] G., "rubbing alcohol."

[2] For G. *räuber*, "robber."

[3] News of Isadora's pregnancy had got about, and there were reports that she and Craig were married. Irma Duncan tells of hearing the rumor while a child at the school in Grünewald. Craig had written to Martin Shaw: "Am I married— now how on earth should I know. I'm told I am by the German papers & the English & American tell me too— & some wild beasts rush up & shake me by the hand— & other wild monsters peck me & flutter— & other animals cackle around. So with all the noises of the menagerie I am left in doubt about it all. Most of these animals speak such a queer lingo— a sort of kitchero talk— a language as unfortunate in its sense, as in its sound. You remember the '3 Jovial Huntsmen'— well leave out the *Jovial*, & we have the inquisitive monsters of today.

'One said he was married
& the other he said nay
He's just a blooming lunatic
that wants his blooming way.'

"Look ye now the only one who besides you has not asked me that disgusting question is my old 'Black.' Black & I have spent the loveliest of all times falling in & out of the sea . . . He is a dear. We are all well & happy thank you— & we hope you are too. I return in a few days to Holland."

The letter includes a sketch of the dog Black. Craig had taken him to Villa Maria and left him there.

Tell Mr. Van Looy[1] I agree with him that you are the most Beautiful Being in the World. The papers came this morning— I read about your Mama in Coventry— She is splendid. I study each day from the Chipiez books[2] & am becoming awfully learned. Did you know that when they built great Pyramids or works in Egypt that they took all the men by conscription to work, like we do when there is war & soldiers wanted! Also, I have developed a positive talent— I am too modest— Genius, for crochet! You'll be sprised—

Wish you were here to listen to the Sea.

When you comin to see yo poo ole Rabbit?

Did you see the fine picture of Brer Fox & Rabbit, ancient Japanese—

Por ole rabbit is now going for a little toddle down to other end of beach—

> Love you your
> Topsy

———— *CD 78* ————

[Noordwijk, probably early July 1906]

Dearest

I thought the enclosed letter might be of some interest— so telegraphed you to see the said Mr. Chubb.[3]

Old Lady kicking up an Infernal Row so must go now & telegraph to Hague for another servant. Old one seems suddenly off her Chump! I fly now to telegraph office— will write you this aft. All my Love &

---

[1] *The Art of the Theatre* had just been published in Dutch by S. L. Van Looy as *De Kunst van het Theatre*, with three forewords by J. C. de Vos (actor), Jan C. Van Looy (painter) and M. A. J. Baur (painter and etcher).

[2] Charles Chipiez, a French architect (1835–1901), was, according to the *Larousse du XXe Siècle*, "one of the two authors of a first-rate work: *l'Histoire de l'art dans l'antiquité* (1881–1893), in collaboration with G. Perrot." Craig wrote to Shaw about this time: "Am reading daily about Egypt. 2800 BC things were complete & civilized there, which means they must have started about 4 or 5000 BC to get ready."

[3] Unidentified.

Good good wishes. Thank you lovely little paper cutter—
Thank You All—

Yours

   Topsy

The old lady is shrieking & banging pots about so excuse haste. Black is glad *he* isn't a Bull Dog,[1] but he's scared to death.

——— *CD 79* ———

Wed. morn
[Postmarked Noordwijk, 6 July 1906]

Dearest

Have had no letter from you since Sunday so am anxious to hear how all gone—
Only the wonderful Bed arrived—
It has a little sign on the side
            "Bett der Toe K"
Did you know that?
It is a very magic bed & the canopy is enchanting— I sleep twice as well & think I'm a Princess!
Have been spending my time with the Bacchae. It goes wonderful with the rhythm of the Sea, and it takes very wonderful words to suit to the sea— Therefore it has been much joy to me.
Let me know how things are going if only a line. Wish I could trip up to Amsterdam—[2] Couldn't I some *dark* night & return the next *dark* night? All my love & wishes to you

      Isadora

A nice nurse called— looks strong & aimable. Will come to stay tomorrow. Mr. Black continues to enjoy himself.

[1] A scribbled note from Craig on this letter reads: "Edit. of 'New York Herald' Paris edition— Buster Brown & his Bull Dog— which accompanied us always day by day."
[2] Craig had come to Amsterdam for the Dutch publication of his book and, according to Edward A. Craig, in the hope of trying to interest the State Theatre in his work through his friend, Jan C. de Vos.

—— *CD 82* ——

[Postmarked Noordwijk, 9 July 1906]

Dearest— When I opened my eyes this morning the old one brought me your letter— a letter from you is like a touch from your hand filled with vitality and gives me new life— also you are dear and sweet to write so often & to send me so many beautiful thoughts and things—

The nurse is very nice, only she comes from a "good family" which is a pity. I must say I am a trifle medieval in my taste. I would prefer six black slaves who would kowtow & do my bidding, with rings on their noses & bells on their toeses—

Elizabeth writes me that the children are going to Leipzig to dance for the Frauenverein[1] there, and that they will be paid— she doesn't say how much—

Each day here the sea has different colors, & I always wish you could be here— wonderful. I found a picture in the Japanese book which is curiously the same composition as "St. Jerome in the Wilderness" that I had on my bureau at Berlin— you remember the Priest with clasped hands before the old sage!

When it says always "at the age of —— he began to meditate"— as if meditation were an art to be learnt. For each one it says always the same. Can *you* sit truly still like on a Lily Pad and *meditate*? I tried it— it is dreadful difficult— I've no doubt it is an art like being a great musician— I had a charming letter from Mrs. Mendelssohn, who is in the country. She says Duse's[2] address is Hotel Jungfraublick, Interlaken, Switzerland. It said in the paper she might come to Holland for the sea! The Queen of Austria used to walk from Zandvoort to Scheveningen on the sands— she often stayed here by the sea. It seems to me wherever I go in the world they tell me the Queen of Austria used to walk there— she seemed to walk everyplace.

[1] G., "women's club."

[2] The production of *Elektra*, for which Craig had designed sets and costumes for Duse, had, in Edward A. Craig's words, "been postponed indefinitely. During one of her practical moments, Duse had concluded that the play would be too elaborate to become part of her repertoire, for which she must have standard-type settings that were easy to pack, and as easy to light in Buenos Aires as in Florence or Berlin." But Craig and Duse had still not escaped each other. Within a few months they were to meet—with interesting results.

I am going for a little walk now.

We have found a photographer in Katwijk— ¾ hr. walk— who developes the pictures. I enclose one of Mr. Black's first introduction to the water— some little children called him.

Certainly [as] you say, to reasonable people death must seem at least as fortunate as to sleep or to wake from sleep— but tell me what state is the meditating Japanese priest in the picture in?— a sort of state beyond life— they seem to live beyond nature— well, unless one can be a Yogi one must live according to one's nature— only the Yogi lifts above all and I haven't *yet heard* of a woman Yogi— (have you?)— and the nature of a woman is being a little revealed to me. It is extraordinary nice. The final revelation will come about the 21st of August, when I'll know more about it. At present I am what you make me— very happy—

> Your
> Topsy

CD 83

[Postmarked Noordwijk, 14 July 1906]

Dearest— I sent asking for 50 gulden— cause my Bank has suddenly written to say I am *overdrawn*— I am *sure* they are mistaken but I must write & have their answer before I can cash another check—

The old one leaves today in High Dungeon & must be paid before she leaves— also Butchers Bakers etc.— so I am telegraphing you again. That's a wonderful Baby you sent me— a real inspiration.

It is windy stormy cold here— I wish I had a hot fire & soft carpets— The waves are 20 feet high

> Wow—

> With love
> *Topsy*

CD 84

[Noordwijk, probably July or August 1906]

Dearest— Many thanks— The money rec— The old one is now *departed* with her black bonnet perched on one side— still in a perfect fury— no one knows why. The nurse has telegraphed to Hague, to her Mother, who telegraphed back that she would send a *good* & *trusty* one tomorrow— Mr. Black is much excited over all these proceedings and howls dolefully unless he is allowed to stay in the house. Since the story of the robber his nerves have been shaken.

The wind is blowing the house down, and the *gentle waves* are dashing 100 feet high or so, but I feel quite cosy in spite of it. I am becoming so learned about ancient Egyptians that *you'll* be *awe*struck—

That Baby you sent is a Masterpiece— *Such* a spirit. Will run put this in post & then sleep after the tremendous excitement of the day.

Did you ever think of returning to the country for *Peace*? Better war against the stormy world than *one* Cook—

You dear, I cannot say ever what I want to you— but you *know*—

Good night

———— *CD 85* ————

[Noordwijk, probably July or August 1906]

That's beautiful that your Mama will belong to the Verein— Mayn't I write and thank her?

As for *You*— don't you ever ever leave your poor Topsy *8*— 1, 2, 3, 4, 5, 6, 7, 8! days without even a picture postcard again. Even a picture postcard would have cheered me—[1]

I didn't send Kathleen your picture but a different one—

My new cook is very ill and the nurse has to sit up all night nursing her— we had to have the Dr. who says she can't be moved for a week at least— I thought it would be nice to have K.[2] I need someone to help me *walk* around a little— It's rather difficult as the nurse must be occupied with the poor cook—

Have you seen the New Moon?

Have you seen my most wonderful article repeated from Schaubühne in Neue Courant?

[1] Craig had gone to London to visit Elena and their children. As Edward A. Craig puts it: "Again the feeling that he was being trapped came over him and he bolted—this time back to England and to Elena."

[2] Undoubtedly Kathleen Bruce, who, as we shall see, did come to stay with Isadora. The date of her arrival is uncertain. There was another K. in the house—Marie Kist, the nurse.

I'm so well that I look like a peasant—
Mr. Black watches the house most faithful and is learning to bark at the
trades people. I'm writing a Big Book *too*—[1]
Come & see me— only 1½ hrs here or ¾ hr in a *Moty* Car— you could
have a fine time coming here in a Moty-Car— Couldn't you— Just come
see yo poo

  Topsy me!—

——— *CD 86* ———

       [Noordwijk, probably July or August 1906]

Dearest— Just rec your letter— you can have no idea how anxious I have
been— *10* days without a line— I thought you were run over by a London
cab— I thought you *ill*— I thought the boat had gone down in the
storm Sat night— I pictured all sorts of fearful things that had happened
to you— till I got a bad fever and the nurse had to take my temperature
every minute. Now I see I was quite *silly*, but you know just at this time
one's nerves are not under control and I couldn't sleep any more or eat.
I telegraphed Shaw to ask if you were ill & no answer. I still don't understand why you didn't send me a *post card*! and you must admit it was
bad of you. However, now I have your letter I can laugh at my fears—
For you dear heart I am so glad you are well, and also glad you see your
dear Mother or see any that you love, and I can only repeat— if there
is anyone you care for very much who feels unhappy and wants to come
with you she can have half my little house with *all my heart*. It will give
me *joy*— and Love is enough for all—

  With all my Love
  Isadora

[1] Perhaps the essay "A Child Dancing." See footnote, next page.

——— *CD 87* ———

[Noordwijk, probably July or August 1906]

Been Walking two hours by the Sea—

Dearest Heart.

What a Beautiful letter—
How Pleased I am
How Happy I am
How Grateful I am
Don't I love you
Aren't you the
           Most Beautiful
O I adore You—
O to see you again
Again—

      Isadora

——— *CD 88* ———

[Noordwijk, probably August 1906]
If you have time bring Temple[1] a few yards
of skito net. She is all bit up.

Dearest

That little boy brought you by mistake a card sent to the Bath house
to order my warm bath for this eve! If you have *time* you might send
the wellenbath[2]— smallest size, but don't bother. You are made of Sun-

---

[1] Temple Duncan, the daughter of Augustin and Sarah. An essay that
Isadora wrote that summer, dated August 22, 1906, "A Child Dancing," begins:
"Seated on the beach at Noordwijik, I look on while my little niece, who has
come to visit me from the Grünewald School, dances here before the waves."
Irma says that Isadora had also invited her and another pupil, Erica, to Noordwijk, but that Elizabeth had refused to let them go—probably fearing the
rumors of "immorality" that were circulating in reference to Isadora and
threatening to harm the school.

[2] Isadora probably means a simple portable sitzbath, the Villa Maria being
tubless.

light, Sweetness & Beauty. Courage— Punch the Horrid Black dragon[1]
in the eye—
Good night

    Isadora

—— *CD 89* ——

[Noordwijk, probably August 1906]

Dearest— I have just been reading a remarkable book "Argent"—
"money"— by Zola. You must get the English translation at once— how
a man in Paris raises a capital of *40* millions for a vast scheme that doesn't
even exist when he begins. It is really *inspiring*— he visits the great kings
of finance in their dens and how he *talks*— wonderful— if I were a man
I'd take the next train & begin! It has inspired me to such an extent—
when he gets the first *25* millions assured, he says— "That is nothing— you
must realize that this first little capital of *25* millions is a simple fagot
thrown in the furnace to start the first fire— That I hope to double it,
to quadruple it, to quintuple it, in measure as our operations enlarge, that
we must have a rain of gold— a *dance* of *millions* if we wish to accomplish the prodigies which we have announced"— or again he says: "One
must have a vast project so that the greatness of it can seize on the imagination. Then the passions will be alighted— life will course, each will
bring his money to it— by a great central magnetism we can draw all—
we can own the earth— Our "Universal Bank" will open a vast new
horizon— certainly never has ambition been more colossal or chances of
success more obscure— but it is just for this reason that we will win."
Heavens— if you had "Mon. Saccard" to work for you, you would have
capital— unfortunately he is in the book. He says to the dreamer— "Bring
me the *good ideas*— I take the financial side— I find the capital for them."
I can't translate but he is fine— would talk the birds off the bushes— he
meets a dreamer who tells him of some marvellous lands containing silver

[1] Probably a certain E. Verkade, in Amsterdam, of whom Craig writes:
"Here was a sly dog, one of a family of able business men. He spent quite a lot
of time trying to convince me— (and indeed, convincing me) that he wanted
to establish for me my theatre in Amsterdam or elsewhere in Holland . . .
How could I tell that he was later on to establish a theatre with some of my
ideas in it, but under his own name?" And later: "Wrote Verkade from Nord-
wijk, telling him . . . to go and boil himself."

in Asia— and on the strength of this idea which isn't at all sure he goes out and lances the "Universal Bank" with a capital of *40 millions.*

Keep Verkade at work— if he has found 1/3 he can find 3/3rds— Then if you had some one do the same in Germany & some one in France to do the same, many a mickle makes a muckle— it is only the first beginning that is hard.

Does Verkade speak French— if so he might trip to Paris. You ought to have twenty of 'em at your finger ends & keep 'em wound up— Paris, Wien— Why, getting capital for you ought to be *easy*— I don't understand why any difficulty— perhaps it is that you need not *one* but a small army of Verkades' or probably that you need one "Saccard." If so you ought simply to insist on finding him— it's only a matter of time— or perhaps you could cultivate a little more of him in your*self*—

Read "L'Argent"

Temple in her best bib and tucker will go to meet you at the train Sat eve—

> With all my love—
> Isadora

Find Saccard!

"He intoxicated himself with his own eloquence and in exposing his vast plan made one believe it was *already sure.*"

Saccard is a great force—

------ *CD 90* ------

[Noordwijk, probably August 1906]

Dear love— Your news would make me quite desperate if it weren't that I have a vague feeling of our father Walt observing us & saying 'keep on'— or as he writes

"Long & long has the grass been growing"[1]

All these tests are just to make you mount stronger and be more secure when you get there. But I would simply insist on V. putting his shoulder harder to the wheel. He *must*— cause he *has* to—

[1] "Long and long has the grass been growing,
    Long and long has the rain been falling,
    Long has the globe been rolling round."
    —*Song of the Exposition*

Shall I send you your mail or keep it here? Telegraph if you want it.
Bring V. here if you think sea air would brighten him—
I send you all my love— Your Topsy.

—— *CD 91* ——

[Noordwijk, probably August 1906]

Dearest Love—

You were come & gone so quick today— so Beautiful— I feel all over
fragrance from you— sleep tonight still near you—
I send you this pathetic mail from Elizabeth who also sent a telegram
tonight saying send her gold or she is lost—
So please send her some to tend to enclosed things.
Good night
Me very sleepy
I guess you are too—
I love you— Your Topsy

THE DEGREE OF ISADORA'S FORTITUDE IN STEADILY WRITING TO CRAIG
with a cheerfulness she did not always feel—the reader will have
noticed that only when he left her without news during his visit to
Elena did she falter—will be appreciated when one turns to the
memoirs of Kathleen Bruce, who left her studio in Paris to be with
Isadora. In performing her merciful errand, Kathleen, an artist but
also an Englishwoman of genteel upbringing (Isadora had even called
her "a nice quiet English girl"), achieved a victory over elements of
her own background:

. . . there came a letter from Isadora from The Hague. It was a queer
cry, childish and pathetic. Would not, could not, I come to her? Her need
was very great, very, very great. I went at once. I found her pitiful, help-
less, and for the first time endearing. "Poor darling, what is the matter?"
"Can't you see?" cried the dancer, spreading high her lovely arms. Slowly

and with many a lie the story came out at last. A well-known personage with a wife, a mistress, children, dissolute habits, and no money, had entranced her body and mind, and her baby was due in a month or two. She had dared to tell nobody, not her mother or her sister.[1] She had danced as long as she dared. She was lonely and miserable. In after years, when the war had given different values to these things, she said and probably believed that she had done this deliberately, and was proud of her courage and independence; but at the time she was still nothing more than a frightened girl, frightened and pitiful. I was torn and shattered. All my inborn prudery, strengthened by my convent upbringing, was terribly affronted.

The sad, queer happenings in the Balkans[2] served not at all to soften this experience. The girls of my nightmare winter there were of so completely different a civilisation that they had seemed lovely wild animals. But here was the dancer, my friend, with a limited education it is true, but speaking my language, sharing my acquaintances, and with recognisable ambitions and ideals. It was a shattering blow to me, who found exultation in audacious defiance of convention coupled with assured self-control. So loudly and arrogantly had I proclaimed that complete independence for a lass was fraught with no dangers whatever, given character and intelligence to back it. I was very young. Bernard Shaw had not yet written "Man and Superman."[3] Daughters were still living with their mothers in dutiful subjection. Well, here then was a situation to be grappled with. My pseudo-maternal heart took my head sharply to task. Get on with the job! Vicariously I figured myself the mother of Isadora's son. It never occurred to me that the expected baby could be other than a son. For the health of this future son the mother must be cheered and cared for. I would not let Isadora see that I was shocked, yes, quite simply and honestly shocked. Never did I let her suspect my rather mean fear lest any of my commonplace relations, with their standard morals, should hear of my aiding and abetting, with sympathy and capacity, the arrival of the illegitimate child of a dancer. In my head I could hear the scorn with which those last words would be bandied from naval mouth to military, from military to clerical, from clerical to old maids'.

"It is easy," thought I, "to have the courage of one's convictions, but these are not my convictions. I must have courage all the same. My dancer

---

[1] Isadora's family certainly knew about her pregnancy.

[2] Kathleen had been a volunteer nurse in Macedonia.

[3] The first impression of *Man and Superman* was in fact in August 1903 (footnote in original).

is a great, a supreme artist. She is going to have a son. He must be born in as much happiness as I can command for him." So it came about that we two girls settled down to a queer, anxious life in a little seaside villa on a lonely foreign beach The days were long. Isadora stitched little clothes like any sweet mother, and was sometimes peaceful and even radiant. But there were other terrible days and nights when a fierce cloud of doubt, fear, and loneliness would descend upon her, and many and many a time she would cry for death and plan suicide. I laughed at her, reminded her of the great triumphs she would return to, and reassured myself by remembering that as a rule it was not the people who talked of suicide who succumbed to it. Nevertheless, there was one horrid night. A press-reporter had tracked the poor girl down, and had come to interview her. Of course she refused, but the reporter hung about the house. She implored me to wrap myself in the characteristic drapery she usually wore herself, and go and run violently on the beach in order to mislead the reporter should he have heard adverse rumours. Unaccountably to her I refused. Unaccountably to me too. It seemed an act so undignified, and yet, in argument, how could dignity be presented as an excuse for so unkind a refusal. So I did make myself look the very counterpart of Isadora. I tripped off to the deserted beach, I ran, I danced, I flung my arms to the sky. I evaded a meeting with the reporter, but made sure that he saw me from afar. I felt no exhilaration from the exercise, but an uncomfortable shame which I found hard to hide. That night I woke in the small hours aware that all was not well. I lay still for some time, telling myself that there was nothing unusual afoot. I heard nothing. Nevertheless, after a little anxious listening I got up and peeped very quietly into Isadora's room. The bed was empty. There was no light in the house. The front door was open. I dashed down our usual sandy path to the sea. The night was not very dark; the sea was halfway out; there was no more reason to look one way than another. But some instinct sent me rushing directly from the house to the sea's edge, and there, straight ahead in deep water and some way out, I could surely see dimly a head and two hands and wrists extended. The sea was calm. I rushed in. The figure ahead did not move. As I neared it, calling, she turned round with a gentle, rather dazed look, and stretched out her arms to me with a faint, childish smile, saying, "The tide was so low, I couldn't do it, and I'm so cold." "Foolish one," said I, my teeth chattering from fear and excitement. Isadora came from the water fully clothed in her ordinary walking clothes. With infinite and patient care for the life of the little son, I undressed and rubbed his mother, filled hot-water bottles, and made hot drinks, murmuring soothing and lullaby-like consolation. "There, there, go to sleep, you're all safe now. You won't even catch cold. There, there. You're warm and comfy now. We'll forget all about it."

Gordon Craig, "unbridled child of mature age," was far from being the ideal man in the eyes of Kathleen, who was soon to find her own ideal husband in an intrepid, stoical, heroic Antarctic explorer.

What a change when, not long after, Isadora's lover arrived without heralding, to stay we knew not for how long! Isadora was radiant and masterful. He was to be treated as the Messiah; everything was to fall before his slightest wish. Our simple fare must be supplemented; wine must replace the customary milk; everything must be turned to festival. My instinct was to fly, but the foster-maternal feeling was too strong. The boy to be born must need me soon. I supposed I must submit to the presence of this thoroughly inappropriate father. Physically, I was bound to own, he was not altogether inappropriate. He was tall and well built, with a mass of long, thick hair, just beginning to turn grey. He had good features, high cheek-bones, and a healthy colour. Only his hands, with the low-bitten nails, betrayed the brute in him. He was gay, amusing, and argumentative; only once or twice did wild outbursts of uncontrolled temper pass with a wave of terror through the little villa. And I, ever mindful of the little life, wondered whether it were taking any harm from these distressing scenes. Isadora herself remained externally beautiful and serene. Endowed always with an abundance of generosity towards those about her, she seemed now ready to forgive, to condone, to accept, to give herself up to ministering to this unbridled child of mature age whose presence so altered our mode of life.

To feed the rare brute well two large live lobsters had been carried home from town for his lunch the following day. They were put in a pail in the pantry with a trickle of water running from the tap. In the middle of the night I woke up hearing hair-raising noises. What was it this time, suicide or murder? I fled downstairs. No light!—but the noise continued. I stood stark-still listening; and presently I heard a door upstairs open, and soon the whole household was assembled with lights and scared faces, to find that the lobsters had upset the pail with a crash, and were now lashing out lustily along the pantry shelves, shattering the crockery to right and left. A ludicrous scene, which united Isadora's lover and me for the first time in hysterical merriment born of relief.

Then one fine day the lover left, and Isadora sank back exhausted into the monotony of the long wait.

Isadora's well-known pages in *My Life* about the painful birth of her baby are confirmed in the following account by Kathleen:

The end of it came at last. The local doctor, a little, fat, middle-aged Dutchman with a stubbly beard, arrived with a black handbag, containing, he said, anæsthetic; this however he left in the hall both then and later. There followed the most terrible hours that I had ever spent. I had seen and heard things grim enough in the mountain hospital, but here must be, I thought, the ultimate agony. Hour after hour I held the hands, the head, the writhing body, the same hands and head and lovely body that had held European audiences enthralled. The cries and sights of a slaughter-house could not be more terrible. That human beings suffer physical pain in proportion to their artistic sensitive awareness must surely be indubitable. The atrocity of the pain suffered by the sensitive organism of Isadora exceeded immeasurably the worst suffering that could have been felt by one of the poor peasant girls in Macedonia.

I knew little of anæsthetics and Isadora less, but in our respective agonies we implored the foreign doctor as best we could to administer them. He seemed to reply only that there wasn't time, he could not leave her to get it ready. So the frenzied agony went on and on. A terrible bungle! But at long, long last, just before final exhaustion set in, the birth came. But Isadora was not at peace, not for a weary time.

More is expected of educated women now in the second quarter of the twentieth century than was expected at its opening; and who shall say whether their lot is thereby improved or not? But one thing at any rate is no longer expected of them; and that is to endure as that woman endured without alleviation. Nerves are brought nowadays to an all but unbearable tension; but opiates and ether are allowed to relieve it. Perhaps it evens out.

And the babe? It was unhurt by it all. It was perfect. I turned from the horror with joy to the tiny, miraculous object. For a moment a hungry jealousy surged through me. Why was it not my son? And then with a dazed surprise I became aware that the little creature was nobody's son: it was in fact a girl! Quite without sense or reason the gladness went out of it all, and the creature, who had seemed a joyous miracle, seemed now an object of pity. It was a fleeting instinct only, and soon I was tending and purring over the queer little atom with that love that passes all understanding—the love of a woman for a new-born babe.

The foregoing account from Kathleen's memoirs of those last days with Isadora at Noordwijk may be supplemented by the actual entries in her diary, which are, in their brevity, perhaps even more moving:

22 Sept. 1906 (Sat.) I. woke me at 5. Dilation pains begun. Got into bed with her & lay there till 8. Got her up— breakfast & little walk.
23. Sun. [Isadora] got up suffering 2.30. Tried to walk outside— awful. Sitz bath— immense relief. 11.30 went to sleep.
24. Mon. 2 a.m. woke. Sitz bath. Labor began. 4.30 woke Ted went for Dr. Van Nes. 5 came. Dr. slept 5 till 8. About 10.30 forehead appeared. 11.15 pulse weakened, instruments— no time for chloroform. Alive— rupture to rectum . . . stitches. Placenta easy— buried it in sand.
25. Tues. Nurse Kist alarmed. 12 walked with Ted to Nordwyck Binnen to buy things. 10 pm found her flushed. 9 went to interview Dr. at his house. He said possibly never dance again & certainly not for 8 weeks.
30. Sun. Left Noordwyck.

In their published accounts, neither Isadora nor Kathleen mentioned the detail of this period of labor and birth that has perhaps, and understandably, caused the reader some surprise: Craig's presence. He had received, in Rotterdam, a telegram from Noordwijk asking him to come at once, yet even Edward A. Craig has recently expressed astonishment on learning, from Kathleen's diary, that he obeyed it: "I never imagined him being on time." But he was; from the event itself he had not bolted.

ISADORA STAYED ON AT THE VILLA MARIA UNTIL THE END OF OCTOBER, writing to Craig in Berlin and Amsterdam.

–––––– *CD 92* ––––––

[Noordwijk, perhaps September 1906]

Dear— Don't you miss the Sea? It is wonderful tonight, with white caps roaring in. The ad. for the book looks beautiful— me very proud— Tried to get up today but was astonished so weak couldn't stand— sat in a chair but felt faint & had to be put back to bed— frl. says it will go better tomorrow.

Baby growing stout & rosy—
Cooks says she looks just like You!
I am as weak as a newborn kitten— Hope will go better tomorrow. I
didn't know about Tempest— what will they do?
Sounds silly to me—
Sea & wind are roaring fine— wish I could walk to Katwijk—
Good night—

> Your
>   Topsy.

Mr. Schlaf evidently thinks we're just *the ones*— as they say in Ameriky—
Black is getting gloomy and *bad*. He *bit* the girl that brought the chicken—
> *Without cause!*
Say! I wish I were on me legs again I do— I'm tired of lying low— I want
to scamper out of this rabbit nest I do— Yr Brer Rabbit— lying *low*—

------- *CD 93* -------

[Noordwijk, probably September 1906]

Darling— Just a line to tell you all is well— sat up a little today & feel
as if I'd been on a 40 mile walk. Will get up a little tomorrow—
Your little Bird peeps in her warm nest very content— Thank you the
pretty pictures— Read the new Egyp. book today— Prayers to Ra— very
Beautiful—
Bright Sunshine— the sea looked like summer—
Nurse took the Baby *Out*, for a Walk—
All my heart's love

> Your Topsy   & your Baby
> wat loves you *forever*

------- *CD 94* -------

Tues.
[Noordwijk, September or October 1906]

Dear Love   Just rec your card, and the magazines made me laugh—
Dear Heart don't be depressed— *You* ought not to— You who have

all of Beautiful and flame in you to light things— Let the dark ones be depressed— but not the Son of Walt— Never!—

Her Royal Highness is fine, sucks away & grows— Me I lie here thinking of you and loving you "And shall not those who love each other become invincible"

Sun is setting—

Good night Dear one

        Your—
           Isadora

——— *CD 95* ———

[Postmarked Noordwijk, 11 October 1906]

Dearest

I sent you today letter from Art Club in Rotterdam—[1]
frl. K. says *very* well known and fine people—
I telegraphed so you would know their name quick—
Dear Heart you mustn't grow glum— while I admit you have had enough lately to make a Hercules glum, still— that's just the reason why you must go at it with more strength and Cheer than ever—
I came in the other bed today where I can look over the Sea— The Baby had a whiff of sea air from window. She looks *fine*—
Black misses you so much that he sits out & *bays* the Moon *day times*, which sounds most dolorous—
If exchequer is so low better try to make some dates for Dec—
Two nice Egyptian books by Budge made today pass quickly—
If you think so we will arrange a wiley & strategic battle against Verkade & Co.— range 'em up—
All my love to you dear—

        Your
           Isadora

[1] There would be an exhibition of Craig's drawings in Rotterdam in November. The letter Isadora forwarded was probably the invitation.

———— *CD 97* ————

[Noordwijk, probably October 1906]

Dear Love—

Here is S[tumpff]'s letter— I don't think it needs such a quick answer, so send it to you to answer—
I sat up & saw you wave your hand at the turning—
I am getting stronger, indeed feel what you said once I would— new born again—
Baby feels fine too—
There is no life but Love—

    Your
      Isadora

If you think any fun to interview the wiley Mr. Grosz, get his address by telephoning to Grunewald.

P.S. Don't you think the *Harlem* orchestra which S[tumpff] offers impossible? The people were already *very* indignant with it last year.—

———— *CD 254* ————

[Noordwijk, probably October 1906]

Dearest— Here is Stumpff's letter— you might accept his 9000 fr. offer in order to have something *sure* for the season— it would make us feel safer —
Baby is fine— I am much stronger— Do not worry on my account. I must just have patience till I can walk— Frl. says the pain will go away gradually—
Am feasting on wine jelly—
Love to you Dearest Heart

    Your
      Topsy

——— *CD 98* ———

Mon eve
[Noordwijk, October 1906]

Dearest— A nice quiet day— Miss Cheribun lovely & quiet— I hope you're finding things all right— Next week I'll be up dancing about— It's good to think of—
Good night Dear Love

> Your
> Isadora

——— *CD 253* ———

Monday
[Noordwijk, probably October 1906]

Dearest— Please don't tear up your letters— but send them— I understand— and it's you I love whether you're jolly or sad— I didn't know by your letter whether you were coming today or tomorrow or not— a good deal of pain when I stand so that Frl. says it would not be safe to walk for a week yet— but we could leave here *next* Monday— Baby shows so much individuality— or so it seems to me— She seems like a real person—
The days go by— I try not to be impatient. Great winds & storms— a letter from Mary.[1] Mme.[2] is still delirious, but will recover— she is overjoyed!
Love to you Dearest Heart— Am reading Budge's Egypt— I wish we could go to that sunny and wise land together—

> Your—
> *Topsy.*

If you're starting telegraph me.

[1] Perhaps Mary Sturges (Desti). See footnote, p. 230.
[2] "Mme." is not identifiable.

─── *CD 99* ───

[Noordwijk, probably October 1906]

Dearest— This morning Bright Sunshine, & post brought me your letter & the magazines. Baby awfully pleased with her portrait, but says she wants that nice whistling back again at once— she's saying it now quite forcible—
Magazines made the day go much shorter— but how sweet & happy your love makes every day. I feel full of it— never so complete as now. Wish we could take a little run down to Borchart's together— How is old Berlin?
Nurse will take this to post—
Good night—

    Isadora

I sleep holding your dear hands in mine—

─── *CD 100* ───

[Noordwijk, probably October 1906]

Dearest— rec a telegram from Elizabeth— 1700 marks— that is about *990 gulden.*
I telegraphed at once asking if you wanted it for Stumpff— Just rec now your express letter so I will send frl Kist to you first thing in the morning with this & the 1700 marks— In spite of my having my opinion of Mr. Stumpff I think it wise to fix this contract as a sort of *Safety* and indeed after you have warred so valiantly in the making of it would be a pity to lose so much precious energy—
Dearest Heart thank you for your word of this morn— and Miss Baby Bunny enjoyed the joke of her picture— she *laughed*!
Don't let this Beastly Business disturb you— which is easier for me to write, probably, than you to feel— it's so very discordant. I think Stumpff & Verk. came out of the same family *surely*—
Took a little walk with Black today—
All my love to you dear— Your

    Isadora

—— *CD 101* ——

[Note in Craig's hand: "The envelope
shows Oct. 18, 1906 when it reached me
in Berlin fr Noordwijk."]

There's a stormy wind and a cloudy sky
Heigh Ho for a Bottle of Rum—
The rain beats hard & the waves dash High—
Heigh Ho for a Bottle of Rum!

I'm feeling real Nautical— with the big storms a raging around like this—
Sure a seaman's life for me— Nufin like the O-shen wave— the Baby feels
it too— she's getting real sailor like— today she said
"Stop my wittles give me a good drink." It's the devil of a storm, but
we're real cosey & warm in here— with the Ile[1] stove— & tomorrow
we're going downstairs & sit with the other stove—
Heave Ho— almost keeled over that time, but here we go sailing again—
Love to you me Darling—
Come & catch the good dried herring in a swishy swashy sea!
Love to you— Feeling *that* Nautical

    Your Topsy—

—— *CD 102* ——

[Postmarked Noordwijk, 27 October 1906]

Dear—

   It's getting very freezy here— If you find any money rolling up hill
send it[2]— for the Landlord says he's coming for it Monday—
Baby is lovely—
Am scribbling this while postman waits—
Cook is going Monday
Frl. says she *must* go—

[1] A Duncan-Craig Irishism.
[2] Craig was now in Amsterdam.

Helas!— as Mounet Sully says— Quel Mal*heurrrrrr*
With Love

    Isadora

——— *CD 103* ———
HOTEL DU VIEUX DOELEN
LA HAYE

[Probably late October 1906]

Dearest— There came an awful wind storm and almost blew the house
down. Frl had packed everything, and all was so uncomfy I thought
Topsy me had better come over here. Frl will go back for things tomor-
row— we packed all your things & your pictures. I will ring you on the
phone about 9 tomorrow and if you say where she is to send the pictures
there is no need for you to go there. I arranged to send the money to
Mr. Land Lord—
I ate everything in sight here & feel much better—
Your telegram just brought in *forwarded here*—
O, Civilization is a foine thing & portyhouse with Bordylaise sauce is
what makes a man—
Snowdrop[1] likes travelling fine—
Please come & see your
                Topsy when you want to
Helas— Just as frl about to send you pictures all boxed & even nailed
down— Enter L.L. with metaphorical Billy Cock Pistol & Money or your
Life— So I can't send Sphinx. Telegraph him his guldens and to express
your box & trunk to you. He's a most disgraceful L.L.[2] Topsy me is
still weak on me pins— Very— and me poor head needs a trifle tonick-
ing— I'd like to hear some good music. If you hear of any Bach going
on tell me where. You better come over to tea pretty soon anyway—
Snowdrop wants to see you

[1] In *My Life* Isadora implies that the baby was named Deirdre immediately,
but in the letters she is constantly called Snowdrop; there was even a question
of registering her legally under that name. (See p. 240.) The first appearance
of the name Deirdre in the letters is on p. 293. For Craig's indifference as to
the baby's name, see footnote, p. 242.

[2] Many years later Edward A. Craig met this landlord, who told him, speaking of Isadora and her friends: "They all thought they were very important,
like kings and queens"—as, in a way, they were.

So do I
The Landlord's address is
    K. de Bes
    Broukhorst straat
    Noordwijk-Binnen[1]
I enclose his bill. The extra sums are for pumping water and stove & repairs. The 35 taken off is for bed & bath & oil stove which he took— I told him we would send it him in next 2 days. You needn't go there yourself unless you are afraid as to your pictures not being packed right.

SO THE LETTERS FROM AND ABOUT VILLA MARIA END: WITH A BABY girl born and blooming; with the lease on the villa expired, and Craig, close-by in Amsterdam, allowing Isadora and the nurse to attend to all the details of departure—including the packing and shipping of his own effects; with Isadora, the nurse and the baby suddenly chased out by a storm from the North Sea, but not in time to escape the "most disgraceful" landlord and his refusal to release Craig's effects until bills are paid; and with Isadora, still disabled, having taken shelter in a hotel in The Hague, suggesting—in a tone she makes carefully casual—that Craig (still only thirty-five miles away) "come over to tea pretty soon."

Before long they were all back in Berlin.

"When at last we saw [Isadora] again in Grünewald," writes Irma, who was still a pupil in the school, ". . . she appeared with a sweet blue-eyed baby in her arms . . . She held the child up for all of us to see and admire, and said, 'Very soon, she will be the youngest pupil in the school.'"

---

[1] The landlord's name and address are written in a different hand.

Duse, Florence,
Neuralgia

IN BERLIN, ISADORA AND CRAIG WERE SOMETIMES INVITED TO THE
house of the Mendelssohns—the cellist-banker and his Italian-born
wife, who had stood out against other local matrons in the matter
of supporting the school at Grünewald—and they were asked there
soon after Isadora's return from Noordwijk. That night the Mendelssohns' friend Eleonora Duse and her daughter were also present.
In 1895, when he had been, as he described himself, "rather a shy
young man" of twenty-three, Craig had seen Duse act in *Camille* in
London; thanks to his mother he had met her, and she had been
"exceedingly practical and kindly."[1] They had not met again during
his work in Berlin for Duse's never-produced *Elektra*, but according
to Craig that evening at the Mendelssohns' he was appealed to by
Duse's daughter: "Oh, *do* help Mother, she has no one to help her."

"At that moment," says Craig, "I was trying to be of some use
to a far greater performer than the great Italian[2]— and, I suppose,

---

[1] See note for this page.

[2] In one of the later additions to *Book Topsy*, Craig tells plainly why he
considered Isadora the "far greater performer": "Whereas Eleonora, Ellen &
Rachel were remarkable interpreters of Ibsen, Shakespeare & Racine, Isadora
interpreted no one at all— she positively created. No one ever denied this—
her detractors were won over to her when she began to dance creatively— & in

she was trying to be of some use to me— for she urged me to see Duse and helped me to arrange a sort of unsatisfactory combination betwixt us. 'What can I be wanted for? What can I do— anything at all possible I'll do it to please Isadora.' And so I did. I was asked to design scenes and the rest of it for *Rosmersholm* which Duse would perform in Florence. I agreed to do that." And in his "day book" for 1906 Craig wrote: "With Isadora to Italy, there to prepare the scene for *Rosmersholm* for Eleonora Duse, chiefly for the sake of Isadora." "The hour," he added later, "was about to strike."

And so it was: for the first time Craig was to have the experience of producing a major theatrical work entirely on his own terms. The Florence *Rosmersholm*—one single evening in the Teatro alla Pergola, December 5, 1906—was a triumph of theatrical art, and the expedition, undertaken "chiefly for the sake of Isadora" (by that Craig perhaps meant that Isadora had persuaded him to risk another venture with Duse for his own possible benefit), was to reveal itself during the next year as a turning point in Isadora's life as well as his own.

They went down by train with Fräulein Kist and the baby, whom Isadora was still nursing. In *My Life* Isadora writes amusingly about her difficulties, especially given her own meager Italian, in acting as translator and general go-between for the two other artists, neither of whom spoke the other's language. Craig, in his later notes, makes the most of the various professional obstacles he encountered in Florence, including Duse's "lack of cooperation." (It is difficult to tell, from his accounts, whether he objected more to her respecting his independence too much—her "helplessness to be of assistance" to him—or too little: he repeatedly ordered Isadora to "keep Duse out of the theatre.") As it turned out, Duse was at first aghast, and then ecstatic, over Craig's soaring, utterly unrealistic designs—"graduated streaks of color, indigo merging into ultramarine, into Russian green," portraying "a state of mind"—for *Rosmersholm*, Ibsen's own scene-description for which specifies a "sitting room . . . comfortably

---

lesser or in greater degree she always danced so. But we who saw her cannot today say what it is she did— what happened was a transformation— a metamorphosis— something more remarkable than anything we had ever seen— & *MORE LOVELY*."

furnished in old-fashioned style." Duse's off-white, trailing sheath apparently made her a similarly unearthly Rebecca West, and Craig wrote a splendid program note emphasizing Ibsen's "marked detestation of realism":

Realism has long ago proclaimed itself as a contemptible means of hinting at things of life and death, the two subjects of the masters. Realism is only Exposure where Art is Revelation; and therefore in the mounting of this play I have tried to avoid all Realism.

We are not in a house of the nineteenth or twentieth century built by Architect this or Master Builder that, and filled with furniture of Scandinavian design— that is not the state of mind Ibsen demands we shall be in. Let us leave period and accuracy of detail to the museums and to curiosity shops.

Let our common sense be left in the cloak room with our umbrellas and hats. We need here our finer senses only, the living part of us. We are in Rosmersholm, a house of shadows.[1]

"[Rosmersholm] shall be made into dream— dream— *DREAM*," Craig wrote from Florence to his friends the van Looys in Holland, and indeed he and Duse together seem to have made *Rosmersholm* "take off" in a mysterious, almost religious way.

After the performance Craig wrote about it to Martin Shaw: "It was a success & is— Duse was magnificent— threw her details to the winds and went in. She has the courage of 25! She, Ibsen and I played our little trio out and came home happy. I have this morning rec'd a lovely long letter from her— she asks me to work with her in joy & freedom & do 3 more Ibsen plays at once. She says 'I will never have any other scenes— any more of that other *horrid family*!' Is it not happiness to find this still alive in the theatre. What I talk— and I think it's *necessary* to talk— is not always what I do. One must shout out *Passage to India*! in order to book travellers to Dover or Maidstone." And in a later letter to Shaw: "The pleasure I got from seeing Miss Duncan watching my work with Duse was infinite— I care not now whether any one approves or disapproves of one point in my plan or a hundred— because I have that which *glows* to *accept* it without approval or disapproval."

[1] See note for this page.

In her enchantment over the Florence success, Duse asked Craig to prepare for her immediately two other Ibsen plays, *John Gabriel Borkman* and *The Lady from the Sea*. Craig returned to Berlin, where he was soon brooding about gaps in Duse's good behavior in Florence, her general undependability, and her irritating habit of constantly changing plans. Isadora traveled to Warsaw for her first engagement since April, and sent Fräulein Kist and the baby to enjoy the mild climate of San Remo on the Italian Riviera. Whatever the financial arrangements with Duse had been, the Duncan-Craig treasury was in a bad state—due chiefly no doubt to Isadora's long inactivity.

The first Warsaw performance was scheduled for December 17. Craig was apparently still Isadora's manager, dealing with theater and concert agents in various cities either direct or through yet another new assistant at Vereinigter Künste. If a manager's chief responsibility to his artists is to relieve them of worry, Isadora's letters from Warsaw confirm, if confirmation be needed, the absurdity of Craig in that role. Besides, Isadora was not well; the baby had been abruptly removed from breast-feeding. Reading the Warsaw letters, one must wonder whether Isadora had perhaps resumed dancing too soon.

––––––– *CD 104* –––––––
HOTEL BRISTOL
VARSOVIE

[16(?) December 1906]

Dearest— Just arrived Completely Capoot, but as manager says postponement would mean big loss I will do my best to dance tomorrow night— rehearse this afternoon— will go to sleep now.

That *frl*[1] sent carpet without saying *what* carpet for theatre or getting any *paper* as one has [to] when things are sent to Russia so it is held at the douane for *300* marks!!

She's almost as big an idiot as I am— I spent one day going half way to Warsaw & back and the next in rushing around all the Consuls American & Russian trying to get a passport— At the last moment almost missed getting train as they said I might be *Jewish*!!!!!

[1] Perhaps the secretary at the Direktion Vereinigter Künste.

Imagine—
Says sale is good so
Cheer up Topsy—
Cheer up Ted—
Cheer up Snowdrop
Everything will be all right pretty soon

    Love
      Isadora

―――― *CD 105* ――――
Hotel Bristol
varsovie

Dec. 18, 1906

Dearest— I slipped into my old dresses & my old dances last night like
a Charm. After rehearsing orchestra all day— & great agony of spirit—
suddenly felt myself dancing like a miracle. *Art* or *whatever* you may
choose to call it— every little finger movement came in its old place. I
was hardly conscious of my body at all— I feel I have cause to triumph
a bit because I had such a terrible time getting here. It was like one of
those heavy dreams where one tries to get places & can't. To cap climax
a toothache began on the train Sat. night— my cheek swollen— I had to
go to dentist yesterday morn. early & have the filling taken out— is better
but still aches some. But last night was a *real Joy*!
The House was entirely *sold out*—
People all over— I wish someone were here to make the *count*— (I feel
a little nervous about it)— but *not you*— I can't tell you what I felt when
I witnessed your wonderful work in Florence. Probably you have no idea
how truly great & Beautiful it was. It was like something supernatural
that a man with a thousand million *geni* at his disposal might create & I
felt conscience stricken too that I had perhaps been the cause of you
wasting some of your time on me— It would be a *Sin*—
I dare not go out as it makes my face swell more. I must go again to dentist!— & rehearse orchestra— The Cold here is terrific!
I bought here at Hotel news-stand a good *French translation* of J. G.
Borkman for you—

    With all my Love—
      Your
        Topsy

——— *CD 107* ———
Hotel Bristol
varsovie

[December 1906]

Dearest Love— I rec. your letter fr Berlin this morn.—your two from
Italy yesterday— The management here sent you an account of the eve.—
without the *expenses* which they presented to me— They said they *would
keep the expenses till the last eve,* but that is the *same* thing isn't it—
"and the expenses of taxes" was *written* on the contract in *red* ink— in a
vacant space— was it there when I *signed* the contract? If not they have
no right to ask us to pay.
I have had an awful time with tooth which still aches a little— no sleep
etc.— and cannot budge out on account of face swelling—
They have fixed the eves. *17* Mon
                          19 Wed
                          20 Thurs
                          22 Sat.
so I will probably return to Berlin Sunday. I await your answer as to
whether I shall sign the quittance of the evenings under these terms or
not. The taxes are *Theatre Taxes* and *Poor Taxes*— did our contract agree
to them? Remember that a *rouble* is *2* marks. The town looks sad enough
here— & I am glad if my dance can bring to some people here a little
joy— all the *best* families aristocrats etc. have left—[1]
I have been reading Borkman carefully.
Heavens what *gloom*—
Macbeth is not like that but full of Life & Fire—
Rosmer[sholm] is certainly a great play if put on greatly— *you* could
probably put on Borkman so as to bring out & make apparent to the crowd
the Poetry of it. It certainly is a poem but unless handled like a poem
will be a *farce* much worse than a musical comedy. Besides I can't see
why D[use] takes it— there is no *solo* part in it— and her company is
too weak— the principal part is J.G.B. himself.

---

[1] Since the Russian repression of the Polish uprising of 1863, the country had
been treated as a mere Russian province, strictly ruled by a military government. Many of the "best" Warsaw families, "aristocrats etc.," had probably
escaped from the bleak Polish winter to such places as Nice and Cannes.

I am so tired I can't hold the pen.
Au revoir Best Beloved. I will see you soon

  Isadora

Be *careful* of your health. Don't be stupid about it— wrap *warm*.

———— *CD 106* ————
         [Warsaw, December 1906]

Dearest— Just rec. your second letter from Italy. Dear Heart, *don't* be
disappointed about D. As I exclaimed & joyfully when I saw your work,
to be Completely Beautiful you don't *need* anyone else mixed up in it—
It will all come— but it will be *complete* not having to *compromise*—
Beauty— Inspiration
  Genius— *You*
not Ibsen. I have been reading Borkman. Of course Ibsen has a sort of
genius but O Damn it all it's just the *reverse* of Beautiful and if D. goes
that way she will wander in Darkness— No— *not* Ibsen— great as he
may be —
  but
  You
you have the divination of *Beauty*.
My Dear I believe with all my life in *your* Theatre and in *You*.
Dam Borkman
Dam— it all
Dam Strindberg
Dam such stuff
it is *Poison*—
No such mixtures for *you*
  No Mixture
Song of Solomon
  Psyche—[1]
   what you will,
but not these grubby darknesses.
No— No— No Ibsen
Come lets do

[1] An apparent reference, together with line above, to ballet projects for
design by Craig.

Psyche
You read Borkman—
you agree *mucky*
Horrid Horror
Lets go *upwards* & onwards—
against all *practical reasons*
I could be glad about D.
> *MIXED*
>> Don't mind it.
> *PICKLES*

——— *CD 109* ———
HOTEL BRISTOL
VARSOVIE

Dec 19th [1906]—
After second performance—

Dear Heart— As much as I joy in your presence I am *glad* you are not here. This is all *too much suffering*. It seems as if the Gods were piling everything on my head just now to prove how much I can stand!— A furious toothache for 3 nights kept me awake. After *6* visits to the dentist he at last succeeded in stopping it today. Now my stomach begins & refuses all food.

I got through the performance some old way tonight but it was awful— To make things a trifle worse the Governor General of Warsaw, his wife & a party of smart officers sat in the box right on the stage which they shouldn't have sold, & made rude remarks. I politely sent them word that as they didn't like it they would find their money at the box office— at which they sent me an apology explaining that they "always made fun of everything— it was just their way."

Well everything may be a bit funny but just at present poor little me is not on the funny side of it—

Dear Love I begin to believe in the Immortality of the Soul. There must be something to compensate for this tragic comic mixture here. There is Beauty— but O it is so hard to reach. There is Love— & yes I guess that makes up for everything.

In our next contract put that *all spectators* must be seated so many feet etc. away from the stage. These people were in *back* of me.[1] They were

---

[1] Here Isadora has drawn a plan of the stage.

not *Polish* people but Russian aristocrats, which means *Beasts*. Never mind. Good night dearest.

> Your
> *Isadora*

------ *CD 108* ------
HOTEL BRISTOL
VARSOVIE

Dec.
[Probably 20 December 1906]

Dearest— This Business part is *Maddening*. The House was *sold out* last night— *crowds standing*.

They brought me a muddled account this morn.— 1700 roubles (*a rouble is 2 francs*) *in house*.

Then a *long* list of so-called *expenses* & *taxes* ending in wanting to hand me as my share *400* roubles— This is obviously absurd—

So I telegraphed you either to come if you could or send a Business man to unravel the mystery. I *did not accept* either account or *money*— said they must justify them with Verein. Künste.

I am frightfully sorry to worry you with this. You might send Mr. G[rosz?] if you don't want to come— Send a ~~thiexx~~ to catch a T*xxxx*. I'm sure you wouldn't want me to accept & sign for 400 roubles!!!—

Tell me what to do?

I am sending this quick express.

Isn't it absurd to have to worry over such idiotic things—

I will dance for *2000 marks* a night *Guarantee*— and then trouble no more about it—

This *Contracting* and *accounting* is *Death* to any *nobility* of life or thought— You agree— It is Brutalizing & directly hurtful to any true work or inspiration.

Just send or come up here & ravel this out & then we'll have nothing more to do with percents—

> All my love
> Poor Topsyme
> Got a frightful toothache
> *Dentist* Ohooooo!

——— *CD 110* ———
HOTEL BRISTOL
WIEN[1]

[December 1906]

Dearest— I think it better that account money etc. are always sent to Bureau & receipted from there as when they bring me receipts to sign I am not sure *what* I might be signing— and if people found I signed one mistake one day they'd bring me *2* the next. When you have *enough* will you send the *2450 marks* to Zehme— and after that when we have enough we'll send the 2000 *lire* to D.— but I'm afraid that won't be till *Holland* will it?[2]

I am having an awful time here really— first the Passport, then the tooth & now the stomach. Fortunately I found that although it refused everything else it took *oysters* so I am living on them & *raw* eggs— but am dreful weak—

The city here is gloom & darkness personified, & I can't go out because of tooth— altogether I am on the point of despair. Hope you are feeling better.

Go & see Mrs. *Mendelssohn. Who knows* what might happen. Anyway when D. comes back from America (if she goes) I'm sure she'll be of quite another turn of mind. You know she has no money at present—
O I must try & sleep now—
Love to you Dearest one

      Your
      Topsy

——— *CD 111* ———

[Warsaw, probably after 20 December 1906]

Dear— It's rather discouraging trying to work with one's own body as instrument. I am too *tired*— it's the air here— you felt it when you were

---

[1] Isadora has crossed out "Wien" and written "Warsaw" beneath it.
[2] Holland is where Isadora was to dance next. Apparently she and Craig owed money to Dr. Zehme and to Duse.

here remember?[1] However I found something quite new for *me* this afternoon— only a little movement but something I have never done before & may be the *key note* to a great deal. The *dance* is *really* a very interesting study.

Poor little duffer me— I need help with it—

Seems as if I'd been up at this North Pole place forever—

Need music—

Musicians will tear their hair about Chopin on *orchestra*[2]— I *know* it—

Mais que faire—

Am anxiously awaiting your next Bulleteen—

Nurse writes Baby is well & rosey

She needs money

Must buy a baby carriage. Better send her— *enough.*

Salary due about 6 months at 60 gulden a month!!!

Wish I had someplace to work.

How about that studio?

I feel so dissatisfied with my work & that infernal Blue Danube.

House *packed*— wily Director put *back* the 3 first rows again, right up with *noses* to podium— & is *beaming* with *elation* which is *suspicious*— But never mind. Resolved: we won't be greedy.

[1] It is not clear when Craig had been in Warsaw. Dame Marie Rambert writes of seeing him there following a recital by Isadora: "The audience got carried away into mad shouts, and she had to repeat the dance [a Bacchanale] again and again. I rushed backstage, pushed aside a tall young man with a leonine mane who was guarding Isadora's door—it was Gordon Craig—and threw myself on my knees kissing her hands and tears streaming down my face." In correspondence, Dame Marie has said that this scene took place "the winter of 1906," and it is possible that Craig came briefly to Warsaw at this time in response to Isadora's summons by telegraph in CD *108*. However, Isadora's words "when you were here remember" make his visit sound less recent. Perhaps they had stopped in Warsaw together on their way back to Berlin from St. Petersburg and Moscow in February 1905. Or perhaps, as Natalia Roslavleva suggests, Isadora is thinking of Poland as part of Russia (which, politically, it then was) and is referring to the St. Petersburg and Moscow visit itself.

[2] Isadora is referring to the indignation, familiar to her by now, of some critics that she should use Chopin's music, even in its original piano scoring, as accompaniment to her dancing. "Chopin on *orchestra*" would be further profanation.

Forgive this stupid letter.
Good night dear Heart.

> Love
>   Isadora

———— *CD 112* ————

[Probably Warsaw, December 1906]

Dear Love— Whenever my spirits get low comes a letter from you like
a ray 〰 of Life. You are the unique life-giver for me— & without
you it would be like the Earth without the Sun— and I confess that when
I am not with you it is *sometimes* like a partial Eclipse— but never a
total Eclipse for you have a way of sending your rays even from afar.
To pass the time last night when I was tired I read that absurd but perfectly delicious story *Manon Lescaut*— fancy I had *never* read it. I also
read a big book— the life of the Dauphine Maria Joseph & Louis XV,
but they are neither of 'em uncles or aunts of *mine*. *Stupide*, as D. would
say. I'm afraid take off the glitter of past times & those people were just
as uninteresting then as they are now.
I had a nice letter from André Beaunier— the young writer who never
never ——— but I will send him your book— he has good taste & will
be enthusiastic.
I work some each day.
Something is on the way but comes *slowly*. It's this music question. I
must settle *once* for all—
>   antique?
>   Early Italian?
>   Gluck?
>   Modern?
>   or
>   None?
You know it's a subject worth thinking about. You have a superior Think
Box in your head than mine— what do you think?
You know it's very interesting because when they compose a *Ballet* the
Ballet Master composes the dances from a list of dances, steps, figures, etc.
from a book— time of Louis XIV or XV. Then he brings this to the poor
musical composer & says "Make me so many bars of 2/4 time, so many

of 3/4, and then so many of 4/4." The musical director of the orchestra (the old one) who composes ballets says that is it quite impossible to compose any music *worth* anything in *that* way. The whole question ought to be worked out by a head stronger than *mine*. I screwed up my nose & thought for a few hours yesterday & evolved the following— or I'll enclose it.[1] Tell me if it's any good— I feel my poor head is very *faible*. But I've found *one* new movement which I think will *stonish* you. Don't delay too long before going to Mrs. Men[delssohn] or she'll be offended. In 3 days I'll see you
won't I
I have before me a little sketch you made on a postcard of a man coming downstream in a little boat balancing himself with a long pole. The least line you make has Beauty & Life— You a Fountain of *the Beautiful* & it flows in whatever comes from you—

   Good night Love

       Your
       Isadora

Frl telegraphed for money— she must buy Baby *carriage*, so send her enough. Says Baby is *well* & *laughs* all day— in sunshine.

------ *CD 113* ------

Saturday
[Warsaw, probably December 1906]

Dearest— Been dreful ill— Dr. says *poisoned* oysters caviar or something— Am up & better now— oil every hour all day yesterday— spare you details— Will start for Lodz[2] tonight. Had just made good resolution to work—
This trip would read like a joke—
You dear Heart— I will be in Berlin Jan 5?
Good St[umpf]f put off dates— I need a week's respite.
This beginning is hard but we'll round the curve all right.

[1] No enclosure has been found.
[2] An industrial town eighty-two miles southwest of Warsaw. Apparently Isadora's Warsaw success had caused the Polish tour to be extended.

Great Things Coming!
Love you dear one—

> your
> Topsy
> > a trifle *upset* but ready for the *start*.

Resolved: Let us take care of our Health—
Please be careful you too.

——— *CD 114* ———

[Warsaw, December 1906]

Dear Love— ☺ That's Topsy me— It seems they're marching about Lodz at present amiably killing each other— 100,000 people have struck, so the soiree is put off. Will I fix it for Jan. 6?— They say things may be quiet by then! I telegraphed just now to ask you—
I haven't had anything to eat for 2 days. If any of the German Ballet was here I should suspect that it *wasn't* the oysters.

Sunday
> Been out for a long drive— like flying through whiteness— feel much better & am allowed to eat again—
Just rec. your letter—
Thank you for the nice pretty ticket dear!!!
Send me a telegram now & then to cheer me up?
Don't forget dear to send money to *frl. Kist, Grand Hotel de Nice*— San Remo— Italia— or Snowdrop will be complaining. I feel like poor old Robinson Cruso— I won't be there to see the new Year in with you—
> *Be Good*

> Love Your
> Topsy—
> > *faithful me.*

—— *CD 115* ——

[Probably Warsaw, shortly before Christmas,
1906. Note by Craig in margin: "This
letter came with Christmas card."]

Darling— Just came home from dancing— Chopin on *orchestra* is such a *Success* that it *frightens* me! Schubert falls quite flat afterward. The *2* Chopin waltzes are really lovely but they take an *awful good* orchestra to play them— ought to tell Stumpff that.

I am very well and not so tired— but it is *hard* to think of new work— one needs a studio & surroundings a bit regular. I worked two hours yesterday but not much result— & I have to *rest* a good deal & get fresh air— rehearse orchestra & dance evenings— I feel something dimly coming— I badly need a musician to help me. You see my life has *always* been such a continual scramble rush & excitement— I would like someone to help me *learn* more about music, and study more *exactly* its different relations to dancing— It is a very interesting subject. I heard the Pathetic Symphonie of Tshaikowsky (how do you spell him?)— Wonderful— Go & hear it when you have a chance. Tell me what you think: does the dance spring from the music, as I think it does, or should the music accompany the dance— or should they both be born together— or How?— Sometimes I think till my poor little head is all muddled— A big library of books— a big studio & a musician— I want.

Your letters are Beautiful— They enter in my heart & suffuse all through me and I feel how completely I am your own—

Here comes my modest repast— Frl. writes the Baby grows stout & well with *red* cheeks so you must find another name than Snowdrop—

Life *is* a bit extarordinary, isn't it—

Good night— full of love for you—

　　Your Topsy

—— *CD 116* ——

[Warsaw, probably December 1906]

Dear— I hate to *bother* you with my affairs when you have so much to think of but this subject of the *music* must be fixed, or it will be the com-

plete *ruin* of me as an artist and eventually financial also— as finances generally fall when art falls in spite of all one can say to the contrary—
I am afraid Reichman[1] is not honest. First he deliberately put back the 1st 3 rows of orchestra— which makes me appear to dance exactly on the heads of the 1st row; and now today when I went to rehearsal I found an *entirely different orchestra*— not even from opera but from some 3rd class theatre here. The director admitted it. How they played was something *Comic*.
He wishes to send the Philharmonic orchestra to Lodz, and leave me with that— of course I refused. So I'm afraid the evening will not take place tomorrow—
I cannot deliberately sacrifice every feeling of art— (or even not speaking of art simply to do things *decently*) for *money*— and even from a money standpoint it would soon mean *no public*.
I *must have* a permanent musical director— Shaw if you like or someone else, but I cannot continue tour without. If I had once a director that was an *artist* we might then organize a *small fine* orchestra— say *8* musicians & I would dance *Every Night* so as to make it possible[2]— for after a few more years like *this* I will be *dead* from anguish.
Evening arranged *with* Philharmonic orchestra the *9th* as they go to Lodz *8* & *10th* but *what* a *nerve*-racking affair.

[3]Mr. Reichman & wife just came in great trepidation to apologise. Said he had thought he could get the opera orchestra etc etc. His orchestra goes to *Lodz* on the *8*— but he will make my soiree on the *9* so as I can have Philharmonic orchestra— That makes me dance the *9th* & *10th* which is not good for me[4]— but I couldn't do anything else—
Dear I hate to bother you but I cannot go on without a *permanent* orchestra director, & after as I say we could make up a very *small— 6 or 8—* but *good* orchestra. If you don't want Mr. Shaw then will you ask Grosz to find someone. I would rather jump into the Sea than continue this sort of thing— It would be *far* easier for me to dance every night in week but one—

[1] Rajchman, the Warsaw theatrical agent.
[2] Here Craig later scribbled a testy note: "—but would you?"
[3] A new page begins here, and Isadora has written: "But read this page first."
[4] Another note by Craig in the margin: "see back '*every night*'!"

Forgive me writing such a Beastly letter but I am almost dead from so much *vexation*.

Perhaps now Grosz has a Concert Bureau he can find a director among his Gob ～～～ lins!

Another thing that worries me is that unless Mr. Stumpff has supplied a very *good* orchestra it will be impossible to play Chopin with it, as the Chopin music is arranged *all solos*— solo for flute, for oboe, etc., and needs the *very best*—

Would you mind having the fr[äulein] write Stumpff this & say that I attribute the falling off of the *audience last year* to the *bad* music— and I really do. People got tired of having their ears murdered.

I will have to have more money here, and as it is impossible to *telegraph* money to Warsaw I will have to take it from Philharmonic.

Again forgive this horrid letter.

> All my love—
> Isadora

———— *CD 117* ————

[Warsaw, probably December 1906]

Dearest— Your letter delights me— it's full of wake-up & electricity That's right—

Keep a spirit like that & everything you want will come to you—

Have just come from rehearsal—

The manager rushed up with some proposition about going to *Vilna*— tour in Pologne— on a guarantee. I told him he must arrange putting off Lodz & all with [Direktion] V[ereinigter] K[ünste].

I have been awfully ill but am well now.

Chopin *all* on orchestra—

One waltz sounds Beautiful.

The Pianists will tear their hair but the public will love it—

Whole programme on orchestra—

Will I arrange or will you the terms on which the Capelmeister is to give us the Chopin music for orchestra— whole programme, as they have it now.

Go softly with *Mrs.* M[endelssohn]— not too much *Business* to *her*—

Ask her to *play* for you. Storm the Citadel *gently*. How about building studio?[1]

Youre as foine a Boy as ever was made in Old Ireland—

You're right about dress suit—

To look Beautiful is also important— also a *hint*: you might change that brown[2]— it's getting a *trifle* just a wee bit ∼∼∼.

> Love to you
> *Isadora*

—— *CD 118* ——

[Warsaw, December 1906]

Dear— These are the last few moments before the New Year begins. I stopped in & heard Handel's Four Seasons[3]— Philharmonic *almost empty*— Great Work— The wonderful *Hunting* Chorus— & then the Wine Pressing dance— and a lovely Spring Chorus— I enjoyed it— and it gave a good zest to the last few moments of the old year— really beautiful— but no one took the trouble to come & listen to it— Queer!

I am waiting for the clock to strike *12* before I sleep— & then I will cry out Happy New Year Ted Happy New Year Snowdrop— Happy New Year Everyone— including Topsyme.

Happy New Year— do you *want* to be Happy—? for a whole year.

[1] Craig was dreaming of founding a school of theater design in Berlin; the Mendelssohns were potential financial backers. In one of Craig's notebooks, on a page of sketches and notes for the project, he wrote: "Speak Mrs. Mendelssohn re the place." And in a letter to "Dear Mr. Lapidoth" in Holland, dated December 17, 1906: ". . . It will interest you to know that Madame Duse has associated her name with mine and will serve with all her heart the idea which my School intends to develop. That is to say I have the spirit of the greatest Actress living for the most advanced idea of The Theatre, even to the extent of getting rid of the actors themselves, which as you know by no means implies getting rid of the great personalities."

[2] "brown suit," Craig has noted.

[3] In one of his notebooks Craig wrote: "The Seasons— by Haydn— Oratorio— Warsaw."

Craig at seventeen, with his mother, Ellen Terry, playing in The Dead Heart, *by Watts Phillips. (Courtesy of Edward A. Craig)*

ABOVE: *Gordon Craig in Brussels, 1905. (The Craig-Duncan Collection)*
BELOW: *Photograph of Craig by Isadora Duncan. Inscribed by Craig: "1906 Holland. Before Deirdre." (Courtesy of Edward A. Craig)*

Isadora in Brussels, 1905. Photograph by Craig. (The Craig-Duncan Collection)

Isadora in Belgium, 1905. Photograph by Craig. (The Craig-Duncan Collection)

ABOVE: *Isadora at the Hotel Metropole, Brussels, March 1905. Photograph by Craig.*
(The Craig-Duncan Collection)
BELOW: *Craig at the Hotel Metropole, Brussels, March 1905. Photograph by Isadora Duncan.*
(The Craig-Duncan Collection)

Craig's drawings of Isadora on the train between Hamburg and Berlin, January 1905.
(The Craig-Duncan Collection)

"Me spring clothes," 1905. *(The Craig-Duncan Collection)*

Craig's drawing of Isadora dancing in Breslau, January 1905. (Courtesy of Arnold Rood)

—— *CD 119* ——

[Telegram, Warsaw to FOOTLIGHTS BERLIN,
received 1.1.07, 12.20 P.M.]

HAPPINESS ENOUGH FOR TRITILLIONS OF YEARS LOVE

—— *CD 120* ——

[Warsaw, January 1907]

Dearest— I am overjoyed with all your news & wait breathless for each new letter. I have always known that marvellous & unheard undreampt-of things were on the road to you. This is a part of the beginning— Have faith in your Star.

I go to Lodz where their bubble revolution is broken this eve. & dance there tomorrow eve. so *unless* you arrange the eve. at Vilna or another here in Warsaw I will start for Berlin Fri. eve. after the performance. The Chopin on *orchestra* was just what the dear audience here liked— wanted. *All* things encored— the waltzes especially created a furor.

You must arrange for *buying* of music— partition parts etc. from the Philharmonic. I am afraid to ask prices. The Kapelmeister very kindly says he will make me a present of the *two* waltzes— but there remain the others. The whole programme which we *must* have is:

1	Mazurka	C dur	
2		H moll	
3		D.dur	
4	Nocturne	E dur	
5	Preludes	A dur	
6		E moll	
7		H moll	
8		D.dur	
	Waltz	Cis moll ⎱	These two he (Kapelmeister)
		Ges dur ⎰	gives us as a present.
9	Waltz	des dur	

(9 pieces to buy)

All that will cost something.
Going out for some air now.

> All my Love
> Isadora

Are there no letters from fr[äulein Kist] at office?
Don't forget to send her money, dear. We owe her about 4 or 5 months
salary. Register letter: Frl. Marie Kist
> Grand Hotel de Nice
> San Remo Italy

—— *CD 121* ——

[Warsaw, January 1907]

Dearest— The director here tells me he is arranging with you to give
the last eve. *here* the *10*— on your same terms. I am pleased as it will save
me the voyage. The Musical Dir. tells me that at *Kieff* he plays to an
audience of *2000* people— I think a tour of all cities of Poland might be
profitable. I enclose you an offer from Ellenfeld, sent me from Grünewald.
My old lady femme de chambre has left me— her husband wanted her
etc.— with many tears—
Yesterday I saw some shooting in the street— One man was shooting after
another man who was running away in abject terror. *Another* had a *4th*
covered with a revolver. The man covered, *grinned* and *gibbered* with
fright, his knees *bent*— & finally turned *slowly* & ran heavily away his
knees giving at every step as in a bad dream. The other finally fired but
missed— it was very *curious*.
I asked the cause & was told indifferently "O Socialists!" Was it not
strange that the man *could not* run quickly away—
I took a long walk today. Sun shining on snow like diamonds— but no
more sleighs— not cold enough!
The other day I visited Melanov, the Chateau of my other chère vieille
Potocka. Very pretty— & I saw the famous little Chinese appartement of
the rez-de-chaussée where my aunt was invited to take Tea! I felt stremely
Historical.[1]

---

[1] "My aunt" may be an echo of the unexplained fanciful mention, in CD *112*,
of "aunts" in connection with Louis XV, whose queen was the Polish Maria
Leszczynska.

I leave night of 10th— no woman in Siberia could be more *pleased*— &
11th will see *you*—

 Good night dear one

 Love your Topsy—

My Chopin dances seem to be giving some of the ladies here Hysteria—
which is the last thing on earth I mean to do. One attacked me at stage
door today— mad as a Hatter—!!

—— CD 123 ——

         Wednesday night
        [Warsaw, January 1907]

Darling— I opened your envelope just now expecting to find a letter
but instead found something so sweet so beautiful I didn't know what to
do so cried over it. How can you write me such words— anyway they
would almost create an angel out of a dustheap, such words as that. Thank
you dear I will try to live up to a little part of them at least— I kiss your
dear Hands. Good night Your

 Isadora

—— CD 124 ——

        [Warsaw, January 1907,
     perhaps only last part of a letter]

Picture of studio Beautiful.
Let's begin—
This is last time I write from here— Thank ye Gods—
Only your beautiful letters have kept me alive—
Yes I want those kisses I do— I'm coming right along—
You'll see me morning of 11th
Love Love Love Your

 Topsy
 a coming—

Get that Brass Band out I'm coming—

AFTER A BRIEF STOPOVER IN BERLIN, ISADORA LEFT TO DANCE IN Holland, where Martin Shaw had come again from England to be her conductor. As the letters show, she now fell alarmingly ill—an occurrence so frightening that when she came to write *My Life* she recorded it as beginning with dramatic suddenness: "The first night I appeared on the stage in Amsterdam, a strange illness overcame me. I think it had something to do with the milk, what they call milk fever, and after the performance I fell prone upon the stage and had to be carried back to the hotel." Though in fact the letters tell us that this illness began with a malaise that sounds menstrual, there are all too many signs of spiritual malaise as well. She had served Craig loyally in Florence, keeping herself in the background of his work, but in the "lovely letters" he had sent her in Warsaw and continued to send her he did not succeed in concealing what might mildly be called his restlessness. After his Florence success, Craig was obviously straining at the leash, and Isadora could not face the implications of what she saw.

———— CD 126 ————

Sunday
[Amsterdam, probably Brack's Doelen Hotel,
January 1907]

Dearest— I arrived pretty tired but seeing bright sunshine reflected in the many little canals & the good cows on the green cheered me. Been looking at Blake's wonderful pictures—
Mr. Stumpff & Mr. Shaw came in a few moments. Both send you kind messages. Mr. Stumpff says your exhibition here was a tremendous sensation & success. Said he wanted you to give something in Theatre here but that you *refused?*— What?—
I gave him a glowing account of Rosmersholm. I will stay *here* as they have given me a great big room & I will have a piano & a *lady* to play on it & practice each day.
    Good Topsy me— so address all letters here—
Too tired to sit up now— falling over with sleep as couldn't last night. Love to you dear one—

        Your
            Isadora

―――― *CD 127* ――――

[Amsterdam, January 1907]

Dear Love— Your packet of Blakes came on awakening & gave me a *tremendous joy*. How strange I have lived so long without knowing anything of Blake, but I am so glad it was so— for the initiation comes so beautiful from *you*— *you* opened to me the *extra* sense of Beauty that I lacked— I always loved lovely things but I remember the first morning I visited your exhibition I felt my *limited* circle had widened its horizon to *limitless*—
Do not tire yourself—
If you don't like your studio any more *change* it— The building where Magnus was has some, very *nice*, with heat, etc.
Get in *Harmony*—
It is so *Precious* & so *Necessary* for you.
I have a piano here this morn. & a young lady to play— Have put piano in the other room so I can't see it or her but only *hear* the music which I find very good & I will soon have a new programme ready—
I will *stay here*— it is more cheerful than Hague— & work—

      All my love
      Isadora

Snowdrop is *well* & *laughs* all day— I am so *glad*. Warm as summer & she all day in open air—[1]

―――― *CD 128* ――――

[Amsterdam, probably January 1907]

Dearest

    Just came home from theatre— just a word to say Good Night. Wish I could say it a *different* way. You not: you connect with Lady of the Sea— don't want Topsy me. Sometimes I wish to God you were a carpenter or so, & I could sleep on your arm every every night— but then

―――――――――――――――――――――――
[1] The baby was still in San Remo.

I would lose the joy of your art which is more. Thank you [for] your beautiful letter of Lady of the Sea. Your sketch is full of inspiration & now that I've seen Rosmersholm I know a *little* more what to expect.

It's rather *lonely* coming back to hotel after dancing & I want the Baby— Everything went smoothly tonight— crowded house— & seemed pleased. Mr. Shaw directed very well & made the most of bad orchestra. I had young girl play 3 hours yesterday & composed a little *minuet* of *Bach*— very *simple*, nothing special, but I think the movement goes well. I will try a *Gigue*.

By the way when you feel you need something *hire* a *piano* & employ someone to play to you— Bach— It is *much* better than going to a concert & one doesn't have to *clap* or hear *clapping*, ugly lights, etc.— great relief. She played me fugues— preludes— & I enjoyed it— Quiet lovely music— Try it.

I have a *big* salon here to dance in & must stay in Amsterdam to rehearse orchestra— besides it's more *cheerful* than Hague— I don't feel quite so forlorn as I would there— so don't tell me go Hague— that old Vieux Doelen is too melancholy— isn't it?[1]

> Good night
> Your lonely Topsy

----- *CD 131* -----

[Telegram,
Amsterdam to CRAIG PALASTHOTEL BERLIN,
received 16.1.07, 6.40 P.M.]

DAY OF JOY PROPHETIC HAPPY BIRTHDAY LOVE

----- *CD 132* -----

16 January 1907
[Amsterdam]

Dear Love—

Today is your precious birthday—
Would I were there— to drink a bumper of wine to your health—

---

[1] The real reason for her not going to the hotel in The Hague becomes clear later.

Frl. sends me word the Baby's health is splendid—I long for her—I long for you—I miss the wonder & the inspiration you add to all the moments. Even the suffering you sometimes cause is joy compared to being without you. Do you think the day will come when I can stay with you & be of some help to your work & so further my own better than by bumping about the country like this? Will it come, a time of harmony & achievement? What do I care for the black houses here without you to say lovely things about them— *You* are the Wine & Poetry of Life— Without you how flat & cold— You make the Beauty *Luminous* to me— If you were going to Italia I might come with??? yes—

Your
Pore
Topsy

———— *CD 164* ————

[Amsterdam, January 1907]

Dear Love— O, how I would long to see our Baby— but Dr. told me to change her milk & bring her to cold climate *now* might be fatal so I don't dare. Frl. writes me she is leaving— She *promised* to stay till March. I will find a nurse here that I can give full instructions to & send her down— I must *see* the nurse myself who is to care for Baby.

Stumpff wants more dates here—
O Darling I am so sad & distracted, but will try & be brave—
Ray[mond Duncan] telegraphs for money— he is at Sans Souci Hotel. I have *not* sent it him— but wrote E[lizabeth] to try & stop him dancing in Berlin.
Too much   Too much—
I will do my best but feel a bit dashed—
I love you dear— Good night

Isadora

——— *CD 129* ———

Tuesday
[Amsterdam, January 1907]

Dear

The sweet strong words of your telegram gave me strength to dance last night as nothing else could. I put them up on my mirror & between each dance they *shone* for me—

This morn. I found I was '*ill*' so have been lying flat all day as it is necessary—

Yes— go & show Duse the Lady of the Sea as it will give her new life to see you—

Mr. Loeser wrote Kathleen that every one in Florence *loved you.*[1]

I got worried about Frl. Kist leaving the 25, & so found a nice reliable nurse here & sent her down there— so feel easier. She rec. the same 60 gulden a month.

If no other engagements are made in this part of country I will be in Berlin the 29th won't I?

The house was *packed* last night— & enthusiastic— but the orchestra is a *disgrace* & *no lime lights*— Stumpff replied there was no mention of them in contract & so he didn't need to supply them!! Awful light— red & white plain electric lights!—

I have been working hard with the pianist but now must lie still— Darling love what a mystery all this life is— & the changing time & all— I sent your boxes from Hague this morn.— & pictures packed well— took me all morning to sort things out. The lantern slides I took out extra & will send you in little packet, as the big things go slow.

That sounds beautiful about London. I am so worried about Ray— he is really rather *stupid* don't you think?

I found all Blake's Book of Job here & bought it— Wonderful— & felt you beside me when I looked at it— I work from your inspiration & I repose on your Love—

    Good night
    Your
      Topsy

[1] Kathleen was then visiting Isadora in Amsterdam. The reference to "Mr. Loeser" is explained on p. 197.

—— *CD 130* ——

[Amsterdam, January 1907]

Dear— My star seems to have been a yearning star & it is decreed I spend my life in longing longing longing. Sometimes when I dance or when I am with you it is *stilled*— yes *you* can still it— but no one else & nothing else, only sometimes my dance. I have been looking at the little photo I took of you in Noordwijk— you are So Beautiful— is it Beauty then which awakes such longing—

No letter from you today!—

Kathleen left this morn. for London— She was very sweet & cheerful. I have been lying down all day as am rather too '*ill*.' Tomorrow I must go to Harlem for rehearsal of Chopin music—

Darling, I am going to bed again now with a book of Blake's Job! What a funny life!!

I want the Baby— I want *more*— *You*. I am filled with yearning & unrest. I have the Madonna you brought me to Noordwijk— she is lovely.

What are you doing now?

Do your thoughts reach me like the Zigzags [?]?

Do you say 'be a sensible Topsy, go to bed & get well'—

I dance here 25 & 28 & then Berlin?

I have to pay the Beastly Bills here *as they come in*— or they would make trouble.

Hotel Doelen— Hague	500	guldens
Prof. Trul.	150	"
Dr. Van Ness	300	"
Frl.	225	"
Hotel here		
9 days	255	"
	1430!!!	
	awful!	

Frl. telegraphed for 450 frs. I had to send it as thought perhaps they were in some difficulty.

Almost the receipts for 2 evenings— dreful— as soon as they stop coming in I will send you all accounts, receipts, dividends, etc. Elizabeth writes she must have 1000 gulden back she lent, to pay House Taxes with.[1]

---

[1] Another debt. The bills from the Hague hotel and Dr. Van Ness must date from Noordwijk and immediately post-Noordwijk days.

O, Dear—
Topsy me go to Bed now, me a little sick which makes me melancholy—
but indeed I will sleep & dream of you— & of *Joy*— and of Baby— few
people have such Beautiful things to dream of—
Good night dearest Love—

———— *CD 133* ————

[Amsterdam, January 1907]

Dear Love— I don't blame you being a bit angry about E[lizabeth] and
the stage managing, etc.[1] it's really too stupid. Sometimes I wish I could
just simply help your great work & stop everything else & be *to you
something*— but Fate has put us in such queer complicated positions.
Perhaps Time will help—[2]
Elizabeth telegraphed me she had made a final arrangement with Harden-
bergstr. and settled for 1200 marks & wanted 1000 marks— so I sent you
telegram. That will *end* H[ardenberg] str[asse].
Also— Old Doelen Hague it seems had written to Stumpff! and *he* wrote
me about it— I didn't want to tell you as I knew it would irritate you—
but *that* is the reason I *won't* stay there *ever* again— I had to telegraph
them the money— 455.36 florins.
Darling Heart, don't let these things annoy you— don't let anything
annoy you— Treat 'em all as mosquito bites. They are nothing. Your
work is God head & nothing can really affect it or hurt it. It will all
come in a Blaze & even your own eyes will be dazzled & astonished—
and all the People will then form in a procession & follow. Lift your
head above the clouds— & *don't* let small things worry you. The more
I live & experience, the more I see of beautiful things like Blake for
instance & Bach's music, the more I realize what the right, the *divine*,
place of Woman is— and it's *not* rushing about doing things— *not*—
No— it's like she is in Blake's pictures.

[1] Elizabeth and Craig were both in Berlin, and as usual there was conflict.
Elizabeth, apparently engaged in winding up the Duncans' lease on the flat in
Hardenbergstrasse, had probably been giving Craig some advice which, unlike
the loan from the school funds, had not been requested.
[2] Craig (years later) in margin: "Time taught— without helping."

Good night dear— perhaps it will come to pass that I may be some day what a great Beautiful dream tells me I *might* be to you.

Your Isadora

———

To this letter, there exists the draft of an answer—whether sent or not is unknown—from Craig.

——— *CD 266* ———

[23 January 1907]¹
(Stumpff was the theatre agent
to I.D. Berlin   in Amsterdam 1944)

Stumpff wires me at the last moment about dates Brussels etc.

I have answered him.

I have no faith in anything for you that can't produce *at least* a guarantee of 2000 marks.

I have told him also to engage Shaw.

Enter into *no* conversation even to say *yes* or *no* to any question about performances— or he sees our position and acts accordingly and takes advantage of you.

He already has got it into his head that Shaw is *necessary*. Too bad— he should be *sure* of nothing but his own guessing.

So you wired to Kathleen.

Duse has wired me— about 6 times— and today I get wire about going to Nice.

Isn't your mama there.

You are quite right— a woman's business is to do differently to a race horse— 6 times round and then once more. And a human man's is the same. But slowly men are growing into something different— and if one doesn't want to be lonely— if one fears to be lonely— one had better join in the race.

Whole point rests on the capacity for a critter to sit or stand alone— most people fear that. It has drawbacks—certainement!

¹ All other headings added by Craig in 1944.

Stumpff's last telegram contained 159 words. What's the matter with him?

Mr. and Mrs. M.[1] come to see my pictures tomorrow morning. I'm sure the prospect is depressing in the extreme. If I had velvet hangings to my walls I should enjoy the sporting farce. For plush speaks— and whitewash is silent. But we shall see. They certainly enjoy their music.

I have done 4 of the drawings for the *Lady from the Sea*— and only like one— and the scene painters are a bit expensive— taking every sou and more of what D[2] pays me. It's queer this idea of an artist working for positively *nil*. It's so *strange* somehow— uncanny— not quite to be comprehended. A good steady wage like Otto[3] gets would be preferable. And when history repeats at the death of each artist this same story it seems to make no impression.

It is so cold here that the streets are *nearly empty* . . the noisy street by my bedroom keeps me restless most nights and I get up sick of it about 7.30 and dawdle at dressing until 9 when my studio is ready and possible to work in.

I hope to find time (I have the fit on strong) to sit down and do 3 or 4 articles for the "Zukunft" . . To draw one's dreams is soothing— but to write out one's (prisoned) convictions is *Relief*. One feels that the drawing only adds another mystery to a great Riddle which no one will ever guess. The words clear up and one feels that if ever they are read they will somehow be a direction— a sort of clock— half past 9—.

By the way Duse will not do "Tintagiles"[4]— she has a new play— It is pitiful— yet she had evidently forgotten Mr. Rosmer and M. Magi and Co. when she spoke of "Tintagiles." Yet even with all this forgetting and changing she is the best of her land.

A word of business.

Has Stumpff paid you— and has he returned you the 1000 guildern which I paid him as caution.

I shall feel better tomorrow and I dare say it will be less cold.

Who came to Amsterdam with Kath?[5] You don't send me much news. I feel always as if I could act better at this end with clear news and facts to go on. It doesn't help me to keep back communication. I would have

[1] Note by Craig: "the Mendelssohns."

[2] Note by Craig: "Duse."

[3] Note by Craig: "Otto was the concierge of the 25 to 40 studios in Siegmundshof 11. 1944."

[4] *The Death of Tintagiles*, by Maurice Maeterlinck.

[5] Note by Craig: "Kath Bruce, Lady Scott."

been glad to have heard that Stumpff had been written to by Vieux
Doelen. But facts are rare things anyhow, and not to be relied on either.

Stumpff has no right to act as family lawyer between us and third
parties. I sincerely hope you told him so and wrote also to Vieux Doelen
and told them so. Meantime I'm the only loser— as I needed my things
and they have been forgotten, I suppose. But I must have them soon as
I must turn to my book this spring

The school[1] it seems must wait. All good things wait— and if 30 years
is worth a fairly good thing a *good* thing is worth 100 years.

I shall then appear "for the first time on any stage" as Yorick.

———

Meanwhile, Isadora's health had worsened considerably.

——— *CD 134* ———
BRACK's DOELEN HOTEL
AMSTERDAM

[Probably 24 January 1907]

Dearest— This is *3rd* day I must lie in bed. Horrid, when I was working
so well—
Patience—
Can't even read as my head swims— Will be all right tomorrow I hope
for evening. No letter today— Such a hotel— silence all day— Wow—
I don't like such interludes—
Silly me, to get so ill—
Can't understand it—
forgive these stupid lines—
Must be content to close my eyes & call up visions of lovely times past
& wait—
Was afraid to *stir* today—
Looked at Blake's Job— till I almost saw apparitions myself— Why no
letter from you?
What you doing?
Dear Love—

———

[1] Note by Craig: "My project for a school for Theatre."

I come Berlin 29th?
What long long hours—
Darling, good night—

    Your *Pore sick* Topsy

Looks as if I were turning into a Blooming Invalide! Frl. writes me
Baby *well* & *rosey*.

If, as it seems, that sickbed letter was written January 24, and
Isadora was to dance the next day, perhaps it was after the performance of the twenty-fifth (her second Amsterdam appearance of the
season) that she "fell prone upon the stage and had to be carried
back to the hotel." The account of her illness in *My Life* continues:
"There for days and weeks I lay in a darkened room packed in ice
bags. They called it neuritis, a disease for which no doctor has been
able to find a cure. For weeks I could eat nothing and was fed on
a little milk with opium, and went from one delirium into another,
and finally into unconscious sleep. Craig came flying up from Florence and was devotion itself. He stayed with me for three or four
weeks and helped to nurse me, until one day he received a telegram
from Eleanora, 'I am giving Rosmersholm in Nice. Scene unsatisfactory. Come at once.' "

Yet this account, like so much of *My Life*, is partly inaccurate—
although, as we shall see, some of its inaccuracy is interesting and
significant. That Craig came to Isadora's bedside in Amsterdam is
evident from her reminding him (see CD *136*) that he had left her
no money; however, he surely did not come from Florence (he was
in Berlin), he certainly did not stay several weeks, nor can one
imagine him as nurse. Duse had been wiring him frequently and con-
fusingly from Cap Martin about her plans,[1] and he had indeed
received—but in Berlin, on January 23—a telegram that asked him

----

[1] To one of Duse's messages, which she had sent in garbled English, there
exists the draft of a perhaps unsent, characteristic reply from Craig: "Dear Duse
engage a secretary who can better translate what you evidently write in
Italian."

to come to Nice. As translated by Edward A. Craig in his biography, it reads: "I have a new play that is very beautiful but I must discuss it with you. Can you come to Nice? I shall be putting on Rosmer February ninth. Duse." In her next letter (the dates are confusing at this point), Isadora refers either to that telegram or to yet another one from Duse to Craig, perhaps sent in Isadora's care.

—— *CD 135* ——

[Amsterdam,
late January or early February 1907]

Dearest— Sent you D's telegram— but you know *you* once in *Nice* Holland would seem an *entirely* different picture to D. She would *see* the glory of it— she gets discouraged by herself. So *please* take wise Topsy's advice, which some instinct tells me. Go to Nice & *cheer up D.* & she will be only too glad to return with you to Holland,[1] I am *sure*—
I feel *much better*— will *surely* be up in a couple of days— no more pain or fever—good appetite.
Perhaps can travel Friday or Saturday—
Do not miss the 9th at Nice—
Haldane Macfall sent you a nice book with

[The rest of this letter is lost]

————————

Craig left Berlin for Nice, via Milan, on February 7. Although she had encouraged him to obey Duse's summons, Isadora wrote later, in *My Life*, "I had a terrible premonition of what would happen to those two when I was not there to interpret and to smooth over their differences." It was before she learned what did occur that she wrote her next letter to Craig—the last of this series from Amsterdam.

---

[1] Craig had been urging Duse to play *Rosmersholm* in Rotterdam and The Hague.

——— *CD 136* ———

[Amsterdam,
probably 7 or 8 February 1907]

Dearest— I am much better— was up an hour this morning— but still some pain so popped back in bed— I am *happy* you are at Nice. Rec. your telegram & postcard from Milan this morning— They write me Baby is not quite well & Frl. says it may be *teeth!*— *already*— Dr. says *perhaps* I may travel Saturday but I'm afraid not till Tuesday— but then I will be *quite* well & *never* be ill again— I telegraphed for you to send me money as you forgot to leave some!

Forgive this scrawl— the nurse objects to more.

All the Love of my heart to you dear— be well & *cheery*— & I will too—

Your
Isadora

———————————

There are two, similar accounts of what happened in Nice. Isadora's, in *My Life*:

Craig appeared one morning in the old Nice Casino, which was horrible, to find that, without the knowledge of Eleanora, they had cut his scenery in two. Naturally when he saw his work of art, his masterpiece, his child that he had laboured to bring forth with such energy in Florence, thus amputated, massacred before his eyes, Craig flew into one of those terrible rages of which he was at times the victim, and, what was worse, thus addressed the form of Eleanora, who was at that time standing on the stage:

"What have you done?" he stormed at her. "You have ruined my work. You have destroyed my art! You, from whom I expected so much."

He went on and on mercilessly, until Eleanora, who certainly was not used to being spoken to in this manner, became furious. As she told me later: "I have never seen such a man. I have never been talked to like this. He towered more than six feet, arms folded in Britannic furor, saying fearful things. No one has ever treated me so. Naturally I could not stand it. I pointed to the door and said, 'Go. I never want to see you again.' "

And that was the end of her intention to devote her entire career to the genius of Gordon Craig.

And Edward A. Craig's, in his life of his father:

[Craig] went round to the old Casino Theatre to see if all was going well. To his horror, he discovered that the stage-manager, on finding the proscenium opening at Nice so much lower than the one in Florence, had calmly cut two or three feet off the bottom of the whole set . . . His fury knew no bounds, and after telling everyone in the theatre what he thought of them in English, with the introduction of various French and German words such as "cretins," "imbeciles" and "dummkopf," he rushed off to find Duse. She could not understand any of his words, but she disliked his outburst and lack of self-control. All was over between them—they would never work together again . . . Duse, who had learnt the hard way, is supposed to have written to Craig philosophically, saying: "What they have done to your scene, they have been doing for years to my Art."

That even after the stormy scene Craig wrote to Duse and had some brief hope of reconciliation with her, is evident in passages from three letters he now wrote to Martin Shaw in rapid succession. From Nice:

I am here having hell with Duse— but hush not a word to a soul— & besides I shall win. The Rosmer. scene was *CUT* down. Pity me a little— yet I care so little, for I want now to fly far beyond all that haphazard work. Yet it is bitter.

From Cannes:

I'm harassed a bit here trying to tame the wild D. Bison or Elk is easier. She refuses offer for Holland. We shall *see.* I'm that determined but without a deep desire (love) to accomplish.

And from Monaco:

I hope I.D. comes here to regain her strength. It's glorious here. I could just sink into it & write well if I had peace for a bit. Still Dooty calls— and Doosie don't reply— the poor dear is just *existing* too.

If the date (February 11) Craig put on that last note is right, and if Isadora arrived in Nice when she says, in *My Life*, she did ("the first night of the Carnival," with the grimaces of the maskers in the streets seeming to her "like the Dance Macabre before ultimate death"), then she was already on her way when Craig wrote Shaw from Monaco. She does not say that Craig was there to meet her; one hopes he was. On the fifteenth he wrote to Shaw about her: she was worried, he said; she had no money; she was sick. "She is so troubled. She's down, *down*."

The reader may sense, as Isadora must by now have sensed (she would scarcely have brought her mother to Nice otherwise) that for Craig the moment had come to "bolt"—the word his son has used about Craig's flight to England during Isadora's pregnancy, and which might have been used about his earlier flights from the same conditions. Isadora was ill, with a baby—his baby—to support: for a bolt, these were even more compelling reasons than a pregnancy. Craig had recently written to Shaw, "You write you hope Miss D. and I are good humoured— I am fighting to be so." Now he fought no longer.

WHEN ISADORA MISTAKENLY WROTE, IN 1927, THAT CRAIG HAD COME flying to her bedside "from Florence," she was revealing the sinister importance she had long since attached to that city. The triumphant beauty Craig achieved there with *Rosmersholm* had greatly accelerated his impatience to be on his own—or what he considered "on his own." As he had written in the closing words of his program note for that production, "It is . . . possible now to announce that the birth of the new Theatre, and its new Art, has begun." It had been a great though short-lived taste of independence. The break with Duse became necessary: her irritating flow of telegrams was an attrition, the mutilation of the set for *Rosmersholm* the culmination. But that break was only a preliminary leap before the great plunge. Isadora's "terrible premonition" in Amsterdam was well-founded.

Had she perhaps been precipitating the crisis herself all along? She had held back nothing, never made herself inaccessible—quite the opposite: had Craig come to find that oppressive? She had supported him, carried him off to Russia, enabled him to live "like a Duke": he had reveled in it—but had dependence become galling to him, his pleasure curdled by the thought of his work? She had had her baby: was that the final trap? In Florence, at his moment of triumph, Duse had said "Not to hang on to past and dead things— to sweep all past away and to constantly renew."

It was to Florence that Craig now "bolted."

From Nice he went first to the French hill town of Vence (a move that was to have a sequel many years later: in choosing a place to spend his old age Craig would settle in the same village that was now his first refuge). But within a few weeks he was in Florence. Friends welcomed him. ". . . when I first found myself in that lovely city," he wrote later about his stay there for *Rosmersholm*, ". . . I was working in the closed-in theatre all the time and barely caught more than a glimpse of the Arno— its bridges— the hills and the palaces— and felt nothing of the miraculous life of the place. Neither its sun nor any of its sounds reached me." Now they did. Among the friends were Martin Shaw, there on a brief visit, and the American art collector Charles Loeser, who lived in Florence and who during Craig's previous stay had "told him that if he ever wanted it, he could always let him have an old villa to live in on the hill across the Arno, with the most beautiful panoramic view of the city." Loeser kept his word. Edward A. Craig tells how:

Loeser and Craig met . . . and, passing over the Ponte alle Grazie and out through the old city gates of San Miniato, ascended the steep slope by threading through walled lanes overhung with gnarled olive trees, still green in February. At last they came to a twisting lane called the Viuzza della Gattaia, and an old, square cream-painted villa with faded green shutters and a roof that seemed to project halfway across the lane. The villa contained many rooms with tiled floors and just a few pieces of simple furniture. There was also a long terrace covered with vines and dotted everywhere with great earthenware jars in which were planted oranges, lemons, and camellias. Craig was enchanted by the place, and the generous Loeser told him he could have it for as long as he liked; an old peasant woman would come in and clean, and make coffee in the morning, and he could find excellent food in the many osterias in the city below. No. 4 Viuzzo della Gattaia became Craig's first home in Florence . . .

"Such a place," Craig wrote Shaw, "vines & olive trees and the peace of nature."

Florence was to be Craig's home for the next seven years: first in Loeser's villa and then in a larger house, Il Santuccio, in the Via San Leonardo, and a flat in the city. There Craig was to devote himself to the theater—"the foolish theatre," he wrote Shaw, "that claims me not at all & yet somehow I continue to claim relationship with it." There he would begin his magazine, *The Mask*, invent his mobile scenic screens, become an etcher, produce the series of woodcuts resembling brass-rubbings that he called his "Black Figures" and that were intended as designs for marionettes, prepare his book of stage designs, *Towards a New Theatre*, experiment with a model stage. And there, eventually, just before the annihilating calamity of the First World War, he would found his longed-for theater school in an old open-air amphitheater, the Arena Goldoni. For the school he would obtain a gift of £5,000 from Lord Howard de Walden, but all the prior ventures needed other financing. For a time there would be money coming in from the Moscow Art Theatre. Ellen Terry, of course, continued to support two of his families. "Ibsen petitions his King 3 times running May June July for £90 to travel for 6 months & was refused twice," Craig wrote to Shaw. "3rd time he got it. Henrik Ibsen had to ask 3 times. I wonder if I tried Albert Edward at £75-10-6 whether it would turn up trumps." That was doubtful; meanwhile, in the absence of King Edward as a benefactor, and before Lord Howard de Walden, there was still—not forever, but for longer than one might think possible—Isadora.

ANOTHER OF ISADORA'S DISTORTIONS IN *My Life* REVEALS THE DEPTH of the wound. Speaking of her days in Nice after Craig's departure and of her resumption of the broken Holland tour in late March, she writes:

I adored Craig—I loved him with all the ardour of my artist soul, but I realised that our separation was inevitable. Yet I had arrived at that frenzied state when I could no longer live with him or without him. To live with him was to renounce my art, my personality, nay, perhaps, my life, my reason itself. To live without him was to be in a continual state of depression, and tortured by jealousy, for which, alas! it now seemed that I had good cause. Visions of Craig in all his beauty in the arms of other women haunted me at night, until I could no longer sleep. Visions of Craig explaining his art to women who gazed at him with adoring eyes—visions of Craig being pleased with other women—looking at them with that winning smile of his— the smile of Ellen Terry—taking an interest in them, caressing them— saying to himself, "This woman pleases me. After all Isadora is impossible."

All this drove me to fits of alternate fury and despair. I could not work, I could not dance. I did not care at all whether the public liked it or not.

I realized that this state of things must cease. Either Craig's Art or mine—and to give up my Art I knew to be impossible: I should pine away—I should die from chagrin. I must find a remedy and I thought of the wisdom of the Homeopaths. And as everything that we wish for very much comes, the remedy came.

And she goes on to tell how a decorative young man whom she calls only "Pim" entered her life and how she immediately swept him off to Russia.

Actually, the "good cause" for Isadora's jealousy—at least, the particular "good cause" to which she refers—probably did not yet exist: writing in 1927, she displaced to this period of her unhappiness the beginnings of the intimacy that she later learned grew up in Florence between Craig and Dorothy Nevile Lees, who helped him with *The Mask* and bore him a son in 1915. And since Isadora's 1907 Russian tour did not begin until December, she certainly did not sweep "Pim" away with her quite yet. (Irma Duncan says there really was a "Pim," though outside the pages of *My Life* his existence is elusive.) Between Craig's flight from Nice and the beginning of the Russian tour there were eight months to be filled, and during those months—especially during the first weeks, when, as she says, her own life was "more burdened with financial difficulties than ever"—Isadora wrote Craig some of her most touching letters. They are the gentle letters of a convalescent, still in love with the father of her child, still unable to believe that their "kissing" has ended, still hoping to share his life.

————— *CD 137* —————
HOTEL DES PRINCES
NICE

[Postmarked 20 Februry 1907]

Dear— I hope you're all right— Four good men & true carried me down
in a chair & brought me over in a wheeled chair. Excruciating pain, but
glad to be here— so *quiet* & I can look right out on the sea. I am in
a good deal of pain— must lie flat.
I feel a bit of a Fool but it's no use fretting over spilled milk, so Patience
Topsy—
The latest torture invented for me is Mustard Plasters— I thought they
were out of date!
Love to you, dear dear soul. I feel a very foolish & inadequate Topsy—
Poor thing
I envy you to see all the Beauty of Florence again— "our Donatellos"!

————— *CD 138* —————

[Telegram,
Nice to CRAIG LUCHENBACH FIRENZE,
20 February 1907]

MUCH BETTER HEARTS LOVE

————— *CD 139* —————

[Nice, probably 20 February 1907[1]]

Dear Love— There's a "Sirocco" or something today— Big Wind—
waves Sky High. I had two awful days yesterday and before, pains like
1700000 devils— but am *much* better today. Mustard plasters all over—
talk about Dante's inferno he forgot to put in a shop labelled "Mustard
plasters."
Yes, you're a Marvel— you're a Naughty Bad Marvel— that's what you

[1] Note by Craig: "Feb. 20, 1907— Nice to me at Florence, Luchenbach
Hotel Metropole."

are. But you wait till I get out of this— I'm going to play Roulette etc. at Monte Carlo!!

Your child, Sir, has a wonderful constitution too— and a *Voice*— and she *won't* sleep— she's a Howling Terror. Aren't you going to get a little barn for *poor little me too*— I notice you don't mention *me*— I'll be coming along in the Wright Brothers flying machine—

About that History of your Life, I suspect it's only just *begun*—

It is now a *month* I've been in bed—

D. has wired me each day to ask how I am— exceedingly sweet of her—

Love to you dear one—

Isadora

If Shaw is willing to wait a bit for salary he might go to Bologna, but if not we will be Stony Broke!

——— *CD 140* ———

[Nice, 23 February 1907]

Dearest— Just rec. your welcome letter—

It kills me to say it but I'm afraid March *10th*[1] is *impossible*— O Lord!—

I am still lying very flat & *pains* all over—

I came "unwell" yesterday 22— so it will be also again (on March 22 till March 26). After that from *26* to *31* is *Holy* week— Good Friday, Sat. & Easter *Sunday* the *31* when no one goes to theatre, but from Apr. 1 is *good* theatre week.

I will be in bed a week more, the Dr. says, & then it will be at least 2 weeks before I am strong enough to walk— practice dance—

All this is despairing— the constant pain & constant powders. I feel a bit discouraged. Last night I was a bit cracky!

Will be better in a few days but I'm beginning to feel a proper rival to Job!

This is the *limit*—

The baby creates universal admiration—

[1] Craig, in an attempt to get Isadora dancing again as soon as possible, had suggested that she appear at the Casino Municipal of Nice in late February or early March; to Stumpff in Amsterdam he had proposed eight performances in Holland, March 10–17 and 24–31.

Thank you for your dear letters— They keep me alive— a sort of cordial reviver. I will write again as soon as I'm a little better.

All my hearts love
Isadora

—— *CD 255* ——

[Nice, probably late February 1907]

My Dear— I still lie low— Aches & pains, pains & aches— Ach!—
No letter from you yesterday or today— always send if only a *card*—
There is too much feminine in my composition— that's it— a silly mixture—
I miss you—
I love you

Isadora

That apple-cheeked Baby with blue eyes seems pretty glad to be alive—

—— *CD 257* ——

[Nice, probably late February 1907]

Dear— Thank you [for] your sweet kind letter— always like *elixar* to me— I can't write today— have been fairly doubled up with schmerzen[1]—
Dr. says *Internal Neuralgia* caused my fatigue of the nerves— Internal Devils say I— Will take a big powder & hope to get some sleep—
Baby *is* lovely—
Take it all Pain & Pleasure it's worth it when I think of you— Good Night—

Poor Topsy

Have you rec. your letters from *Cooks*— if not telegraph me *"No."*

Love

—————

[1] G., "pains."

—— *CD 141* ——

[Nice, probably late February 1907]

Dear— It is very sweet of you to write often— it brightens up the day. I can't budge an inch. The Dr. now says it's a form of nervous prostration. What next? He has just been here— he says no performance possible till the first of April! Otherwise he says I would only fall ill again & hints it would then be profitable commission for the Undertaker!

I am taking extra strong powders & can't read. Your letters & the dear baby keep me from despair. The Baby is beautiful & so intensely alive— I will probably be better in a few days—

I am getting ashamed to regale you always with my pains—

> With all my love
> Isadora

I will write better tomorrow

—— *CD 142* ——

[Nice, probably late February 1907]

Dear Love— Thank you— the etching is charming— you are wonderful to do it so quick—

So you have a Villa— Bedad!— It sounds very imposing—

I sat up an hour today. How little we value Health when we have it.

Fräulein has found a quiet hotel up on the hill overlooking the sea— 12 frs a day— an improvement on this. If Dr. allows I will move— Nice is a silly place.

This getting well is very difficult. I still take these powders which make my head continually spin—

A tedious business—

It is such fun to see how Baby resembles you, & she has beautiful strong hands like yours.

I look at the Baby & look out over the sea & think of you— & if my poor body is racked with silly pains my heart is filled with love & love— & so it's all right.

> Your
> *Isadora*

———— *CD 144* ————

MONT-BORON PALACE HOTEL
NICE

[February or March 1907]

Dearest— We moved up here on the hill. I am still in bed but enjoy this heavenly *quiet*— our windows look over the sea across a grove of orange trees.

Dear, you need not worry about me. It is true I am still somewhat ill & a good deal of pain but your power of giving me joy is so great that the dear lines you write me make up for all else. It is perhaps just from having to lie so still & being so much in pain that I have more joy— it sounds a bit Irish but it is really so— life dulls things a good deal & this being in a way half out of life Love shines more clear— So don't worry about me— *I'm not unhappy.*

I'm glad Mr. Loeser is nice— is he as witty as ever? Kathleen said she'd be going to Florence in March— Will she be waving seductive lanterns at you from neighboring chimney pots— if so I'll pull her hair—

Your etching was charming— in all you put your hand to you put Beauty— Whatever medium—

Baby is in great health & spirits. I will be soon—

All my love
Isadora

———— *CD 145* ————

Sat.
[Nice, probably 9 March 1907]

Frl & Mama are at dinner. Baby sleeps. I lie here waiting for the next post to bring me a letter from you— Why is it that even the sight of your handwriting on paper is life to me— I don't know. Why this constant longing for you— Is it that you have really made me a *part* of you— Are you my pulses & my blood & do I only exist because of you— and if you turned from me would I die— & do I exist when apart from you only by your thoughts of me— Can this be so— The last few days I have felt like a bird under a glass globe suffocating— Is your love air to me— would I smother to death if you ceased to give it— does my spirit beat itself to death out there trying to get to you & leave me with nothing but a body & a dulled brain——— Someone knocked. My heart jumped up & down & I have your letter— only to touch it with my fingers & life comes rushing back to me— How sweet it is to hold your letter & to read it again & again. My whole being wakes up— it is like food to the starving.

O— who is this Bocaccio whose reading seems to satisfy you so profoundly? Well, I've never read him, but I have a feeling he's an enemy & I wish Savonarola had had him burnt on the pile of Vanities & not an Edition left—

O I tell you I have no caution or care, & if I don't see you soon I will pull myself up by the roots & throw myself into the Sea—

I have been in bed all day with neuralgia The Dr. laughs & says it is all nerves——— Then what are nerves? I can't move from pain & the Dr. says "It's neuralgia— just nerves— nothing."

Well then— ?—

Now I am better—

Will I read Bocaccio? eh? I'd like to be where I could kiss your hands & let you do all the thinking for two— Is that laziness or a sort of inward necessity of sex— Are you going to be a sage? Once I danced, yes then I was more like "tree or wave," but now I feel just the *beginnings* of being a woman— just the beginnings. The others at my age arrived at it long ago— & I begin to feel it's a d—— pesky thing to be— Yes Infernal.

The Baby has not little dainty taper fingers. She has hands exactly like yours— a feminine thing with hands like yours. What sort of a mixture of character will she have? She has suddenly given up crying & instead spends hours uttering piercing shrieks of wild joy! It is as if she had suddenly woke up to the pleasure of life.

The neuralgia pains have suddenly left me— Queer— Gone as suddenly as they came—

What are nerves— are they little demons who when they find the soul forces weak rush in & strike with pitchforks all over?— & did a thousand little spirits jump from your letter just now as I opened it & demolish them all? Anyway theyre gone & your little spirits having sent 'em forth will all nestle cosy in my heart all night sending messages of pleasure out at each beat.

Come nice growly Tiger— Eat me up so that Ted can be a really sage [*sic*]— for till I'm eaten I'll do my best to destroy that wisdom— Come Eat me— Put your lips to mine & begin that way—

[No signature]

—— *CD 256* ——

[Possibly Nice, March 1907]

[Incomplete letter]

If we were two free spirits flying in air— or two wooly sheep cropping grass— but *what* a mixture! I love you— I don't spose I'd cook for you, keep house for you— I've no doubt I'd be Happier if I did— but I never learned how— & besides you'd walk off— why the very *Goo* of a Baby makes you look for a Time-Table book— You don't want a wife much or even a woman, but a sort of *Geni*— that's what you want. I'd *like* to be what you want but I was made a silly sort of dancing dervish— and now that Baby— she has hands just like yours & looks like you— she has you in her & I love her for that— & me in her too— & all our ancestors— Ye Gods!— I wish I could spread wings & be your *Geni* but I

—— *CD 147* ——
MONT-BORON PALACE HOTEL
NICE

[March 1907]

Dear— It isn't one night I "lie loving you" but every night & when asleep I dream of you— Sometimes I feel that with each breath something leaves me & goes to you as I lie here quite still in the nights—

My strength is coming back— but this is the difficult time when I am so weak— I went a little outside the garden gate today— & I am quite straight again.

Frl. brought me some good stories of Gorki's but in French— You would like them—

You will have to find another name for this bouncing *red*-cheeked Baby.— I wish I could read to you— I must practice to read better. Getting well is really hard work. My spirits feel equal to anything & then I find my feet dragging & body like lead— Enough to make one Swear Horribly. I am so impatient to be strong— I want to feel the earth spring under me again— I do not wish to die just yet or even by halves— but repeat me those magic words— say you love me & my old husk will fall off. I will bloom up anew for you

Your Isadora

——— *CD 148* ———
MONT-BORON PALACE HOTEL
NICE

[March 1907]

Dear— You send me poems that are caresses & words that are like kisses or a flock of little soft birds that fly down & nestle in and all about me & take away my senses. If you write me like that I will not wish to grow well but only to lie here with those delicious words nestling in my throat & my heart & singing me conscious only of Heaven. You cannot know what joy you give me— No you cannot know it— my heart is over-flowing & I cannot write to you.

Indeed I wish too that I had some work detached from my person. It isn't that I don't love *work*, but that wandering about & all— I can't bear to think of it. It was good enough before I met you, but now—

For before I met you I was not *born*.

Tomorrow if the day is warm I am to walk in the garden. I am full of grateful love to you. I kiss the pages on which your hands have rested & I kiss your dear strong hands that know so well to make beautiful things— I like to think of you in Florence where one's eyes rest always on loveliness. I can't help thinking that many of the old 'spirits' rejoice that you are there. They must be glad that your eyes rest on their works. Mr. Bernard Shaw seems to be worrying in London about the 10 commandments— but I think Mr. B.S. is blind to that Beauty which includes all and is *one* Commandment. I don't know what the ten Commandments are— but I kiss each one of your dear ten fingers—

Your Topsy

——— *CD 149* ———
MONT-BORON PALACE HOTEL
NICE

[March 1907]

Today I walked in the garden certain I love life. This is like being released from prison. All the smells of the earth were so good to breathe— I wanted to kiss all the plants & dance— too weak yet but *soon*. Yes life is delicious— not to pass any more days lying flat in a room— & I have days & weeks & years to live still— how good— and

some day I will see you & touch you again— Yes, life is overwhelmingly good. I will be near you again & if you like me you will kiss me— but I must grow strong first, bathe & dance & grow strong— completely this time and no more *ill— Never again.* I have had enough of this bugbear of illness. I will be always *well* in future—
Good night—
I shut my eyes & see you.
Good night— who knows but what my thoughts travel out over the blue sea to Italy & straight to your cottage & to you— for I often feel a force coming to me which I am sure is your sweet thought taking care of me.

> Good night—
> *Isadora*

——— *CD 150* ———
MONT-BORON PALACE HOTEL
NICE

[Postmarked 11 March 1907]

Dear— Today Frl. & I took quite a long walk up the mountainside, so I am nearly quite strong again— out in the warm sunshine all day with always the blue sea & blue sky. I am beginning to feel as fresh again as the day I was made in the Garden of Eden. I have a wild desire to go on a walking tour— to stride over the earth with a pack-sack— Where is our little house on wheels?
Our Baby is becoming as noisy in her joy as in her woe— she has wild moods of mirth— waves her little arms & legs. There is a little doggie in the next room only 4 months old— he also jumps & barks & seems delighted to be alive. Eternal renewal— live over & over again. It is Love— it is Beauty & from that you produce Beauty & that is the highest still— I have been reading Gorki but he makes me afraid— & I always think that in life just as in gymnastics the chief thing is to have Confidence. Imagine an acrobat who felt *afraid*— he would fall on the first turn— so I won't read Gorki— he makes life seem like a great terrible *trap.* That isn't good & I'm sure it isn't true— and if it was it would be as mean to inform people of it as to ask some fellow who was gaily walking the tightrope to 'look down' & make him lose his balance. He writes splendidly, but what ails them all— Ibsen, Strindberg, Gorki? Mon dieu!

Shelley & Keats begin to sound like nursery rhymes beside them— Tennyson & Longfellow like the babbling of Babes. Only one holds his own— *W.W.*— He's all right!

Never mind. They will clear away all the debris some day and the truck,— make an open space & give you a chance to show them Beauty— It will be the beginning of a new epoch. Great Heavens— this world needs it. I will be very glad to see what you have been writing.

The walk today has made me quite tired. I will sleep now. I lie here alone & shut my eyes & go into darkness— sweet & soft— but in spite of Gorki I feel quite *safe* & I do not feel alone— I feel your Love. Good night to you

    Your Isadora

—— *CD 152* ——

Saturday
[Nice, March 1907]

Dearest— A funny wind here yesterday blew me to bed again with neuralgia all over— but it can't last more than a day. Has Stumpff fixed the dates in Holland yet? I think I better be up there a week beforehand to rest from the journey. Tell me where you think the best place for Snowdrop. She is in splendid health— cheeks like roses— & says *Mama*— is so proud of saying it that she says it all day long. The last few days I have been filled with an unquiet longing about you— I hope it is unfounded & that you are well & happy. When I am separated from you for any length of time I begin to have a queer feeling of not being all there— as if my soul were hovering in the air over my head ready to fly to you— a strange feeling. There is a pigeon shooting near here for *sport*— as each bird flies from the box it is shot— if missed it comes back to the keeper to be shot at the next time. It is perhaps that at each shot a little pigeon soul flits off to seek its next incarnation.

The sea is sparkling with whitecaps today— that means I must hide under the covers away from the bad wind.

No letter from you yesterday. I hope for one today. My *Munee* is giving out— perhaps it is better I should start for Holland before I am quite bankrupt?— What do you think? If you think so I will start next Wednesday or so. Also, the Dr. says it would be better to stop over a night on the way.

Well— I'd rather go to Florence.
Forgive me for worrying you but that's what I was put on Earth for—

> All my Love
> Your Isadora

------ *CD 153* ------

[Nice, March 1907]

Dearest— Almost quite well— will be able to practise in a few days. If it were not that the Dr. is still giving me treatment which he promises will make me well forever I would leave Nice as it is a silly expensive place. I have been reading the Life of Zola— one reads what one can find here. All the part where he is poor & starving he is interesting, but when he becomes too well off & turns out books so many a year to order of publisher it is no longer interesting. But he had great Force & Courage. I went to town today as they would not give the 500 frs telegram to Frl. K., but when I went they said I must go to American Consul for identification & the Consulate is open only mornings. As we were walking along the principal shopping streets we saw a man who really looked *sane* & pleasant in the midst of a lot of lunatics & ladies who resemble Birds of Prey of a most disagreeable sort. He was selling books. I stopped & bought one— I send it to you— I like the picture with the tent. After all, he seemed the only pleasant-looking human being in the Boulevard. Dear heart— & have you found a peaceful nook? I couldn't help thinking your letter sounded rather hard on Noordwijk, where doors did slam & Topsy *did* chatter & make a noise.[1] My heart felt a bit sore, and I wondered does he want me ever— even in *another* cottage?— for my part, a cottage near Florence would be Paradise enough.[2] Here Nature is lovely, but not the *Beauty* of Florence— that is different. The lines of the hills there are so full of meaning— or is it Giotto's dome which makes the Beauty?[3]

I have much joy to be well again. Life must be a good thing, otherwise

----

[1] Note by Craig: "Well deserved" (obviously referring to his complaints, not to Isadora's reproach).

[2] Note by Craig: "You would stop for 3 weeks at most."

[3] Note by Craig: "But dear Giotto didn't do the dome."

why this spring-upward feeling when life comes back. The beating of
my pulses is a delight to me & I *want* to dance again. After 6 weeks lying
flat every action seems fresh & exciting— but I am very prudent & go
to bed at 5 o'clock.
Our Baby is a darling—
and she is like you.
The Bird likes to live with his mate in the nest— even the Lion stalks
about with his lady at his side— but you— O— you— You say go away[1]
disturber of the Peace, I shall live with my dream—
Good Night, dear— I love you

    Your
    Isadora

———— *CD 159* ————

[Nice, March 1907]

Dearest— Your two articles arrived this morning. How good of you to
send them to me. I found a quiet nook in the garden & read. I find them
Beautiful & their chief Beauty that they are written & kept entirely in the
world of *Idea*— the *Idea pure*— I see that your stay in Florence has been
of great benefit for I feel a *Harmony* in your writing much more complete— The only critic[ism] I could make is to go still more slowly, for
instance to enlarge much more the 'Visions' which you no doubt intend
to do. Certainly you should keep on writing & writing. What you have
written about the Hill is also *exquisite*— All in all these two seem to contain more *Breadth*, Harmony & Purity of Idea— than any of your previ-

---

[1] Note by Craig: "I don't say 'Go away'— but I do say 'Stay by me & give me
that pin.'— & you talk big about giving me the Earth & fail— then why not
try a pin that I ask you for." His word "fail" refers to Isadora's inability, later
in the year, to fulfill a promise of financial support she had given him.

Craig's draft letter already quoted (p. 189), which contains not a word of
affection, and Isadora's reference in the present letter to his complaints about
Noordwijk make one wonder what his letters to her at Nice were like—the
letters which she persists in prizing and praising and taking comfort from. To
use Isadora's language, it "kills" one to suggest it, but: was his chief interest
now, perhaps, that she should resume dancing—and earning—as soon as
possible?

ous writings. They are only fragments, but continue in that way & you will have a Superb Book.[1]

I will send these back to you as you ask— They gave me a great deal of Joy—

I am slowly getting strong— I practice a little each day. The beginning is like breaking stones. One loves to work when once begun, but it *is so difficult to reach the right state to begin*[2]— sometimes I wish I might dissolve into a mist rather than begin again— The feminine spirit has a *special* aversion to entering in that land of abstract idea where work is— Indeed only a few in History have succeeded in doing it alone— & then only through suffering, & I object to suffer.[3] To *wrench* oneself from Time & place and self & enter where time & place & self do not exist— that is a great pain— but then also a great reward. Is anything comparable to the feeling of having come in contact with that eternal idea of Beauty— a wrench, an awful suffering, a feeling of battering for ages against an impassable barrier, & then suddenly & sharply a glow, a light, a connection with the idea like entering into a God— a happiness indescribable, triumphant—

That's what I feel when I try to work, only many times I get only as far as the suffering & battering & then a blank fall to despair.[4] That there is so much pain connected with so simple an effort I put down to my sex. Now a man works *easily*— it flows from him naturally[5] more like a God— Baby grows sweeter each day— a laughing, crowing & happy little creature—

I am afraid I cannot *live* without you— I'm afraid it's not merely a figure of speech—

What think you?

        Good night my Love

     Your
     Isadora

---

[1] A note by Craig in the margin says: "In 1911 it appeared— in 1944 in France." He refers to the enlarged edition of *The Art of the Theatre*, which was first published in England and the United States in 1911 and in France in 1920; later in France in 1942, 1943 and 1951. (See note for p. 349.) Arnold Rood identifies the essays mentioned by Isadora as "The Artists of the Theatre of the Future" and "The Actor and the Uber-Marionette," both of which are included in the book.

[2] "is . . . begin" underlined by Craig with note: "*true.*"

[3] Note by Craig: "*Oh* dear Topsy."

[4] Note by Craig: "With all artists it's so."

[5] Note by Craig: "Does it!!"

—— *CD 154* ——

[Nice, March 1907]

Mama & Frl. have gone walking. The Baby is sleeping. I have been enjoying a lovely hour of Peace. I have your engravings before me on the table & I have been dreaming over or rather *into* them— I found it very beautiful— but you seem to be disappearing up a high flight of stairs into another land.

Some time after:
Baby Boo woke up & screamed lustily. Now she's trying to grab my pen & upset the ink. I must go find her a Big Bottle of Milk. She takes the wildest interest in watching the pen go along, but her unruly presence is disastrous to consecutive thought or indeed any thought at all.

Evening:
I put the Baby on the floor on a pillow & did my practicing. She watched every movement & then tried to do the same, kicking her little legs. This aft. I went for a long walk with Frl.— I think it makes me strong.

Now I began this letter to tell you how Beautiful I found your etchings— especially *the two*— but now Frl. & Mama are at dinner. I am trying to hold the bottle in one hand & write with t'other & the Baby acting as if she was intoxicated— yelling Ma Ma— which she now says perfectly between swallows. So I will wait till next post. The man has just brought me your dear letter. Yes, I wouldn't mind dancing B[eethoven] if he has a really first class symphonic orchestra— *not the Utrecht one*— it wouldn't be fair. Every orchestra has the notes—

The Baby has got hold of a newspaper and is waving it frantically in the air trying to knock over my ink. I will have to leave Mama & Frl. here on account of financial reasons, & send to them afterward.
As for you— you must follow what your *Demon* says, I would not dare say— you know what I mean— (the Baby is now howling like a veritable Bogie. There— I turned her on her Tummie & she stopped— now she's trying to chew the end of this paper— Well, that's a kiss for Papa—) I can't live without you: that's true. I think my Body & Soul contains parts of you & I long for you, but I'd rather you be a million miles away from me & know you *happy* or at least happy you know what I mean[1]—

[1] Note by Craig: "Yes. My wonderful Topsy— yes! yes!— but don't you protest too much?"

than close to me & unhappy—
Here comes man for letters.
Good night my Love—
My own heart & soul more than Brother Helper friend *All*—

> Your
> Isadora

—— *CD 258* ——

[Nice, probably 21 March 1907]

Darling— I have had a funny day— am about to sleep— between laughter
& tears. Tomorrow night I start for Amsterdam. Am ordered to rest a
night on the way— so will arrive Wed—
Your engravings are extraordinary. The *movement* is so wonderful & the
light— if you are finding things like that you better not stir—
Alas— poor me— my heart is torn to pieces— & still I am alive—
I cannot write tonight— I feel too many & too queer things—
I love you—

> Isadora
> Snowdrop too.

Can two people be one
There are lots of clever & prettier people in the world than I— *Heaps*—
if I turn [out?] to be jealous of them all I will soon be dead— from the
strain—[1]

—— *CD 155* ——

[Nice, probably 22 March 1907]

Dear— I was going to start for Holland today but became unwell, so must
put it off till Thursday & must lie quiet till then. A fit of darkest Blue
despondency lasting 48 hrs is now explainable. How silly! I am a very
funny made toy & I suffer a good deal of mental or is it moral misery
over nothings.

[1] See footnote, p. 229.

The Baby is turning into the most *good natured* & *contented* little Being. She hardly cries any more at all. She laughs & crows & lets me sing her to sleep— as sweet as an angel. She is sitting up in an armchair beside me gravely watching my pen— always happy if I let her watch me eat my dinner— takes the wildest interest in everything about. Lovely little Baby born of your kisses— I never grow tired looking at her & thinking of the Wonder of it. She is a great teacher & I learn from her each day Religion, Science, Philosophy, History of the Race. Miss Professor Snowdrop.

I haven't seen you for 6 weeks! a pretty long time!— & I've had no letter since Sunday!

I have been reading Histoire de Ma Vie de Georges Sand, 4 Volumes— but she tells a good deal of *Histoire* & leaves out the *Vie*. However even without that it is interesting for the wonderful men that she writes about, especially Chopin. I would like to be someplace near a good library this summer—

What do you think! The Baby has been saying Ma Ma as I told you, but today she said Pa Pa— !—

That's *you*! ! !

Tremendous excitement.

Frl. has just brought me my ticket— Riviera Express, which starts Thursday morn. & arrives Fri. eve.— all the other trains were full. Well, pray for me!

I've been writing you about six letters but all so blue I tore them up— I'll feel better tomorrow. I'm going to bed with a book on the "Psychologie des Grands Hommes."

Good night dearest heart. Blessed be the day of our next meeting—

Love Isadora

———— *CD 156* ————
MONT-BORON PALACE HOTEL
NICE

Friday evening
[Good Friday, 29 March 1907;
postmarked Nice, 30 March 1907]

Dear— I am just starting for station. There was no train yesterday— all very crowded. Good-bye blue sky— sunshine— & Baby— O— I don't like it. I wish I was going toward you instead. How joyous I would be then— how I would *fly*—

No I am well again— funny funny life—

Couldn't you find me a wee bit cottage[1] in Florence *too*. I promise to devote myself to the study of divine Philosophy & not to bother you at all—

Good night, darling. I will think of you all night long in the choo to te choo tonight—

> Love your
> Isadora
> a little if you can—

Now Isadora resumes the Dutch tour broken off by her illness in early February.

——— *CD 157* ———

BRACK'S DOELEN HOTEL
AMSTERDAM

Sunday eve.
[Easter, 31 March 1907]

Dear— Just arrived. Trying to reconcile Spirit to Matter— I am one ache from head to toe but will take two powders & go to sleep— will surely awaken tomorrow fresh as the Spring Time— the Tulips are out. I must not write now as I am dropping with fatigue, but tomorrow— One look in your eyes— one kiss on your lips & I sleep— cradled, confident & happy in your Love—

> Your Isadora

'While your branches mix with mine & our roots together twine'

——— *CD 158* ———

[Amsterdam, 1 April 1907]

Dearest— I arrived last night & sent you a line, but your dear letters were only brought over from Stumpff's this morn., so when I opened my eyes I found the sun shining & your letters & I felt great and happy.

---

[1] Isadora has drawn a cottage here.

Dear, you ask what you give me— but you *know* what you have given me— what you give me every moment— Life— Great Beautiful Shining Life which is Love— What the Sun gives the Earth— that's what you give me. My soul is but the reflection of the rays of your love— & this is always growing more & more intense— I feel my body & soul becoming divine— through you. I would give myself to you a thousand thousand times till all passed into flame—

I have passed the day in looking at Blake's books. I left them here & now they seem quite new to me— & in intervals reading over your letters. I thank you that you wrote to me about N.[1] I have often wanted to speak with you about her. I *know* it is a good heart & filled with love for you— and I have often thought of her and I thank you because it shows when you write to me so that you have forgiven my stupid jealousy of which I have been many times ashamed— but I swear to you there is not a vestige of it left. Perhaps it was the pain of the Baby which cleared it all out— only love is left— & I am so grateful if you write me all your pains— & so proud that you *can* write to me. Couldn't you find a pretty place for her in Italy or South of France that she might rest in the sunshine & get *well*— Tell me what you think & let me help any plan— There is so much unnecessary pain in life that should not be— I have the picture of Raphael that you brought me, up before me— There is Breadth— & I have your little study of flight "Bach" remember— & I think I'll dance all right tomorrow, although I feel somewhat frightened.

Tell me what I can do to help you about N. What I wrote you to London[2] I meant & mean with all my heart— I mean I can't write what I mean but you *know*. It's just Love Love Love— the God of Love— & the Kingdom of Love— we will enter it & all who you love with us—

> Your
> Isadora

---

[1] Nelly (Elena Meo).

[2] Probably her letter from Noordwijk offering to share the Villa Maria with "anyone you care for very much who feels unhappy and wants to come with you." (See p. 142.)

——— *CD 160* ———
Hotel du Vieux Doelen[1]
la haye

[Postmarked Gravenhage,
3 April 1907]

Dear Love— Baby has got me in the habit of waking early— 6.30. To hear the birds sing & read "How Sweet is the Shepherd's Sweet Lot"[2] is a good way of beginning the day.

Everything went well last night. My legs were a bit weak & wobbly, but I took great joy in dancing & thought of you & danced to a Harmony of Love. I felt but the visible symbol of your love— & the evening past in dream like unreality. So when I came back to my room alone I wondered if I hadn't only been *dreaming* that I had danced. Your telegram came to me just before I went on the stage— and I rose to your message & thought— *You* point out to me incomparable heights & you teach my spirit to climb— I love you— I am *made* of your love & your thought & nothing else. Without you I would never have gone further than the door. You *opened* the door for me— I feel so rich from you, but what can I give you in return— Can the Created being return something to the Creator— Body & soul you have ploughed deep & sown & they blossoming & bearing fruit only from your sowing—

What can I ever be to you in return?

You said in your telegram "see no one"— & very fortunately I don't have to. Once I had to come in contact with horrid people & talk about contracts & dates— but you have taken that off my shoulders—[3] & now I float in & dance— only— feeling your protection all around me like a big wall— I live in *exquisite isolation*. I would I were some God who could do for you what you do for me— Your

Isadora

[1] Isadora had apparently decided to forgive this hotel for dunning her.

[2] William Blake, "The Shepherd," in *Songs of Innocence and Experience*.

[3] This statement, blatantly contradicted by the news in letters written only a few days later about the "contact with horrid people & talk about contracts & dates" that she was indeed forced to have because of the loosely written Dutch contract, is so illuminating of her way of writing to Craig at this time that little discussion is necessary. Her persistence in saying that everything he does is wonderful, and the contrasting moments when she can no longer pretend that this is so, are two of the elements that make the letters after Craig's bolt so touching.

——— CD 161 ———

[Amsterdam or The Hague, April 1907]

Darling— Poor Topsy me is having a pretty rum time. I manage to dance, but have neuralgia all day. Can't read, write or anything. The Dr. keeps saying it's nothing but over-excitement & gives me asperin— says it will go way.
Are you Coming here?
   I don't dare ask—
I have to pay bills here. Whew!!! & telegraph Mama 1200 francs, as the bill there wasn't paid when I left. I will send you what remains tomorrow so that *all* will not be swamped—
Ooooooooooo
I don't like this!!!
No letter from you for *three* days.
Darling, when do I see you again?
Rainy & cold here & Neuralgia—
Poor little me.
The enclosed letter arrived— it was addressed Craig *Grunewald* only I opened it by mistake seeing only the *Grunewald*. It had been wandering round the earth a month or two— it asks for articles for some paper.
Please write me— I feel so missabel but when I get a letter I brighten up.

   Ooooooooooo   Your pore
                      Topsy

——— CD 162 ———

[The Hague, probably 12 April 1907]

Darling— In bed all days with this horrid neuralgia— dance nights— funny combination! I've been writing you letters & *tearing* them up— neuralgic letters—
Rain & storms here— *dark* & freezy cold—
Stumpff showed me contract "Pay after performances" which he swears is *not* after *each* perf. So pays when he pleases. Am not yet paid for Hague for instance which *was April 8th*.[1]

---

[1] For a list of her performances this time in Holland see p. 221.

Frl. Kist said she must leave—
So I told Mama take Snowdrop to Berlin till I can take her summer. It
will cut off all that immense expense at Nice. In the meantime I will go
Berlin till time to go Sweden.

Tonight last night here— Harlem— & it is too melancholy here. The
other eve, at stage door a lady called out "Why don't you come to
Manchester— the people want you there—"

She afterwards wrote & said I had a good public there— might be a hint.
I have been reading a big "Popular Astronomy"— I stopped at the *10*
movements of the Earth & remained wondering. Well you might go up a
Galileo tower[1]— it would be nice to watch the stars from Florence—
This neuralgia is affreuse—

Three kisses from you might cure it— Dr. says over-excited nerves—
Boo—

What a stupid world— & what a marvellous interesting Earth & Stars &
Sun & Moon— but the Town of the Hague— a correctly damp & miserable place—

Dearest Love— I would write to you what I feel but I better not— it
is too impatient— & the writing of it would be apt to make me take
the next train—

I will be anxious to hear of N's health— bring her down in the *Sun* &
she will get well— or what can we do? Heaven knows there are *no* com-
plications which Love cannot make simple— for me I am ready to be
simple— simple as the primitive earth & sky— I feel full of Love &
nothing else. Suffering is caused by a misunderstanding of love— Plato
might as well never have written his glorious Republic, since no one
pays any attention to it— Just read it over & you will see why N's heart
don't beat right— it's lack of *rhythm*. Is it your fault, my fault, the fault
of Civilization & its rotten ideas— Can't we mend it? Can't we do something? All the answers lie in Plato's Republic clear & simple, so plain—
Why not follow them? Why not?

Don't laugh at your pore Topsy— she means well.
All my heart & body burns perpetually with love for you—

>   Your
>   *Isadora*

---

[1] Not far from Craig's villa were houses lived in by Galileo and a recon-
structed medieval tower, the Torre del Gallo.

——— *CD 163* ———

[The Hague, April 1907]

Dearest— Your address in Florence is so long[1] that it costs about 12 frs. every time I telegraph— Can't you make it a bit shorter— Cook's for instance—

You seem to be mistaken about the dates here. They were:

Amsterdam	— 2 —	paid 1000 florins
Hague	— 4 —	" " "
Utrecht	— 6 —	" 750 "
Hague	— 8 —	" 1000 "
Leyden	—10 —	" 750 "
Harlem	—12 —	not yet paid

Stumpff refused to pay the nights of the performances but sent the money 2 or 3 days afterwards as he pleased, & made a great favor of it because he showed me the contract which reads "Payment to be made after the performances" which he insists means after all of the performances & not after each performance. This morning he sent a bill to me by his man, which included

> orchestra   400 guldens
> Mr. Shaw   140   "
> something abuot Brussels— I forgot how many guldens—

I refused to accept it saying the orchestra & Shaw should be paid by *him*. He then showed me the contract, which says "Mr. Stumpff is to *engage* orchestra" & said "engage" does not mean pay— & the contract says nothing about *paying* orchestra." After this extraordinary statement I again refused to sign paper—

I'm afraid that contract isn't worth much—[2]

O— dear I hate to write you such silly things— but I don't know what else to do—

Never mind them— let Stumpff revel in his old guldens—

I will go up to Berlin as this hotel simple robbery—

I will send you by Bank tomorrow what is left of the fray— and I will send you a list of my expenses, etc. Indeed I have made *no* bills— but

---

[1] The full address was Viuzzo della Gattaia 4, Viale Michelangelo, Florence.
[2] Craig was responsible for it.

there were old ones— the hotel, Dr., nurses etc. etc. etc.[1] Forgive this Stupid letter. The 2 extra dates on contract were scratched out in lead pencil—
I will close this beastly scrawl & write you a proper letter tonight—

>   Love   Your
>   Topsy

Never mind old Beastly Stumpff— we'll come out some paltry gulden ahead anyway—

—— CD 165 ——

>   Tuesday
>   [Berlin, probably 16 April 1907]

Dearest Love— Just a line to tell you I arrived safely. Have gone to bed & will stay there a few days. I telegraphed you today. I fled from Holland to escape the Cold, the Gloom & the Hotel Bills which were overpowering me. Here the Baby is comfy & costs nothing—
I long to see you. I find all this [a] very rocky road—
Stumpff *refused* to pay me any of the 1000 florins deposit— & also the 750 of last eve. in Harlem—
I was dying to take the train to Florence & if I hadn't been feeling so ill I could not have resisted going to you, so much do I long for your comforting presence & sweetness—
I will rest & be better tomorrow.
Baby is rosy & lovely—
O my Love when will I see you—
Good Night

>   Your
>   Isadora

She ends the story of the Dutch tour with a painful accounting, in slightly erratic arithmetic (which must have infuriated her lord and master if he caught on to it), of income and outgo:

[1] Bills dating from her February illness.

----- *CD 166* -----

[Postmarked Berlin, April 21, 1907]

Dear— Since coming to Berlin I have had a good rest— & I feel so *well* again. I take long walks in the woods with Temple & we both dance for joy of all the opening buds. I was really ill & suffering in Holland from perpetual neuralgia— Now I am glad to be alive again.

I rec. Holland

Apr.	2	Hague	1000
"	4	Amsterdam	1000
"	6	Utrecht	750
"	8	Hague	1000
"	10	Leyden	700
"	12	Harlem *nothing*	

4500 gulden

& *no* deposit—

I *sent* or *spent*

Hotel Bill Amsterdam	288.00
(1 week plus 2 weeks left on *Feb.*)	
Hotel Bill— Hague	25.00
R R fare	12.50
Dr. bill from Feb.	35.
Carfare, tips, miscellaneous expenses	30.00
Sent Mama	481.00
" "	250.00
Hotel Utrecht	6.00
R R fare	29.50
Sent to Florence	750.00
Old Doelen Hotel, bill including tips & carriages	360.00
Paid Shaw for Italian music	140.00
Ticket to Berlin	40.00
Hotel bill Harlem	25.00
R R fare	6.00
Nurse Kist	350.00
Back pay & money which she had paid— Hotel bill at Ospedaletti, Italy[1]	

[1] "Italy" is written in Craig's hand.

altogether	2907.50
received from Stumpff	4500.00
	2907.00
	1492.50[1] gulden

which I have left in my purse at present. You can see that I only paid
things which *urgently demanded* me to pay them—
The carpet & music I have all right here with me & ready to start as
soon as I hear from you when & where—
As for Mr. Shaw, if he was in a "wild rage" he dissimulated it wonderfully— he came to see me the day he left & was amiability itself. As for
talking to Mr. Stumpff I saw him only once & then we spoke only of the
Chopin programme. There was no discussion at all & I don't know what
you mean. My telegram 18 to 23 was in *answer* to yours asking bad days
in May— they will be *about* from Mai 18 to 23. I am sorry to trouble
you with all these things—
It is a beautiful sunny morning— I will dress & go out for a walk—
My heart is full of Love for you—

    Your
     Isadora

———————

The next letter, sent by Isadora in Berlin to Craig in Florence, was
forwarded to him at the Grand Hotel, Stockholm. Just after she
mailed it, she must have had a telegram from him giving her the
"Sweden dates" she asks about, and—whether he stopped off in
Berlin and traveled on to Stockholm with her, or whether they
reached Sweden separately—they were together (Craig says in a
marginal note) when the letter finally reached the Grand Hotel.

[1] An adding machine would show a slightly different total, and some of the
details differ from those shown in the last letter from The Hague.

—— *CD 167* ——

[Postmarked Hallensee, 25 April 1907;
arrival postmarks: Florence, 27 April,
and Stockholm, 2 May]

Dearest— I have thought every day that you would arrive— didn't your last letter say you were coming—
The last 3 days I have had to be with Baby every minute— she is very uneasy since the change of nurse & I haven't slept a wink for 3 nights— She had a little fever & I was so worried, but now she seems all right again. I want so to *see* you again— just to look & look at you would be joy enough. Did I ever have the supreme joy of touching you— my head turns dizzy at the thought. I feel starved for a sight of you— I walk out in the woods, I enjoy everything, I love everything, but it is you I want. I have thought you would be here before my letters could reach you but I will send this on chance— only I hope you are on the way—
Cold & windy here— rain all the time— but we might keep dry in a Bedaq [?].[1]
I wait to hear from you the Sweden dates.
Miss Brouckère came to see Baby. Says she is the image of you. That is not strange, as my whole being is reflected through & through with you— Send me a telegram when you come— I love you love you & love you.

    Your
      Isadora

Have you rec. all my letters?

——————

The reunion in Stockholm at the beginning of May (or in Berlin on the way to Stockholm) was the first since Craig had left Nice for Florence in February. Isadora gave eight recitals in Stockholm between May 4 and 15. During that fortnight when she and Craig

---

[1] It has been suggested that "Bedaq," which is one of several readings of a curious example of Isadorean calligraphy, may be a variation of her more usual "B*xx*"— perhaps an acronym of some kind.

were together, was the "kissing" resumed? If so, it was the last. Their way back from Sweden—Isadora to Berlin, Craig to Florence —led them through Heidelberg, and there, as we shall see in the next chapter, something important took place.

"Click Goes the Apparatus"

In one of Craig's several unpublished, later-written accounts of his relations with Isadora after his flight from Nice to Florence—all self-justifying, and many bitter toward Isadora—he mentions the time they were together in Sweden in 1907, and tells of what came after [CD *340*]:

> From the first day that I met her (in 1903 I think) until 1907 I saw her continually. In all that time I never spoke of working with her—although she now & again touched on the possibility of dancing in a stage which I should arrange for her. I did not want to do this; & I managed to evade the suggestion every time it came up. But one day when we were near Stockholm the thing was touched on again. I remember we were driving (horses, no dam machine)— it was in 1906 or 1907— & we spoke of a beautiful performance in which she would take part. "I will slip in— do my dance— & slip out, & your performance will go on— then I will step in later again & do my other dance & again step out." This I thought was the very way not to collaborate to any worth, but I saw a certain practical something about her notion. But I didn't like it.
>
> We were soon after that in Heidelberg. There we spoke of marionettes & building a theatre which could be built up & taken down & travelled. "Very well then," I said. "I will go to Florence— do the work for Duse[1]— & begin this work for you myself."

[1] Chronology confusion by Craig here.

"Yes, & as I have the 8 or 10 dates arranged for Germany," she said, "I will keep you sufficiently supplied in funds to pay your 2 workmen & to get wood & canvas & do the rest."

This was not an immense undertaking— her receipts might be anything between 3000 & 8000 marks per performance & she would send 1000 marks per show to let the work go on.

I went off to Florence— waited, not a word— not a mark arrived . . . I waited & began work— I got 2 men to commence— one a young artist from Bordighera gave up his house there on the strength of my assurance & dammé if Madame Duncan didn't let me down & him down & what's worse sent no word of excuse.

From that day I have never forgiven this: I don't mind what anyone does or says to me— but if they in any way show disrespect for my work once I am at work (when warm at it) then click goes the apparatus & it's all over between me & whoever has played me the trick.

But in a note in *Book Topsy* Craig says, in the self-contradictory language he was now increasingly to use: "I already knew after that strange farewell in Heidelberg in 1907 that all was over between us as lovers although I promised myself & the Gods that the love should remain & increase"— in other words, that the apparatus had already clicked, in one sense at least, well before Isadora "played the trick," the following summer, of showing disrespect for his work. The estrangement between Craig and Isadora was certainly not caused by any single click of an apparatus, but Craig's belief that Isadora "let him down" after Heidelberg, and "what's worse sent no word of excuse," is certainly at the bottom of much of what his treatment of her was to be from now on. How valid that belief was, the reader will perhaps be able to judge for himself.

Craig is the only source of information for what took place at Heidelberg (there is no mention of it by Isadora), and in one of his notes he says he wished "Isadora had not listened to Elizabeth in Heidelberg in 1907 spring." Now, to "listen to Elizabeth" always meant, in Craig's parlance, to listen to anti-Craig advice—advice which was undoubtedly Elizabeth's repeated reminder to Isadora that not only should the financial needs of the dance school take precedence over Craig's needs, but also that Isadora's own dancing and teaching career needed far greater support than anything Craig could provide. Craig came eventually to believe that Elizabeth was basically responsible for the direction Isadora's life was soon to take: her move to Paris, her connection with Lugné-Poe, her years of luxury with Paris Singer—all of which, in Craig's view, led straight to decadence and her tragic end. To Elizabeth, Craig continued to be the "Bogie man"; there are indications that following his bolt to Florence she lost no time in trying to turn Isadora against him by hints about other women,[1] and Craig was always unbelieving when, in her own occasional letters to him, or in Isadora's letters, he read that Elizabeth sent her love. In a note on a letter sent him by Elizabeth shortly after the episode in Heidelberg, he wrote: "Elizabeth une 'être dangereuse' de Balzac— anyhow an enemy by intention or through folly to I.D. & EGC. June 15, 1907." [CD *294*] But if Elizabeth contributed, as she may well have done, to the deterioration of Isadora's relations with Craig—which were now to begin a steady decline—hers was not the dominant role.

In *Book Topsy* Craig gives another description of the "plan" for Isadora and himself that he suggested in Heidelberg:

Now while she often spoke of our working together I never spoke of it until 1907. And in 1907 she failed me— as you will hear. I never spoke of OUR work because I did not see how I could fit her into the kind of thing I did— *Acis & Galatea* & *Mask of Love*, etc. & I did not contemplate fitting into what she did— for I saw no possible opening— what she did was complete as it was & in my eyes much more marvellous than any phenomenon I had ever seen on a stage. Isadora had such a powerful influence on the public that I would not even have risked placing a Shakespearian play before or after her performance acted by fine actors. Fine acting beside a magnetic personality is swamped by the personality . . .

The only thing I thought which could be put before or after Isadora's dancing was the *Marionettes*: for the Marionette competes with no one & is the antithesis of the actor, singer & dancer.

So in 1907 when I had thought about things carefully & after 100 assurances from I.D. I said to her that I would go to Florence & there prepare the marionettes I had in mind (see my Black Figures) and would she really support that preparatory work by a tour of abends [evenings] in Germany— "Yes yes yes— yes yes yes"— The tour was planned by us

---

[1] Perhaps Isadora's words on p. 214 about "lots of cleverer & prettier people in the world than I," and about jealousy, hint that Elizabeth had already begun to do this.

to begin at Mannheim & to be under the direction of Augustin her
brother— & as soon as it was over she was to come down to Florence
with the bag of gold & see what progress had been made.— "Meanwhile
I'll send you 1000 marks a week— will that be enough to pay the men?"
"Yes! heaps enough."

I went. No 1000 came— no letter for some time[1]— I wrote— no
reply— I began to go mad— Three years I had kept still & now when I
moved . . .

It was quite in the nature of things that a dancer, who is at the same
time an actress, should work with a metteur-en-scène— it is a common
occurrence— And the better the performer & the better the plan of the
metteur-en-scène the greater chance of a fine success.

Later came a few letters full of enthusiasm for this or that . . . but no
good sense— & not one regret for having failed in her part of the unwritten agreement—

That the "agreement" remained "unwritten" was not Craig's fault.
There exists (ironically enough, preserved by Craig himself) a pair
of "provisional contracts" [CD 267] in Craig's hand, drawn up in
Heidelberg, which illustrate the cloud of egotism—burgeoning so
vastly as to distort or blot out feeling and, to an extent, reason—that
so often enveloped him.

| | Heidelberg |
| Provisional contract | May, 1907 |

| | Messrs _____ |
| Miss Isadora Duncan | Mrs. Sturgess[2] |

Messrs _____:

Mrs. Sturgess agrees to engage Miss Duncan for 5 years to appear in
America and Europe.

Not less than 100 performances a year. Not more than 150 (except by
agreement).

---

[1] But see p. 251.

[2] Presumably this is the Mrs. Sturges who under her name of Mary Desti
wrote a book after Isadora's death called *The Untold Story: The Life of
Isadora Duncan*. But in it Mrs. Sturges indicates that she did not see Isadora
between Bayreuth in 1904 and Paris much later, and makes no mention of any
discussion, in 1907, of her "engaging" Isadora in association with "Messrs
_____" (presumably a management firm, to be chosen).

Miss Duncan to receive 7000 francs a night payable after each performance.

The agreement to be terminable at end of 1st season of 100 nights but if continued to continue on same terms as before.

Miss Duncan does not dance on what is called "Bad days" nor on Sundays.

Miss Duncan to dance only in the theatre which will be⎫
carried from town to town for the service of her art and which ⎬ EGC's
will be erected within large halls which are not used as a rule for⎭ part
theatrical exhibitions.

Scenic effect will also be according to her wish.

Orchestra to consist of not less than 30 instruments and 1 capelmeister. Should her Beethoven programme be given, the orchestra must be augmented to the necessary number of instruments.

A small chorus of (boys') voices will be necessary.

The places and halls to be visited must be settled by arrangement with Miss Duncan or her representation.

Polizeiliche Erlaubnis.[1]

EGC—

(Heidelberg)
1907

EGC—   Messrs _____:

5 years.

140 performances per year.

EGC to receive 500 dollars per performance.

The plays or productions: *"Bethlehem" "Temptation of St. A"*

Messrs _____ to supply EGC capital to produce these to the amount of 25,000 dollars (£5000) for each production.

No more than 2 new productions to be invented and made each year.

Messrs _____ to supply EGC sufficient capital to construct in wood and canvas 2 portable theatres— consisting of stages— raised platforms for seats— walls of canvas— antirooms— carpets for same— lighting appliances— entrances— etc., the sum to be not less than 15,000 dollars (£3,000)— and not more than 20,000.

Messrs _____ to pay salaries travelling and all expenses etc. of company of 40 performers. 6 singles, 30 chorus, and necessary staff to work the scenery and lighting for the production— These salaries to be paid through Mr. Craig and his representation.

[1] G., "Police permission."

Everyone concerned in production to be engaged by Mr. Craig.

(House in portable theatre same as general carries with him on a battlefield!!) (For this idea, worth 20,000 dollars worth of reclame, Mr. EGC asks nothing.)

Polizeiliche Erlaubnis.

EGC

In other words, by combining Craig's descriptions of the project with the "provisional contracts," one gathers that Isadora was to appear during the next five years exclusively in conjunction with various dramas acted by large marionettes (among them a *Temptation of St. Anthony* and Laurence Housman's nativity play, *Bethlehem*, which the Purcell Operatic Society had produced in London in 1902), and was to be subject to the conditions listed. These conditions, the sums mentioned, the language itself—all are so preposterous that if Isadora's "listening to Elizabeth in Heidelberg" which Craig so regretted consisted of her being dissuaded from considering the "provisional contracts," one can only congratulate her. Even as mere drafts, the contracts suggest more than just the fantasy of Craig the *metteur en scène* characterizing Craig the man of affairs; more than a case of "leaving one's common sense in the cloakroom" for the attainment of beautful effects, as with *Rosmersholm*: they reveal a distorted will to rule over his universe and its denizens.

Despite the new warning signals in the contracts, one fears that Isadora did indeed promise—as Craig said she did—to support a "plan," not too clearly detailed, which he now returned to Florence to execute: she would keep him in funds while he was "warm at his work." If her recent letters from Nice and Holland are touching, those that follow her promise in Heidelberg are lacerating. We are presented a picture of a great dancer, recently desperately ill, driving herself to dance (first of all, trying to find engagements in midsummer[1]) through a new period of worry and depression, almost to the point of another physical collapse. And this out of continuing devotion to the father of her child (whom, of course, there was no question of his supporting or helping to support)—a man who,

---

[1] As she herself was to write Craig: "I committed a grave error in judgment in thinking I could be able to make money in summer— something I have never yet been able to do in my life."

though he remembers their past love and esteems her art, now addresses her primarily as a money-earner, duty-bound to use her art to provide him with funds. When she doesn't send them—can't send them—she is "failing" him.

We have an idea of Craig's answers to some of the fifty or so letters Isadora wrote him between her return from Heidelberg to Berlin and the end of the year, when she went to dance again in Russia, from a number of existing drafts in his hand. These will be printed, in whole or in part, in their places—they begin a little later in the summer. Some are marked "unsent"; others were presumably sent in recopied, perhaps different form.

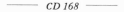

——— *CD 168* ———

[Berlin, June 1907]

Darling Dionysus— Life without you is Horrifficc Horifficcccal— Dates fix themselves & vanish in the most irritating fashion—. . . Gus[1] is in Karlsruhe today. He is working hard. Things will come all right but slow— Lucerne is trying to vanish after appearing dazzling as the Top of Mt Rigi with a sunny guarantee— but we'll fix 'em— Poor Gus doesn't sleep for rushing all day— I dance here tonight but must eat now & then sleep . . . I have been directing orchestral rehearsals till dizzy— but Gluck always Beautiful— Met Prof. Thode[2] for a few moments— he said my work had made 'Grosse Forshritt'[3]—

If it is too hot in Florence take a little house by the sea & perhaps in the early dawn Aphrodite will come out of the Blue to you & help you breathe love into your Marionettes . . . I send you programmes— posters not finished yet— I will send you a line each day— I am living at present in the love & the thought of all you would wish—

    Isadora

[1] Isadora's brother Augustin.
[2] Heinrich Thode, art historian, who had been "intellectually in love" with Isadora at Bayreuth in 1904.
[3] For G. *Grosse Fortschritt*, "great progress."

─── CD 169 ───

[Baden-Baden, June 1907]

Dear— I am just home from the theatre but *not* a good house. They say the real season will only be here in a month!!— His Majesty the King of Siam! sat in a box— he must say More Western Madness—! Gus will see the Kur[haus] director in the morning & try to arrange for a *big* open air affair in July or Aug. Gus is really working hard, but this time of year seems fatal— Lucerne was all fixed but suddenly drew back. Gus says he had better go about & visit all places himself. We are trying to fall over things too much in a hurry. All the hotels are empty here! . . . Falling asleep now will write again in the morning—
Good night darling— all will go forward for our great Plan

    Never fear—
     Love Isadora

─── CD 170 ───
BADISCHER HOF, HOTEL ET BAINS DE LA COUR DE BADE
BADEN-BADEN

[June 1907]

Dear— Thank you for the lovely cards— Evening & Bach passed off nicely but owing to His Majesty— Siamese— not a large house— only 2019. & over a half for expenses (hall, orchestra, etc.) & hotel bill almost 700!— that is including wagens,[1] telegrams etc. etc. but I found it enormous— have to come to a more reasonable hotel here & hope to do better all round. Fixing this tour seems like running up the rapids of the Neckar.
Still we have now
    Baden   June 7
    Lucerne   " 13
    Zurich?   " 15
      waiting answer
& Krolls Berlin for June 28.
Also started for the open air performance at Mannheim for July &

---

[1] For G. *Wagen*, "automobiles" or "carriages."

waiting to hear from Wiesbaden & some other places. It is not at all going as *quick* as *I* desire & I go crazy with impatience.

It rains perpetually— if it weren't for the books I don't know what I'd do— I am reading the Trojan Women of Euripides. Would it not be a wonderful one for Marionettes— Do you know if any better translation exists— This one is a rhymed jingle, but even in spite of that carries one completely away. Only perhaps it is too terrible. It would almost cause too great a strain of terror & pity. It is even heart-breaking to read.

. . . I'm going to take a little rest after traveling. Will write later. All my love & many things unsaid perhaps unsayable—

Isadora

———— CD 173 ————

[Wiesbaden, June 1907]

Dear Love— I was so happy over the letter from your dear Mother— I cried over it. It was too good & sweet of her. I wrote a little note to thank her— I am so *Happy*. I want to spare you the recital of all our troubles. We were sent for to come *at once* to Stuttgart[1] to give a big eve. with children in Hof Theatre. Travelled all day. Arrived. Intendant had just been put in prison for fighting a duel & everything *all off*. Came here as thought it best center— Hope to arrange with Curhaus here. Lucerne all fixed & Zurich for 13 & 15— guarantee suddenly backed all out, but am sending Mr. Mery[2] there to see if can be fixed on again. Pfeffer must have made some mistake as Lucerne man wanted me to dance on a sort of Variety eve. I could keep on writing you the details for hours— but *now* we hope everything will begin smoothly. Berlin is *fixed* for June 28— Waltz programme & children. Mannheim in open-air theatre is being fixed for July— Mr. Mery is away visiting Lucerne, Zurich, Hamburg, Ostend, Marienbad, Franzensbad, Karlsbad etc. etc. and lot, letters & telegrams to all these places having met with *no* reply— but Mr. Mery seems very confident that he can fix them. So much for Business— it is dreful slow but will come out all right—

[1] She had sent him a picture post card [CD *171*] from Stuttgart—a photograph of the bass baritone Theodor Bertram in full fig as Wotan—with the message: ". . . Hail Hero! *You*."

[2] Mery, and Pfeffer in the sentence following, are unidentified agents or intermediaries.

I think we will be able to make it hum during July & Aug.

I fell asleep over writing this last night, so much r.r. journey— Sent you a postcard[1] yesterday of Curhaus here— am to have answer from them today. Heavens— it is up-hill work & each one flies before us like Will o' the Wisp— The Children & Elizabeth have returned to Berlin. If the 28 is a success at Krolls we will also give the 30th— Mr. Mery has an enormous lot of energy & says he will fix this tour or die in the attempt, but theatre directors who are contrary enough in the winter seem to be simply the limit of cussedness in the summer. Write me a cheering word from another land than this Deutschland— Haven't had a letter from you since Baden & have been traveling ever since— However, I think things will go now— I am about to order tea & arise— it is 7.30 & all the birds are singing like mad. If we receive a telegram today we go to Bad Ems[2] to dance there Fri. eve. Then if good news Lucerne will go on there.

Here's my Tea—

Poor Topsy—

Love—

———— *CD 175* ————

PARK HOTEL

MANNHEIM

[June 1907]

Dearest— It is very hot & dusty. I couldn't make anyone see the importance of this affair here, so I came over & am trying to do it myself. It would be a great thing here— fully *5000* people could be seated in the open air. The Burgermeister called on me yesterday— he is very enthusiastic & will put it before the committee today & give me answer this afternoon. They would pay all expenses, reclame, etc. & the prices for entrance for *Ausstellung*[3] would be raised for that evening. Thou-

---

[1] CD *172*.

[2] From Bad Ems she sent him another picture post card: "Just arrived. *Fixed* for Sat. eve.— all will go well now. Write to Englischer Hof here. Love."

[3] G., "fair," "exhibition." On picture post cards which Isadora later sent to Craig, showing the exhibition grounds, this one is called a Jubiläums-Ausstellung (Jubilee Fair); what the jubilee commemorated is not said. Mannheim was an important commercial and industrial town on the Rhine. It was here, as

sands & thousands are each day visiting Ausstellung. There is a big sheet of water & I proposed to Burgermeister your idea of stage in middle of water— he thought it wonderful—
I have seldom in all my life spent a more disagreeable time since— since you left, but if this is a success here I will feel all right. I telegraphed you yesterday to know if when things are fixed up here I should meet you somewhere or go to Berlin until performance there 28. Must do one or other as money is given out. Those small affairs in Heidelberg & Baden only paid hotel bill—
I now wait your telegram.
No letter from you for 6 days— since Baden.

        All my love
           Topsy poor Thing.

—— *CD 176* ——

                           [Mannheim, June 1907]

Dear Love— I am waiting at station restaurant for train— Berlin. Tomorrow morning I will see Snowdrop! Do you get all my letters? I sent just one from hotel. Sometimes I think I'm wonderful clever at doing things & sometimes I think I'm an awful idiot. Anyway no one would budge for this Mannheim thing & I have done it. It waits to see if the results will be good.
My letters must seem *wooly* to you but you know the state of mind. When the contract for this *first* fête is once definitely settled the others will come easy.
The place is like this—[1]
That's not a good picture, but gives you slight idea. They will make a *Big* raised platform over the fountain— The terraces slope away from the water so—
There is room to seat as many thousands people as could ever come. At present the fountain is a big colored light fountain. The Ausstellung is right in the *middle* of town. The Burgermeister exclaimed "Nothing will

---

Craig later remembered (see pp. 229–230) that Isadora's tour for the benefit of the "plan" was to *begin*. Isadora herself, in her next letter, will refer to the Mannheim performance as "this *first* fête."
[1] Here, as at end of paragraph that follows, Isadora has drawn diagrams.

ever have been seen like it"— and I added "Since the days of Louis 14."
Then he felt just like Louis 14 hisself!—
Now I wait contract. Do fix a telegraph address so I can telegram you
things— He will have *orchestra* in a ship *just* as you said!!!!— & chorus
of white-robed maidens— Last days of Pompeii will be nothing to it!—
    Anyway I've learnt a good deal about Ausstellungs. They have *one*
restaurant alone put up at a cost of *130,000* marks— make it on Beer
alone—
Darling Heart I kiss you—

    Your Topsy—

──── *CD 177* ────

Monday
[Berlin, June 1907]

Dear Love— Just arrived & received your dear letters which cheered
me. The Porter had paid no attention to my orders for forwarding letters.
It is a treat to see Snowdrop again— she has grown *very* stout & *hearty*.
Your letters do me much & Beautiful good— and put all within me in
Harmony again—
I go to dance in Kiel on the 25th & here the 28th— Mannheim continues
to send good tidings. I think there is now no doubt it will be for the 13th
June[1]— & other evenings following. There is place to seat *5000* people—
Think of that.
Gus is dear & good but not very *quick*—
I spoke just now to E[lizabeth]'s Russian friend. She is very nice. She
says the Moscow Kunst Theatre people are very anxious to meet you—
Gorki is now in Naples—
She says they are excellently trained servants but need a Master— Was
very enthusiastic over your work & I said I will find one of your books
for her—
Things are beginning to go forward but we always need that *Business*
man . . .

─────────

[1] Isadora's error for "July."

——— *CD 178* ———

Tuesday
[Berlin, June 1907]

Dearest— We are having the usual old trouble about permission for children to appear for 28. I just visited Frau & Herr Humperdinck[1] (he will see Hilsen tonight & ask again). They asked after you, & Herr H. remembered meeting you & spoke about your work with very sweet understanding. He and she seem to live in very sweet & pleasant atmosphere. I told him you lived in the *Stars* & he said it was the only place for Artists & Poets. They are coming here tomorrow to see Baby. A letter from Mery saying he is having much trouble to fix dates— but *hopes* he has Zurich

> Berne
> Lucerne
> Interlaken

fest.[2] He will now go to Marienbad etc. but I have *more* faith in the open-air performances & as soon as Mannheim is fest & fertig I will begin another— Hamburg is also a good place for open-air fest[3]— . . . It is cloudy & rainy here but Baby is rosey & strong—
Elizabeth has your postcards tacked up about her Bureau— She refers to you as "Her darling Teddy"!— but she also insinuates you are kissing another girl now!!— but I told her you had not time or liking for such things & only her being my Sister that you deigned to notice her at all— but she replies "Humph." She's very naughty![4]
When Mannheim is really *signed* I will sleep better o'nights— Shall I look for a Business man? Gus is a dear but asleep—
The *Grune wald* here looks a bit melancholy—

---

[1] Englebert Humperdinck, composer of *Hansel and Gretel*. He occupied a high academic position in Berlin and could perhaps bring influence to bear on the management of Kroll's Opera House or the police. The trouble about getting police permission for the children to dance would seem, from a later letter, to have had less to do with child-labor laws than with "nudity"; the Empress was excessively puritanical. Also, Irma Duncan says: "The Prussian School System tried to enforce their educational standards which included religious matters, church attendance, etc."
[2] G., "certain"; with *fertig*, in next line, "signed and sealed."
[3] For G. *Fest*, "celebration."
[4] Note by Craig: "Naughty? only that?"

Your little book of Japanese pictures gave me joy— Elizabeth says to
call the Baby
        Amida
after one of the pictures— the loveliest. The Berlin Police came & said
she must have a name!!! refused to anmeldung 'Snowdrop'— said it
wasn't a real name. O these Berlin Police, finally anmeldunged
        "Snowdrop zum besuch"[1]
She just says "Pa Pa Ma Ba Ta Ta" over & over again— but I say Love—
Love— Love & I *feel* it
        for *You*.
        I *love you*

            Isadora.

[Postscript by Elizabeth]
Dear Teddy
    All is lovely here do be happy a bit too.

        Love Elizabeth[2]

    ────── CD 179 ──────

                                        [Berlin, June 1907]

Dearest Love— Mannheim has accepted— 4000 marks guarantee & all
the money from all the seats sold. They pay reclame, building expenses,
orchestra & everything. It is fixed for *July 12*.
I have been dancing all afternoon— am composing a new Strauss waltz
& making studies for a new programme. The seats here for 28 are selling
well— if ausverkauft[3] we will book another evening.
There is nothing to do here but sleep & work— & talk business & so I
do each alternately with all my might— I am up at 6.30 or 7 each morning!!! Life is in general so dull without you that there is no temptation—
& difficult things come easy— When I feel I can't stand it another
moment without seeing you I go & work till I am tired out— & then sleep

---

        [1] The meaning here is that the police, after refusing to accept the name
"Snowdrop," finally consented to register the child's presence in Berlin as
"Snowdrop, here on a visit."
        [2] Note by Craig: "I am happy enough in my way— but I don't trust you—
you'll corrupt Isadora."
        [3] G., "sold out."

& wake up the next morning feeling fresh & hopeful. Will you come to Mannheim & show me how to dance in middle of water? Such a joke!— orchestra in a boat!!! No letter from you yesterday or today— Please write me if even a little line often, it keeps me in *Harmony*.

Baby is wonderful. She creeps all days— *won't* keep still— climbs up on all the chairs & stands saying Aa Aa Aa. Such *life*—

When you find it too hot in Florence why don't you go to Lido & *bathe*— If I could only fly there & back here only to dance— It is a bit wooly to pass the summer like this— Grunewald is *Melancholy*—

I leave 24 for Kiel

dance there 25

here 28

Then we are waiting to hear from Marienbad etc. for 1st week in July— Mannheim 12—

The *entire* Switzerland (no season July) is being booked for August & Sept. It seems always as if we were standing still— but summer is an almost impossible time to do anything. Mannheim send their reclame for this eve. *all* over *Germany*, so when it is a success it will be easy to fix others—

That's a good plan for Dublin to London etc. but who on Earth is going to manage it—

Darling Love this is all fearfully dull— & you write me letters where the words dance & kiss, and full of Wonderful Star Spaces— Well I will surprise you with some new dances—

How I should love to be in a gondola with you in Venice gliding down the Moonlit Canals under the low bridges with visions of Churches & Palaces on either side— Would you like it?

But underneath this dullness I am very happy— I feel our plan is being accomplished— fearfully slow— but surely—. Gus is getting more & more excited over your ideas of Marionettes— he now sees them in the air & all about him. If you could once get all the materials for that little Theatre altogether in ship-shape order— It will be a little seed from which your greater will spring . . .

—— *CD 180* ——

[Berlin, 17 June 1907]

Dearest— No letter from you for 3 days!!!— Horrid— Forgive my stupid letters— I try to follow all the advices in your red & blue letter— only *you* know how difficult all is—

A rehearsal at Kroll's today— before mine they were rehearsing Carmen
on the stage— it was like Bedlam let loose—
. . . Will you come to Mannheim on July 12?
Dearest Please write me—
I am "not well" today so will be all right for dancing on the 2ᵗth.
Did your Mama get my letter to her— I hope she was not displeased. I
feel love for her— I feel I see something of her in Baby— How mys-
terious & Beautiful the recreating is—

I have so great joy in her— My Love these are *difficulter* days for
Topsy than perhaps you think— but I am happy in looking *Forward* . . .

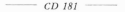

——— CD 181 ———

[Berlin, June 1907]

Dearest— I was so glad to get your letter & card— but I don't like the
idea of *Headache. Please* go to Lido & swim for a week & be quiet—
otherwise you will get ill. I'm afraid it's too much hot sun in Florence.
Now please do what Topy says— go to the sea where the breezes are.
. . . Yes— *gerade*¹— the Plunder. That's what I'm asking for too. They
are scouring the map of Germany for dates but summer is a difficult
time. But our Plan does not rely on summer alone, but can be carried out
in autumn— I want now that Mannheim is fixed for 12 July to try the
open-air theatre in Dresden for end July.
. . . Snowdrop's (do find the child a name!²) latest is the music box.
She sits & claps her hands in time to the music of "Papa, Mama" Polka—
in wildest delight.
Didn't you get my letter expressing my joy over the Walt Whitman
manuscript?³ I wrote one. I often take it out— alone— and look at it, &
think how wonderful it is— the paper left, & his vanished hands—
Good night dear heart— I dream of Future— Your most loving &
obedient Topsy.

¹ G., "exactly."

² Craig wrote, in the draft of a reply: "Miss Kist, the baby's nurse, sends
me 'informations' of child I shall call Snowdrop— you may call her Artemis,
Diana, Sappho, Sophocles Duncan Craig IF you like."

³ Craig had apparently sent Isadora one of the Whitman manuscripts his
mother had brought him from America.

Craig: A design for Elektra, *1905. (From* Towards a New Theatre)

My Beliefs: My reaction to Haeckel
1905

1. I believe in makebelieve
2. I believe that the principles of the art & the theatre are more important than the star actor ~~and~~.
3. I believe that it may be difficult ~~if anyone thinks to~~ to some people to credit this — because —
4. I believe that star actors feel more important than anything else in the world.
5. I believe that the star ~~system~~ is now on the decline, ~~and I believe this because I judge by comparison with other things the~~ Darwins theory of evolution leads me to believe this.
6. I believe that ~~except for the stage~~ theatre has never been so ~~inspired as~~ artless as it is today.
7. I believe that we are on the eve of a renaissance.

ABOVE: *A page from one of Craig's notebooks, 1905. Inscribed by Craig: "My reaction to Haeckel." (The Craig-Duncan Collection)*
BELOW: *Craig in Florence, 1907. (Courtesy of Edward A. Craig)*

Isadora reading Ernst Haeckel's Anthropologie. *(The Craig-Duncan Collection)*

Just a few of my old sketches please me now — you'll find I'n said which

I like this sketch ∆o —
It was drawn in 1905 in Dresden in the Central Theatre from the top box — Proscenium
on the left side of the house when looking towards the curtain
if you're in the stalls.
I took the top box as it was empty — (it generally a useless spot) —
& from this box during an interval I sketched the audience
The arched "windows" are not windows but looking glass —
& there reflect the audience of this top gallery —
It is a good theatre device & enlarges the appearance of the galleries —
& also increases the strength of light —

It would be impossible to give any notion of the effect produced on these
audiences in Dresden + other German towns by I. D.
at this period in her career as a dancer — as unquestionably
THE dancer of her epoch. Since Taglioni there had
not been one such — & since I. D there has been no other.
And I doubt whether D was ever more herself than in these 1905 – 1910
years — (It was in 1914 that the first of the Big wars came along)

Craig's sketch of the Central Theatre, Dresden, during Isadora's
performance, January 1905. Notes on opposite page added in 1939.
(The Craig-Duncan Collection)

Villa Maria, Noordwijk-on-Sea, Holland. (The Craig-Duncan Collection)

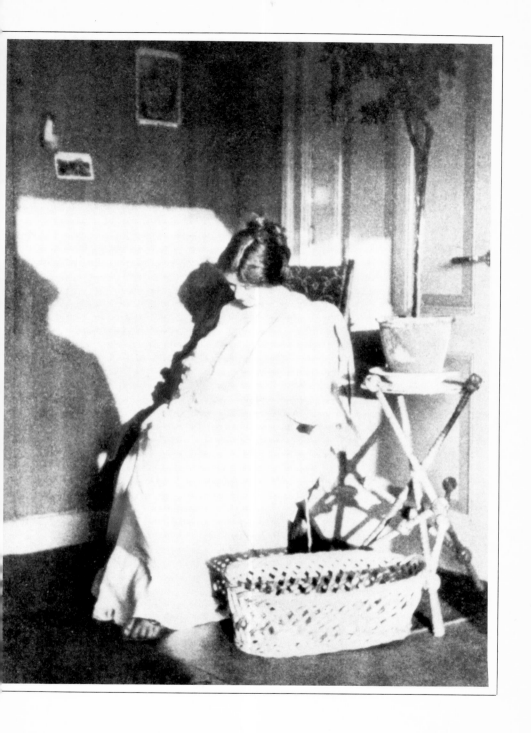

Isadora in the Villa Maria, 1906. (Irma Duncan Collection)

ABOVE: *Isadora and Deirdre, circa 1908. Inscribed by Isadora to Craig:*
"Love from your Baby & Me," with Craig's comment at the top: "I would have said to
you look down at Deirdre & that would have made a perfect picture."
BELOW: *Deirdre, five years old. (The Craig-Duncan Collection)*

——— *CD 182* ———
GRAND HOTEL GERMANIA
KIEL

24 June 1907

Dear Love— Just arrived 11.30— falling over with sleep.
Very cold— Electric lighted ships in harbor— very gai here apparently—
Emperor here! 6 hours journey— Very tired— Will be back in Berlin
26th.
Great effort!
Yes, but where's the Plunder, that's what I say . . . ?!

——— *CD 183* ———

[Berlin, June 1907]

Dearest— Kiel, alas, proved one of Mr. Sach's amiable & periodical illusions. *1000* marks *gross* receipts in house— just paid chemin de fer &
hotel. I danced nevertheless as best I could & the small audience shouted
themselves hoarse in an effort to make up in enthusiasm what they lacked
in quantity. 4 Japanese officers were present & they invited us on board
their Man of War & there entertained us most charmingly with Japanese
wine & little cakes. The sailors were practicing Jiu Jitsu on deck. The
ship big like a small island— all black with the red flag— really splendid
& inspiring. The German Men of War— a light new grey— not at all
imposing.
The Japanese officers expressed great enthusiasm for my dancing— said
I should have music "like Japanese music with lines & rhythm." The
visit to their ship was a splendid experience. They were so gracious &
courteous & exquisitely considerate, neither stiff nor familiar but just
perfectly poised & *kind*. They gave us little silk Japanese flags as sou-
venirs— were so pleased because I said Japanese wine was exquisite— it
tastes delightfully of Bamboo sticks & flowers—
6 hours journey back to Berlin— am rather tired— & we have been having
all sorts of difficulties here. Sticky men had broken into your studio—
for Frl. Hosler's *Klage*[1]— we brought it to a lawyer but am afraid must
only pay— also another sticky man, a frame-maker. Police directors

[1] G., "legal complaint"—apparently for unpaid rent.

ordered a special rehearsal this morn. We put all the little girls in long dresses & he looked in vain for a single leg— he asked me to dance also, but I told him that was *quite* impossible. He created an awful atmosphere & has given me nervous pains galore. As if that wasn't enough they've called up that *eternal* Gerichtsvollzieher's case[1] again for 9 o'clock tomorrow morning & threaten to send the Police if I don't come. How can I dance in the evening with *that* in the morning? That & a few more Schwierigkeiten[2] make life here anything but angenehm. Berlin is simply impossible with these things. Your studio looked as if snow had fallen, with sticky papers. But don't worry, we will get them off all right. How Elizabeth goes along in this sort of an Inferno I don't know—
She keeps up against it with really wonderful courage.
They are even attacking me again on the taxes question—
The only bright spot in all this is Snowdrop, who continues to flourish & looks more lovely each day—
I try to take a book & read & be quiet sometimes, & when your letters come I have an hour of joy. O, I will live through it— but the summer is evidently no good— date after date comes back to us "unmöglich." They all suggest October instead. If Mannheim is a great success other places will be more ready—
Darling, forgive me all this stupid letter. One gets in a *Stimmung* here that is impossible for man or beast— a sort of fever of bumping one's head against a stone wall. I do not send you the details of all the places that have disappointed us—
The sale for tomorrow is already 1600 so that looks well—
Cheer up Poor Topsy— & it rains & pours here continually. I feel like some poor Spirit banished from Paradise to wander in a difficult Inferno . . .

———— *CD 184* ————

[Berlin] 29 June 1907[3]

Darling— A wonderful House last night. They shouted from the first number & made ovations all evening. We will repeat the evening next Friday— but on terms of 50%, we making the *extra* reclame. This will

---

[1] Isadora had been subpoenaed (G. *Gerichtsvollzieher*, "marshal").

[2] G., "difficulties"; *angenehm*, same sentence, "pleasant"; *unmöglich* and *Stimmung*, below, "impossible" and "moods."

[3] Craig, most of whose own letters are undated, has noted here: "Am staggered— she gives a date!"

be the *first* time we have ever succeeded in making a *Berlin* theatre go on *percent*, so [it] is quite an *epoch*-making date. There was over 4000 in house last night— we made *net* about 1500.

That would be all right if it was done *3* times a week— but only *once* isn't enough. The papers say I have made *Grosse Fortschritt!* "Her Art has ripened" says Lokal Anzeiger— & Börsen Courier, an ancient enemy, wrote an eloge.

There are no dates between Berlin & Mannheim although Gus has almost worked himself into brain fever trying to book some, but it really seems impossible at this time of year. I was hauled off to their awful court early yesterday morn. & feel tired now from all the excitement. Dearest will you come to Mannheim on the 12th because I really don't think I can exist much longer without seeing you. Gus keeps his books in perfect order & as he hasn't made dates enough refuses to take any salary whatever but Hélas the enormous expenses eat up everything. He is now making a mighty effort to book *August solid*, 3 dates a week.

It was very nice to see how the Berlin people had not forgotten me. The Theatre director said 4600 was an *unheard* of high receipts at this time of year— & the house shouted like one person—

Elizabeth says my work has improved *twice* over—

I feel it myself— for I dance rich from all my love from & to you—

The mail just came— Your pictures— they are splendid—

They redouble my longing to see you. You *will* come to Mannheim? Yes! Poor Gus is getting awfully discouraged about the lack of summer dates— he tries so hard.

I am too tired to hold a pen— I will put your pictures before me & fall asleep . . .

——— *CD 185* ———

[Berlin, late June or early July 1907]

Darling— Thank the Gods I leave diese liebe Berlin Schule etc. on the 8th for Bad Neuenahr—
Southwards—
Also Besser—[1]

[1] Isadora, obviously under strain, has had enough of "the dear School" and of rainy Berlin; since the direction she will be taking, if only as far as Bad Neuernahr, is southerly, "that's all to the good." Perhaps, with the Hardenburgstrasse flat given up, she was living at the school.

What your pore Topsy suffers from "Schwierigkeiten" you will never know— Never mind— We will book next season then all will be well. I send you all my Love— I walk in the Traurige[1] Grunewald— I love you— but lack eloquence at present.

    Your
      Topsy—

Have been reading Salammbo— of Flaubert— wonderful.

—— *CD 186* ——

[Berlin, late June or July 1907]

Dear— Summer in Berlin is *not* Paradise. So viele Schwierigkeiten[2] I can't even write about them—
I dance July 10, Bad Neuenahr— but making[3] money in summer is like trying to hold water in a sieve—
I am making a new Programme— beautiful music that Shaw sent from Florence. I work, but need inspiration. Baby is lovely & wonderful. I leave here Monday the 8th.
Your last letter wasn't marvellously sympathetic, but I suppose no one can appreciate difficulties except those wading in the midst of them.[4] The ones here are *Wooly*. Well— I spose it's Life. I have much joy in my dancing & I suppose that is joy enough— only when one gives so much *out*, one demands something *in*. Couldn't we meet 2 weeks by the Sea— perhaps Venice?
I'm afraid financial things won't turn to much till the season begins— the Summer seems Impossible.

[1] G. *traurig*, "sad."
[2] G., "so many problems."
[3] Craig crossed out the word "making" and wrote in "saving."
[4] Craig has written on this letter: "What is the matter— what's the matter? Difficulties?— What difficulties?— We, you & I, are doing a *set task*— you your part— I mine. & the rest working to cue. Is it possible you have mixed some other task with this new one of ours? Drop everything but this one thing. *Then* you *cannot* fail— & difficulties cannot interfere. If you do *other* things you will wreck *this* one. I expect to hear in few days of success— no more 'Difficulties'— Kiss."

Mrs. Mendelssohn came to see me today & admired the Baby. I think she has it not in her power to do more. Everyone else is out of town . . .[1]

To the above there is a draft reply by Craig in which the phrases of affection seem like blatantly added ornaments.

—— *CD 269* ——

[Florence]

To ID from EGC. 1907[2]

Sweetheart mine— a wee lecture bowered in kisses all the time my letter (kiss) you say is not marvelous sympathetic (kisses) and no one can appreciate difficulties (kiss) except those wading in them— (kisses). *Sympathy never pulled all those guns over the Alps in 1792*!!!!!! Sympathy sits down at those moments and lets her (kiss) Disciplined sister step forward— (kiss) And so far as I can see Sympathy has caused you to waste a few thousand marks instead of saving at least a few thousand— (kiss). It is *not* discipline to *begin* and then to say "I'm afraid financial things won't turn to much till the season begins" when you've had receipts amounting to

Heidelberg—	2000	?
Baden—	1500	?
Kiel	1000	?
Berlin	3600	
Mannheim	4000	
etc		?
	12,000	—

---

[1] Especially considering Craig's later demand that Isadora get money for him from their friends, this sounds as though he had suggested that she beg from Frau Mendelssohn and others.

[2] Heading added later by Craig.

There is another draft by Craig written about this time.

———— *CD 268* ————

[Florence][1]

June, 1907.   To pay my people I wrote articles,
                                              sold etchings, and bookplates.

(To ID from EGC)

Well darling, I hope *your* regiment is now working under you better. My regiment is the strongest I have yet had. My stage— masks— all being *made*. It has been an awful if enjoyable time to get it so far— *time* always gets round one somehow— and regular weekly payments go out and more come in. I have asked Daily Mail 2000 marks for rights of "Letters to Ellen Terry." I hope your regiment is working better. You must do several "man"-ny things.

        1st. You must call your cashier to you and must say to him *this*:

You must   "The object of this tournee is to make a regular *profit* at each town— *not* to cover expenses, or lose. If your expenses—

say all   grand total per week— exceed your takings, or even just come

this   up to your takings, *you are to reduce the expenses*— I expect you to hand me *never* less than 500 marks profit after *all expenses are paid*."

        2nd you are to say to him:—

          "If you wish to know how to reduce the expenses— take a list of each item and reduce each by 5%. Do *not* reduce these following: *Printer's Bill.*

                        Carriages for Lady.

          but reduce all the rest:

          Hotels— eating— Expenses in Theatre or Hall— salaries; and stop the leaks (the 10-mark and 15-mark expenses which mount up to 200 in quick time.)"

He is to do all this— and to bring you never a littler *profit* than 500 marks when performance is finished and you are going on to next town. Unless you keep this RULE you'll reach October with only 3000 marks in hand.[2]

[1] All other headings added by Craig in 1944.
[2] Note by Craig: "This happened!!"

My darling— As I told you my regiment are a picked lot, and are working in good order.

I hope I shall not have to disband them all in a month from now— for I could only with *greater* difficulty begin again after another reverse. A river is a river— and succeeds and wins to the sea because of its *incessant* flow— but it becomes only an old lake and reaches never the sea when hills are all around and it has to stop— bump— bump— and bump. Never before in my experience (and I have had some fine flings) has the work been going so *steadily* and *productively*— my small staff here of 8 are all bending backs together— pushing together— to rule and in time— with caution—

That will only be broken if one day a part of it breaks away.[1] The part may be Jones who rebels (he can be replaced) or the part may be me— and I shall only break the rhythm if I have to stutter out "Haven't any more OIL for machine." Obvious reply of all the hands: "How the ——— Hell can the darned thing go on then" and then they will say "You shouldn't 'ave begun Govenor if you couldn't come up to time every pay day."[2]

and then I shall throw up the sponge.[3]

When I have more to "*show*" here— more figures and lights and scene, *it* will gain capital for us— for it will convince. Till then for the 1st salaries and material we rely on your Lieutenant relieving the fort with an occasional 2000 marks—

My young friend Carr is proving his worth. He doesn't get a large £10 salary— I pay him £3 a week and he is doing the work of 10 men and keeps asking for more *work*. I think the whole army is doing magnificently— from my darling Banner— *you*— down to my excellent little drum— the "Mask." Did I tell you it was in the press[4]— 3 numbers August–Sep. Oct— *in 4 languages*[5]— Whew!! Wait and see. It covers its own expenses, and so is an excellent and well behaved little drum and valuable for its *tone*.

How's our Elizabeth? and what is she doing: she mustn't "walk by herself" too much—[6] I guess planning to give us all a theatre apiece and finding when the day arrives that the SHAPES don't fit any of us.

[1] Note by Craig dated August 1908: "I.D. broke 1st. Padgett 2nd. Carr third."
[2] Note by Craig: "They did. (1908)"
[3] Note by Craig: "I didn't. (1908)"
[4] Note by Craig: "proof sheets only."
[5] Craig has crossed out "In 4 languages" and noted "only in one 1908."
[6] Here Craig has drawn a *cat* walking alone.

Let me hear from you. Pull your regiment together— don't make 'em
more *enthusiastic*— insist on them being more systematic.

Possible takings— 1300
Expenses   — 800
                   ———
        Profit   500

x Possible takings *must be put low* in *all* your minds
x That will lower and control the way and quantity you spend
xx That will *ensure* a profit
LOVE AND FORCE TO YOU.

In speaking of business with Guss use the Socratic method— make *him*
explain how profit is to be secured. But don't tell yourself you KNOW!!
essence of ignorance and Folly is *"I know"* . . . *"Tell me"* essence of
wisdom! isn't it. May I play at tutor to my darling— will she speak her
lesson pretty. Kisses all over you— and a flow of vitality from here
to you.

———————

On her way from Berlin to Bad Neuenahr, Isadora had to break
the journey at Cologne (Köln), whence she sent Craig two post
cards [CD *187, 188*]: "Breakfasting at K. between two trains— Very
sleepy. Cathedral in a mist— Beautful— Love" and "Write Kurhaus
Theatre Bad Neuenahr." It seems to have been her first visit to
Cologne since their happy conversation in the stationery of the Dom-
Hotel in January 1905.

——— *CD 190* ———

[Bad Neuenahr, 10 July 1907]

Darling Love— What is with your foot?[1] O— dear— Take Wings
instead—

———

[1] Note by Craig: "I had broken my foot." This flippant remark of Isadora's—
"Take Wings instead," in reply to Craig's news that he had broken a bone in
his foot—is perhaps a first show of exasperation with Craig and his incessant
difficulties.

Let me know each day how you are.—
Terrific journey here—
Arrived half asleep— to be kept awake by Military Band! playing Tann-
hauser!— outside my window— Heavens, it's madly gay here!
Dance tomorrow eve—
Will write you tomorrow when I wake up—
Love to you—

  Isadora

  Mother
   of
  Snowdrop
   &
  Beloved
   of
    Ted— but not dead yet— That is, it began to sound like a
           denkmal.[1]

THE "FIRST FÊTE" FOR THE "PLAN" TOOK PLACE AT MANNHEIM ON
schedule, July 12, 1907; from Hamburg, where she next went to
dance (traveling almost entirely across Germany), Isadora wrote to
Craig about it. There is a hint in this letter of something that may
have been in Craig's mind when he wrote later that the failure of
the plan was "all Elizabeth's influence"—for here Isadora points out
to him that the children from the school, who appeared with her at
the Mannheim fête, had to be paid (probably only for expenses).
Craig may have thought that Elizabeth, as the school's directress,
overcharged, thus cutting down on what Isadora could send to
Florence. In an earlier letter we have seen Isadora speak with momen-
tary impatience of the school, but her commitment to it—and the
unpleasant consequences for her of the debts that Craig had left in
Berlin—may well have made her withhold more money for Berlin
expenses than Craig thought proper. However, we see that she did
send him a thousand marks from the Mannheim receipts; thus his
statement that "No 1000 came— no letter for some time"[2] is a
mis-memory.

[1] G., "memorial."
[2] See p. 230.

Despite Isadora's pleas, Craig had not come to Mannheim; his draft on the following two pages shows that he had expected her to come directly from Mannheim to Florence, apparently with the "plunder"; in this letter she tells why she did not do so.

——— *CD 192* ———
ROTTERS PARK HOTEL
HAMBURG

[Between 12 and 24 July 1907]

Dearest— After all the enormous effort— Hurrah & Huréh— after paying all expenses— Children, Capelmeister & everything— I have only a little over 2000 marks left!! I send you 1000 & keep 1000 for running expenses. I dance here on the 24th— am trying to persuade the Kur[haus] director to arrange it for open-air, for the weather has turned hot— just *after* we wanted it hot. I think a Böse fée[1] must be watching over my doings this summer—
There seems no possible way of any dates for August, so will try to spend that by the sea— with you if you like?
No letter from you since the 12th. Write here till the 25th.
I have been quite desperate over the impossibility of making any money this summer. The only thing to do now is to rest, & make next season *good* from Oct. on.
Gus has gone to Berlin to see if he can hunt up some sort of Business man— Mr. Fisher recommended a Mr. Salter there. I would have run down to see you these 10 days only considered expense, & also 'not well' so must rest. The Mannheim affair was exciting to the verge of nervous prostration. Fancy dancing in the middle of a square while 20,000 people looked on.[2]
They want to give a Big Fête there in Sept. Would you like to suggest your doing anything for it— If so send me a rough plan for idea— expense etc. & I will put it before them. They would not however go to *very* much expense . . .

[Letter incomplete]

    [1] G. *böse*, "bad"; F. *fée*, "fairy."
    [2] Isadora sent Craig six picture post cards of the Mannheim "Jubiläums-Ausstellung," showing the elaborate layout. She wrote: "Yes, that's just about how it was on a larger scale— 20,000 people stood or hung onto roofs— Never thought people *could* be so ornery. Hélas!"

—— *CD 195* ——

[Hamburg(?), July or August 1907]

Dearest Love— I don't know any more *what* to write you. I hate to send you disappointing letters, & I can't send any other. Have been trying to fix more dates— but no success. The next one I have is for open air in Baden— Aug. 24. My money is at an end— I will have to fly to Berlin where I can at least get my board till then. This summer is quite desperate. Frl. Kist has gone home & I had to send money for new nurse. Gus flew off to America sending me word of his going only from the boat.

The best thing I can do is to find some manager to fix next season & make money then— it is quite impossible *now*.

I should have known that summer is *always* a rum time.

. . . I wish I could get in the train & come to you, but I'm afraid that would only be making things worse, as I would not then have enough money to get back to Baden on Aug. 24.

This is a very rummy way to spend the summer, & I feel tired to tatters. It is all very rum rum rum— extremely rum— I had better go to America & find a millionaire or so— for this dancing business seems to make board & lodgings only— & very lucky in summertime to make even that. Can't your dear Mama find us a millionaire?—

    All my love
    Isadora

———————

Craig, suffering from his "broken" foot and from acute shortage of funds, now wrote to Isadora saying that he desperately needed 6,000 marks, and asking her to get it for him from Dr. Zehme or elsewhere. A draft in his hand reads as follows:

. . . Please answer my letter Isadora about the 6000 marks. Or is the ship to go down once more— If so I go down with [it] & then goodbye to all such rush work. Do you always do what Elizabeth tells you? Or any other stray influence? What has made all these tours utterly unproductive? & why in Walt's name was I fool enough to start? I could have waited until doomsday. You can never know! So why should I talk & try to show you. You don't seem to realize how serious this thing is. How can you write me about *everything* except the one thing we all thought was what you are working for.

In a few days I shall have to pay out 2000 marks or close up & end the whole affair. That would mean 3 or 4 processes as I have contracts with my workers. I am laid up still with a foot red hot & I read at night instead of sleeping— Ice in bags makes foot pleasant at times. It's about 14 days I've been laid up & I could take it easily except for the weight of the money affair hanging like a hell in the air— flames downwards.

It's unfortunate just now. And then I expected to see you the day after Mannheim— but I suppose you have lost the map— or your head— or some other trifle—

         ah well—

No— I am not well— or I could not see any but beautiful pictures.

And didn't you say you were doing some "grosse sache"[1] with me? Or did I dream it. Well then, where's the "grosse sache"? This end is going ahead with fearful & divine energy & success— *fearful* to me & to see, because I see by side of it the words "useless— for Isadora has forgotten."

So much for "grosse sache"— No— no— but you see how ill I am—[2]

Isadora had to make it clear to Craig that she could not borrow, and she did what she could to save the contents of his Berlin studio from confiscation.

———— *CD 194* ————

[Berlin, July or August 1907]

Dearest— I do not write as I am a bit distracted. Between the bills & the mosquitoes here life is not Gai! You and I are not very practical people, but this summer our impractibility is the *limit*. You will have to tell

---

[1] G., "great things."

[2] Craig later annotated this draft: "Written in Florence 1907 to I.D. in Germany who had promised to support the work & who had made a tour with that end in view— PROMISED ME! It was the 1st time I had told her I would prepare some theatre thing if she would help a little— & she promised."

your people there that they must wait till winter— there is no other way. I stopped at Gautzsch to see Dr. Zehme, but Mrs. Zehme was away, & other circumstances made it impossible for me to ask. My Banker here wouldn't lend me anything if I was dying! My only comfort is the Baby, who is very wise & sweet & laughs all day—
Every now & then everything at your studio is attached— I asked Mr. Magnus to help me pack your pictures & take them out of danger of further attachments, but they refused to allow us to move them without lawful written permission from you. I asked him to write you & explain. I thought to carefully pack pictures, books & clothes & either store them or put them in a small room somewhere under another name—
I must pay 100 marks to raise the attachment today or everything will be sold.
Gus left for America because he rec. a letter from Frohman[1] offering him a better part. Frl. Kist lent him the money for his ticket.[2]
I feel dreadfully anxious about you. I will try & send at least 200 marks or so tomorrow if I can get them— at present things look much bluer than this paper, but Summer cannot last much longer. I have to go through a treatment, otherwise the Dr. says I will not be able to dance next winter. Can't you insist on Mr. Loeser doing Something?[3] The Dr. won't let me practice so I can't continue on my new programme. I console myself with the Baby & ancient philosophy— also contemplating the Japanese pictures is a good panacea. The summer here chiefly consists in rain & thunderstorms. I wish I could write something to comfort you— I can only say try & let things stand for a couple of months— in Oct. it will be simple to make money.
I committed a grave error in judgment in thinking I could be able to

[1] Charles Frohman, the American producer, who was to sponsor Isadora's first American tour in 1908. Augustin Duncan later became well-known as an actor and director in New York.

[2] Note by Craig: "absurd!"

[3] Note by Craig: "Mr. Loeser— Whew— what a hope!" Apparently relations had cooled between Loeser and Craig since the loan of the villa in Viuzzo della Gattaia. Craig had recently moved to a larger villa, Il Santuccio, 35 Via San Leonardo. "Opposite Il Santuccio were a couple of smaller villas," writes Edward A. Craig, "and in one of them D.N.L. [Dorothy Neville Lees] found rooms where she lived and typed, and tried to keep pace with Craig's literary output."

Loeser's meticulousness, precision, and pride of ownership, all of which Craig may well have offended, are illustrated by an account of his disposition of his paintings by Cézanne. (See note for this page.)

make money in summer— something I have never yet been able to do in
my life—
Please send me always if *only* a line— You can imagine I don't feel very
quiet about you—
Dearest Dreamer, this is a pretty silly world & I'm afraid you needed
someone a bit stronger than your poor Topsy to help you.[1] All my
heart's love to you— it can't do you much good though can it . . .

———————

So it was, calling him "Dearest Dreamer" at last, saying he had
needed someone "stronger" than herself, that finally, in so many
words (yet, one feels, not fully facing the finality they implied
even though it was she herself who said them), she admitted her
heart's love was not what Craig needed—or wanted.

For a time she still struggled to help him as he wanted to be helped,
and to write as before.

——— *CD 197* ———
BAUR AU LAC
ZÜRICH

[July or August 1907]

Dearest— They have given me one of our old rooms here which makes
me extra homesick for You—
It is Thunderstorming as usual— very Beautiful lake ruffled with white-
caps— Am going over now to try & arrange about lights & curtain. The
Eternal question— O dear— 'Why was I born with a different face?'[2]
Write me—
I feel one billion five thousand & 6 million miles away from you—
I will try for a week in Venice after Baden—
Must have something or will die— too much German summer & this con-
tinual travelling—
Write me . . .

[1] Note by Craig: "All this is Elizabeth's influence."
[2] William Blake. See note for this page.

———— *CD 196* ————

Baur au Lac
Zurich
[July or August 1907]

Dear Love— Your letter from *some wheres*— you don't give the address— just arrived. I'm afraid you don't get my letters! Otherwise you
would have rec. the one asking you to write here— so I will send these
lines reg. to make sure. Did you rec. the 200 marks from Berlin? I
haven't written much because I have been so frightfully disappointed
with this summer. If I had been able to send you what I wanted & felt
your plans progressing as you wanted I would have written *chapters*. I
do so want to see the first number of the Mask, & I'm afraid you haven't
been able to get it out.[1]
I wish I was up in the Marble Mountains too—[2] Fashionable?
It is Horrific here—
I dance Munich 20 & 22— address Hotel Continental—
Pray the Gods some sheckles come in— at present the entire firm is
Bankrupt. Can't I see you after Baden 24th? I must run & dance now—
Oooo————!
I don't like fings, & the poor verkauf[3] isn't good, they say—
That too—
Oooo————
No wonder I can't write—
. . . *Why* didn't you put your address? I must send this to Florence . . .

———— *CD 198* ————
Badischer Hof, Hotel et Bains de la Cour de Bade
baden-baden

[Between 24–30 August 1907]

Dearest Love— Every fibre in my being wants to take the train & come
to you but I am not coming for reasons. I see before I can help you I

[1] The first issue of *The Mask* was to appear in March 1908.
[2] Craig had perhaps been visiting one of the Tuscan seaside resorts near the
marble quarries of Carrara.
[3] G., "sale."

must become a great deal stronger myself. I am going to devote myself
to one thing now, & that is— Bank account.[1] Nothing can be accomplished
without a sure foundation of *Capital*—
Danced here in open air— of course it *rained*, & the *next* day *hot*. What a
climate—
Mr. Magnus is much better than most agents we have had, but I am
trying to find a responsible manager to book next season quick & solid.
They have asked me to drive in a decorated carriage in the flower fest
here! Perhaps I will. I dance Zurich 30, & Munich Sept. 1 & 3.
I am now about 2000 marks in the bank— it's all a bit absurd— I ought to
have 100,000 & more, & I mean to *very* soon. Watch Topsyme—
I'm awakened to the necessity of Capital & I'm going to get it—
Send me a sure address & I will send you a check—
Darling heart— what a summer!
Baby is splendid . . .

——— *CD 199* ———
GRAND HOTEL CONTINENTAL
MÜNCHEN

[Postmarked 5 September 1907]

Dearest— I have been spending my time here rehearsing my orchestra &
attending the Wagner festspiel— a sort of Music Jauche[2]—
I dance again tomorrow night & then have no other engagements. I am
much in need of a rest & if possible from financial standpoint I will come
to Venice & bathe for a week— Will you meet me there?
I went to see the Intendant of the Opera about the Kunst Theatre here—
for 1908, but he couldn't give me much information. I will see some other
people— It is simply astonishing the utter lack of intelligence everywhere— We are living in a sort of Dark Age—
The principles of Beauty & Harmony are completely ignored—
I remarked the audience here & what goes on on the stage seem about on
the same level—
I don't know what hotel I will stay at in Venice but will register my
address at Cook's—

[1] Note by Craig: "So she went on to Venice!!!"
[2] Very pejorative: "musical swill."

I am longing for a sight of the Sea— to lie on the Sands—
My public here is small but enthusiastic—
Will you meet me at Venice? Yes . . .[1]

———————————

There is an unsent draft answer by Craig.

———— *CD 271* ————

To Isadora—
Sep. 15, 1907

[Florence][2]
Not sent.
Sunday

This printing[3] done upstairs— nothing wonderful— but considering the machine, creditable.

I sent you a telegram last week in answer to your asking me if I didn't want to come to see you in Venice— didn't you know, that you asked? I sent telegram to you c/o Cooks. Did you remember *you* gave me that address?

I am going down to the city to make drawings of the wooden models of the Duomo made by the architect— and which are preserved in the museum. They assist me very much, no masters being about to go to.

The more I see of the structure of these old works the more I see that one must reverence the *least* manifestation of these old artists— not merely skip on to the *greatest*— not to India except through Persia— not to Persia but via Greece, not to Greece but through Italy— not even to Italy but through Germania— till one comes back to starting in Dull old Britain and slowly *slowly* creeping Eastwards— so that one fine morning, one can catch the sun napping. I suppose I shall hear from you soon. I shall be only glad to hear that you are at last rested— all nervousness banished— and all restlessness gone— I am no more restless— no

[1] Note by Craig: "No."

[2] All headings, except the word "Sunday," added later.

[3] The letterhead: a drawing of trees and the words "35 Via San Leonardo Firenze Italia."

more nervous— I *hum* like a sphere which has got into its acre of firmament and goes *with*, not against, the rest of the constellations.

Only true loneliness which is not seen, not felt by others but is an *internal, eternal joy* can submit to play the game for its own sake— the sake of the *game* not the sake of the *goal*. The game is to encircle the earth, to press one's lips upon the face of the world— that is called "thanking one's maker," or "filial love." Only that is LOVE. All else is Death. Where are those who with me will encircle the earth? without persuasion, to share the lovely and responding face and *lips of the world*.

Indeed indeed *alone*.
EGC   Whoop!

————————

Meanwhile, Isadora had arrived in Venice.

————— *CD 201* —————
HOTEL ROYAL DANIELI
VENISE

[8 September 1907]

Dear Love— I am so *tired* if I don't rest I will be ill— Don't you want to come here— It's most divinely beautiful. If you don't I'll come & see you as soon as I get my breath—
Only the faithful Fanny [illegible last name] is with me here. I travelled all last night— am dead tired & *hungry* for Beauty & it's lovely here. If you were only here— well if you don't come I'll come & see you as soon as I'm alive again. I've seen only tiresome things this summer, & now O the Heavenly domes against the Sky— I feel like a mortal transferred to Paradise—
Art & Nature both together here—
O— wouldn't you like to ride with me in a Gondola?
Address me Cook's Bureau, Piazza San Marco, as I won't stay in this hotel.[1]
Love Love Love—

Isadora

[1] Perhaps a reference to its high prices. But an international diva like Isadora had to stay in a *"palace,"* and who can begrudge her the Danieli after the summer she had passed?

------ CD 202 ------

Venice
[September 1907]

Dear Love— Do come here if only for 2 days, it is so wonderful—
Venice at its loveliest beyond mortal dreams—
I bathe in the sea & am feeling so much better & stronger. If at the end
of the week you don't come I will & see you— *if*[1] you want me. Do you?

Your Topsy—

O the Sunset & the Moonlight— all a bit maddening—

------ CD 203 ------

[September 1907]

Dearest— the sky & all red!— O Wonderful City— Do come here if only
for 3 days?[2]
It is so lovely—
I am intoxicated with Beauty— Sun— Color— & the swish of the Gondola waves—

Your
Topsy in Venice
I love *you*

------ CD 204 ------
HOTEL ROYAL DANIELI
VENISE

[September 1907]
Will stay here after all
as all else crowded

Dearest— Have been living in a dream of Blue Sky & Sea on figs &
cream! It is so good after so much Deutschland!

[1] The word "if" is underlined fourteen times.
[2] Note by Craig: "How had I 1000 lire to pay for 3 days to & from Venice?"

I was famished for Beauty— It is wonderful here— You ought to see it all. I dined last night with the Princesse de Polignac[1] . . . I sat next to Prince Francis of Teck. Topsy me in High Life!

The days glide by here like the gondolas— Wish you were here— Write me . . .

In the insouciant air of this letter one senses for the first time a significant blunting of Isadora's sensitivity to Craig's situation: he had been too long insensitive to her own.

I then decided [Craig wrote later, in another account of his life in Florence] to go on with the work but alone. Immediately I took a house— took assistants— started "The Mask"— cut my "*black figures*"— & began to ascend a far more difficult path than any Isadora was aware of.

It led away from her. About a month later she suddenly arrived in Florence: expected to find me willing to go on working with her— but she seemed to me like a sort of stranger & [in] spite of all her dear old attractions nothing could make me look on her as anything more than a wonderful dear thing, across there *on tother side of a river*.

There I put her since there she seemed to be & I never crossed over to her again.

It was by visiting Craig in his Florence workshop, and by being totally rebuffed, that Isadora was made to face at last the reality of her own recent words: that her love was, to Craig, no longer of benefit. After a certain number of days (apparently about two weeks) "glided by" in Venice, she had taken the Florence train. She had not seen Craig since "the strange farewell in Heidelberg" in May or June; since then she had been struggling for him. She spent only twenty-four hours in Florence, and it must have been the most wretched day of her life—so far: other, worse days were in store for her. It was her last day by arrangement with Craig. All later meetings were to be occasional and chance.

"She was here one day," Craig wrote later [CD *273*], "and went

----

[1] Nee Winaretta Singer, daughter of the sewing-machine magnate. Isadora had danced in her house in Paris.

away in tears." And, ". . . She [had] come to Florence & seen me at
work with my group of assistants . . . I had found it impossible to
kiss her as in the grand days— before Elizabeth & Augustin had
come near her to distort everything which our unity had meant to
us both from December 1904 till now . . . She had gone away crying
from the San Leonardo studios, I sitting by her side almost heart-
broken too— seeing her down to the station in Florence off to Köln
or Berlin or somewhere— all dreadfully sad to us 2 and all Elizabeth's doing." And yet again: ". . . we had parted, she in tears—
I do not weep outwardly except for joy. It was as she left my house
in Italy, Il Santuccio, and drove with me down to the station, that
she wept. Maybe she had heard that the tears of a woman soften
the heart of the man who loves her and whom she loves— but I gave
no sign that I had seen any tears: from head to foot I suffered, but
my cloak hid that."

Isadora's only known reference to that day in Florence is the
following letter.

—— *CD 205* ——
DOM-HOTEL
KÖLN, DOMPLATZ

[October 1907][1]

Dearest— A very long journey— with rain outside & tears inside. Köln
looks personification of Gloom— in rain & mist & soot. Thank the Gods
that you have Something Beautiful to look at about you— one forgets
how horrific it is here— I have a room with magenta wall covering!
Mr. Magnus arrived here all right & Stumpff will keep the contract in
spite of his threats. It begins Oct. 7— in Hague. I will send you the other
dates tomorrow. Dear Ted you have a funny effect on your Topsy!
You fill me with a Longing & Pain that are terrible. I felt I would rather
die than leave Florence, & each jog of the train was like torture. It is
probably better that I am not there. I have no strength when I am near
you— I only want to fly into you & die. It is the music of Tristan that

---

[1] Note by Craig: "She came & I couldn't say 'how late you come'— but we
had been parted at Heidelberg by Elizabeth & 'ambition' & I was *alone*. This
she must have seen & felt—"

you do not approve of at all, and it is the most horrible suffering— I am *two* people really, & each would be fairly decent if the other wasn't there but the combination is frightful—
Your house in Florence is Beautiful— there is nothing in it but it is filled with Beauty— I can't tell you all I think about it—
I am very tired from the long journey & will tumble into bed now— All my heart's love to you— & what I can't express—[1] . . .
Remember me to Mr. & Mrs. Carr— They are *splendid*.[2]

> Your
> Isadora

In addition to showing her, in Florence, that their "kissing had come to an end," Craig had apparently preached to Isadora the merits of a life of renunciation. The terms of his sermon are not known, but Isadora wrote him rejecting it.

[1] Note by Craig: "My darling— I know— I had shown you that our kissing had come to an end because I felt mortally hurt— FORGIVE ME I PRAY YOU— I too had a heart."

Although this might indicate that even Craig, in later years, felt an occasional twinge at the thought of that day in Florence, he was adept at finding explanations of his behavior that were soothing to himself. In a note written in May 1943 he says:

> I think that I deliberately made her think ill of me. I think I did this that she & I (she whom I loved and I who I knew she loved) might get out of our muddle— *we were getting in each other's way*. Strange but true— for we were made for each other. She couldn't fit in to me— I couldn't dream of her doing that— Her genius could fit into nothing— & although *like a woman* she wouldn't have minded at all if I could have fitted into her place of things, I was not able to do that. She would later have seen the distress that such an act would have brought about & then there would have been no redress. So there was only one thing to do which was to slowly make her critical of me & this I did. I think that's what was behind her move to Paris & the subsequent life she led there. It was better than what might have been— a life together *because we feared to part*.

[2] Michael Carr was a painter. He and his wife had come to live with Craig— "the proposal being," says Edward A. Craig, "that Carr, who was a very practical man, should help Craig to construct and manipulate the model stages for his experiments, while his wife looked after them both and filled in time by translating from the Dutch an enormous book on the history of the Javanese shadow theatre."

------- *CD 206* -------
HOTEL DES INDES
LA HAYE

[October 1907]

Dearest— I have been having awful time with Mother— Wild horses would not hold her & she has left now for London. I spent a small fortune in Drs. & nurses trying to hold her to no avail—

I leave tomorrow to dance Leeuwarden tomorrow night— Groningen the night after, but business is not good here. I rec. only 400 gulden for Rotterdam last night— Stumpff keeps railing for a new programme but where have I had the time or peace necessary to make one.

No dear I don't approve of your "give up Life to have it"— it sounds too Christian— & anyway it's a good enough plan to begin when one is sixty—

Go & see Duse & be *nice* to her— Don't expect such wonders of people— our ancestors were only lately throwing coconuts at each other's heads & swinging by their curly tails—

I am pretty tired— will go to bed—
I love you any way & every way . . .

Your Isadora

There is a strange draft by Craig in reply to Isadora's "Don't expect such wonders of people."

------- *CD 272* -------

Florence. October 17, 1907

And so I expect too much of people.[1] And I forget the fact that we have only begun to emerge from the ape stage.

Emerge do you call it most wise one. Rather do I think we have gone back a stage or two since we hung by the tail and caught fleas as an art.

[1] Note by Craig: "How can I expect too much when I have daily proof of more than I expect—?

Then we animalized unconsciously.

Today we are conscious about it all— and are no less animals.

Today rather than be patient with our comfortable conscious ape tricks we should fire up and at any rate paint a little romance, a little picture of an Ideal—

Even the savages did that— and called it God—

No Darwin*ism* for me, though Darwin for ever—

NO, Baby Isadora; all things which can reason (even a little bit) *Desire* a God— an Ideal— and no amount of calm materialism can drive that out of man.

Woman as a rule being the most material packet of goods in this earth, makes a good effort to kill the Desire for an Ideal.

So she would create Peace Congresses— and is now creating Socialism and is trying to break the man of his worship of king— monarchy—

SHE

stars and gods— that he may have no other gods but *HER*. And she will succeed until she reaches the artist and then she will utter a shriek and like the Sphinx— will throw herself off the Cliff—

Commonsense— conscious materialism— are fine things— but they are the dough of the bread and need leavening—

I could tell you some fairy stories— but you don't believe in fairies do you. You believe in monkeys—

Bless your simplicity.

I am (or should be) fully aware that a long and tedious meandering upon a worn-out theme can only create a feeling of passionate weariness in the listener— but I write more to see my own writing, and to create a feather feeling in myself, than to attempt to awaken sympathy for that mood in you.

Besides, you detest a servile affection for any special mood— you are generous to all your moods, are you not, Rainbow?

You were put in the heavens as a sign to all the moods Red, Blue, and Yellow that they could unite without loss.

And, Rainbow, you will not vary will you— and you will not command the seas to become red— nor the sun to be come blue— nor the thistles and the weeds to become reasonable.

You will leave all as it was left.

No?—

"No. I have neither seen nor heard from Madame Duse. I suppose she is in Paris— occupied in forgetting her promises of 1906. I have not heard from her since I left Nice last March."

The above goes into our diary.

Ah, it is only a blunt & idiotic truth— — but never mind the book shall glow with beautiful & intelligent truths also. Such as "Isadora made a promise in 1906 1907 and kept it. That was because Elizabeth helped her to remember." The page will glow with brightness— —

No. Madame Duse is not a lover of the art of the Theatre— she loves herself . . . How right that is too—

It justifies the Art. & it justifies all the *wreck* which I hope shortly to make of the old theatre & *all* its inhabitants. But before I begin I must go to the mountains— & clear & clean myself from all the moths & spiders & webs which try to play at "Fool" with me. The cold will freeze them off & they'll *die* & then I shall tingle & be warm *inside*.

How wise to believe as you do— what one sees—

How *Rash* to swear in what one has not seen as I do— but how exhilerating— how dangerous too— and how sweet—

I swear by all I see not— I *love* all I do not see— that keeps me in a state of natural intoxication. But you consider that to be both child's play and humbug. But do you want me to murder and hang and quarter all around me and myself. No— leave us our dreams for the sake of our lost tails— In remembrance of our lost forests— for by our Dreams we recreate a gross nature into an ideal paradise. And when our existence can be one long and unbroken Dream then— Happiness—

[Last part of page torn off]

———————

Two more drafts by Craig were written about this time.

——— *CD 273* ———

[Florence][1]

I.D.   Oct. 24, 1907

Not sent. Rec'd. a loveless letter from her— so why send this—

Profound Comrade.
   dear Topsy
      I have to announce to you that I have today made a new recruit.

[1] Other headings added later by Craig.

He is about 20— another Ducci[1]— he was drawing my caricature on the white walls of the Piazza when I discovered him. He had collected a crowd. He drew with a lump of charcoal.

Shamefaced at having been caught in the act, I had to put him at ease by drawing his portrait on the wall— huge success— delight of crowd. Oh— I'm getting on. Always believed I was for the crowd.

Next day I sent Ducci to make enquiries of him. He is motherless— fatherless— homeless— hopeless not a bit of it— but pennyless.

He is now dressed in one of my old suits and boots— sandals later when we can afford them.

He is to become our Cook and assist the carpenter. He will also finally become our scenepainter. For he handles charcoal with courage and joy.

He tells us his father left him long ago— if true the sooner all fathers leave their sons the better for the sons. So it would seem. He is under Ducci's supervision and has only a trifle better food and warmth than usual— No sudden changes for my boys— no no no. Wise owl Edward! He is content to stay with us for LIFE— no contract. For food and clothes and house and as he says an occasional penny extra for himself. He seems as if he was in Heaven—

But isn't it lucky for me— for he can and does work like a Trojan, and all these women cooks are asses and talk and cry and mope and demand 30 lire per month at the striking of the clock.

Soon I hope to have a house of men and all the dear little ladies safely interred.

Then we shall be asked out to dances— me and my brave Mike [Michael Carr]— Ducci and Bruno and the rest— and we shall all learn to flirt pretty with de gals.

You don't write to me I notice. You don't forget me, do you?

I should be very much tempted to fall into many states of love here, even in Florence, if I did not remember that I am Gordon Craig.

Did you know that.

And when I remember that I care no longer for the grape or the other fruits. And then my pleasure is a pain— and I sigh and say "Well there *is* a girl for Gordon Craig but only one— all the others are for Teddy and

---

[1] The first Ducci (Gino) was a postman and an amateur printer who had his own small printing press. He installed his press in Craig's villa and worked at odd hours on small jobs like letter-headings, pamphlets and bookplates. (EAC, 233)

I am no longer him. And if that girl doesn't love you, you would be a fool to try and fill her place: leave it empty: it's easier."

And so with another sigh I cross the bridge at a swinging step.

And Gordon Craig sends his greetings to that girl Isadora Duncan and wants to know more. He wants to know more about Isadora Duncan. He has heard a lot— and knows just a little but would like to know much more— though, he dare not hope— ALL. Only the Journalist wants to know *all*. "*All*" is completion and repletion; and the point just *short* of all is intoxicated somnambulism. That's Heaven.

Isadora Duncan I love you— and I ought not to say it— for it is almost ALL.

There is a landscape out through that window in front of me. A landscape . . . rather call it a Heaven too. I have now moved into the room which you had[1] and am very comfortable there— my table faces the side window— my bedroom close at hand.

Downstairs the Theatre has grown so fat and fine that it or I had to leave— so I left. A performance is to be ready in 4 weeks from now.[2] The order has gone forth— and all the workmen are on their metal. We shall but call it an experiment for it is no more than that. It is rather childish perhaps— and perhaps children will take to it. If they do I defy the critics— and announce on my Posters

> FOR CHILDREN
> TO NIGHT
> SOMETHING TO SEE
> Via San Leonardo. 35

Anyhow profound comrade "Battles *are lost* in the same spirit in which they are *won*." are they not? How goes your battle my champion? Are you winning? Send your thoughts occasionally to Gordon Craig— more of them. I know the old ones— now *more*. The old words were lovely— now more. New words— new thoughts— always eternal birth— just for Gordon Craig his sake.

AMEN.[3]

[1] Note by Craig: "Yes. She was here for one day and went away in tears. I remember. EGC. 1944."

[2] Craig does not say what this performance "for children" was to be.

[3] A long note by Craig follows [CD *270*]: "This letter of October 24, 1907 and others of Sep. and Oct. Nov. Dec. were written by me when I lived at Il

——— *CD 274* ———

[Florence]

To I.D. Oct. 27, 1907[1]

Write no more to me— Think about me no more— I no longer exist for
you *since that for which I live is less than nothing to you.* I am ashamed.
Red hot with shame that I ever thought you part of that. All my letters to
you lie here unsent. I shall write more I believe— I fear. I believe too I

Santuccio— San Leonardo just outside Florence. It was a house with a lot of
olive trees at the back; and an open piazza in little, a square one, led onto these
trees which were on a gently sloping bit of hill. [Here Craig has drawn a
diagram of the "piazza in little"—the farm courtyard.] In this Piazza the
peasants worked and made their stacks of hay or piles of beans or barrels of
olives— Each season a new work was begun with clockwork regularity— I had
a small garden of my own.

"I moved from Loeser's cottage to this place on . . . anyhow before September 15th, 1907 . . .

"Had some chairs and tables and empty boxes. Bought some 2nd hand beds.

"It was up hill from the centre of Florence— I walked it often— to supper
in F. and back at night. ¾ of an hour's walk. I was youngish—

"It was at the house I made the 1st black figures— Hunger was it? Hamlet
and Demon. Electra. Moses. Hecuba. Dancing girl. Girl with Ball etc.—

"It was from this house I sent Mrs. Carr to speak with Mme Duse (as Mrs.
Carr was a perfect French conversationalist) and sent D. a present of some
etchings. (See here enclosed letters)

"It was here I began to make the screens and stage— here too I prepared
many essays etc. for the Mask and many wood cuts for same— (not yet out
in 1907— appearing in March, 1908—)

"So it was here that I did some good work, and a good deal of it.

"It was here I experienced what it meant for friends to fall away—

"This young man Bruno was a good lad but wishing to impress me he staged
a burglary one night acting the burglar and chasing said burglar and being
wounded by said burglar— the window door was broken in— all in confusion
but nothing was stolen.

I did much good work here at San Leonardo."

[1] Heading added later. On the envelope of this draft Craig has written:
"Oct. 27th and October 28th 1907. Now in Moscow I reread this Oct. 27, 1908.
I remember—! but only as in a pointless dream— nightmare."

shall not send them. It is all my fault— Now for *this* instant I am beyond all misery miserable— disgusted and bruised to death— & Now——I forget.[1]

Sometimes I have thought so much to ask advice from you, and then I knew you could not advise. Advice must be command: and commands must be *Technical* to be of any value.

All men even the duffers know about *Patience*— and development of character and the rest— to become HARD like stone says Nietzsche— to become generous and warm like fire says Walt and both inspire but neither *show*.

I want the man or voice or vision that will *show* me in hard photographic fact how to do that jugglery of turning water into wine.
[Part of page missing]

I begin to think there is a regular barrier against allowing me either to produce as I like or to write as I like.

If the productions are impractical the writings are essentially harmless.
[Part of page missing]

What is the matter with England that only its *Socialists* may be *progressive*. Why don't they admit *Reform* rather than later be swallowed by Revolution. It seems stubborn ignorant and strangely short sighted.

———————

Craig writes in one of his later notes that after their farewell in Florence Isadora became "quite as rudderless as she was before we met— 1904." Post cards he received from Groningen and Utrecht in Holland, and a letter from Warsaw (a city she had already found depressing in the past), convey the feeling of interior hollowness she was undoubtedly experiencing as she resumed her tours.

[1] This first portion of the letter exists also in a second draft, almost identical.

————— CD 207 —————

[Post card, Groningen to
Florence, October 1907]

En route— Rainy— rainy— rainy— dancing like a Marionette in fits—
Topsy

————— CD 208 —————

[Post card, Utrecht to
Florence, 10 October 1907]

On the way to Rotterdam— been up since six o'clock—Love Topsy

————— CD 209 —————
HOTEL BRISTOL
VARSOVIE

[November 1907]

Dearest— I am returning to Berlin tomorrow after 3 evenings here. You
haven't written for an age and your last letter was rather enigmatic.
I have been en fête perpetual here— champagne & dancing— it was the
only alternative to suicide. The only way possible to stand Warsovie
was to be continually *drunk*!
I will be now a week in Berlin without dancing & dance again at Munich
the 20th. I will see Baby tomorrow again. I saw her a few hours passing
by Berlin. She is wonderfully strong, in perfect Health, & *Sweet*—
Mama insisted on taking the steamer to America & she is now on her way
there. She has cost me a small fortune & now I think dear Brother Gus
may take care of her for a time.
You do not write me so I don't know what you are doing— Did you see
Duse? & how is she? I will write you again from Berlin— address me
Palace Hotel.
My Head is a bit dizzy—
I have been living here exclusively on champagne & caviar & dancing

the Mazurka with *10* young Polish Counts— all of them quite mad.
I send you my Love—

    Your
      Topsy

Beside the word "*drunk!*" in this letter Craig has written, "Oh—
big Fool." But he must have known that Isadora was trying here to
impress him with her desperation: she had never before written in
this way. He knew that she liked champagne but drank it to enhance,
not spoil, performances. There is no evidence that at this time she
drank to excess, though the post card that follows does seem to have
been written at a moment of not too happy conviviality. Isadora's
drinking habits have been the subject of conflicting reports. Letters
written by her toward the end of her life, when there was considerable gossip about her drinking, show her often distraught, at times
even suicidal, but never as an alcoholic. According to both Irma
Duncan and Victor Seroff, the gossip was greatly exaggerated. Mrs.
William A. Bradley, who with her husband was closely associated
with Isadora during her last years until her death (the Bradleys had
encouraged Isadora to write her memoirs and were her friends and
literary agents), has said: "I do not think that one can speak of
alcoholism in Isadora's case. It was after the loss of her children and
her separation from Singer that she began to seek occasional consolation in the vague forgetfulness that comes with drinking. But she
did not drink when she was happy, and when she was dancing. She
certainly liked Goebler champagne and drank it when she could, but
particularly during her last years, when, no longer dancing, she was
unhappy and felt herself somewhat forgotten. Alcohol was for her
a *remedy*, a pleasant remedy, and she so considered it: she refused,
for example, to allow any to be given to the young piano-accom-
panist, Yasha, whom she had brought back with her from Russia,
saying that he was not unhappy and had no need of it."
On November 20, 1907, Isadora danced in Munich; on the picture
post card of a restaurant, she sent Craig, among the more or less

coherent messages[1] of her table companions (two of them her sister Elizabeth and the agent Mery whom she has mentioned earlier), one of her own [CD *210*]: "O Ted—Forgive me—I am sowing the wild oats I forgot to sow in my youth—Topsy."

"Unkind—& *foolish too!*" Craig noted on the card, and he composed a censorious, semicoherent reply, which he may or may not have sent.

———— CD 275 ————

[Florence]
November, 1907.

Elizabeth— SNTG whoever that is— Snowdrop and Isadora I greet you all back again— My hand is steadier than the whole 4—judging from the writing of the 4.

(1) Oats wild or any sort are greatly necessary to be sown. Sow on Isadora— you know how useful oats are— so many bray out that they hunger for them.

(2) SNTG— you say there is nothing so difficult but life—. That is essentially German but neither Bismarck nor Bach ever were heard to say so.

(3) Elizabeth. being more *faithful* than a woman was ever expected (or able) to be you must win all our *admiration*. My love— my love— if it wasn't for the houses in between. I am the one who is building the houses on the corpse of my ancient love and which rise as a growing barrier between me— and my love—

   This will not be understood by reading.

(4) Lastly Snowdrop. sending love through her mother— the love has its little feathers all covered with the chaff from those tame wild oats——

   Silenzio my Snowdrop! it is not necessary to say a word. Adio amici mio—

You seem to be eating and drinking well— I hope your socks and shoes have no holes in them— I look forward to meeting you again— but you must have keen eyes or you will not recognize me.

[1] The other messages are, or seem to be: "2 + 2 = 5 oder [or] 3— Mery"; "Dear Teddy, here is your Elizabeth"; "There is nothing so difficult als [as] life! SVYG"; and, in Isadora's hand, "Snowdrop— Love."

2 + 2 make neither 5 nor 3
2 + 2 make nothing— 1 makes everything

1 is the only Impersonal number. Personality and Art are opponents. This is shown to be true by looking back across History.

The Impersonal and an empty stomach suits art— suits Life— suits everything but the entirely idiotic and trembling ME. Me little me or great me that is the Personality

[The above two paragraphs are crossed out and the following is written across them]:

if I may be permitted to advance a theory 2 + 2 make nothing. 1 alone makes the Earth and all that there is in it.[1] And if I may be again humored I would advance ½ a Reason for this. That better-half Reason is, that the figure or number 1 is an Impersonal symbol. Personality absorbs. Impersonality creates. Forgive my conclusion and don't think about it.

A few days later, from Stuttgart, Isadora sent Craig another picture post card [CD *211*], saying: "You don't write me any news of you . . . address Grünewald— Baby is lovely."

To this also Craig composed a reply, one which shows him at his most uncompromising about his art—and, toward Isadora, at his most unkind and disingenuous.

———— CD 276 ————

Florence   Saturday
To Isadora   Nov. 30, 1907

You send me a postcard my dear girl to say that I don't write you any news of myself.

But I never have from you a list of future addresses. Most tours, when managed by a real business man like Magnus, are able to announce where they will be at *least* a month in advance. Even when I tried to rise to the

[1] These words are difficult to read; they might be: "and all that therein isn't."

Impresario occasion, I was able often to let people know 3 weeks in
advance where to write to on a given date—

You see *then* I should be able to write and give you the longed-for
news of my acts, if I were warmed to it by receiving even the news of
your whereabouts. I sent a letter to you to München, "*Hotel Vier
Jahreszeiten*," and one to Elizabeth. You had better write for them or
some booby will get them instead.

Now that I know you have been in Stuttgart I can easily find you by
sending to Berlin— isn't it?

And will give you all the views that is good for you to hear.

To the beautiful Madame Duse I sent my good ambassadress Mrs. Carr—
who speaks clear and quiet French— I sent her with a letter— 2 letters—
and 6 of my best etchings. Duse made a tragedy out of the whole parcel
and made me most most proud (of myself) by refusing to look at or
even open the parcel of etchings. This is quite the Dumas *Junior* style—
NOT the old and greater man. On getting my parcel returned to me
unopened, I sat and wondered why she was so tragic about it for she
told Mrs. Carr she thought I was a god-sent genius and necessary for
the stage and all the rest of the stuff and cried and said she wished
she could make it easy for my work to be done under even fairly comfortable circumstances— *wished* she had 100,000 francs— *wished* she
could help me— etc. etc. *and yet would not look at my etchings in which
lies my soul.* And I— I feel twice as strong as ever.

Bye the bye— she also confounded Mrs. Carr by speaking of US, you
and I, as if we were separated— What could she mean? How? Why?

I will not offend her intelligence and her heart to say that she is upset
by my letter to the London and American papers— I send you a copy
here.[1] She must let some time pass over her brow and cool it with its
truth and then she will understand that I love neither my work nor
hers— nor myself, nor her, but *IT*, the Theatre which is *degraded daily
by us all* and which bears all, and is a *Beauty*; and which some one must
speak up for and with *truth*— and entire truth—

She Duse is unwise to believe that I should be grateful for 100,000

[1] Craig's "Letter to Eleonora Duse" was printed in the Washington *Post*,
Sunday, December 1, 1907, in conjunction with an article about his work in
Florence by Francis Cotton, apparently one of the "not a few" young American writers he says had come to see him there. Both are interesting statements
of Craig's ideas about actors, marionettes, the spoken word, movement, and
stagecraft in general. The letter was reprinted in the first issue of *The Mask*,
and later (1919) in Craig's book *The Theatre—Advancing*.

francs. I should be grateful for her hand: a friend's hand. She is not honouring the enormous difficulty of the situation of the theatre by thinking it is to be made whole by plaster. The Theatre is dying— and I believe I alone am in a position to say what must be done— for so far as I can see my position is *an entirely free one* and I am not hedged in by a single compromise. I no more care for a success of the hour or the day than I care whether my friends desert me when I most need their love and assistance.

If they confound the personal me with the impersonal artist me, then I am only bitterly sorry. I thank God I am spared this bitterness more times than not. Unless my friends and championers and followers love and follow me— the real live *me*— not "*Teddy*" you know— or as Rozinay of Budapest put it, "Gordon"— but me, unless they follow me, all is impossible so far as even remembering their names— for how can what is not and never has been remember anything.

Except for my life as artist and I hope as more to be, I am non-existent. I say "do this" or "this *must* be" and a fool thinks I am suddenly grown angry and a wise man knows I am in love with my ideal and sees nothing else and likes me *better*. When I speak with fiery beliefs the young fellows would die for me, and Duse only mistakes it for so much angry noise. She mistakes a cry of pain and triumph in pain for one of anger— (Yes— a silly woman whom I supposed was wise.)

I should have been grateful to have found she left that to the fools— But she is to be excused as she is no longer 20 nor even 24.

The case of the Theatre is a violent one and needs a violent remedy. I find my friends all the same wherever I go, and my friends are the best blood in the Earth. From Spain and Budapest lately have come two young writers both keen and now afire with the flames of the hope of rescue to the Theatre. From Finland another— and from America not a few.

I am far from well for I have had so little to eat lately but *feel* splendid on it really. I rather hope to keep up the meagre diet and also rather expect to have to. It cuts both ways and suits both ways.

I go out to dinner whenever I can in my old clothes and good Lord much in tatters— sandals— and everyone is as kind as *English* can be at times. And I have issued a Portfolio of Etchings— only 30 copies even to go out. £16 or 400 Francs per Portfolio— and with that Carr and his girl shall be paid and fresh wood bought and Lunch— The little pricking difficulties of finding a new house in a month from now, and paying my poor and faithful old Ducci (when I think of his regular Post as Post-man and his possible Pension as Postman I utter a wail and a whoop!)

these sink into insignificance beside the deeper heart crumblings which are going on in my own house— my own box of a brain fed by nice warm heart blood— and getting or trying to get trim and hard for the winter months of life.

For my winter months have begun early— the frost has nipped all the old buds— buds were always sentimental nonsenses of spring sweetness— and I am ever so old today— just the right age for the task.

And now you have my news.

I want no help from the pocket. I want all the *hands* . . of friends. I can take care of the pocket business right enough, for it is the easiest part of the problem.

I am no longer afraid of anything— except that the love of my loves in which I trust— except that:

this very love may turn to hate:

unconscious love to unconscious hate:

unconscious kindnesses to unconscious acts of unkindness. — And that we all suffer under—

Well then

let us think neither of ourselves nor of one another but only each of his Ideal— and "let the bloody battle begin." The biggest Ideal must win— Life— Intensest joy— it cannot lose this—

I can let this hastily written letter go at this— At least you will not wilfully misunderstand it and put me down as crazy— You used to think Raymond crazy and you were wrong— be good better [*sic*] to yourself about such things.

————————

"If [my friends] confound the personal me with the impersonal artist me, then I am only bitterly sorry" . . . But we have had ample opportunity to see that those two "me's," and others as well, exist in Craig so closely intermingled that not to confound them is all but impossible. Because of the cruel presence of one of those "me's" in this draft, one can only hope that it—the last existing communication from Craig to Isadora for the year 1907—was, as seems to be the case, never sent.

THROUGHOUT HIS LIFE CRAIG WAS TO WRITE OF ISADORA—IN TERMS now glorifying, now reproachful. In his reproaches, she is the uncomprehending one:

She was a strange, lovely, strong creature, but it seems that I was the stronger. Perhaps she wished to see me at her knees, at her feet, and there she did not find me. I *stood*; no matter what pain I may have felt, I stood. And it is this which at first attracted her, then puzzled her—came to astonish her—and finally . . .

Whatever I may have suffered, as men ever suffer in love and, when they are artists, suffer doubly, she did not see it . . .

But when he writes about their meeting, one savors again the joy of the first letters of Isadora from St. Petersburg and Germany:

Our meeting first of all was, as I have already written, a marvellous coming together. Not because I saw in her someone who fulfilled my ideas of the perfect dancer, the interpreter of unspoken things, the Figure of Figures for the stage. That may or may not have contributed some slight extra-ness to what I felt in 1904 in Berlin. That coming together was so little to do with art—theatre—dreams. That coming together was a marvellous thing. No small words or thoughts can tell of that. How so? How shall I say how?

Suppose one had been in a world with ones other half—once—and that world so wonderfully perfect; and then suppose that world had dissolved and time had passed over one, and one had woken up in another world—but one's other half not there. One would have taken to the new existence as cheerfully as possible, to one's new state. If once one had been a king and now found oneself just a boy in a house, eating and being spoilt, one would fit into all that; and as good things came along to make things more and more jolly and gay, one would have come to find the new world quite pleasant. Then one grew up, began to work, fell in "love"—a fall indeed—picked oneself up and one would soon be laughing again. Years go by, and one seriously becomes in the true state of love. But Life, making sport of us, makes it difficult: it becomes more difficult—but one lives. Life wins. Then, suddenly, the marvellous happens—that other half is standing beside one; she too has found her way, after all these centuries and over all those hills and rivers and seas—and here she is—and here am I. Is not that marvellous? It is quite "impossible," being so very marvellous—with what a cry we come together . . .

"She was filled with enthusiasm (besides genius) for her work at 20— 25— 30," Craig wrote. "But slowly she began to wink the other eye." That Isadora's work gradually deteriorated from lack of enthusiasm after she turned thirty—that is, after the break with Craig—does not seem to have been the case: it will be up to future biographers of her later years to tell the tale. But if she temporarily felt that she was, in her tours, "like a Marionette dancing in fits," the events of the preceding months were to some extent responsible. That the battering by Craig—by the tornado of egocentricity that was Edward Gordon Craig—had permanent effects on her personality and way of life is indubitable.

The love that was born in Berlin and snuffed out in Florence was never definitively declared by either Isadora or Craig to survive only in memory. Neither of them could forbear to speak, from time to time, and in varying ways, of their "love that would endure forever"; in one of the later pages of *Book Topsy*, Craig says: "To *us* then our love seemed & was after 1907 & later after 1909 a big torturing thing— so desperate a thing that at times we felt quite mad." The fact that neither of them found another love partner of even remotely comparable radiance, as they proceeded to lead separate lives and yet remained in touch, did endow their bond with a special kind of permanence. What the remainder of this volume will recount is not the full details of the career of either of them (that must be left to biographers), but rather their subsequent meetings— in person, in thought, and by letter—and the continuing influence of their association on each of them.

From now on they were to see each other only occasionally, and the remaining letters that Isadora sent to Craig refer chiefly to three episodes that involved them both: her bringing him together in 1908 with Konstantin Stanislavski, the director of the Moscow Art Theatre, for whom he would prepare the production of *Hamlet* that remains his most famous work; the death of their daughter Deirdre ("Snowdrop") and Deirdre's half-brother Patrick in 1913; and an emotional reunion between them in Rome in 1919. The year after that there were a few notes written in Paris; then all is silence between them except for two isolated, one-way missives just before Isadora's death, which will be related in their place.

Isadora, Craig and Stanislavski

In December 1907, about two months after the farewell in Florence, Isadora left Berlin for Russia. She gave three performances in St. Petersburg, whence she sent Christmas and New Year's telegrams to Craig. There is a draft reply from him to Isadora, with a barbed allusion to what he probably with some justice considered—and what Isadora's next letter shows that she herself was perhaps beginning to consider—her thralldom to Elizabeth and the school.

––––– *CD 277* –––––

1907. Late December. Florence.[1]

Christmas over thank God—
    Now for the play.
And thank you for remembrance telegram— I could only write to you to Berlin as I didn't know your address— I see it's St. Petersburg— Besides I haven't had any money for quite a long time & have had to borrow &

[1] Date and notes added by Craig in 1944.

now that's all gone & I have been obliged to give up the villa.[1] Where the theatre can be put I do not know. It was folly to commence— utter folly to dream of being born— what I could have been thinking about even my stars cannot tell me.

Still all is well— quite quite well— for I am actually alive— & the Carr's staunch in all the difficulties—[2]

I think we can say one is lucky so long as one is alive & can walk, see & smell— the smell of the wet streets invigorates— the beauty of the wretchness in the streets invigorates—

For to speak with reason nothing golden can come of my work until a businessman comes along—

Everyone is & has been as kind to me as they could be— they have visited my work & been pleased & said so— what more could I expect.

I alone know how good it is & how bad— I alone realize how long it will take for one man to lay the *foundations* of the work.

Duse has been very kind— she has not come to see me— nor sent me any word about the great things she spoke about last year— but she did *speak* about them[3]— that you remember— & in that she *intended* kindness—

Florence is paved with tender hard stones—

"— — when I look each one starts; when I speak I offend

Then I'm silent & passive, & lose every friend"[4]

And I hope you are having a carefully planned tour so that Elizabeth's school can flourish— flourish— & so that you can be happy in that.

For my own failure so far at this superhuman task I ought to blame no one but myself— Everyone has been angelic to us— some throwing us bones now & then, upon which we have pounced ravenously— I have been invited to Budapest where it appears they spend thought about that mare's nest The Theatre—

[1] Note by Craig: "Via San Leonardo." In his biography of his father, however, Edward A. Craig says (p. 241): "It was getting very cold on the hill, so Craig found warmer living quarters in a flat in the city, overlooking the river Arno and adjoining the famous Ponte Vecchio—the new address was No. 2 Lung' Arno Acciaioli; but he still kept Il Santuccio going, with an old carpenter coming in to help on sunny days."

[2] Note by Craig: "the Carrs not for long." Edward A. Craig says (p. 241): "Michael Carr and his wife were not paid for weeks, and Michael was so run down from overwork and undernourishment that they had to leave."

[3] Note by Craig: "to I.D., to Mrs. Carr."

[4] Concerning these lines by Blake, see note for p. 256.

As if my work had anything in common with anything on the boards of the Theatre.

Indeed it is so clear to me that no one who loves beauty can enter a theatre—I used to hope in a kind of hopeless way that this was not so—but I give in entirely—I was wrong—the theatre needs no beauty—no Law—"its Vulgarity increases, it will ever fall into nothingness"—to caricature poor Keats' lines.

Whether or not the above letter was mailed, Craig did telegraph Isadora to St. Petersburg, and during the Russian holidays she wrote him a pair of letters that vary the same themes.

——— *CD 216* ———
GRAND HOTEL D'EUROPE
ST. PÉTERSBOURG

[January 1908]

Dearest—Here I am at the North Pole—I have a week free on account of holidays here. Am spending my time reading the History of Ivan the Terrible & rushing about in a sleigh over the snow & ice. Everything here reminds me of you & I would give a good deal to have you open the door & hear you say "Topsy!"

Baby is lovely. She is beginning to walk & talk & *dance*— she turns solemnly around in a circle saying Wau Wau & that is her dance.

I don't know if you are in Florence. You wrote saying you might be coming to Berlin. Did you rec. the two checks I sent from Munich bank?

I spent two wonderful mornings in the Hermitage—remember the Rembrandts?— & will go again tomorrow—but how much more glorious things were when you showed them to me—

Magnus does his best to do business for me, but my business seems a very impossible thing—Here I have given three evenings for a *fix sum* of 1500 roubles an evening. Imagine our astonishment when we learn the Impresario takes in 6700 rbls a night!—and here the hotel, voyage, etc. are so expensive. There isn't fearfully much over—

I went to see an awful play in the Kunst Theatre— all copied from
Aubrey Beardsley's pictures & played against *black velvet* with very
little light— it was *ghastly*— made me quite ill.[1]
Everything is snow here & it is dark at 3 o'clock & so cold one can
hardly walk out. I go each morning to a Swedish institute for gymnastics
in order to keep alive—
Then I buy books & read—
What a funny life!—
I don't write to you, because you seem so very far away, & your letters
are not very human or easy to understand— but you are almost always in
my thoughts except when I am very intoxicated & in a merrie company
which I frequent now & then from sheer despair—
Send me one word that I can read— just say "Topsy I'd like pretty well
to see you" (or something like that)— but perhaps you wouldn't— & I
wouldn't blame you— I'm nothing but a silly old dancing dervish, always
en route— I can't help it— it seems to be my cussed fate, & I haven't
been able to help you much either for your life or your work, but
Patience— perhaps I will be able to some day—[2]
I give one more evening here the 9 of Jan. & go the 10th to Moscow
(Hotel National), where I will give 4 matinees, as they could not get
the theatre for evenings— until about the 20th when I will return to
Berlin. Duse is coming here— perhaps I will see her in Moscow. I sent
you a telegram Chrismas & New Years— did they reach you?
The young Editor of that Moscow magazine[3] called on me & asked your
address— we talked of you over an hour— he seems very intelligent &
nice—
The waiter has just brought my lunch & then I'm going for a long drive
in the snow—
Love to you dearest— if I ever allowed myself to long for you life would
be impossible, so I don't allow it— because I've got to go on dancing— it's
my cussed fate— but I love you— & I am & always will be your

      Topsy

---

[1] Note by Craig: "So it did me when I saw it."
[2] Note by Craig: "No— only in 1904 & 5."
[3] Note by Craig: "Lykiardopolos." Michael Lykiardopoulos was, or would
become, secretary of the Moscow Art Theatre.

——— *CD 215* ———
GRAND HOTEL D'EUROPE
ST. PÉTERSBOURG

[January 1908]

Dear Love— I waited all day today for your telegram & was so Happy when it arrived. Everything here is freezing— something unthinkable, the cold. I have a week free on account of Holidays here. Was for a long sleigh ride today— The horses are wonderful & go like the wind, but what a sad landscape— long, long stretches of snow & finally the Sea— all frozen. I asked myself when I saw it— Why am I a dancing dervish & why am I up here at the North Pole?
I have been talking all afternoon to a big manager here about your work— You see I talk of you, I think of you always— but when I go to write to you I am overcome. Never mind, I'll write anyway— perhaps you'll come to understand what I wish— but I feel such an idiot. The same old ratatat of telegrams come in from Mama & from the School— send 1 thousand send 2 thousand at once— etc. Darn it all, School & all—
Your telegram reminded me of one I rec. from you 3 years ago when I was here & you in Berlin— & I had only known you 2 weeks or so! How I longed to get back to you, but that longing was a small thing to what I feel now. Only I feel I have been so inadequate— but I hope & hope & hope— & it must come— it will—
I will write if you like even if my letters sound idiotic. I read all last night "La Mère" of Gorki— it is the best I have read of his— & beautiful. He is at Naples, ill.
Write me if only a line. I will be 11th of Jan. till the 20th Hotel National, Moscow.
Baby *walks* talks (a little) & *dances*—

    Your
    Topsy

———————

It is not clear whether the "big manager" in St. Petersburg, with whom Isadora talked about Craig's work, was Konstantin Stanislavski, the director of the Moscow Art Theatre, but it was during this visit to Russia that Isadora and Stanislavski met. "During our talks about art," Stanislavski says in his autobiography, *My Life in Art*, "Duncan continually mentioned the name of Gordon Craig, whom she considered a genius and one of the greatest men in the contemporary theatre. 'He belongs not only to his country, but to the whole world,' she said, 'and he must live where his genius will have the best chance to display itself, where working conditions and the general atmosphere will be best fitted to his needs. His place is in your Art Theatre.' I know that she wrote a great deal to him about me and our Theatre, persuading him to come to Russia."

In his copy of *My Life in Art*, in the margin beside Stanislavski's "I know that she wrote a great deal to him about me and our Theatre . . ." Craig has written a note that says, churlishly and untruthfully: "hardly a word." About that, Isadora's next letter, written when she was back in St. Petersburg after performances in Moscow, speaks for itself.

––––– *CD 214* –––––

Address for six days—
Grand Hotel d'Europe, St. Pétersbourg
[January or February 1908]

Dearest— I have been waiting to find the time to write you a long letter about the Art Theatre in Moscow, but have been so very tired these last days. It is the intense cold exhausts one & then it grows dark at 2 o'clock— makes one feel like living underground like Siberian miners— or moles—
Mr. Stanislavsky, the régisseur of the Theatre, is a wonderful man— really Beautiful & Great— I talked with him many hours about you— He says he would love to have you come & be régisseur altogether, as he prefers to *act*. The plays for this year are all fixed, but he says if you came next August & prepared a piece Aug. & Sept. to be given in October, then if you liked & all went well you might stay with them—
They are wonderful people all of them & he is Beautiful. So kind & unassuming— a *really great* man— I have never met anyone like him—
He asked if you would write to him. I told him he should write to you first— he seems shy— said he would write you a long letter but that it would take him a couple of weeks to compose it. He wanted me to tele-

graph & ask you only to come & visit them & see if you liked them— but I didn't think you'd care to come for anything not sure. He says he would give you a perfectly free hand in the Theatre— that the actors would all follow your directions as to movements, etc. & that you could do what you liked & take all the time you liked to do it in—

All the people belonging to the Theatre are so simple & sweet & un-assuming. There are 300 pupils in the School. I told him 6000 gulden for two months. He said he would put it before the directors. He said after-wards you could take a troup from their Theatre & go on tour—

He said "Tell Mr. Craig we are very simple people, that we care nothing at all for ourselves but very much for Art & that if he will come we will all be glad to follow his ideas."

I can only repeat that he is great & simple & Beautiful— such a man as one doesn't meet with once a century—

I showed him your book & he thought it very beautiful—

He is very anxious for you to come. He is a bit afraid of your prices— The Theatre is not very rich—

I received all your letters from Grünewald in a packet & your other letters followed & I felt me very rich—

The Baby is *walking* & talking— I long to see her— & I suffer in not seeing her— but one cannot have everything & I have to pay a big price for being so 'truly famous'—

I have been reading Russian authors— Turgeneff— Tscheckoff— Tol-stoi— Gorki— all with strength & somber Beauty but O dear how sad—

This contract which promised brilliant things— The Manager says simply "I can't get theatres" & puts dates so far apart that almost everything is taken in expenses. It is always so, & what with School, Mama, Baby, my bank account never rises higher than 2000 marks!!!— but they tell me I'm a great success!

I have a wild not yet defined plan to go to Egypt!—

I dance in Odessa— which is only *18* hours from Constantinople which is only *one day* from Alexandria— I think I could make quite as much money there as here— at any rate I couldn't very well make less— & O the Joy of the Sun— Would you join me for a look at the Pyramids?

How's the lovely Polonaise?[1]

---

[1] Note by Craig: "The talk about the Polish lady— i.e. Mme. Muttermilch [*sic*], whom I saw twice & at a distance— was I confess to annoy Topsy for going so far away. I.D. is expecting me to drop my work & follow her to Egypt!!!! great Gods what is her head made of?"

Beware, take care—
Is she really so lovely— really truly *lovely*? & what had you better "do about her"?— Well, I guess neither you nor I but the lady herself will decide that. Ladies generally do & there's no much stopping them. If you can spare a month for the Pyramids, say so, and we'll make a rendezvous by the Sphinx.
I am very tired— will go to bed now. Love to you, dearest Heart— Polonaise or no Polonaise be happy & gather to you all the joy that you meet with.

>   I love you always
>   Isadora.

———————————

And Isadora wrote to Stanislavski in Moscow: "I have written to Gordon Craig. I told him about your theatre and about your own great art. But couldn't you write to him yourself? If he could work with you, it would be *ideal* for him. I hope with all my heart that this can be arranged."

WHILE ISADORA WAS IN RUSSIA DANCING AND TRYING TO ADVANCE Craig's cause, Craig drafted a letter to his friend De Vos in Holland which speaks of work, Isadora and Duse, and gives news of Ellen Terry, who had recently married James Carew, a young American actor. (She announced this, her third marriage, to her son on a picture post card showing herself and Carew at Niagara Falls: "1 March 1907. Dear Duck— This is Jim & me— we are married— long ago— You don't mind much, do you? You are happy that I'm happy, aren't you? . . . We had to keep it secret until we left off acting before American audiences— not caring to be a kind of circus. James Carew is an American— only 32 & a half but as old as the hills. I love him very dearly. I neglect no responsibilities.")

—— *CD 278* ——

2 Lungarno Acciaiuoli[1]
Firenze, Italy
February 13 or 14, 1908

Ich kann nicht gut Deutsch lesen— und schreiben— gar nichts— aber in Englisch will ich schreiben— kann und will[2]— My dear dear De Vos— I could "Howl— Howl— Howl— oh they are men of stone"[3] & women of salt— the old legend of Lot's wife who looked back— & then the pillar of salt— a chrystalised ocean of *tears*— . . . .

But I have nothing to complain of— the world leaves me— each step of my way friends fall away from me, & new friends meet me & fall away in their turn— & so the march proceed[s]— [my] only fear is that I shall be true[4] to what I love— if only I could be less true to it less agony would wrack me.

You know that I write of the work not of myself.
I should write with more patience but that you speak in your letter so feelingly & I spring forward & utter one howl—
          h o o o w w l
Yes— we have an agent for Holland. I shall have the name sent to you tomorrow— I hope he will be energetic—

Did I tell you I had built a small theatre model here— It is a beauty— built by our sweat & blood & strength & with no more than a finger's worth of outside help—

In your letter you write of
          Isadora[5]
& that's all I care to speak about—
Have I broken (gebrochen) with Isadora, you ask. Dear De Vos, you better than all else know that man does not break with love because he

---

[1] Note by Craig (added, with all his other notes, in 1944): "At this address I had but one room." Another note, at the top of the letter: "To my friend DeVos of Holland— an actor aged maybe 56." Unless Craig had heard of his mother's marriage before she wrote him the news on March 1, he has dated this letter too early.

[2] G., "I cannot read German well— or write— not at all— but I will write in English— can and will."

[3] *King Lear*, V, 3. Craig had played Oswald to Irving's Lear in 1892.

[4] Mistakenly, Craig later inserted "un" before "true."

[5] Craig has surrounded the name Isadora with drawings of flowers.

can not. That whether it is light or dark or good or wicked— cold or hot— a heavy or a happy love— it is love; and when that is said or done, all is said & done & is unalterable. I love Isadora & I love this burden which I am carrying— & though it will kill me (& it assuredly will) I shall love it for ever.[1]

At one time I *dreamed* that Isadora was by nature (or even perhaps by love) bound up with this labour of mine— this fight for the freedom of our theatre— & had she liked she could I believe have taught me to do better what I am doing only to the best of my own ability—

But little Isadora is very little & very sweet & weak & she has to do whatever her impulse tells her to do at the moment. And sometimes it is one thing, sometimes it is another— & all that she does is right[2]— & then besides she has her sister & her school which absorb all her time & attention— & then too she has to keep moving— first to Berlin— then to Moscow— then to Munich & then to Stockholm— So how can she have time to think quietly about anything— or to work with me—

Madame Duse too.

When I last saw her she said she *wanted* to do wonderful things. To act nothing but Shakespeare & Ibsen— To alter the barbarous part of the stage— & she said that on her return from South America she would do it all— & with me—

But well known women (even men) seem not to be able to do the *one thing* which would make them doubly great.

What a lot of talk, De Vos: what a lot of talk— Eh? Don't I talk? Isn't it awful—

But believe me, my friend, I am doing much more than talking here.

What result it will all have I do not know— I hope & keep on & on . . .

I have not a franc in the world at the moment I write— because I cannot act as impresario to Isadora for *ever*— that would kill me.— and so I make enough to pay for food & for 3 workmen— carpenter— assistant— & a third— I make etchings & sell them *when I get a chance* & I make bookplates— & even design table covers or wallpaper— *anything*— so that this *damnéd-blessed* work may proceed.

And I am publishing this "Mask" & it will pay for itself— *just* pay for itself— and we shall be happy.

————

Isadora came here to see me— she wanted me to give up my work & go rushing round the world with her— God, how lovely— but she does not

[1] Note by Craig: "As a matter of fact the burden, the work, saved me."
[2] Note by Craig: "I think."

understand that I cannot— I seldom hear from her because I think the Italian post eats her letters— and my letters to her get eaten by her school. When you see her give her my love—

Do you know that my dear little mama has just married again— how wonderful— & is *desperately in love*— We are a queer family— Can you read any of this—?
I have no photograph to send you— or I would send.

     Gordon Craig[1]

ON FEBRUARY 23, 1908 (WESTERN STYLE), ISADORA GAVE A GALA performance of her *Iphigenia in Aulis* dances at the Maryinsky Theatre in St. Petersburg, once again for the benefit of the Society for the Prevention of Cruelty to Children "under the august patronage of her Imperial Highness Grand Duchess Olga Alexandrovna." This time children danced in some of the numbers: Isadora had brought the pupils from Grünewald for the occasion. Irma Duncan tells of the children staying in St. Petersburg two weeks, of their being given candy by Pavlova, of improvising a solo for Kchessinska and her guests in Grand Duke André's palace, and of all the children being taken to visit the Imperial Ballet School. It was about this visit that Isadora wrote in *My Life* of the ballet school children looking at the Duncan pupils "as canary birds might view the circling swallows in the air." After dancing with the children in Helsingfors, Warsaw and Lodz, Isadora returned to Berlin, but only to prepare for still another visit to Russia—this one an extended tour.

[1] Note by Craig: "1944. It was to DE VOS & HEVESI of Budapest I dedicated my most important & my best essay 'The Actor & the Uber-Marionette.' DeVos wrote a bravely ringing foreword to my 1st small book on the Theatre to appear in the Dutch language, & for this I always feel grateful to him."

——— *CD 218* ———
HOTEL ADLON
BERLIN

[2 April(?) 1908][1]

Dearest— I arrived here from the North Pole today & am seeing the Baby
for the first time since three months— She is so splendid— rosy & strong—
walking about & dancing on her toes & talking. I have been sitting all day
only looking at her. I wish you were here to see her. You would be so
delighted with her & she is the image of *you*— I am so overjoyed to see
her again—

Forgive me for not writing for so long— Life is so queer— & difficult
sometimes to write. I was ill a week in Warsovie, in bed with fever &
neuralgia. I found your letter here & if it was not that I have a contract
to dance in Kief on Monday next I would take the train tomorrow &
bring the Baby to see you. But it is all so difficult. I am trying to make
enough money to rest from June to October without dancing & stay
quiet some place with the Baby—

Your letter made me anxious that you were not well, & so I sent a telegram and am waiting for the answer—

The Baby is having a fine time dancing about & singing "Das Leben ist
so schön"[2]— I hope she will always find it schön— she looks like a duck—

I leave next Thursday night to dance Monday eve. in Kief— after that
Odessa, then Carkoff & Rostov— & if it is a success further— I have made
a contract with a Mr. Zeller, the manager of Duse in Russia—

My dear just consider that I have been steadily *travelling* ever since
I saw you last. I wonder even I have any sense left at all— & up in Russia
in darkness & snow all the time. I took to a bit of mild [wild?] dissipation
to keep from suicide! It was 6 degrees below zero when I left Russia—
bundled in furs.

I talked a whole week before last about you to Stanislavsky. He is a
really great & Beautiful person— He wants you to come there but was
frightened at the price. The Theatre is poor— He says always he will
write to you. He impresses me as Carrière used to— a great simple beautiful soul— He asked if you couldn't come there & visit them. I told him
the journey was a trifle long for a visit—

[1] Note by Craig: "To me in my one room, 2 Lung Arno Florence."
[2] G., "Life is so beautiful."

If you liked him as I do he would be a great joy to you. He said he would be quite willing to give you entire control of what productions you wanted. I wonder how it would be if you came together. He is a great & Beautiful person— it might be wonderful—

The Baby had her picture taken & I will send you one tomorrow— how she looks like you— it is astonishing. I want to call her the first Irish name you found— Deirdre[1]— do you remember— I think it's a good name, don't you?

This is the new hotel— it is *cheerful*. Dear, you *must* do something about your studio. *Please* give me or Elizabeth or *someone* the right to take & store them[2]— it is so dangerous the way they are— or you ought to come up & see about it yourself if you don't want anyone else to do it—

Baby is asleep— looks so sweet— I wish you could see her. I love you although you may think my way of showing it a bit strange. There are times when I can't write— if you ever ask me I'll tell you why some day— if you like the truth— but what is the truth— it's all an illusion. But the Baby isn't an illusion— she's *lovely*. I kiss your dear hands—

Your   *Isadora*

There is a draft of a reply (unsent) by Craig.

———— *CD 279* ————

April 1908
— One mood—[3]   Not sent

A letter from you, from our Berlin— Gods & devils all embrace each other to see my unearthly happy smile as I hold your letter—

Tonight as often at night I am ill— that is the word which means

---

[1] The first appearance of the ill-fated name "Deirdre" in the letters.

[2] Craig was still keeping some of his drawings, etc., in the Berlin studio so often visited by bailiffs.

[3] This heading was added by Craig in 1944 (as were the other headings) apparently to balance the "Another mood," which is in the original draft.

lonely— hemmed in by the Furies— seeing before me at a glance the huge futile Road & the continual finger posts which point— upwards.[1]

And at night the silence conspires with the one who is lonely— Together they hatch the most unearthly & vivid plots— But *never* that feeble plot suicide. And in the morning— dear little phantom *tomorrow*— tonight it looks like a baby, so small & so far away— all remembrance of Hell vanishes with glimpse of the new Heaven— only the hair is a little whiter & the dashing smile a bit more dashing.

That is enough record of the evening & the deadly night— It is a bad record but Nox was a strange mother— tomorrow a fresh (delusive) & joyous show— a sketch of the pageant of my daily life— a happy, frisky, *coquettish, proud* life.

Another mood.[2]

And one day when I ask you why you do not write often— often— often— you will tell me (you say) the truth— that is a promise.

A little or a large truth—???

"A truth to heal us— & another to guide us & another truth to cheer us—"[3] all in one.

That will indeed be *THE* TRUTH that is no illusion (you say it is— oh-oh)— all else IS.

No, you see that the Baby is no illusion because she heals & cheers. That which pains & robs or trembles isn't truth. So tell on dear spirit— you cannot frighten me out of my bit of knowledge.

Do you give me pain— oh no— no— no. For to give it [to] me you must first have it— & to have it must be that I caused it—

therefore it is I who give myself pain—

You give me nothing but—— yourself, covered with the wounds I have given you—

How sad, how sweet & how untrue— the bitter sweet untruth of myself— but even then Truth is no illusion— for you are & were beautiful without me, & that knowledge is my last & supreme happiness.

And was I and am I even beautiful to you without your love— that then is the illusion you write of?

---

[1] Here Craig has drawn several posts ending in fingers pointing upwards.

[2] Note by Craig: "To Topsy. Not sent. This must be 1908 in reply to hers from Berlin, Hotel Adlon, April 2."

[3] Note by Craig: "Quoted bitterly from the page I wrote about her for Insel Verlag. c. 1944." No such page has been found. Perhaps Craig wrote more about Isadora—for the Insel Verlag album of drawings—than was published.

Oh how great happiness still seems to belong to me in thinking of the Truth which for me is represented in you—

ISADORA'S WORDS TO STANISLAVSKI ABOUT CRAIG WERE EFFECTIVE. "I began to persuade the Direction of our Theatre to invite the great stage director to come so as to give our art a new impetus forward . . . I must pay full justice to my comrades. They discussed the matter like true artists and they decided to spend a large sum of money in order to advance our art. We gave Gordon Craig an order for the production of *Hamlet*." The contract called for payment to Craig of 500 rubles a month (purchasing power of approximately $1,250 in 1973).

What Craig first received from the management of the Moscow Art Theatre, according to Edward A. Craig, was a telegram at the beginning of May asking him if he would be interested in discussing the production of "a play."[1]

The telegram arrived [Edward A. Craig says] at a moment when Craig had just decided to work out the whole of *Hamlet*, as an exercise, on his model stage at Il Santuccio, and he immediately wrote to say that he was interested. Simultaneously, he heard from Magnus in Berlin that Reinhardt wanted him to produce *King Lear*, followed by *The Orestia*, and from Frederick Whelan in London that Beerbohm Tree was interested in an idea that he had put forward—that Craig design a production of *Macbeth*.

Craig revelled in this sort of situation, for he liked to imagine he could act the clever businessman, when in fact it was a role that least suited his talents. He sent telegrams to all, saying that he had "important deci-

---

[1] There exists a telegram [CD *217*] from Moscow, torn and mutilated, with the address and date missing: ART THEATRE OFFERS YOU TO ARRANGE PEERGYNT AND OTHER PRODUCTIONS [FOR?] TWO MONTHS WHAT CONDITIONS CANT PAY MUCH GOOD OPENING FOR [YOU?] WIRE REPLY RUSSIA—ISADORA NATIONAL. Craig has underlined "Can't pay much" and noted, "Oh— oh Isadora." And he has written on the telegram, "Replied 'Direktor communicate with me direkt— would not object . . .'" The remainder is illegible.

sions to make about productions in Germany and Russia," or, "England and Germany," as the case might be, and "what offer were they prepared to make?" Tree was not in any hurry, and wrote saying he was willing to wait until Craig could come over for a discussion. Reinhardt telegraphed an agreement to pay 2,000 marks for the designs for *Lear*—if the sketches arrived by August 15—but Craig was not in a mood to be hurried and let time slip by as he played with the idea; eventually it was too late and the scheme came to nothing.[1]

Craig was not to go to Moscow to begin work on *Hamlet* until that October, 1908, and the production would not open until January, 1912, after he had visited Moscow four times. Throughout those three years and more he seems to have been paid his 500 rubles a month by the Moscow Art Theatre.

In the meantime, Isadora, her Russian tour ended, wrote him about other matters.

———— *CD 220* ————

[Apparently Paris, June or early July 1908]

Dearest Ted—I have been travelling all over Russia & the Caucasus—stopped a few days in Paris & start for London tonight with all the Chil-

---

[1] Isadora, whom Craig told about the various offers, wrote him [CD *221*]: "About the Reinhardt letter—I am sure you would make the Orestia beautiful. Your *terms* are more than reasonable. If it comes off I will sit in a Box every night & enjoy myself all winter & *refuse* to dance a step! Reinhardt's letter seemed very polite & properly appreciative."
But what Craig had cavalierly told Reinhardt was that he should "get sketches from Magnus," and an August 11 telegram from Reinhardt in Berlin to Craig in Florence reads in part: YOUR REPRESENTATIVE [MAGNUS] ANNOUNCED SINCE FIVE DAYS . . . THE LAST REPETITIONS FOR LEAR TAKING PLACE IN 10 OR 12 DAYS WE ARE UNFORTUNATELY FORCED TO RENOUNCE ALSO THAT WE REGRET IT THE MORE THAT WE HAVE ALL DONE ON OUR PART TO REACH A CONSENTMENT NOW WE ASK DEFINITE DECISION IF YOU ACCEPT ORESTEIA OR NOT. By the time Magnus finally reached Reinhardt, it was too late. This was Reinhardt's last attempt to work with Craig. As Edward A. Craig says, "Had Craig combined forces with Reinhardt instead of with Stanislavsky, the theatre today would have had a richer heritage."

dren— Wish me luck! We open Duke of York Theatre July 6, under
Charles Frohman[1]— it has all been arranged inside of one week & I
feel dizzy— *10* days travel from the Caucasus here & ten nights. The
Baby is here with Miss Kist, & she is a perfect *Love*. She dances like a
Duck & speaks *everything* & says "I'm going to see Papa." You will be
delighted with her. I had her picture taken the other day & will send it
to you next week. If we only have a success in London— I am frightened
to death— Pray for us. I telegraphed to Berlin to send me your books . . .
over to London—
Write to me Hotel Cecil— & send me a lot of copies of the Mask, for
which I will send subscriptions.[2]
Think of all the things I want to say to you & can't, & know that I love
you & will bob up serenely & show you some day—

> All my love
> & Baby's
> *Isadora*.

— CD 222 —

[Postmarked London, August 3, 1908]

Dearest Ted[x][3]— I don't know why I dont write you[x]— I think of you
almost all the time[x] & I talk of you the rest of it— but it seems almost
impossible to write.[x] Meeting your Mother has been a very great thing—
She is so marvellous— so Beautiful so kind— She was like a great Lovely
Goddess Angel to me[x]— & the two nights she came to the Theatre I
danced as in a dream.[x] I was so excited at her being there & applauding
me with those dear hands— it was almost too much—
I have had very very nice audiences here— as nice as anyplace— & it
has cured the terrible fear I had of London engendered by almost starving
to death here 8 years ago. I particularly adore to rush in motor cars about
this town where I walked & walked & walked so many dreary miles—

---

[1] Note by Craig: "Chas. Frohman *failed* to make her a financial success in
London & America."

[2] Note by Craig: "Always returned."

[3] At each point marked x in this letter Craig wrote—apparently at the time—
"lie" or "all lies" in red ink; later he crossed out each of these in black.

The whole visit has been most satisfying & my dear it is a shadow to what will happen to *you* here when London wakes up to you. The Mask is fine & astonishes me every month anew.ˣ

You ought now & then to put in a light or humorous article & now & then a poem— or a local critic— What I mean is don't keep it too much on the same tone—

I leave London tomorrow for Ostend to get a breath of Sea Air— will be Aug. 6 in Paris, & on the eighth I sail with Mr. Frohman to America. It seems a funny time of the year to open in New York, but he says I must get there before these dozens of copies[1] who are all sailing on Sept. 1. Your Mama says you are coming to Berlin in Sept. Couldn't you come— that we could meet before I leave. I mean to find you some millionaires in America.ˣ It would be a joy to see you meet Baby,ˣ & if you can spare the time I think you ought to come & have a talk with your Topsy before she sails the briney deep—

If you haven't the change on hand telegraph & I will telegraph it—ˣ Telegraph me when this reaches you[2]— I can't write— I want so to talk to you— I will telegraph you from Ostend—ˣ³

> With All My Loveˣ
> Your
> Topsy Isadora

for ever yoursˣ no matter what else she seems & will prove it one of these days—ˣ

———— *CD 223* ————

[Post card, Cherbourg to Florence;
arrival postmark, 10 August 1908]

Dearest Ted— Did you get my long letter?[4] Sailing— Baby, all in blue, came to see me off— She is *sweet*. Come up & see her— *do*. All my love—

> Isadora

---

[1] Isadora is probably referring to Maud Allan, an American dancer who was giving performances imitating her style.

[2] Note by Craig: "no address."

[3] Note by Craig: "not done."

[4] Note by Craig: "Yes— saying 'I will telegraph.' Lie."

With Isadora Duncan and Ellen Terry meeting at last, and with Craig's particularly virulent comments not only on the meeting itself but on other details of Isadora's life at the time, one is struck again by the similarities between these two women who played such leading roles in Craig's life. Both beautiful, both famous, both enchanting privately and electrifying on the stage, both unashamedly bearing children outside marriage to the men they loved: a mother who had still been giving him an allowance of £500 a year when he was twenty-four "so that he may be laid hold on by his whims & fancies whilst he is very young (he's a baby)," and who since then had been supporting two of his families; a mistress who danced herself half to death to support their child and further his work. After the years with his mother, Craig may well have thought, on finding Isadora in 1904, that the world would be full of such women for him. But he never found another. Elena Meo was a woman of refined beauty, devoted and maternal, but unlike Ellen and Isadora she was not a blazing comet, nor did she wish to be; indeed, her great value to Craig lay in her quality of what is called "selflessness": her near-anonymity, her gentle, quiet constancy and fortitude—nobility, in fact. Nor were the other women in his life, admirable though they may have been, demigoddesses like Ellen Terry and Isadora. Now his mother had married, at sixty, an American actor of thirty-two (four years younger than himself), and Isadora had, to use his own word, "failed" him. There was something about the conjunction of the two women that he could not tolerate; the savagery of his repeated "lie," "all lies" dashed onto Isadora's letter about his mother in London is found again in the drafts of several letters he wrote to Isadora about this time—one of them so abominable that he himself later wrote on it: "EGC beastly hurt— & disgustingly cruel."

———— *CD 280* ————

to I.D.[1]   July 1, 1908

Having forgotten me so long why should you wish to remember me now?

It was to find some answer to this that I walked along the shore by the sea & thought & thought & found every answer but the true one.

[1] Both headings added later by Craig.

Petty answers— oh no *Not true*— & proud answers— practical answers and thoughtless answers—

Would you know how I argued with all these— how I took *our* part & how they poured their replies upon me.

There is no answer.

Only love is enough— & Love is only enough.

[1]How great a humbug the voices would whisper me that you are— how mean a humbug they would whisper I am.

How paltry— worldly— unsimple

un   intelligent

the voice would make us out to be.

That I should be unintelligent doesn't frighten me much but that you should be, makes me turn & recommence my attack against these voices.

Don't I speak simply enough. Have you ever loved anyone—? What did you feel like when your thoughts or remembrance suggested that he or she was (to you) less than perfect.

That he or she could be a box containing a little love, & that you yourself could be as small a box—

This & more, like actual voices in the wind, blew round my head ears eyes as I walked along the beach looking & longing to hear or see you.

Having forgotten me so long why should you wish to remember me now?

Why, man alive, you are merely an atom in the life of this lady. Be less vain— desire to be less, even than an atom in that life.

Having forgotten me so long why should she wish to remember me *now*?

Why, idiot— she can make some use of you now— she is above all practical— I won't say commercial motives—— it might suit her to make some little use of you, or your name, or your hat, or your manservant or maid servant or anything that is yours . . . why not.

------ *CD 281* ------

[Florence]

You said you would wire from Ostend— you haven't.

Stanislavsky is near you there.

You don't know why you don't write to me, you say—

I know—

[1] Here Craig has drawn a shore, with waves.

It's all right— I'm sure.

When you do write you evoke the old picture— & there it hangs a picture for ever—

When we are young we extract happiness & laughter out of these visions— & later we find in the same visions a *treasure* which is more than happiness— it pours on us— pours— rains like a torrent of the hardest sharpest ice hail from the terrible vision— strikes us— burns— freezes— creates us—

I cannot come to see you—

You will have a great & happy journey to America & back I hope— When you find the millionaires you say you'll find for me— keep them for yourself & your plans. You have & have had & will have unending difficulties and will need all such things to assist your hand— & what you don't need Elizabeth will (by right) demand— & what Elizabeth don't get Raymond has a right to— & then there is your poor lone old ma & Gussie likes a leg up of £20 now & then

& *I*— I like all or nothing—

so I ask you for respectful remembrance for the best part of my old pride—

> my scrap of work which is not now or tomorrow or while you are alive to even know if it's full of love or only full of trick. I suspect trick in all of it— so now to begin— & again begin— never ending— beginning———

It will give you some pleasure to know that I am not forgetting to provide for needs of life & am making money for my boy and girl who you know of—

It is a great kind of idiotic satisfaction to find they are being trained well & that never since I left them in 1903[1] have they made it difficult by a single word for me to keep on the same course I determined on on saying goodbye— I have not received the like *kind* of support since I

---

[1] Craig had, as we know, left Elena Meo and their daughter Ellen in London in 1904 to go to Berlin. The "boy" (Edward A. Craig) was born in January 1905. He had now brought them from England to Florence, but he did not stay with them long. As Edward A. Craig says: ". . . no sooner had they found another flat in the Lung' Arno Acciauoli than he started to prepare for his Russian trip . . . A few weeks later he was on his way to Moscow." The money Craig was making "to provide for means of life" was probably the 500 rubles a month from the Moscow Art Theatre. One could scarcely hope for anything more purely Craig than: "I have not received the like *kind* of support since I was born— They have no clothes & little more than bread & milk for food & I call them Damned Great & splendid."

was born— They have no clothes & little more than bread & milk for food & I call them Damned Great & splendid.

Has anyone ever helped you work like that— no not even I who tried for a time to obliterate my self and only succeeded in pretending to the obliteration— I think Walt is right & that the unheard of & unknown Hero's are at the top of the ladder—

Here's my hat off to them anyhow, & to you as a *known* Heroine.

—— *CD 282* ——

to Isadora.   Florence, August 1908

EGC beastly hurt— & disgustingly cruel— 1944

My poor child,

Try not to feel the separation from us all so keenly as you are doing. It will kill you—

I am very very sorry for you.

I think he must have been off his head don't you— off his head.

Great success to you— and keep all the millionaires you find for yourself— you need them.

It must be awful to leave Elizabeth, Raymond & your baby—

But you have your Art— Ecco! And your bread—

Nietzsche tells us that he admires an artist so modest in his demands that he . . . asks only these 2 things.

But don't read Nietzsche— He speaks truth, though he despises women for being LIARS—

—— *CD 283* ——

[Probably Florence 1908]

You have had a scene of blue [curtains] made which creates in people who see it the impression *that it is my work*.[1]

---

[1] Craig made two notes on this letter: "To I.D. 1909. 'Her famous blue curtains'— see Sewell Stokes & McDougal's books on Isadora"; "1944. She quite unaware of any blundering: esprit de corps not I suppose quite unknown to her— & yet here when no longer near me she forgets *I had repeatedly said no* to her when she asked me to design a scene for her dancing." For more about Isadora's blue curtains, which obsessed Craig, see p. 305.

My mother went so far as to be "enthusiastic" to me about it.

I am utterly ashamed of you for doing this— or permitting this— and I am furious.

I obtained a description of it & how & where it was made.

Do you announce it in the programme as the work of an imitator or as my work— or perhaps you do not mention it but merely let it be ru-moured without contradicting it— or allow it to be supposed that you thought of it— "*alone I did it.*"

In any case it is a direct case of piracy— a thing you despise.

    Amazing!

You may say that it's not so important as all that.

It is just as bad & unkind an act as if I were to get some girls & put them in dresses like yours & let it be rumoured that you had trained them for me. The public would not know any better & would think the fools possessed your genius—

You have removed from yourself the right to deride the Maud Allens of the variety stage.

    Oh, Isadora————

And now I give you the use of that scene, & the right to copy anything of mine you choose— and in any way to do anything which will help you no matter how much it hinders or hurts my work.

  I cannot do less.

  I wish I could do more.

ELLEN TERRY ONCE REMARKED TO HER GRANDSON ROBERT, ONE OF Craig's older sons: "I considered Isadora too temperamental for your father . . . and what is more no woman should fall in love with a perfectionist—ever." But that Isadora was not "lying" in saying that Ellen Terry was something of a "great Lovely Goddess Angel" to her in London is evident from Isadora's letter itself (and from Irma Duncan's memory of the great actress taking the children "to the zoo, then to see Peter Pan and The Pirates of Penzance"). And that she returned Isadora's warm feelings is reflected in another letter written by Isadora that year from New York. (At first, on that visit to the United States, under Charles Frohman's inept direction, Isadora had little success, but the tide turned and with Walter Damrosch as conductor she triumphed in appearances with the New York Symphony Orchestra in the Metropolitan Opera House and on tour.[1])

[Probably New York, Autumn 1908]

Dearest and Sweet Nell. My heart leapt for joy when I saw your letter—How gracious and kind of you to write—

I don't know where to write to Ted[2]— he did not answer my last letter so I think did not receive it—

Whether I write or no my heart goes out to him always wherever he is— I long for him just as I long always to see his Baby but I don't dare to think of it— or I shouldn't be able to live at all—

That there is a Glorious Future waiting for him of that I never have had a doubt— It has seemed a long time for him to wait but it will only be the greater when it comes.

I will sail about Dec. 20th and dance in Paris— January— then to Budapest— February till March I go to Russia— I hope to steal a little time and come over to see you— Perhaps Ted might be there too— what a rejoicing we could have—

Where shall I write to Ted— I feel so much about him that I can't write— when I take up a pen— it all comes over me— choking— I can't write— Well perhaps we can all sit about the same table some day soon and drink to his Health and Glory.

He always looks wonderful— All the light and beauty of the World— That's what he is— *You* are the only one who understands how I love him— it will all come right some day.

> With all my love.
> Isadora.

Isadora did return to Paris in January, and under the aegis of the French actor-director Lugné-Poe she appeared during February and March in a series of immensely successful matinees at the Théâtre de la Gaieté. Craig was not then in Paris, but the renown of those 1909 matinees prompted two comments from him, written at different times and characteristically different in tone.

[1] For Isadora in New York in 1908, as seen by J. B. Yeats and some of his friends, see note for this page.

[2] He was probably in Moscow.

This time she did most decidedly "conquer" Paris. The French know what is lovely— not merely lovely to look at— but what is wonderfully lovely in its whole being. A great musician, painter, poet, a great actor or actress & a great dancer— & Paris found Isadora to be the greatest dancer, the most perfect embodiment of the dance, that had ever moved within its walls— she was Dance itself— not Ballet— not a Dancer merely— but the very Spirit of Dance.

But in a note [CD *342*] written on a Théâtre de la Gaieté program for Isadora's matinee of March 1, which he somehow and sometime procured, he sourly returned to the matter of the blue curtains, apparently forgetting that he had already reproached her for using them the year before in London.

It was here & at this performance that she first used the great blue curtains which followed my designs as may be seen in my "The Art of the Theatre" . . . & which I had made in 1901–2–3—
She pretends [in *My Life*] that she used them in 1904 in Berlin at the Hochschüle where I saw her dance for the 1st time in December. She did not use them then.
. . . These matinees were a tremendous success & led to one tragic mistake after another . . .

The first "tragic mistake" (as Craig calls it, and in many ways he is right) brought about by the 1909 spring matinees was Isadora's accepting the "protection" of a millionaire—one of the breed of whom she had jokingly told Craig she "meant to find some" (for him) in America. It was in her dressing room at the Gaieté that she was first visited by Paris Singer, younger brother of the Princesse de Polignac in whose salon she had once danced, and like the Princess an heir to Isaac Merrit Singer's sewing-machine fortune. Soon Paris Singer would begin to play the roles in Isadora's life which he was to fill for the next several years: Maecenas, lover, father of her son. Later we shall see her trying, through him, to persuade Craig to realize some of his visions in a well-paid theatrical project. Shortly after she and Singer met, however, she had to leave, sometime in April, for another engagement in Russia. Stanislavski was in St. Petersburg (the Moscow Art Theatre was giving a season there) and so was Craig—now on his second visit to prepare his *Hamlet*.[1] On her arrival Isadora sent Craig a note, inviting him to what would be their first meeting since the parting in Florence.

—— *CD 224* ——

[Written on envelope of
Grand Hôtel d'Europe, St. Pétersbourg,
probably April 1909]

Thank you for your note— I have just arrived, have no one with me but a young lady secretary— will you come in one half-hour—

Isadora

It was an evening soon thereafter that there was enacted, during and after supper in Isadora's suite in the Grand Hôtel d'Europe, what Craig later called a "tragi-comedy."

To go back a little, Stanislavski tells in his memoirs of how, on his first meeting with Isadora, "We understood each other almost before we said a single word"—understood, he meant, each other's artistic ideas. In *My Life* Isadora says that she soon wearied of Stanislavski's constantly talking to her of art:

One night I looked at him, with his fine handsome figure, broad shoulders, black hair just turning to grey on the temples, and something within me revolted at always playing this rôle of Egeria. As he was about to leave, I placed my hands on his shoulders and entwined them about his strong neck, then, pulling his head down to mine, I kissed him on the

---

[1] On his way to Russia, Craig had apparently stopped in Berlin to empty and relinquish his studio. There is a draft [CD *284*] on his old Direktion Vereinigter Künste stationery, with the printed heading (SIEGMUNDSHOF 11, ATELIER 33, BERLIN, N.W. Telegraphic Address: FOOTLIGHTS), later dated 15 April 1909: "The last evening here— alone— Well? I thought there was something to be said— & I find nothing to say— but a pain— a pain." In 1944 Craig added a note: "I can say now— It was here in Atelier 33 that she & I passed those wonderful days & nights in 1904."

mouth. He returned my kiss with tenderness. But he wore a look of extreme astonishment, as if this were the last thing he expected. Then, when I attempted to draw him further, he started back and, looking at me with consternation, exclaimed, "But what should we do with the child?" "What child?" I asked. "Why, our child, of course. What should we do with it? You see," he continued in a ponderous manner, "I would never approve of any child of mine being raised outside my jurisdiction, and that would be difficult in my present household."

His extraordinary seriousness about this child was too much for my sense of humour, and I burst into laughter, at which he stared in distress, left me and hurried down the corridor of the hotel . . . Many years later, I told this story of Stanislavsky to his wife, who was overcome with merriment and exclaimed, "Oh, but that is just like him. He takes life so seriously."

Stanislavski continued to resist Isadora. "I love you, I admire you, and I respect you (forgive me!)— great artist," is the way he puts it in one of his letters to her.

What happened the spring evening in 1909 when Isadora, Craig, Stanislavski and Isadora's secretary met for supper in Isadora's suite has been described by Craig in the later pages of *Book Topsy*, written in 1944 and, like most of that notebook, never previously published. The account should be prefaced, perhaps, with the remark that although Craig clearly wrote it in denigration of Isadora, it is printed here in the expectation that the reader will experience quite different feelings.

Have I written elsewhere of the tragi-comedy she thought fit to stage in the Hotel d'Europe in 1909 when she came from Paris (& Paris Singer) to St. Petersburg & invited Stanislavsky to supper—

Anyhow it was a Parisian idea in the Parisian style, and the result of Lugné Poë & Elizabeth D. & all the agents' desires to make lots of money out of the sale of one more dancer. Had she not listened to Elizabeth in Heidelberg 1907 spring she would not have agreed to go to Paris under direction Lugné-Poe (whom a year or so later she told me was an Apache of Montmartre) & would not have absorbed there the cynicism which (by April 1909) she was poisoned with.

Yes, April & May I was at St. Petersburg— & in April she arrived— *At the very hotel she had stayed at in 1904* (I in Berlin) during *our great days* when I was in Berlin.

I suppose seeing herself there & seeing how she had been tricked by Elizabeth, by Paris, by Poe, she thought she could do no better than play the whore, or pretend to, & so fixed on Stanislavsky—who *resisted* her superbly with a caution quite remarkable to observe.

She had brought with her a Miss S—an American or a Scotswoman—& we 4 sat down to supper in Isadora's large private sitting room—I remember those rooms of hers— [Here Craig has drawn diagrams.] Round the table in the corner we 4 sat & as soon as the 1st bottle of Champagne had been finished she began to encircle S's neck with her arms— & began to kiss him— he objecting most politely all the time—& she refusing to accept his objections.

When I could stand no more of this rotten performance in front of me I did not go Bersack— but getting up I took the other girl S by the arm telling her I had something to say to her *privately*— & mysteriously I drew her into the small room . . . with the bed in it— I locked the door so that no one could come in any way & soon enough a lot of babble first at one door then at the others & a turning of door handles made it clear that I.D. & C.S. were not getting on as she had hoped. Her reason for offending me in this way I could not & still cannot fathom.[1] Anyhow while door handles twisted & knockings on the doors went on I drew the young S. girl down on the bed & whispered "lie quiet & let us pretend to be so occupied that we do not hear them." S., who had not lost her head but who had no objection to resting quietly with my arms around her, lay still. Soon the noise died down & awhile later we heard C. Stanislavsky going away & I.D. decidedly in a quiet bad temper. She went into her bedroom . . . & then quietly tested the door handle but found that door locked too. Then apparently she lay down on her bed— anyhow quiet followed. "Come on," I said, "let's go out & drive in the snow." We slipped very quietly out . . . into the passage— went down— called a sledge— and off we went. Now we were well thrown into each other's arms, for S. had a growing fear to return alone to face I.D. & I certainly had no wish to hold S. So we drove on for ½ an hour— an exciting cold hot drive— & she seemed to like to get closer & closer to me. So I decided to take her back to the hotel— engage a new double-bedded room & pass the night with her. At first she protested very slightly but a minute or two later began to talk of love. The word may be sweet— but I'd prefer if females who take it on & put it off so lightly would talk of lust & not use the word love. However, now we went to the hotel & ordered a nice

---

[1] Later note by Craig: "Why she & S had left their banquet to jumble at the handles of the 2 doors is inexplicable except that she suddenly felt jealous."

room to be got ready—& off again for more drive because she wanted to buy "things"— what "things" never mind. I didn't ask, but she stopped at a chemist & came out with "things." Did we stop at other places— I forget— but I recall our room— her very white body for she had no night dress & the long talks we had between the kissings. Every now & then a fearful twinge or wrench came to me— but I had only to recall I.D.'s behavior with C.S. to banish these thoughts & to return to this exquisite white girl who babbled of what she knew nothing & seemed to feel nothing— for she lay accepting all I gave her & giving no return of energy— no passion— she was apparently in church while in bed.

Next day. It was fairly late in the day when the girl suddenly jumped out of bed & began to dress hurriedly— fear of I.D. again assailing her & fear of being left behind in St. P. also assailing her: for I.D. & she were leaving for Berlin or somewhere in a westerly direction after luncheon hour. Somehow nothing of all this concerned me, so furious I had been with I.D. for her beastly behavior with C.S. at supper. I let S. dress, kissed her, told her to write me, at which she looked toffy-eyed & glu-glued a bit & off she ran full speed to save her bacon.

I being "numb & void" dressed slowly & ran & ordered lunch to be ready in the smaller of the 2 dining rooms & in ½ an hour was seated enjoying an excellent dejeuner— *alone*, I thanked the Gods.

Finished I looked at my watch & found it was near the hour spoken of yesterday for I.D. & S's departure by train— so I went to the Hall & there sure enough were all the signs of departure & the two women descending by the lift or the staircase. Outside a sunny snow day & a sledge waiting— into which after a few very casual words they entered.

As I helped to arrange the rugs I could not help saying with polite smiles that I hoped she had passed a pleasant evening anyhow. To this she said neither a yea or a nay but, as was her custom, when utterly bouleversé, she uttered a brief sermon— said she, "Try to emulate the virtues of the good *good* man with whom we supped last night,"[1] & signing to the coachman to jolly well drive on she drove away. These sudden bursts of damnèd hypocritical sermonizing *rarely* seized her— but

---

[1] Note by Craig: "This in a Pagan— for she professed paganism, & really was no christian— was so especially ludicrous if astonishing. It grew, as I say, into a habit with her to suddenly lecture those who had got the best of her ON HER OWN GROUND— & to lecture like Pecksniff or the Rev. Mr. ———. This I think was the only occasion on which she lectured *me*, but she never could get in a rage with anyone (so far as I know) & this preaching took the ugly vacant place of hearty rage."

when they did one stood staggered & uncertain whether to weep, laugh, howl, or shoot: to see a professed "Pagan" preaching like a Plymouth Brother. Anyhow off she went by train to join Paris Singer, her millionaire in whose millions she so thoroughly believed & whose millions she came to curse:[1] but of this Sewell Stokes writes in his little book— of this & much else.[2]

By this time, one's confidence in Craig's capacity for sustained human sympathy has necessarily flagged, and one even suspects the term "tragi-comedy" that he applies to the episode in the St. Petersburg hotel: Does it really reflect anything more than awareness of his own prowess at telling comically the story of a scene which was to him—the consummate actor—tragic in the sense of being, in his own words, "a rotten performance"? Assuming that it all happened as Craig described it[3] (Isadora kissing Stanislavski and attempting to "draw him further" a few months after her rejection by Craig in Florence; her seizing of the opportunity to caress him openly in front of Craig almost the moment she and Craig met after a year and a half of separation), did Craig really not see, as Isadora flaunted herself before him—"trying to make me jealous," as he says elsewhere [CD *340*]—that beneath the "rotten performance" there was the wound?

Isadora, feeling more "philosophical," wrote Craig at the end of her Russian stay.

[1] Note by Craig: "One must not forget that she hoped to get so many millions that she could help all those she loved— her brothers, her sister, her scholars, & many artists whom she supposed needed such help— why she even writes me that she is going to America to get millions so that I can have my theatre & everything I need. She went: Frohman the manager: either it was a fiasco or she spent so much of the takings there was nothing over in her purse on her return. In any case I heard no more that time about having my theatre & all I needed. But the good intention was in her heart, all the same."

[2] Sewell Stokes, *Isadora Duncan; an Intimate Portrait*. London, Brentano's Ltd., 1928.

[3] For Isadora's version, as printed in *My Life*, see note for this page.

——— *CD 225* ———

[Postmark illegible, somewhere in Russian
territory, 24 April 1909 (7 May Western
style); arrival postmark, St. Petersburg,
26 April 1909 (9 May); addressed c/o
Theatre de l'Art, Theatre Michel,
St. Petersburg"; correct name of theater
("Mikhailovsky Teatr") added in Russian,
apparently by post office]

Dear Ted[1]— I dance here tonight for the last [time]— & leave for Paris,
arriving Monday morning. If there is anything I can do for you in Paris,
let me know. Address c/o Mrs. Sturges, *10 rue Octave Feuillet*. I am overjoyed to get back to Baby— for in spite of a telegram every other day I
always worry about her when I am away. I will have the beautiful photo
you gave me framed & put over her bed that she will always know that
her wise Mama chose some one pretty nice for her Papa & be properly
grateful to me. I hope my studio will be ready in Paris so that I can work.
I am thinking always of your representation of Hamlet, and when I close
my eyes I see the Vision of Beauty which your model of the scene gave
me. It was beyond everything marvellous & lovely—
I am feeling much better & rested & philosophical— been reading Hero-
dotus— charming. I want *very much* to have your English landscapes—
I have an idea of a room to be devoted to them— Could you send them to
me in Paris?— Let me know what you think. Of course I want you to
consider me exactly as you would any other purchaser—[2]
With good wishes & love

    Isadora[3]

———————

[1] Note by Craig: "Once 'Dearest'— now a Parisienne it's 'Dear Ted' & will
I sell the pictures to her. NO I will not sell." On the envelope he has written:
"A grievous letter."

[2] Note by Craig: "You may want *that*— but that I cannot do."

[3] Note by Craig: "This was in April 1909! but then in 1919 in Rome we
walked all night close!!!!! ourselves."

How does one read, exactly, Craig's indignation about Isadora's asking for the "English landscapes"? Those landscapes held particular memories for both of them—they had hung, the reader may recall, in Craig's 1904 Berlin exhibition, where Isadora first visited him ("All in white she walks round with me & looks at each drawing . . ."). Why was it "grievous" of her to ask to buy them? "NO I will not sell": if Craig had heard of Paris Singer at this time, was his objection to being paid with Singer's money? But Isadora was herself not now penniless; the New York Symphony appearances had been a success, and even before meeting Singer she had taken, in Paris, the studio where she had "an idea of a room to be devoted" to the drawings.

In St. Petersburg Isadora knew that her life would—or could— take a new turn as soon as she returned to Paris and to Singer. The flaunting of herself before Craig in the hotel: if it took place, was it not a last offer of herself to him, as an alternative to beginning something new and dubious? As asking for the drawings might perhaps express a wish to have always, whatever her new life might be, a reminder of that day in Berlin?

So it was that Isadora "went off by train to join Paris Singer, her millionaire in whose millions she so thoroughly believed." She had not yet had time to believe in them thoroughly. And one feels that in St. Petersburg she may have made a desperate effort, unrecognized by Craig, to continue to believe in something else.

The Death of the Children

Despite what has been written about him in *My Life* and elsewhere, Paris Singer, Isadora's millionaire, remains a shadowy figure. In his patronage of the arts he had as an example his sister Winaretta, Princesse de Polignac, but in his playing of that role one does not sense the Princess's delicacy and flair—qualities, some say, which she had imbibed from her husband, a true musical connoisseur. Singer once spoke *of himself* as an *"homme de goût"*—which at once arouses one's doubts—and his best-known attributes remain his wealth and a tendency toward suspiciousness which wealth seems to have engendered.

In the present volume his part is minor: he is Craig's successor, the man to whom Isadora turned after Craig let her go. On May 4, 1910, at Beaulieu-sur-Mer, after a winter spent partially on a yachting trip to Egypt, Isadora bore him a son, Patrick Augustin Duncan, on whose birth certificate the name of the father is left blank, only "Isadora Duncan, *artiste*" appearing as parent. Singer provided lavishly for Isadora and both children, and for a time she prized the luxurious living after the strain of the preceding years. But they were often separated during the years of their liaison—in part because of Isadora's dancing engagements, but also because of the clashes of temperament[1] and her eventual impatience with "Society" which sent Singer off on long absences. And he had other obligations, including five children by a wife whom he was divorcing.

During the summer of 1912 Isadora tried to include Craig in a splendid plan that Singer had conceived for her: the building of a theater in Paris to give her, as he said in one of his letters, "the possibility of showing your work in its complete form." This would include performances of several Greek tragedies in their English translations by Gilbert Murray, with dances by Isadora and her pupils (Isadora had written to Murray and asked for the rights). Singer bought a parcel of land in Isadora's name in the rue de Berri, off the Champs Élysées, and commissioned the architectural firm of Huillard and Süe to design the theater, which he planned to call "Le Théâtre du Beau."

Isadora was in Munich and Bayreuth for part of the summer, but Craig was in Paris. On January 21, his spectacularly designed and directed *Hamlet* had finally achieved the first of the four hundred performances it was to be given by the Moscow Art Theatre; on the crest of the wave of international celebrity it brought him he had been taken up, following an introduction from Count Kessler, by another great Parisian protectress of the arts, the Comtesse Greffulhe, who was trying through her many theatrical connections to have his talents used for the greater glory of the French stage, perhaps in a huge production of Bach's St. Matthew Passion. Singer, who knew from his sister of Madame Greffulhe's imperious ways and love of "exclusivity" in her artistic pursuits, respectfully asked her permission to propose to Craig that he be the architects' consultant in planning the stage of the new theater—an idea that certainly came from Isadora. When the Countess consented (none too graciously: "I should not be very glad if public opinion should think first of Craig as the architect of a theatre, instead of being what I believe he could be with your advice and mine, it is to say a very great artist able to produce an immense and new effect of art"), Singer wrote to Craig and went to see him (the first, and perhaps the only, time they met), offering him a fifty-thousand-franc fee if

[1] See note for this page.

he would furnish "plan, section and elevation to scale of the stage
. . . take up the question of stage lighting . . . and supply the architect with any information he needs for the construction and equip-
ment of the stage."

On July 30 Craig wrote his acceptance: ". . . this is exciting work,
& should therefore begin at once, for first sparks are the most valuable and indicative part of a new fire." But Singer was shrewd enough
to characterize, in a letter to Isadora, Craig's reply as "perhaps a little
over-enthusiastic"—probably basing his opinion on a gratuitous suggestion or two that Craig had included: "I wish to ask you, before
I finally set to work, whether I could not be of service in helping
you to frame the programme . . . A theatre should start with a programme CLEARLY laid down, and follow it faithfully— this prevents attempts on the part of individuals to interfere with the natural
course of the stream. These individuals who act thus are only the
performers . . . I would earnestly urge you to exclude from your
counsels all and every performer."

Singer and Isadora had intended, once the theater was completed,
to offer Craig part-time use of the stage he himself would have
designed: it is not known whether Craig was told so. Soon the newspapers began to print, about the projected theatre, stories of which
this one from the *Daily Mail*, October 29, 1912, is a sample:

MISS I. DUNCAN'S THEATRE

The foundation stone is about to be laid of the theatre which Miss Isa-
dora Duncan, the well-known exponent of Greek dancing, is to build in
Paris. A site has been purchased in the Rue de Berri, off the Champs-
Elysées, and the theatre will probably be opened in 1914.

The structure, which will be modelled on the lines of ancient play-
houses, will be ideal from the point of view of seating accommodation, and
good seats at popular prices will be a feature. Miss Duncan intends to stage
Greek tragedies in a vivid and artistic manner. The pupils of her school
will form the chorus for the pieces, and the venture will be supported by
well-known poets, musicians, actors, and actresses. No effort will be spared
to make the theatre a real temple of art.

The site has been purchased by Mr. Paris Singer, the American millionaire philanthropist who is providing Paris with a new institute of medical
research.

After the appearance of a number of such articles, Singer received what will—alas—surprise no reader of the present volume: Craig's notice of withdrawal.

[n.d.]
Morley's Hotel
Trafalgar Square
Dear Mr. Singer   London, W.C.

... Thinking over your proposal to me I am afraid that there being no contradiction made by you in the Paris & American Press that the theatre you intend building is for Miss Duncan I am led to believe that the paragraphs are correct—

Now although anyone might be honoured to build a theatre for Miss Duncan I have made it one of my rules lately to work for no performer however highly gifted or eminent, & I cannot break it.

This therefore will make it impossible for me to go on with the idea. I am very sorry— & I had hoped things would have been different.

With good wishes
  Yours sincerely
    Gordon Craig.

It was yet another of Craig's refusals to work except alone, and yet another case of everyone else being wrong. "This leaving it all to the last minute characteristic of I.D. & group," he scribbled on a calling card left him, after his acceptance, by the architect Paul Huillard, begging him to make an appointment to discuss the plan of the stage because blueprints had to be submitted for police approval before a certain date. "I forget if I saw M. Huillard," Craig has noted beside it, "but I did deny through the newspapers that I had anything to do with said theatre." His notes of this time contain numerous caustic references to "Isadora and her millionaire."

Craig was well out of it this time, for the "Le Théâtre du Beau" project soon foundered, one of the causes being the Police Department's urging Singer to heed the already very vocal opposition of the residents of the "essentially quiet, bourgeois neighborhood" of the rue de Berri to the construction of a theater in their midst. In London, Craig found more than better fortune: he achieved the realization of his dream—the establishment of his long-desired school of the theater.

He had discovered in Florence an old, disused open-air theater, the Arena Goldoni, which he immediately saw to be perfect for his purpose, and now the prestige conferred on him by the Moscow *Hamlet* enabled him to obtain subscriptions. Elena Meo, resettled with the children in London, emerged from her usual obscurity and helped canvass for funds; there were many modest contributions, and finally, early in 1913, Lord Howard de Walden, a wealthy lover of music and the stage, gave £5000 to begin the school and promised £2500 a year toward its support for the next two years. On February 27, 1913, Ellen Terry's birthday, the press announced the opening in March, at the Arena Goldoni, of Craig's "School for the Art of the Theatre."

With Isadora now living in France and planning to open a new dance school in her studio at Neuilly, Elizabeth's management of the German school had become total. After a time she chose a co-director and moved the establishment first to Frankfurt and then to Darmstadt, rechristening it "The Elizabeth Duncan School: Institute for Physical and Scientific Education." Relations between the sisters were strained, but in the spring of 1913, at Isadora's request, Elizabeth brought six of the older girls to dance with Isadora in the Châtelet and Trocadero theaters in Paris. Rehearsals began. Isadora and her two children were living at Versailles.

Now came the horror that divided Isadora's life in two.

——— *CD 227* ———

[Telegram, Neuilly-sur-Seine, 19 April 1913; to Gordon Craig, Arena Goldoni, Florence]

OUR LITTLE GIRL DEIRDRE WAS TAKEN FROM US TODAY WITHOUT SUFFERING MY BOY PATRICK IS TAKEN WITH HER THIS SORROW IS BEYOND ANY WORDS I SEND YOU MY ETERNAL UNDYING LOVE = ISADORA

The story of the tragedy of April 19, 1913, has been told many times. Deirdre, Patrick and their nurse were being driven to Versailles by Isadora's chauffeur from her Neuilly studio, where she had gone to rehearse after they had all, including the pupils from Germany, had a "children's lunch" in Paris with Singer, who had just returned from one of his absences. At a spot where the Seine embankment had no parapet, the car stalled; mistakenly leaving the motor in gear, the chauffeur got out and cranked, as one had to in those days; the motor started, and before the chauffeur could jump in, the car rolled down the embankment into the Seine. Newspapers all over the world printed macabre accounts by the would-be rescuers of how the car was found to have traveled halfway across the river bottom before stalling again; of the attitudes of the three bodies found immersed inside it; of Patrick's being rushed to a hospital because for a time there were still faint signs of life.

On Isadora's telegram there are a few words scribbled in Craig's hand: "always Have courage. THEY are happy & eternal too be sure be sure." Presumably this is a draft of his reply, or perhaps the reply itself, and on the twenty-first Isadora wired him again.

——— *CD 228* ———

[Paris, 21 April 1913;
to Gordon Craig, Theatre Goldoni, Florence]

YOUR WORDS AS THEY ALWAYS HAVE DONE BRING ME COMFORT AND IF THERE IS COURAGE FOR A GRIEF LIKE THIS I WILL TRY AND FIND IT LOVE TO YOU AND YOURS TED = ISADORA[1]

—————————

Craig had, one is relieved to see, telegraphed quickly. But there were those among his intimates who were not sure he would have sent any message at all. The following telegram reached him in Florence.

[1] Note by Craig (perhaps his reply): "We are all very near you. Rest."

―――― *CD 305* ――――

[Tenterden, England, 21 April 1913;
to Edward Gordon Craig (address missing)]

HOPE YOU HAVE SENT WORD OF GRAVE SYMPATHY POOR THING LOVE
FROM ELENA AND MOTHER

On this telegram there are two notes, both scribbled by Craig: "Why should you doubt that?" and "They don't understand what she & I were always & always will be. It's the insularity of our old land does it." But though the insularity of old England may have been the cause of many a misunderstanding, one cannot hold it responsible for Elena Meo's and Ellen Terry's doubt as to whether the man they knew so well had sent a message to Isadora on the death of his child. Sixty years later, the reader may recall, Craig's son was to express surprise on learning that Craig had been at Villa Maria for Dierdre's *birth*: "I never imagined him being on time."

Craig wrote Isadora on the twenty-third.

[Postmarked Florence, 23 April 1913]

Isadora my dear— not I alone but all of us, feel we claim some share of your sorrow— and take it.
Dear— dear—
You are bearing all the grief which would have been theirs— then dry your eyes for them.
Be sure the Gods are looking at you now.
& I am sure you are bearing yourself nobly.
And as all their little griefs fall to your share now, so also does all their pride & splendour become yours again by right.
Dear and great Isadora now is your time—

To say I love you would not cover the whole—
I take your fingers your hands in mine & I pray a great prayer.
"Have a good dream" says my little girl in England to me each
night
& she standing with me with her heart towards yours, bids you have
a good dream—
Take our letter to rest with you— we are all of us unseen but
together near very near you.

      Ted

In a message now lost, Ellen Terry had also urged Craig to go
to Paris, to see Isadora, to attend the funeral of his daughter. On
the twenty-eighth he wrote his mother:

But Mother dear, where have all the letters gone to that I wrote you. You
write April 24th from the Farm as though I had not written to you.
Why should I go to Paris? Did I ask you? Well I soon made up my mind.
    Why should everyone weep?
    and why many things?
    Isadora herself does not weep— and everyone writes me she commands
the situation—
Did I ask you in a letter whether I might write to her
    I can't remember asking— *time* seems to have altered— gone quicker
or slower or something.
I am a dull thing at best for I seem to have a work to do which has a
regular beat ′′′′′′′′′′ but there are times when even my dullness slips its cables.
And I do think one needs to be fairly dull to get a machine well started—
′′′′′′′′′′— and so at 8 o'clock each morning I am at work and
I end at 8 in evening and a little more work after supper— & this
early to work used to be easy to me when I was alone once before in
Florence— the time when all those etchings poured out rapidly— they
were all done in about 8 exciting weeks— when I was alone— a few
people called here or there but no one near me.
And now a different work has begun— begun before this tragedy— &
the beat of the machine should not be broken. It had begun— let all
things assist it then— if it broke I don't know what would be. So thoughts

— tears— remembrance— longing to go— longing to fly— longing to break— to dive— all these longings must be kind & sensible to me & come & patiently move ' ' ' ' ' ' ' ' ' '

I have my quiet hours too— at night— the window open— the peace— space— looking like the place we call heaven— all asleep— work done— oceans of something trying to get loose & drown the city & this town— & also journeying through the space to Paris in an instant— to London— to many places & people—

So is it needful to say I wired to her at once— she to me— once twice three times— & I wrote & wrote— but travelled swifter than all wires all letters in person— or what we know is US—

it isn't needful for me to say anything— you must know that as your son I should not forget *such*.

What I feel & see I cannot talk about— even here.

I see many many things—

I think I asked you if I should go— actually go in person— to Paris— but soon after I sent the letter (& one had no time to *think before* sending) I made up my mind not to actually go— I was there, that was enough, & I know now that Isadora knew.

> To work
>
> Love
> Ted

I had a letter from Kessler yesterday. I had written him to go & put 2 flowers— he went & took two bunches of white lilacs on the white coffins. He says "I laid them down thinking of you & feeling so deeply deeply for you & poor Isadora" etc. He writes very feelingly & describes the ceremony.

"There was a most beautiful moving ceremony in the studio, *the most moving ceremony I have ever been to.* Nothing, but exquisite music. Grieg's 'Death of Aase'— then a piece of Mozart that seemed to embody the tripping of light children's feet on soft grass & flowers, & a wailing infinitely moving melody of Bach. I thought my heart would break. Poor Isadora behaved splendidly. She knelt hidden behind her sister & two brothers on the balcony. Then the coffins were carried out through the garden all strewn with white daisies & jessamine to the white hearses drawn by white horses. Everything most admirable in taste & restraint— & others who have seen her tell me she is really *heroic*, encouraging the others, saying *'there is no death'*— Everybody in Paris is moved to the depths of their hearts."

Queer nice Kessler. I thought you would like to hear the news he sent.

"ALL THAT," SAYS VICTOR SEROFF, ISADORA'S LATEST BIOGRAPHER, "happened at a time when the war in the Balkans had come to an end—1913. The Turkish Army had left Greece in a devastated condition. Raymond and his Greek wife, Penelope, were going there to help take care of the refugees. Supported by Elizabeth and Augustin, they suggested to Isadora that some preoccupation would be beneficial for her state of mind and that she should accompany them to Greece. Isadora agreed, and Elizabeth took the six girls back to Darmstadt. Leaving Isadora with Augustin on the island of Corfu, Raymond and Penelope went to Epirus, the most devastated province."

On May 15, Craig wrote again to Isadora, on Corfu.

[Florence] 15 May 1913

Isadora dear— I never shall be able to say anything to you. It's a mysterious thing but when I begin to think of you or speak to you I feel as though it was as unnecessary as if I should speak to myself.
This feeling grows.
And as I seem to be a man mad about something outside myself— I no longer count.
A glimpse of myself— if I dared to lift a veil— might kill me.
I have left myself (so it seems to me who dare not look) & what is me is a bag of sawdust with a head on one end & two leaden feet 'tother end— & so on—
I seem to be outside myself, supporting myself by one arm or by the hair— like a bunch of furies— & with some strength too for I have serious things to attend to, get done, & then go.
My life as yours has been *strange*— you are *strange*— *but not to me*. And my darling I know how you can suffer & not show more than a smile— I know your weakness which is that of a little, dear little fool— for I, a big fool, have looked at you.
I know your strength too— for I who can taste strength have seen all yours— never was there one so weak or so strong as you— and all for Hecuba—
My heart has often broken— large chips (you couldn't have noticed them, for I as you, will never show those)— to see your weakness—

My heart has often shaken with *terror* to see your strength. For my heart
and your heart are one heart and an utterly incomprehensible thing it is.
I want to be with you— & it was only to say that that I write so much—
And as I am with you, being you, what more is there to be said—
Let us not be sorry for anything— or where should we begin. You and
I are lonely— only that.
And no matter how many came— or shall come— you & I must be lonely

———

Of all Craig's letters written to Isadora and actually sent, this and
its predecessor, mailed to Neuilly, are the only ones known to have
been preserved. A letter she sent him from Corfu suggests that he
may have written her at least once more at this time.

——— *CD 229* ———

Villa Stefano, Corfu
[Dated by Craig, 31 May 1913]

Dear Ted— I answer your letters every day— every moment— but how
can I *write* it— Yes, I remember that evening by the sea. I was very unhappy— or thought I was— now it seems as if I were dead & looking
back upon my troubled self I wonder how I could have troubled so—
Do you remember I sent you a little picture of Deirdre sitting on the
Great Temple at Karnak— looking up so calmly & sweetly— That is how
she was— more & more bright & sweet & gay— She would never have
agonized through life as I have— when I looked at her I always thought—
mine is all broken pieces & disaster— hers will be beautiful & Complete.
Raymond is working for the refuge people in Epirus— he took me over
there with him last week. It is pitiful, those poor people with all their
houses burnt by the Turks— and *nothing* left— crops spoilt— huddling
for protection under the trees— forty villages in this condition—
We have bought tents and provisions and are going back to erect shelters
for the children. It is terrible to see the results of war— no one trying to
help these poor people— If we can save some hundreds of little children
I will say Deirdre & Patrick are doing it for me— We live while there

on a little boat as there are no houses— and I lie all night looking up at the stars— Sometimes towards morning I see a marvellous liquid shining one— I think my self is there— what is left of me here— only a poor shadow—

Write me here— letters will be brought to me— Send me if *only* a line— to hear from you *lifts* the agony and puts me in a strange world of Beauty in which Pain seems to turn to rapture—

      Love
       Isadora

    On Corfu, Isadora heard from Elena Meo, answered her, and wrote again to Craig.

6 John Street
Adelphi
London

June 19th 1913

Dear Miss Duncan— From your letters to Ted I feel that you perhaps did not get the letter I wrote you at the time of your trouble— or perhaps as I signed "Elena," & not "Nelly" you may have thought it was Ted's sister— but Nelly is only a pet name of Teds & my mother-in-law.

I have so much & so great a sympathy for you & am very very sad at your troubles— a trouble so great that words become almost foolish— Poor little Deirdre— do not for one moment think I am so narrow or so small that I could not love her— & little Patrick too— dear babes— I could have loved them both— If you were here in London I would come & see you & perhaps help you bear your sorrow— I have suffered too & can often feel for you very very much— & would help if you would let me— should we ever meet.— In one of your letters to Ted you asked for a photograph of us— here is a little one taken in the country.

I have some work I am doing for Ted here— & will be here a month longer before joining him. If you come to London will you come to see me—

Your sorrow is the saddest thing I know— but try to bear up & keep strong.

    Elena Craig

———— *CD 230* ————

Villa Stefano, Corfu
[Arrival postmark, London, 7 July 1913;
addressed to "Mrs. E. Gordon Craig, 6 John Street,
Adelphi, London, England]

Dear— How sweet and good of you to write to me— Your first letter and your second came to me at the same time— The first had been mislaid by those who opened the letters. Yes I have always thought of you as "Nelly" and I have thought so much of you— Some day if we meet I will tell you— I can't *write* it—

I have been with my brother walking over the mountains in Epirus— walking fifty miles a day and sleeping out under the stars— just to tire myself— and then it is better to weep with the stars looking down on you— than in a room. We visited some of the villages burnt by the Turks— poor people with their houses & crops destroyed— if someone doesn't help them they will all die of misery. I am trying to organize some shelters for the children there. We return there next week. The poor little children there, so sad-eyed and forlorn— and the poor women with nothing to give them—

I loved the pictures you sent me— Something in the turn of the little Boy's head like Deirdre— How she would have loved to play with them— She was so filled with joy and romping— Patrick only a Baby but he toddled after her everywhere— Some mornings she would come to me dressed in a little white boy's sailor suit and say "Mama I'm not Deirdre today I'm *Jack*." She was so strong and gay like a boy— only when she danced she was like a little fairy. Yes you would have loved them as I love *yours*— What dearer joy is there in all the world than to love them— ours or others— even those poor little dirty starved children in Epirus have some divinity in their eyes like Deirdre, like Patrick— ~~perhaps~~ it is the same divinity—

As for me— I feel as if *I* had died with them— what is here left seems such a poor shadow— what shall I do with it— all my life gone— and my work too— for how shall I ever *dance* again— how stretch out my arms except in desolation— If I had only been with them, but the nurse had my place—. It is so dear of you to say you will comfort me and if anything *could* be a comfort it would be to feel that Love comes to me from you and Ted and your little ones— Yes I take the hand you hold out to me so sweetly— and kiss it tenderly and Love you and bless you. Yes,

I will come & see you— if I can— and even if not I will feel often that
I am with you—

Isadora

———— *CD 231* ————

Villa Stefano, Corfu
[Arrival postmark, Florence, 8 July 1913][1]

Dear Ted— Yes Nelly wrote to me— but her *first* letter was mislaid
amongst hundreds of others— and I only received it two days ago *with*
her second— Very sweet and Beautiful of her— and I answered. I don't
know about the purpose of the War— but to help those poor starving
mites over there does something to keep me from dying in my desolation
and despair— and then I think Patrick and Deirdre would like to see those
little ones eating & singing— and who knows perhaps among them we are
saving some great Spirit for Future times— anyway what else can I do—
My own work gives me such dreadful pain— even to think of it— and
all my life seems like a fine ship on the rocks and no hope of ever going
another voyage. Also my poor head won't work right any more even to
write to you— Dear— Beautiful Wonderful Spirit— You are creating
the only world that is worth living in— *The Imagination*— This so-called
real world is the refinement of Torture— and if it weren't for the escape
the Imagination offers it would be Hell indeed. You go on opening the
door— releasing poor souls from the Inferno of *Reality and Matter*— lift
them up out of "life" into the *only life* up where the spirit can fly—
freed from this abominable bad dream of matter. This [is] only a bad
dream, a mirage— *You* find the only truth— freed from these infernal
appearances that are *Shams*. I know that all these so-called Happenings
are *illusions*— Water cannot drown people— neither can going without
food starve them— neither are they born neither do they die— *All is*—
and the Eternal truth is only seen in precious moments by such spirits
as Phidias— Michelangelo— Rembrandt— Bach— Beethoven— others and
Yourself— and it is only *feeding* with such glimpses that is of Importance
— all the rest is semblances, illusions, veils— I know that— but what will

———

[1] Note by Craig: "(after Deirdre & Patrick were drowned). 23rd June 1913,
Corfu time. Reached me July 8, 1913."

you— At the present my poor Body cries out and my mind is clouded—
I can only see Dierdre & Patrick skipping and dancing about— and then
lying there all white & still and cold— and shriek within myself *"What
does this mean?"* All illusions— I know they were but the appearances of
Beautiful Spirit—
Beautiful spirit existing everywhere needing no Earthly manifestation—
Beautiful Spirit there for us to find to portray in Eternal Images— to
light others— but I am all torn to pieces & bleeding— I wish I could see
you a few moments— Bless you

>   *Isadora*

Did your Mother dearest receive a letter I sent to her—

IN *My Life* ISADORA TELLS OF SINGER VISITING HER BRIEFLY ON CORFU
and leaving without farewell; of her having to escape from the misery
of the refugees, traveling to Constantinople with her sister-in-law
Penelope, then going to Switzerland and to Paris, where, in the
studio at Neuilly, she "wept for the first time." To remain there
was unbearable, and in the late autumn, taking with her the British
pianist Hener Skene (whom Singer had employed as musician on
the yacht trip to Egypt), she drove to Italy. She makes no mention
of a visit she had made to England before that, in September. Craig,
who seems to have been visiting his mother in England at that same
time, or at least using her address, clearly knew of Isadora's presence,
but apparently they did not meet: a letter she wrote him reveals the
failure, though not the details, of a meeting that he did arrange—
an encounter between Isadora and another of his "principals."

—— *CD 232* ——
SAVOY HOTEL
LONDON

Monday
[2 September 1913; addressed to
Gordon Craig, Esq., Ellen Terry's Cottage,
Small Hythe, Tenterden, Kent, England][1]

Dear Ted— I am sorry my telegram was so blundering that you did not understand it— I am half mad with grief and pain and I wanted to feel your Mother's arms about me— as I used to dream they were before Deirdre was born— and to feel that dear pity & love that *she* gives that no one else has known how to give me since their death.

Your *own* Nellie has no place in her heart except her all-absorbing ferocious & jealous love for you— and that is why I did not come in to see you.[2] In your Mother's arms I found what I was hungry for and which I think has saved my reason in this dreadful time when it seems giving way— I am sorry if you don't understand. Be silent awhile— Think of the morning Deirdre was born & perhaps you will— and if you can't understand at least pity me—

   Isadora.

Perhaps the realization that she was meeting the mother of two of Craig's healthy, living children had overwhelmed Isadora. The consequent fiasco of the visit so angered Craig that he drafted a harsh reproof.

[1] Notes by Craig: on envelope—"BAD very"; at head of letter—"Something went very wrong here— I sent Nell to meet her & Nell's report & hers *clash*. How small that is but how human . . ."

[2] Note by Craig: "Yes— & you selfishly tried to win a place in her heart by pushing me out— vain attempt. Selfish attempt— selfish desire—"

—— *CD 288* ——

[Probably England, early September 1913]

In Nelly's heart there is room for the world so long as the world does not push itself in by pushing me out.

Isn't that right?

Can you find a word to say in defence of a person man or woman who would call for sympathy & help from her, by attempting to draw it *away* from me. Oh.

You who know so well how to be a great woman don't let sorrow make of you merely a person who cries over her self . . & is bitter towards those who won't cry at all.

I have always always wanted to help you— & you have never understood. Now again I want to help you & you won't be helped.

It's not arms— not lips— not eyes— not anything touchable that will suffice for what you hunger for— only one thing will & that you won't have.

Perhaps later—?

————————

Whether or not such a letter was sent to Isadora, Craig's resentment of her behavior, whatever that may have been, is evident from a note he wrote to Elena from Paris a few days later, on his way back to Florence.

Paris 7th Sept. 1913.

. . . I thought I would go & see the river where the little girl went over— so I drove down there & got out & dropped grain of the white heather Teddy gave me. I didn't want to call at the house up the road— but the place still has tragic signs— Very tragic— can't explain but there are marks, clear & speaking . . . It was a silly business all that with ID— but you did your part well and are a dear good Nelly . . . Mama dearest that which is called my *love* is yours.

Papa

IN NO OTHER CONTEXT DOES THE UNBALANCED ASPECT OF CRAIG'S nature so balefully manifest itself as in the fact that he several times asserted that Isadora had been so careless of Deirdre and Patrick as to be responsible for their deaths. Here his transference of guilt is at its most wildly apparent. His neglect of all his children was close to total. Edward A. Craig has written of his father: "He never felt any responsibility for his children. He had done his bit toward creating them and now it was up to the mother regardless of expense —health—etc. . . . He was a great artist with a superb imagination but he wasn't a father, a husband, or . . . a real lover. Romantic yes."

Even before the fatal accident, Craig had hinted, in a letter to Elena, that the children were being allowed to live dangerously: "By the way did you hear that those two children of I.D. escaped suffocating in London. I have met a man who saved them. It's a very strange story." Nothing more is known of that incident, though after the drowning Craig refers to it again [CD *340*]: "She had children & could not abide firm & protect them: they were drowned— but not before they had already nearly been burnt alive or suffocated. This is not 'Fate' unless you are dam careless & she was dam careless." Later he wrote: ". . . After her child died 19— that child she wished for & did not know what it was when she'd got it— lost it in a river— & failed to see it was her own fault— her not really wanting it more than all else— Ran or walked around the world bewailing the loss she could have prevented— millions of women do prevent it." In his notes, Craig several times repeated that charge against Isadora:

Never need she have lost her loved children had she realized that to have children entails having obligations. *Someone* must care for them— & that someone is always MOTHER. This truth she never seems to have faced up to— She let them be looked after by governess or whoever was at hand— the joy & the pain (if pain there be) of doing all that herself she seems to have missed. Never could they have died as they did die with their MOTHER watching. She simply failed to watch— & I believe her grief loses its worth since it was her own fault. It was a punishment of the Gods? was it— there certainly is something Homeric in it— but somehow her tears do not grieve me— they make me cross with her.

Isadora was not maternal. She never showed the slightest motherly tenderness or helpfulness— the kind which children of 3, 4, 5 respond to—

the only kind. She tried to dominate Dierdre [*sic*]— her calm with her was not yielding & dear in the least— it was cold & quite unnatural. Strange this & true. And when I came to Paris & saw our little girl, instead of the baby running to me she frowned & looked at me critically— and I who in half an hour can win the heart to my heart of a child I love, could not bring Dierdree [*sic*] out of an artificial rather ominous kind of slumber.

This refers to the first time Deirdre, then six years old, had seen her father since, in Irma Duncan's words, "she was a babe-in-arms." Just as he perpetuated his own illegitimacy in most of his children, so Craig repeated with them, in varying degrees, his father's almost total absence from his own life. Craig may well have had a winning way with children when he chose, but Isadora's words to him, written when Deirdre was an infant, doubtless paint the true picture: "Why the very *Goo* of a Baby makes you look for a Time-Table book." Much of Isadora's life and art was involved with children, and there is every indication—even from Craig in his less punitive moments— that she loved them. Like most mothers who were professional women (Ellen Terry among them), Isadora necessarily employed nurses and governesses— as, in those days, did most well-to-do mothers even without professions.

Finally, in a note entitled "Topsy & I: Murder," which was written after Isadora's death and sounds partially deranged, Craig says, after suggesting that Isadora herself had been murdered rather than accidentally strangled by the famous long scarf catching in the wheel of her automobile:

When some years earlier her two children Deirdre & ———— were drowned like puppies in a sack, how was it done? An automobile was used— the man who sent it off towards the river was an experienced man— he was not IN the car he managed to start it going while he was out of it— & let it go— didn't catch it up (I think I should have done that)— let it waddle down to the riverbank bump, over the brink— fall into the water & even then this well trained man wasn't trying *in* the water to break windows or doors or to do anything. Was this too— murder? A well paid murder.

So, in the matter of the children, did Craig's stunted feelings find their outlet in macabre fantasies. The degree of the attrition of his feelings may be excruciatingly illustrated by a remark he made in France, in 1929, when one of his elder sons, Robert Craig, had to turn the car in which they were riding into the Loire to avoid hitting a bicyclist. "We emerged safely, and continued our journey," Robert Craig reports. "The unflappable GC did not turn a hair. 'That was presence of mind, Bobby, and we are obviously not intended to suffer the fate of little Deirdre,' was the most he observed."

THE CORRESPONDENCE BETWEEN ISADORA AND CRAIG AT THE TIME of the children's death, and his subsequent letters and notes about her, despite the sharp contrasts of tone, make them seem in constant touch, and it is difficult to realize that throughout this time they saw each other almost not at all. Craig says [CD *340*] that one of the few places he saw Isadora after the episode with Stanislavski in the St. Petersburg hotel was "in Florence, when I had my school"; that occasion seems to have been in the autumn of 1913, following Isadora's first and last meeting with Elena in London.

Isadora says in *My Life*:

I went over the Alps and down into Italy and continued my wanderings, sometimes finding myself in a gondola on the canals of Venice, asking the gondolier to row all night, another time in the ancient town of Rimini. I spent one night in Florence where I knew that C. was living, and I felt a great desire to send for him, but knowing that he was now married and settled down to a domestic life, I thought his [my?] presence would only cause discord and I refrained.[1]

One day, in a little town by the sea, I received a telegram which read, "Isadora, I know you are wandering through Italy. I pray you come to me. I will do my best to comfort you." It was signed Eleanora Duse.

I have never known how she discovered my whereabouts to send the telegram, but when I read the magic name, I knew that Eleanora Duse was the one person whom I might wish to see. The telegram was sent from Viareggio, just on the opposite side of the promontory from where I was.[2] I started at once in my auto, after sending a grateful reply to Eleanora to announce my arrival.

[1] Craig was, of course, not "married," nor was Elena even in Florence with him (though Dorothy Nevile Lees was).

[2] By "promontory" Isadora (or her "editor") means "peninsula"—namely, Italy.

The night I reached Viareggio there was a great storm. Eleanora was living in a little villa far out in the country, but she had left a message at the Grand Hotel asking me to come to her.

Despite this passage, there are a few letters from Isadora to Craig, and two drafts from Craig to Isadora, that seem to belong to this time and which show that Isadora did not "refrain."

—— *CD 233* ——

Villa Rigatti, Viareggio[1]
[Postmarked 17 November 1913]

Dearest Ted— Ever since your last letter I have been trying to write to you— in vain— I can't find words— You will never know where I have been down in the depths of Hell— nor what I suffered the night I didn't come in & see you— Some things will always be a mystery to you— but good— *You know that I think you the Best Thing on Earth— & the most Beautiful* and always will— I was on my way to Santi Quaranta[2]— I stopped here & have been staring at the Sea ever since— It's the only thing that does me any good— If you ever feel it come & look at the Sea with me—
but I can find no words—

    Love
      Isadora

———————

Craig did not go to Viareggio, but there exist two drafts of letters he perhaps sent in reply to her invitation. One is written on the stationery of his old Siegmundshof studio and recalls their first, sunlit morning there.

[1] Isadora says in *My Life*: "As I was pestered by strangers always staring at me in the [Grand] Hotel, I took a villa." Viareggio is not far from Florence.
[2] An Albanian port opposite Corfu, now more commonly known as Agii Saranta, or Sarande. Isadora, "rudderless," had apparently intended to rejoin Raymond in his work among the Greek refugees.

——— CD 287 ———

[Florence, 1913][1]

Your beautiful letter like your beautiful self— I hang on every word—
read over every word you ever write numberless times even as I heard
what you said that early morning in Siegmundshof numberless times—
like a singing chorus over & over— over & over— & *saw* you not a human
number— not one but numberless— a whole Host— White sun— and so
great & lovely *was that* and *is this* that no matter what storms, demons or
miseries have come or might come between those high times, nothing
could destroy the love I have for you. Dead ten thousand times it springs
from its grave with a laugh everlastingly. Not knowledge nor folly nor
anything but one thing calls it up.

Show your Beauty to me & you work a miracle. Hide it from me & you
only make a darkness— but darkness always has passed and always will
pass— & we will find light no matter how dark it be.
So when I think of *you* & *see* your beauty everything comes in place—
mist rises— sun comes out— warm— it's God isn't it?

———

Craig's other draft in reply to the invitation to Viareggio is longer,
and speaks of his school.

——— CD 285 ———

Sunday— Grey & unhappy.
[Florence, 1913]

I considered— oh long after the impulse— & I felt I could bring you
nothing more than you already have— & so I decided not to come to the

---

[1] Notes by Craig: "I found a piece of my old paper to write to her on." "To
I.D. 1913— after the tragedy." "October, 1944, Paris— Yes— & this of early
morning even today is as vivid as today is." The envelope is addressed to
Isadora at Viareggio.

sea & the sands today— As I had hoped to do— arranged to do— & even longed. And because I longed to come, not to go is not wrong.

If I could have brought you anything which I consider valuable it would have been different. And there just lies my unhappiness.

My hands are full here— having a thousand pounds or two the vultures are flapping— Hell opens to let them out attracted by the stench— and what armour have I— ?

I look around———

Anyhow

I *was* with you on the sands— I said "at 10 come down to the edge of water & walk towards Forte dei Marmi." & I overtook you at 10.30. And I took not your hands nor your feet but I put myself down under the ground on which your feet walked— & I put myself lower still & still down until I came to a place where it was so dark that only misunderstanding is darker— & there I am— my heart took me down.

And there it is good for me to be— do you see? I never knew so dark a dark that couldn't be broken— so I wait to see.

But it is grey & cold today— stove gone out— & I shall go out to my caffé— my warm place of mild relaxation.

Shall order a "caffé expresso"— anything but express— drink it— a background of goodnatured ugliness— tables— chairs— waiters & common folk— everyone known— no one known— everyone & thing like big unnecessary dream all nodding & smiling— papers rustling— noise of feet moving—

& S O L I T A R Y

in middle of it all

& trying to forget too beautiful things— lest I *feed on remembrance*— our poor useless heads, hearts, bodies— Stop thinking— *useless*. Only one thing not useless—

In a ship going down the mean fools think only of themselves & the dark & the men & women think for everyone & glow.

We are all of us in a ship going down— & it is necessary dearest Isadora that we - - *WE* - -[1] by love think of everyone else.

You are a woman so enlightened all but one tiny spot & there leather is not denser— I enlightened & much leather—

And your friends? Is there one really *friend-friend-friend*, triple friend, who belongs to you— If he's a he or she's a she, say who she or he is & I'm his friend or hers—

---

[1] The rays around "*WE*" are in yellow paint.

And you— If I say to you "this is *my* friend" will you not be able to be the friend of my friend?

I haven't so many.

WE are damned few, but if we're not WE we are merely the mob howling & raving like lunatics up & down the deck.

I loved you Isadora— you know it. We grew intoxicated— 'orribly & loverlyly we grew sober— worse— and I love you now just the same as ever only more so— ever more & more— anything else is a lie— but I don't agree with the fellow who thought there was nothing like leather & the leather in us is detestable—

Do you know I have the task of Hercules to get through. Do you know I have taken on my back *a school*—

You'd never dream what it was *teaching me*— I am the sole pupil. My dear— I am determined to learn how to carry shawls for people's cold feet— how to wrap them up— hold & tie chairs to the deck— bring & carry for them— read the weather reports in a quiet voice— & never a word about bad weather—

and this while we are going down.

(They don't know it.)

SCHOOL FOR THE ART OF THE THEATRE[1]

ARENA GOLDONI – FLORENCE – ITALY

DIRECTOR: E. GORDON CRAIG

The hardest task I ever set myself— this— to admit *others* to work with me— & to *help them*— not yet even knowing them— *near me*!!

I don't take "pupils" any more. I began it & fired them all out— rapidly[2]——— but I have 21 people working with me & I have *to give them my time*— out of 24 hours it's one hour apiece & 3 over. In this way I am broken up into pieces.

Is this what you would call my folly? Would it be here that you would tell yourself you know better than I?

I want to know this—

[1] The arrow points to the printed heading of the school, on p. 3 of the letter.

[2] Edward A. Craig writes of the Arena Goldoni: "It should have been called a workshop—not a school—for that is what it turned out to be." Some of the school "rules" drawn up by Craig perhaps account in part for the lack or disappearance of "pupils": "It is understood that every member of the School undertakes not to join any other school of a similar nature, no matter when or for what reason he should leave this one"; "'Opinions' are wanted neither inside nor outside the School"; etc.

Consider that even with time against me chance is so great (blessed or cursed) that it provides for the man who dares time to this extent—Death!

or

Life!

How silent & dark it is here— solitary too. Oh for you to fly just like some bird against the window glass— indeed, dear, I am so great a fool, I sometimes look up expecting to see your spirit at the window— that you should fly over here seems only reasonable in spite of all knowledges of the material.

Have done so for years— wanted you. You don't know how I have worshipped you, thinking of you as having wings— Yet you must know in spite of anything what *we are*— I mean what is ONE in us.

No— perhaps it's what we are *when you will*— perhaps it's only your magic, not mine at all. I feel almost sure of this.

Yet I still tell myself it could not & cannot be difficult or hard for you to have willed to be of me— or has it to be a *transformation*— and have I only *thought* that you were from the beginning of the world always a part of me.

Others are good & kind & helpful to me & faithful & obedient & unselfish— & I am none of these but you seem part of me— don't you know I always felt that—

Was that all wrong— & is it— whatever happen[s]? And if you are & were a part of me I then am a part of you— no matter whether the smallest of [*sic*] the worst part or the heaviest & the best— or the funniest!—

Answer me some of these questions & talk to me— if you need something, consider how great may be my need—

And don't be *jealous*— because if it's grander to be jealous & defy things rather than placid & sit in a row, still, dear, it's *DIVINE* to be nonjealous— especially since it's "for Hecuba"— in the play— the band playing— & the ship going down.

Always always always & always returning & returning never able to alter come the good pictures of you to my mind— No wind seems able to blow away these light pictures. Incessantly they come back— I see a star— liquid— a balcony— two balconies— some trees— a convent— a road— a tune is being played— a light in a window— a train rushes by— all these visions covering many years mix & become Real.

[1]*Last.*

No— what I have to say is this— isn't it. Can you forgive me for all

---

[1] CD *286* begins here.

the bad things? & can you forgive me for trying to live without you? You see I can't.
So can you? It would open the sky for me.

Two notes from Isadora indicate that they did meet, later that fall, in Florence.

——— CD 234 ———

Grand Hotel, Florence
Room 22
[Autumn, 1913]

Dearest Ted— I am passing through Florence— If you would *like* to see me come tomorrow afternoon about *6*— But if it would give you too much pain— *don't*— Let me know in the morning— Myself I am in a strange state beyond anything human I think— I am on my way to Rome— & then perhaps to Egypt— to Karnak to rest in that Great Temple that I sent you once a picture of with little Deirdre sitting there looking up so calm & sweet.
With Love

Isadora

——— CD 235 ———

[Probably same as preceding letter]

Yes I should love to but *Please* won't you come & dine first— We[1] dine at *8*. Just send back a verbal yes— My Spirit feels some *healing* & *light* since seeing you—

Love
Isadora

They did not meet again for six years.

[1] Hener Skene was with her.

10

The Last Letters

ISADORA WENT ONLY AS FAR AS ROME IMMEDIATELY FOLLOWING THAT meeting with Craig in Florence in 1913. There a telegram from Singer reached her, offering a splendid building at Bellevue near Paris, and full financial support, if she would return and open a new school of the dance. She accepted, and with that return to Paris and the inauguration of the school at Bellevue there begins yet another chapter in Isadora's life—not the last, but one of the later chapters. With the death of the children, it introduces the period for which she has been most widely known, because it was then that she began to be frequented by some of those who later wrote their books about her—almost the only books which, along with the hectic, confusing patchwork of *My Life*, have up until now existed. As Craig put it to Irma Duncan (whose authoritative *Duncan Dancer* is in a different category) when the books began to appear: "It's the fashion for books to tell of ID after she got to Paris." Too many of these accounts have taken their chief substance from *My Life*, from gossip, from the writers' acquaintance with the later Isadora only—the Isadora who gave birth at Bellevue to her third child (fathered, she says in *My Life*, at Viareggio by a Michelangelesque stranger, and alive only a few hours); the Isadora who separated from Singer and took later lovers; the Isadora who in the 1920's lived and taught in the Soviet

Union, married the gifted, dipsomaniac Russian poet Sergei Esenin and returned to harangue Western audiences about the glories of the pre-Stalin regime; the Isadora of the last, debt-ridden days in Nice; the Isadora who died her famous death in 1927, saying to her friends as she stepped into an auto, *"Adieu, mes amis, je vais à la gloire,"* only to be instantly strangled when her long scarf caught in one of the wheels[1]: the Isadora of all that has been portrayed in some of the books and memoirs like some disjointed, flamboyant creature born only in middle life. No biographer has yet properly fused the elements, early and late, into a psychological portrait of the essential Isadora: the artist who danced and the woman who died at fifty. It would be a labor of years, but the result might be a masterpiece— if the biographer were himself or herself an artist. Craig recognized this in one of his letters to Irma: "So Dougie [Alan Ross MacDougall] is to issue a Biography of Isadora. Wellwell— well—That's easy— the difficulty is to write it as it deserves— as Montaigne or Byron might have written it."

The present volume, which it is hoped may be an aid to such a biographer, now approaches its end with Isadora's last few letters to Craig.

In January 1917, when he was living in Rome (he had had to abandon the Arena Goldoni when Lord Howard de Walden cut off funds because of what he considered wartime priorities), Craig happened to reread one of the letters that Isadora had sent him in December 1904, just before leaving Berlin for Russia, and was inspired to write (and perhaps send) one of his drafts—once again full of echoes of their first days together.

[1] In 1969, when a film based on Isadora's life was playing in New York, department stores advertised their long scarves, with macabre salesmanship, as "Isadora scarves."

Jean Cocteau wrote at the time of Isadora's death, "Isadora's end is *perfect*— a kind of horror that leaves one calm."

—— *CD 289* ——

[Rome?]
January, 1917[1]

"We were born in the same star & we came in its rays to earth— & for a little I was in your heart & then I wandered far away & now I am back— that is our History. No one could understand it— but us—"[2]

Everyone is calling you to hurry— you are packing to go to Russia— oh, my love— You write me two immortal pages & through fogs & fires & terrors those two pages will remain immortal. For the thing in your heart was that which *they don't know*— & *only I know*— which you forgot & which I forgot for we always were so forgetful— even in 1904— even in 904— even in 4— & even before—

And we were so *fond* of each other— not mad at all— only mad when anyone else came near— and we are not mad— 'all the world but thee & me.' I can't write— but I am seeing you as you were & do not see any change at all— I was nothing— & you were you— but we were what no one[3] could understand— everything.

I have only reread one letter— because I do not want to die suddenly[4]— Love like Poison does not kill if taken little bits & little bits.

I can't be sure you have an old letter of mine (I have every scrap— ribbon— ticket— letter & card you ever gave me) but if you have *one*, look at it now & see some of the old eternal wonder. Never mind who else is there. I shall not harm them & no one here shall be harmed by you— but we are once more, & eternally, together— I don't *ask*, my Isadora; I remember the sun which streamed in on us in Siegmundshof & I know— I don't say anything to you I'm only singing dear—

(People came in talked loud— & have gone out this moment—)
I continue easily— nothing can disturb me. It is raining outside— it's dark but I hear it. "I will always be grateful to you," you wrote, & with such fine bold writing— bold & *even*— not like mine irregular. But our differences do not matter— "Joy & love unspeakable," you wrote— Oh, my wonder— what do we not know— you have not suffered. I have not suf-

---

[1] The date is part of the draft. Craig has included it in a later note, written at the top of the page, which reads: "On rereading one of her letters of 1904 on [*sic*] January 1917."

[2] Note by Craig: "1904 Xmas. Your words." (See p. 31.)

[3] Note by Craig: "— not even ourselves."

[4] Note by Craig: "all the rest wait like pearls down sea to be dived for later."

fered— yet we could say so if we wished— *we do not wish*. "Until I
return to the Heart in which I was born," you wrote, & I 12 years later
add "in which I was born too"—

That is not my Heart but *our* heart.
Your letter is the Magic Book— & the pages glow with Truth— a thing
everyone doubts & I don't doubt at all.

Spite of pride, & lots of little cloudy things, your words are just as
though spoken now— today— I swear they are spoken now & today—
It is the old Ted who does not wait till he is dead to tell you this— all
others may do as they think best but we will do better— better than all.
We continue speaking from heart to heart— hearts which for five minutes
of eternity were silent— we were asleep.
Isadora— Isadora Isadora
Where is the man or woman on earth who will rival me in my right &
my joy in repeating that name.

It becomes like a new element— Earth, Air, Fire, Water, Isadora— &
all the four are summed up in the fifth—[1]

All because of the original beauty— the beauty of those days, those
beautiful big days.
There are others, & there have been others & all these others live still &
are in our arms. Whether small or great we carry them— we can & we
will—
Our hands clasped— both hands— they lie between us— nursed by us.
The sheet of paper on which you write is even larger than this— such a
document as no other possesses or can ever possess—
If ever I have wept those tears were all joy, & all become now streaks
of sun— if ever I have hurt you I have hurt myself far more— you have
never hurt me—

All this neither leads forward nor backwards— it only stays us where
we were, where we are, & ever shall be.

I am not merely something which loves you.

I am you— you are me.
We have only one need— the love & forgiveness of others.

We will meet— our two persons— & we will go hand in hand somewhere— wherever we may meet— & we will not even say to the Earth
"We have mastered you" but our cries will be heard by all living things,

---

[1] "Thou hast as chiding a nativity
  As fire, air, water, earth and heaven can make . . ."
    (*Pericles, Prince of Tyre*, III, 1)

& the sound of our hardly moving feet will make the earth tremble for joy—

You are as beautiful as you were a thousand years ago— You are no day older— Indeed I *swear* you are 12 years younger—

"Darling until we meet again— until I return to the Heart in which I was born— *Your* Isadora."

Your words

And mine

    Your Ted

and forgive me what seemed like pain & tears. I have nothing to forgive, & everything to remember.

———————

But they did not meet again until one day in Rome, in the winter of 1919, Isadora discovered that Craig too was in the city.

—— *CD 237* ——

[Postmarked Rome, 12 December 1919;[1]
addressed to Sig. Edward Gordon Craig,
Hotel de La Russie, Rome]

Dear Ted— I am passing thru Rome leaving Sunday and have just heard that you are here— I should love to see you if you are free— telephone tomorrow— or send me a word—

    Isadora

Hotel Excelsior
Rome— *Dec. 10.*

———————

[1] Note by Craig: "Evidently reached me on the 12th . . . *after* she had joined me on the 12th at Café Greco."

That night, as we shall see, they walked the streets of Rome together in emotional reunion, and Isadora wrote him on each of the next two days.

—— *CD 238* ——

Saturday
[Rome, 13 December 1919]

Dear Ted— For so long I have only turned my head looking back & weeping for the past. Now when I see you Life seems again full of Hope & Joy & Enthusiasm, & everything seems possible, Even a Future! *Do* come to dinner— let me feast on you— I need it—

Your Isadora

—— *CD 239* ——

[Envelope of Hotel Excelsior, Rome; 1919][1]

Dear Ted— Woudn't you like to hear a Beethoven Symphonie today at the Augusteo? I have a box. If so, come & lunch & we will go together & hear Music Worthy of You. If you are engaged, join us[2] at the Augusteo or come after— but *please* come. I am longing to see you—

Isadora

It was apparently after receiving her note of the thirteenth, and before receiving the one of Sunday, that Craig wrote out a long draft—the latest dated of all his surviving drafts of letters to Isadora.

[1] Note by Craig: "By hand. Dec. 14th 1919— Sunday."
[2] With her was the pianist Walter Rummel, nicknamed by Isadora "the Archangel."

—— *CD 290* ——

[Rome, 13 or 14 December 1919][1]

Most dear— all is well . . never better.

You— YOU— have no need of me—

All the bad pains of imagined sorrows— for sorrow is not real— all these hours & days come around me at this hour & give me kisses so sweet that —— —— ——

You know.

Don't forget—

you are a great being—

Act as you have always done— greatly— my beloved—

& when in doubt— go one better.

[2]Roma

As I cannot come tonight to dinner, my dear dear spirit, suppose you let me write enough to serve as a sleep bringer—

You are right in all you write— or say— or do— & for you life will never be anything but full of Hope & Joy & Enthusiasm— because of no other reason than your dear self—

---

[1] This seems to be a pair of drafts—one quickly abandoned, the other completed. They are preceded by a separate page on which Craig has written the following notes:

Memorandum made Oct. 5, 1944

EGC & ID in Rome

1919 Dec. 12th Friday— she came

    13   Sat   "

    14   Sunday   "

    15   Monday   "

    16th Tuesday she goes— to Paris

It was in December 1904 we met Berlin on the 16th were photographed together. (12. 13. 14. & 15 were close together) This she remembered in 1919— but I forgot.

The first, short draft, all on one page, was headed by Craig in 1944: "Sunday December 14th 1919 Rome—"

[2] Here begins the second draft, headed by Craig in 1944: "Sunday December 14th, 1919. Answer to hers of Saturday & Sunday with ID & flowers woodcut mark." (The last words refer to Isadora's having written both her Rome notes on correspondence cards bearing the device, designed by Craig, reproduced on p. 110, which she had continued to use even on her French stationery.)

You think that it is I who in some way aid that— all that: if I do, then I am again happy as in 1904— when you first gave me the key to what you write of— Joy . . . hope—

but it is you who are the possessor of the greatest of secrets & you who are invincible—

It is almost more than a marvel that during this life I have known you— & that you have been the revelation of many a blessing which has come to me—

"The past"— "the present" . . . "future" . . . all these are words which have some meaning when used in speaking of most people— *they have nothing whatever to do with you*—

They have not touched you, nor can they—

There is no one who knows like you how to find paths unknown to others— "paths which no man trod"—

& your paths & mine go along in some queer way quite close & lead to the same place— but when we tread the SAME path it's nowhere we find ourselves going to.

Are you already asleep!   ?——

Dear dear dear Isadora . .

All the hours days & years with their sorrows of regret dance near me at this moment with LOVE in being able to speak to you at last— a little. All the bad days with their longing & longing crowd on me here & now & chatter & tumble over each other clambering up & crying around me that they didn't mind the awful pain if you smile & don't mind—

Don't you see it is YOU & not me— it is you who count— & merely to think of you & know you love me (& hear you say so— once or twice) gives me all the inspiration in the world— all I need— *an ocean*.

I talk silly! let me talk!— it's not everyone who can do it so well.

Go to Paris— build there your idea— I will build here— when both are built we will somehow unite them—

No?— then we will not . . just as you will.

And . . besides . . it don't matter: for you & I will not be consulted—

You are one of the greatest of beings comparable only with— no one.

Act like a great being my beloved—

That is to say act as you always act— & when in doubt— go one better.

As you are invincible you cannot fail—

Go to sleep & say it was I prescribed the magic when you wake.

My countless thoughts be around you all the time—

   "Ted"

————

Craig later called his walk with Isadora in Rome the night of December 12, 1919, "a walk of a lifetime," and wrote about it in his notes in several different ways:

Then came the terrible trial for me— for she made the attempt . . . to once more unite with me & rebuild our shattered dreams. That was in 1919 in Rome. It was lovely & like her 1904 self to try— but I knew it would be wrong— an error in every way— yet still we LOVE.

I loved her— I do so still . . . My excitement when I knew I was in Paris and she too— or in Rome and she in Rome too— or wherever she was— that was a huge excitement. But . . . I had no need to tell myself "Be firm— she is coming— now, no weakness."

We hurt each other— we separated. *And then we had to suffer for it* . . . When later on we came together again for a brief moment in Rome (1919) (the night of December 12, Friday) we were both at the very last point of endurance— so it seemed to me: for I judged from the joy I felt of seeing her again— (she too). (This to a day was 15 years after we had first met together.) We walked & walked arms linked in the darkest Rome (it was as we passed an occasional shaded lamp, for the lights were dimmed in Rome, that I turned my head to see her dear face.)— we talked of nothings as we walked & again our hearts SANG— we were weeping as we walked but we walked all that away & ended smiling. Just to stand together was to us supreme intoxication. We didn't ask "have you suffered" but we certainly knew— she wrote me in Rome— there is a card somewhere— I answered it— but what I *first* wrote I did not send— I have it— It may explain what we felt— what I felt.

Back in Paris, Isadora wrote him again of the good their meeting in Rome had done her.

———— *CD 240* ————
CLARIDGE'S HOTEL
PARIS

Friday
[Postmarked Paris, 20 December 1919;
addressed to Hôtel de Russie, Rome]

Dear Ted— It was a joy to meet you. For years I suffer from Neu-ras-then-ia which malady translated means Incurable Sorrow & Heartbreak.

I rush about the world trying to find a remedy— There is none— but nevertheless it gave me much joy to meet you & made me believe in hopes of other spheres—

Paris is crowded with foreigners & Barbarians— spending enormous sums of money in a perpetual whirlagig of fox-trot jazz bands. There are *four* in this hotel, who play the same tunes morning, *noon* & all night— The poor Archangel[1] is distracted & we don't know where to go or how!! I spend hours talking with lawyers trying to get something from the awful muddle at Bellevue.[2]

We went to a performance of "Edipe" at the Circus which was appalling. Everyone shouted & bawled & hundreds of Dalcrozes hopping about naked & athletes walking on their hands— Fortunately I met a friend in need who administered to me a bottle of Champagne in the entre acte— otherwise I would have died of it. The actors walked about the aisles on the toes of spectators shrieking like a Zoological Gardens let loose. They say this is the influence of Reinhardt— *Merci*—

I hope to settle Bellevue & return to Rome or Egypt. How wonderful it would be to walk with you in the Temple of Karnak—

There are some indications of it at the Vatican Mus.— but there is even more in certain drawings of yours. Makes me believe in reincarnation. Perhaps if we went to Karnak or Abydos we would find our former ghosts— who were probably les très chic types & knew better how to adjust themselves to this Earth than me—[3] I hope to settle my affairs here by the first week in Jan.— In the meantime this hotel with four orchestras going at once— C'est gai!—

Please send me a line— & tell me also if the Marquise & Mr. T. turned out anything. I think Mrs. McCormick is right & dreams are more im-

---

[1] Note by Craig: "W. Rummel."

[2] During the war, Bellevue had been turned over to the French government for a hospital, and later it had been used as a school for soldiers organized by the American army. Now Isadora was trying to raise money to restore it. Her efforts failed, and eventually it was sold to the French government at a low price.

At the time of the war, much of which she spent in North and South America, Isadora had conceived and repeatedly performed her stirring dance to the music of *La Marseillaise*; Arnold Genthe's photograph of her in one its impassioned poses is perhaps her best-known portrait.

[3] Note by Craig: "My dear— my dear—"

portant than so-called day life— only you need a good income to appreciate this theory.[1]

A thousand good wishes to you & love

from Isadora

The next spring, 1920, Craig was in Paris for the publication of the first French edition of *The Art of the Theatre*, and he seems to have attended one or more of the performances that Isadora was giving jointly with Walter Rummel in her attempt to raise money for Bellevue. "These performances have been given in the teeth of every catastrophe & impossibility & without a sou," she says in one of the notes she sent Craig at this time. ". . . Glad enough to come off alive & pay the Eternal Hotel Bill." [CD *245*] She introduced Craig to various people prominent in the arts in Paris: "I have invited Mrs. Romaine Brooks & Miss Barney[2] who want to give a reception in your honor— They know all Paris & are most enthusiastic for your work." [CD *246*] Particularly she saw that he met Firmin Gémier, the idealistic actor-manager who had once formed a *"théâtre ambulant"* and was now organizing the Théâtre National Populaire.

——— *CD 247* ———

CLARIDGE'S HOTEL
PARIS

[Dated by Craig,
April 5 or 6, 1920]

Dearest Ted—

I think it absolutely *necessary* for your career in Paris that you have that dinner jacket & I think it will bring you good luck. There is a fine tailor

---

[1] Mrs. Edith Rockefeller McCormick was the daughter of John D. Rockefeller. Craig had met her in Zurich and she had bought a number of his pictures and etchings.

[2] Romaine Brooks, the American painter; Natalie Clifford Barney, the American writer.

in Place Vendôme, as the Archangel says his is a grump. I rang you up today but you were out[1]— I am writing to Gémier— Ring me up *here*.

Love Isadora.

This is the latest dated of all the extant letters from Isadora to Craig; with it their correspondence ends characteristically—on a note of her generosity. It was her last attempt—naïve, perhaps, in the detail of the dinner jacket—to repeat the success she had had in Moscow: the successful bringing together of Craig and a working, visionary theatrical producer. In later life Craig was to pay her efforts in this direction a tribute that was condescending and adamant about "compromise," which here he calls "ambition," and which as we have seen would sometimes have been no more than cooperation:

You know she was as silly as many women are & thought she could persuade me (the artist in me is a terror to change by an inch) to a life of *Ambition*. Now ambition is of all things the very worst—*so* attractive— offering all sorts of devilish prizes— most men fall for it. Wolsey the silly ass cardinal did[2]— Napoleon— not *Lincoln* nor *Walt W*— not any true artist— I mean true to the guns. Gauguin stood firm, Van Gogh; Bernard Shaw flopped. The old painters of Italy & Spain all over the shop stood firm— they were innocent— it never entered their heads to be *ambitious*. Only nowadays has the virus spread & look at the result! Anyhow my great darling thought ambition was quite a nice thing— she was quite without guile & of course what the blessed darling felt was that it would lead to such a success for me— such wealth— etc. etc. She was, of course, wrong— it leads always only to sorrow, pain & death.

[1] Notes by Craig: "I was at Hotel des Deux Mondes, Ave. de l'Opera." "She enclosed a cheque for 2000 *fr* which I took back to her— When lunch was over I remember she begged me to have a suit for 'little Ted'— & this 2000 shall start off Ted's fortune."

[2] In 1892, Craig had played Cromwell to Henry Irving's Wolsey in *Henry VIII*.

ISADORA WAS TO LIVE SEVEN YEARS AFTER THAT REUNION IN PARIS, and there is no evidence that during those seven last years she and Craig ever met again.

In a letter [CD *242*] written to him just before he reached Paris that spring, she had said: "I have ordered your book but it has not come yet"—words that could refer either to the forthcoming *De l'Art du Théâtre* or to a pamphlet, printed in London that year in an edition of thirty copies for private circulation, called The Foreword to *The Theatre Advancing*. Let us hope it was the latter, and that Isadora did eventually see it, for it contains a tribute to an unnamed dancer:

You play no little dramas with others. You are alone—you enter and fill the stage with any figure you choose—and as many as you choose . . . your imagination peoples the place; just as in his lovely scenes the great Appia seems to pack his empty platforms with a hundred, hundred angels—and to start them singing when he chooses. This is the power of Imagination—you both possess it . . .

Your great power (the power not yours but which yields to you) enables you to move your hand and we seem to see lilies or roses or lilac growing—"when lilac first in the doorway [*sic*] . . ." You turn towards the right and by the force of your imagination you project for us a group of three who seem to advance towards you: you turn from us a little and the dark comes on—you turn a little more, evening; a little more and it is night.

It is the power of Imagination, not your power, and you possess some of it—enough to convince a world and baffle a nation.

I have seen you bring palm to palm silently and head the cymbals— cymbals which sang rather than clashed. I have seen your shoulders move bending and heard the thunders of an old story rolling up around you. You have lain your hand on the earth obediently obeying the old Fate, and I have seen the earth open as a smile spreads and drench you in yellow light. You were more than three hundred years old as you bent to obey and you rose up a young woman.

You who alone have the secret of this magic will never tinker with the twopenny tricks of the trade.

Just as it was pleasant that the Isadora-Craig correspondence should end on a note of Isadora's generosity, so it is good to close this volume with that tribute from Craig to Isadora, and with other indications of his concern for her. In 1925, hearing that Isadora was in financial difficulties, he wrote to Singer in Paris through a friend, "suggesting," as he himself says, "that he [Singer] send her £5000." [CD *340*] The friend was dilatory, but by the time Craig's letter reached Singer in Florida, the millionaire had already, on his own initiative, sent money anonymously to Isadora, from whom he had long been separated. The next year, the next to the last of Isadora's life, Craig says he acted again: "I was only once able to be of service when she was in difficulties— that was in 1926. I read in 'Daily Mail' that she was being sold up & called for help from all her friends. As I had 3000 francs at the time I sent a third of it to her— it was all I possessed. I rec'd no acknowledgement— but someone told me that I was put into the newspaper as having sent." [CD *340*]

In the great number of pages both published and unpublished that he devoted to Isadora throughout the rest of his life (he died in 1966 at the age of ninety-four)—some of them scurrilous, some revelatory of his own periodic disequilibrium, others perspicacious, admiring or adoring, and all of them written with the literary gift he possessed among his great repertory of talents and kinds of artistic imagination —it is Craig himself, the man whose ego wounded Isadora so grievously, that comes closest to providing a biography of her written "as it deserves—as Montaigne or Byron might have written it." Among the most romantic of these pages is a manuscript found only recently, an expansion of a section of the early *Book Topsy* written by Craig in 1943, when he was seventy-one. It is an account of a "Christmas walk" with Isadora several days after he had first seen her dance and visited her in her dressing room—their walk through the streets of Berlin as he led her to 11 Siegmundshof for their "marriage night on the floor of the dear studio," December 17, 1904.

I and Isadora strode along arm in arm around Charlottenburg & in & out of the paths of the Thiergarten . . . We two, she & I walked & walked: it was Xmas & we hadn't any engagements: neither had she engaged herself to me or I to her: we just held together arm linked in arm heart to heart because we couldn't help it— we didn't think, because we knew: we could hardly feel, because of joy: we walked & walked. You know I suppose that she walked from the hip— easily . . never tiring: you know I suppose that I was just so in my walk. It was in our work that has arrived. If it has not, I must wait here until it comes and rescues us. If it does not come, I will throw myself into the sea—

De tout coeur
Isadora

The desperate cry was answered; the rescue check did come. The letter is all the more poignant for a reader of the present volume because of the stationery on which it is written. It is that of a Trouville seaside café, whose printed letterhead dominates the page: TOPSY SUR LES PLANCHES ET PAVILLON ROYAL—"Topsy on the Boardwalk . . ." Her old love-name, her present extremity—and Isadora choosing to combine the two in a note which, without naming him, tells us of whom she was thinking as she wrote.

—— *THE END* ——

Isadora Duncan

A BBC Radio Talk by

Gordon Craig

Isadora Duncan[1]

I HAVE SOMETHING TO SAY ABOUT ISADORA DUNCAN. IN FACT I HAVE a good deal to say of her, but that can wait and take its place in my memoirs. The something I have to say now is that she was the first and only dancer I ever saw—except for some in a street in Genoa, and some in a barn near York. Isadora came to us in the first years of this century. When she died it seemed to some of us that dancing ceased. Dancing and ballet dancing are two separate things. The world raved about her for several years—as it will rave, and often ignorantly; and then it actually forgot her.

People called her a great artist—a Greek goddess—but she was nothing of the kind. [Hah!] She was something quite different from anyone and anything else. I always thought how Irish she was [I hope Dublin will be listening], which means, how full of natural genius which defies description: but she had more than that. Yet she had the tip-tilted nose and the little firm chin, and the dream in her heart of the Irish who are so sweet to know. And in her eye was California, and this eye looked out over Europe and thought well of what it saw.

What more she had, no one will ever describe. She was a fore-runner. All she did was done with very great ease—or so it seemed,

---

[1] Partially printed in *The Listener*, June 5, 1952; printed here with some of Craig's ad libs in brackets.

at least. This it was which gave her an appearance of power. She projected the dance into this world of ours in full belief that what she was doing was right and great. And it was. She threw away ballet skirts and ballet thoughts. She discarded shoes and stockings too. She put on some bits of stuff which when hung up on a peg looked more like torn rags than anything else; when she put them on they became transformed. Stage dresses usually transform the performers [don't they], but in her case it was these bits which actually became transformed by her putting them on. She transformed them into marvels of beauty and at every step she took they spoke. I do not exaggerate.

I shall never forget the first time I saw her come on to an empty platform to dance. It was in Berlin, the year 1904—please make a note of that, somebody says it was 1905—the month December. Not on a theatre stage was this performance, but in a concert-hall, and you know what the platforms of concert-halls were like in 1904.

She came through some small curtains which were not much taller than she was herself: she came through them and walked down to where a musician, his back turned to us, was seated at a grand piano; he had just finished playing a short prelude by Chopin when in she came, and in some five or six steps was standing by the piano, quite still and, as it were, listening to the hum of the last notes. [Quite still . . .] You might have counted five, or even eight, and then there sounded the voice of Chopin again, in a second prelude or etude; it was played through gently and came to an end and she had not moved at all. Then one step back or sideways, and the music began again as she went moving on before or after it. Only just moving— not pirouetting or doing any of those things which we expect to see, and which a Taglioni or a Fanny Elssler would have certainly done. She was speaking in her own language [Do you understand? Her own language: have you got it?], not echoing any ballet master, and so she came to move as no one had ever seen anyone move before. The dance ended, and again she stood quite still. No bowing, no smiling —nothing at all. Then again the music is off, and she runs from it— it runs after her then, for she has gone ahead of it.

How is it that we know she is speaking her own language? We know it, for we see her head, her hands, gently active, as are her feet, her whole person. And if she is speaking, what is it she is saying? No one would ever be able to report truly [or exactly—extraordinary, isn't it], yet no one present had a moment's doubt. Only this can we say—that she was telling to the air the very things we longed to hear and until she came we had never dreamed we should hear; and now we heard them, and this sent us all into an unusual state of joy, and I [—I] sat still and speechless.

I remember that when it was over I went rapidly round to her dressing-room to see her, and there too I sat still and speechless in front of her for a while. She understood my silence very well; all talk being [quite] unnecessary. She was tired after her dancing, and was resting. No one else came to see her. Far, far off we heard applause going on [still going on, still going on]. After a while she [stirs, she] puts on a cloak, shoes, and out we went into the streets of Berlin, where the snow looked friendly and the shops still lighted up, the Christmas trees all spangled and lighted, and we walked and talked of the shops. The shops, the Christmas trees, the crowd—no one heeded us. Time passed, time went on.

Some weeks later on she thought she could found a school of such a dance; or she said she thought so. She had forgotten what her much-loved poet Whitman had said: 'I charge you that you found no school after me . . .' Very cautious was that poet, and he often uses this word 'caution' in his books, as you will have noticed.

Isadora caused the rash enthusiasts to imitate her, to do it well or to do it badly, but she laboured very long to create a school, talking much for very many years about it all, getting girls into a school-house and putting her sister Elizabeth (a very clever woman) to train them. The first result of this showed well; I saw this first showing at a matinee at the Kroll Opera House in Berlin, where, after dancing her own dances, turning towards the wings she called her little pupils to come to her and please the public with their little leapings and runnings: as they did, and with her leading them the whole troupe became irresistibly lovely. I suppose some people even then and there began reasoning about it all, trying to pluck out the heart of the mystery. But I and hundreds of others who saw this first revelation did not stop to reason, for we too had all read what the poets had written of life and love and nature, and we did not reason then; we read, we wept, we laughed for joy. And so it was at the Kroll Opera House that day—we all wept and laughed for joy. And to see her shepherding her little flock, keeping them together and specially looking after one very small one of four years old, was a sight no one there had ever seen before and, I suppose, will never see again.

This is something she did towards forming a school [only something], just as Blake's first two verses in the 'Songs of Innocence' are but something; the whole great singing follows. And as surely did the whole great dancing of Isadora follow after these first wild, lovely steps. Unlike weeds, schools are things of peculiar slow growth; but in this way for ten or more years she projected the dance for us to take with us in our heads and 'in our heart's heart, Horatio'.

Was it art? No, it was not. It was something which inspires those men who labour in the narrower fields of the arts, harder but more lasting. It released the minds of hundreds of such men: one had but to see her dance for one's thoughts to wing their way, as it were, with the fresh air. It rid us of all nonsense we had been pondering so long. How is that—for she said nothing [, you say]? On the contrary, she said everything that was worth hearing; and everything that anyone else but the poets had forgotten to say. Yet hers was a divine accident.

How did she do it? Ask a poet how he makes his verse. Yeats answered: 'I made it out of a mouthful of air'. He is right. [Isn't that magnificent?] You may find that an unpractical answer, but do you get any further if he tells you, like Baudelaire, 'I made it always by reading the dictionary'? 'Words, words, words'; it is about all the poet has to work with; so give your son a dictionary if he fancies he will write verse. But tell him, also, what Yeats said. Yet you think by sending your girl to a ballet school you will help her to dance. You will not; you will hinder her. What must she do then? [Why—] She should do what Isadora did: learn what it is to *move*: to step, to walk, to run; few people can do these things. Did it ever occur to you? First the thought, then the head, then the hands and feet a little, just move, and look around, watch all which is moving. Tell that to your daughter. For dance comes with movements; but there are no first, second, and third positions unless you are drilling for a soldier, though after all each dancer will make his own first, second, and third positions if he wants to, but they must be *his own*.

How long did it take Isadora to move? [Well,] About five minutes (that is no answer, yet it is the only true one anyone can give); and then she taught herself how to move this way, that way, every way. But not according to the teaching of Noverre, or of Blasis or Petipas or any of the famous ballet masters. This took her many years to learn. But I [do] believe that that forgotten man, Del Sarte, helped her through his book. Once I found a copy of this book in her room when I was looking for a trunkful of books I had lent her. I did not find the trunkful, so I took this one. Many thousands of people in America and France studied this book by Del Sarte, and yet very few of these thousands ever gleaned any secret from its pages. A word or two to a genius like Isadora is always enough, whereas one hundred thousand are thrown away on [those dear] duffers.

What is it she lacked? What was it she had? She had calm. She had no vanity. She had no cleverness—by which I mean no clever little tricks of the trade—little or no understanding of the arts, a great comprehension of nature and perhaps rather too much ambition.

I have heard Christian Bérard [You know who he was] say that he only saw her dance in 1926, or thereabouts, when she was no longer slim. 'Fat', he said, without a shade of contempt or criticism. 'Quite big—fat'. But he added this: 'I never saw such movement in my life—a transformation took place when she began to move'.

He and I were in a small and empty restaurant on the Boulevard St.-Germain, when I asked Bérard had he ever seen Isadora. It was the first time I met him. He was not given to excessive solemnity, though he was one of the most serious of the artists of his day, the day which ended far too soon. He was a very great stage decorator, though 'decoration' in his case is somehow the wrong word, for his thoughts were to create places on the stage which had not been seen before; and this he did, places peopled with figures not seen before either.

So when the admirable Bérard spoke of Isadora Duncan, and with such gentleness, and only yesterday, when nearly all Paris has forgotten her [—dreadful—], it said a great deal to me; and may these my words about her say something to you.

Bibliography and
Acknowledgments

(Only the principal printed and manuscript sources consulted are listed, in some cases with the abbreviations used in references to them in the notes.)

PRINTED

BABLET, DENIS, *Edward Gordon Craig* (Translated by Daphne Woodward). New York, Theatre Arts Books, 1966; London, Heinemann, 1966.

CRAIG, EDWARD, *Gordon Craig: The Story of His Life*. New York, Knopf, 1968; London, Gollancz, 1968. (EAC)

CRAIG, EDWARD GORDON (see also Ostrom, below), *Index to the Story of My Days, 1872–1907*. London, Hulton Press, 1957. (*Index*)

———, *On the Art of the Theatre*. London, Heinemann, 1968.

———, *Towards a New Theatre: Forty Designs for Stage Scenes with Critical Notes by the Inventor Edward Gordon Craig*. London and Toronto, J. M. Dent and Sons Ltd., 1913.

———, *The Theatre—Advancing*. Boston, Little, Brown, 1919; London, Constable & Co. Ltd., 1921.

DUNCAN, IRMA, *Duncan Dancer: An Autobiography*. Middletown, Conn., Wesleyan University Press, 1966. (*Duncan Dancer*)

DUNCAN, ISADORA (see Ostrom, below).

KENNET, LADY—KATHLEEN, LADY SCOTT, *Self-Portrait of an Artist*. London, John Murray, 1949. (Kennet)

KRASOVSKAYA, V., *Russian Ballet Theatre at the Beginning of the 20th Century*, 2 vols. Leningrad, 1971. (In Russian only.)

MACDOUGALL, ALAN ROSS, *Isadora: A Revolutionary in Art and Love*. New York, Nelson, 1960.

MANVELL, ROGER, *Ellen Terry*. New York, Putnam's, 1968; London, Heinemann, 1968. (Manvell)

OSTROM, NICKI NOWLIN, "The Gordon Craig–Isadora Duncan Collection: A Register." *Bulletin of The New York Public Library*, Vol. 76 (1972), pp. 181–98. (Includes bibliographical indications.)

RAMBERT, DAME MARIE, *Quicksilver: The Autobiography of Marie Rambert*. London, Macmillan, and New York, St. Martin's Press, 1972.

ROOD, ARNOLD, Catalogue: *Edward Gordon Craig, Artist of the Theatre, 1872–1966. A Memorial Exhibition . . .* (Introduction by Donald Oenslager). New York, The New York Public Library, 1967. (Rood, Exhibition)

ROSE, ENID, *Gordon Craig and the Theatre: A Record and an Interpretation*. New York, Frederick A. Stokes Company, 1932; London, Sampson Low, 1931.

ROSLAVLEVA, NATALIA, *Era of the Russian Ballet*. London, Gollancz, 1966.
———, "Stanislavski and the Ballet" (monograph), *Dance Index*, No. 23 (1965).

SEROFF, VICTOR, *The Real Isadora: A Biography*. New York, The Dial Press, 1971; London, Hutchinson, 1972 (Seroff)

SHAW, MARTIN F., *Up to Now*. Oxford University Press, 1929. (*Up to Now*)

STANISLAVSKY, CONSTANTIN, *My Life in Art*. Boston, Little, Brown, and London, Geoffrey Bles Ltd., 1924. Reprinted Harmondsworth, Penguin Books, 1967.

TERRY, ELLEN, AND SHAW, BERNARD, *A Correspondence*, Christopher St. John, ed. New York, Putnam's; London, Constable, 1931. Reissued by Reinhardt, 1949. (Terry-Shaw)

YEATS, J. B., *Letters to His Son W. B. Yeats and Others (1869–1922)*, Joseph Hone, ed. (Memoir by Hone and Preface by Oliver Elton.) London, Faber & Faber, 1944; New York, Dutton, 1945. (Yeats)

MANUSCRIPT

I thank the following institutions and individuals for permission to quote from the manuscript material indicated in their possession or under their charge:

The New York Public Library at Lincoln Center, The Dance Collection: The Craig-Duncan Collection (CD)

Irma Duncan Rogers and The New York Public Library at Lincoln Center, The Dance Collection: The Irma Duncan Collection

The Humanities Research Center, The University of Texas, Austin: The Craig Archives (Texas)

The University Library, Department of Special Collections, University Research Library, University of California, Los Angeles: The Craig Collection (UCLA)

The Bibliothèque Nationale, Paris: Collection Gordon Craig

The Cambridge University Library and Lord Kennet: The manuscript diary of Kathleen, Lady Kennet

The Museum of the City of New York: Theatre and Music Collection

Howard L. Holtzman and Leon Bahr: Isadora Duncan Memorabilia (HLH-LB)

Arnold Rood: The Arnold Rood Collection (Rood)

Donald Oenslager: The Collection of Donald Oenslager (Oenslager)

In addition, my thanks go to the following for valuable help: Wayne Andrews, William Abrahams, Boris Alperovici, Leon Bahr, Fredrika Blair, Mrs. W. A. Bradley, Laetitia Cerio, Morton N. Cohen, Douglas Cooper, Robert Craig, Angus Duncan, David Farmer, Jane Friedlaender, Penelope Gilliatt, Norbert Guterman, Elizabeth Harrower, Lillian Hellman, Howard L. Holtzman, William Justema, Pauline Kael, Alfred Kazin, Manuel Komroff, Vera Krasovskaya, Louis Kronenberger, Dan H. Laurence, David Lees, Therese Marberry, Roger Manvell, Norman Marshall, Donald Oenslager, Genevieve Oswald, John Ramington, Irma Duncan Rogers, Arnold Rood, George Seldes, Victor Seroff, Lynn Strong, Ben Syfu, Robert Sonkin, Henry B. Thielbar, Robert Wennersten, Mme. Olivier Ziegel. And to the following institutions: The Library of Congress; The National Gallery of Art, Washington (H. Lester Cooke); The State Theatrical Museum of Leningrad (G. Z. Mordison); The Hermitage Museum, Leningrad (Albert Kostenevich); The Baker Library, Harvard University Graduate School of Business Administration (Anna S. Longfellow); The British Broadcasting Corporation; Dansmuseet (The Dance Museum), Stockholm (Erik Näslund); S. Fischer Verlag (J. Hellmut Freund); The Museum of Modern Art, New York (Library and Department of Film); Yale University Library (Richard Warren, Jr., Curator, Historical Sound Recordings); The New York Public Library (The Theatre Collection and many other departments);

The New York Society Library; Stanford University Library (W. R. Moran, Archive of Recorded Sound).

I thank the following publishers and authors' representatives for permission to quote from the listed works:

Alfred A. Knopf, Inc., and London Management: Edward Craig, *Gordon Craig: The Story of His Life* (published in England by Gollancz). Copyright © 1968 by Edward A. Craig.

E. P. Dutton & Co. and Christy & Moore Ltd.: J. B. Yeats, *Letters to His Son W. B. Yeats and Others* (published in England by Faber & Faber).

John Murray (publishers) Ltd.: Lady Kennet—Kathleen, Lady Scott, *Self-Portrait of an Artist, From the Diaries and Memoirs of Lady Kennet—Kathleen, Lady Scott* (1949)

Oxford University Press: Martin Shaw, *Up to Now.*

Liveright: Isadora Duncan, *My Life.* Copyright renewed 1955 by Liveright Publishing, New York.

Notes

Notes

p. vi / The "series of manuscript notes" is from a private collection.

p. ix / The three quotations on this page are from, respectively, a letter from Craig to Martin Shaw (in Texas, as are all the Craig-Shaw letters); a private collection; and Craig's BBC radio talk on Isadora, 1952, partially printed in *The Listener*, June 5, 1952.

CHAPTER ONE

p. 3 / *two films*: Isadora Duncan, *The Biggest Dancer in the World*, starring Vivian Pickles (BBC, 1966), and *Isadora* (title later changed to *The Loves of Isadora*), starring Vanessa Redgrave, 1968–69.

p. 4 / *see her dance*: Texas.

p. 4 / *her father's early disappearance*: But before his disappearance the talented, unstable Joseph Charles Duncan had written, among other poems, one which, Isadora says in *My Life*, "was in a way a prophecy of my entire career." She probably means the poem "Intaglio: Lines on a Beautiful Greek Antique," which is printed in *Outcroppings*, a selection of California verse edited by Bret Harte, and of which two stanzas have been reprinted by Sheldon Cheney in his edition of Isadora's *The Art of the Dance*:

> On the temple-crownèd summit
> Breaks again the rising day,

Streaming with its dawning brightness
Down the waters of the bay!

See, the centuried mist is breaking!
Lo, the free Hellenic shore!
Marathon—Plataea tells us
Greece is living Greece once more.

p. 4 / *a small house in San Francisco*: The city of San Francisco has placed a commemorative plaque on the building now on the site of Isadora's birthplace, the northwest corner of Geary and Taylor streets. Of the inaugural ceremony on May 31, 1973, Irma Duncan, who delivered an address, has written: "It was a real 'Isadora Happening,' with some young girls in tunics and bare feet dancing on the sidewalk to music by Schubert, in the roaring traffic, to and in her honor. Speeches, cheers, tears. Isadora would have loved it! It was, literally, right down her alley! Amazing how her name can still arouse the people. I finished my speech saying: 'Her memory will not be dimmed by time.' " (Irma Duncan, correspondence)

p. 4 / *rhythm of the waves*: copy of letter from I.D. to Paul Kennaday, 12 May 1925. (Irma Duncan Collection)

p. 6 / *Frau von Parmentier*: taped interview with Hedwiga Reicher, by Howard L. Holtzman and Leon Bahr. (HLH-LB)

p. 6 / *Red Indians*: *My Life*, 134; quoted in Seroff, 60.

p. 7 / *persistent labour*: EGC to Martin Fallas Shaw. (Texas)

p. 7 / *personality*: small notebook by EGC, formerly in the possession of EAC.

p. 8 / *The Fate of Eugene Aram*: an adaptation (1873) by W. G. Wills of Thomas Hood's poem, *The Dream of Eugene Aram, the Murderer* (1831). Henry Irving often recited the poem. There exists an earlier *Eugene Aram, or, St. Robert's Cave*, by William T. Moncrieff (1832). (Rood)

p. 10 / *Beerbohm noted*: David Cecil, *Max*; quoted in EAC, 99.

p. 10 / (Footnote) *Ted caught socialism*: As printed in Terry-Shaw, 75, the passage is punctuated ". . . He is susceptible and catches most things, against the advice of my friends. I allow him . . ." but that is almost certainly a misreading of the autograph.

p. 10 / (Footnote) *approximately . . . $12,000 in 1973*: Mr. Henry B. Thielbar; Ann S. Longfellow, Reference Department, Baker Library, Harvard University Graduate School of Business Administration.

p. 14 / *Kessler had seen*: This passage and the other quoted passages that follow are from EAC, 178–88.

p. 15 / (Footnote) EGC to Martin Fallas Shaw, 2 January 1905. (Texas)

p. 16 / *together*: In the Craig Archives, Texas, one can read the correspondence—Brahm indignant, Craig lofty (at times top-lofty) though polite to Emil Heilbut, Brahm's conciliatory assistant.

p. 16 / *above ground*: EGC to MFS. (Texas)

p. 17 / *Yeats*: "To a Friend whose Work has come to Nothing."

CHAPTER TWO

p. 19 / *it was spoken*: small notebook by EGC (as above).

p. 20 / *GENIUS too*: *Index*, 256–7.

p. 21 / *one writer on Isadora*: Fredrika Blair (work in progress).

p. 21 / *Book Topsy*: Texas.

p. 23 / *BBC radio talk*: 1952; partially printed in *The Listener*, June 5, 1952.

p. 24 / *his copy of* My Life: Bibliothèque Nationale.

p. 25 / (Footnote) *There was a whole room for me*: *Index*, 275.

p. 25 / (Footnote) *destroyed*: Jane Friedlaender, correspondence.

p. 27 / *a chilling way*: That the displeasure of Isadora's mother, particularly, was something to reckon with in these early days of the affair is illustrated by a letter from Elise de Brouckère to Craig [CD 291] dated Berlin, 4 January 1905:

Dear Mr. Craig

I did *not* ask the Schweitzers about Mrs. Duncan and I shall not ask them, as I don't want to know. I could not stand up for Isadora as I have done several times before in similar cases, as I am getting tired of it all. I should always stand up for a friend, but Isadora is not my friend, and I don't see why people should not have the courage of their acts. Why should the legend go about that Isadora spent those nights with me? I was most surprised to hear it, and said quite openly that I knew nothing about it. Except the night of the excursion to Potsdam Isadora has not slept here. Please don't answer me. Let us not speak about it. I am always pleased to see you, and I hope you shall come and see me.

E. de Brouckère.

Beside the words "as I have done several times before in similar cases," Craig has written: "Oh fie, Miss E de B." And in *Book Topsy*: "Miss de B then wrote me a letter— which is not fair to Topsy— even if it be true & I hardly think it is true." In fact, there is no indication that there had been "similar cases."

Mrs. Duncan must have been valiant, if perhaps a little frightening. When she lay dying in Paris in 1922, Elizabeth wrote to Isadora, who was in Moscow [April 11; Irma Duncan Collection]:

Dear Isadora:

Called to Paris by three telegrams from Raymond, I arrived within forty-eight hours to find our mother waiting with a shining face and in great beauty of expression for the final parting with her children. That she made this long journey from California for this purpose I know— otherwise she would never have had the strength. She has a great courage and beauty— fresh and young she looks as I sit watching her fight her last on this earth. Her eyes are closed— She cannot speak but I have sat now eight days watching the extraordinary expressions passing over her— Just wonder fills me and I am surprised to find us, her children, so small. We are all so small beside her simply heroic lines. Why have we so disappointing littleness. She would certainly have wished us other—

She has been the giver. We should all be here with her together— It is my great regret that we are not big enough— She passes on as ever The Leader.

     All Love
       Elizabeth Duncan.

Mrs. Dora Gray Duncan died the next day, April 12, 1922.

Considering the emotional circumstances, Elizabeth may be forgiven her presumption, certainly springing from very deep jealousies and resentments, in including Isadora in the "smallness" of Mrs. Duncan's children.

p. 29 / [*December 19*] *She comes at 12*: This paragraph is a later addition by Craig.

          CHAPTER THREE

p. 37 / My Life: pp. 161–2.

p. 37 / *Bloody Sunday*: Andrew Rothenstein, *A History of the USSR* (Harmondsworth, 1950).

p. 38 / *Very esteemed Fräulein*: HLH-LB.

p. 38 / (Footnote): Mme. Natalia Roslavleva kindly writes from Moscow, "Our new encyclopedias say: 'Aisedora Duncan (properly Isadora).' Krasovskaya, in her book, uses *Isadora* purposely, to establish the proper thing, but for the general reader she still is and will be 'Aisedora.' Essenin knew she was Isadora, but called her 'Sidora'—it is a kind of peasant version, it sounded very charming. When I speak to Russians, I say 'Aisedora'—there is no other way, otherwise they will look inquiringly at you and make round eyes."

The Russian pronunciation of Isadora's name is also mentioned in Seroff.

p. 40 / *Diaghilev has paid them tribute*: quoted in Arnold L. Haskell and Walter Nouvel, *Diaghileff, His Artistic and Private Life* (New York, Simon and Schuster, 1935), 167n.

p. 41 / *conspiring*: N. S. Shebuyev, "The Beethoven Soirée," in *Teatralnaya Rossia*, 29 January 1905.

p. 41 / *From a reading of the notices*: Much about Isadora's debut in St. Petersburg and its aftermath is told in the numerous reviews and articles in St. Petersburg and Moscow newspapers and journals during and after her 1904 visit to the capital. A number of these, together with full or partial, more or less rough, English "working" translations of most of them, are in The Dance Collection of the New York Public Library, available for the first time outside Russia. Most of the original texts, together with explanatory notes, are the gift of Mme. Natalia Roslavleva, to whom I express particular thanks for procuring them for me from Russian libraries. The "working" translations are basically by Norbert Guterman, to whom go equal thanks.

The trend of the articles might be summarized as follows:

Subsequent to the all but unanimous immediate acclaim accorded Isadora in the press for her two performances, a number of purist music critics who had from the outset considered it sacrilegious that the music of the masters be "interpreted" by a dancer, and ridiculous that Greek myths be associated with the music of nineteenth-century composers, were galvanized into vocal opposition; in two articles in the "serious" journal *Slovo* (*The Word*), 15 and 18 December (old-style), and in other articles elsewhere, Isadora's art was strongly attacked on those grounds. It was to counteract what he considered the blindness and injustice of those articles that Alexandre Benois, who loved ballet, and who himself had many reservations about Isadora's "illustrations of classics," published his critique in *Slovo*, 23 December, the finest of all the critiques of Isadora in Russia and an evaluation of what she had to offer the ballet. In addition to the excerpts quoted in the text, one more might be cited:

Miss Duncan advocates a new life in the dance. Perhaps she or her principles could regenerate our ballet. A few years ago, when the theatres were under the direction of Prince S. M. Volkonsky, a group of painters (they were still young at the time) planned to stage Delibes' ballet *Sylvia*, which is musically speaking a work of genius. All the planners were genuine admirers of our official ballet; they worshipped it; but when the new staging began to be worked out in detail, it was immediately obvious that the admirers were going to be destroyers. Already then we aimed at something like Duncan's ideals. The drawings of the ballerinas' costumes, executed by Bakst, directly reproduce Duncan's costume, which he saw only much later. Trying to work out the choreography and the dramatic scenes of the ballet, I continually met with insoluble problems of reconciling the existing routine with the dream I had before me. To translate the Hellenic beauty of Delibes' music into dramatic action while keeping all the conventional turns of the present ballet, to reconcile antique dance with today's amusing, perhaps piquant, but certainly unruly hodge-podge, seemed to me an insuperable difficulty. All my friends and the others who shared my ideas felt as I did—we, the admirers of the ballet, while trying to reform it were in fact destroying it.

p. 44 / *Well, here it is*: Novoye Vremya (*New Times*), 15 December 1904, signed "Y.V."

p. 44 / *It would, of course, have been not only strange*: Birzhevyie Vedomosti (*Stock Exchange Journal*), 15 December 1905. (By Valerian Svetlov)

p. 46 / *Natalia Roslavleva*: Roslavleva, 76–7.

p. 46 / *in Lydia Krasovskaya's words*: Krasovskaya, Vol. I.

p. 46 / *The music of Chopin*: Birzhevyie Vedomosti (*Stock Exchange Journal*), 15 December 1904. (By Valerian Svetlov)

p. 46 / *Rejecting the dead formalism*: ibid., 16 December 1904. (By S. Rafalovich)

p. 46 / *Alexandre Benois has written*: Slovo, 23 December 1904, pp. 5–6.

CHAPTER FOUR

p. 53 / *On the fifth*: confirmation of this date and of many others is found in HLH-LB.

p. 62 / (Note) *after first saying no*: Duncan Dancer, 10 et sq.

p. 62 / (Note) *Craig's comment*: Index, 270.

p. 63 / (Footnote): EAC, 81; small notebook by EGC, formerly in the possession of EAC.

p. 64 / *she may well have seen*: confirmed by Prof. Jeremy Aisenstock via Yuri Slonimsky. (Natalia Roslavleva, correspondence)

p. 65 / *Auer*: Auer wrote his account of the evening in a self-defensive letter to the St. Petersburg newspaper *Rus*. (Natalia Roslavleva, correspondence)

p. 65 / *almost the kindest words*: N. S. Shebuyev, "The Beethoven Soirée" (as above). Fredrika Blair has found one favorable review of Isadora's St. Petersburg Beethoven concert, by L. Vilkin, in the magazine *La Balance*, issue of 25 January 1905. Later, Isadora danced frequently to the Seventh Symphony in the U.S.A.

p. 65 / *Stanislavski*: Stanislavsky, 505–6.

p. 66 / *Moscow* Daily News: for this and other details concerning Isadora's St. Petersburg and Moscow performances of 1905, my thanks to Natalia Roslavleva. The article in *Iskusstvo* is in No. 22560 and signed "Mich. S."

p. 70 / (Footnote) *Elizabeth had power of attorney*: HLH-LB.

p. 72 / [*Magnus*] *suggested*: EAC, 205.

p. 73 / (Footnote) *Much later Craig wrote*: note by EGC on CD 265.

p. 73 / (Footnote) *most inclusive editions*: Alfred Kazin, correspondence.

p. 74 / (Footnote) *recorded by Martin Shaw*: *Up to Now*, 63.

p. 74 / (Footnote) *gas had been turned off*: EAC, 193.

p. 75 / (Footnote) *Duse*: EAC, 202.

p. 75 / (Footnote) *Irma Duncan tells us*: *Duncan Dancer*, 27.

p. 78 / *He wrote later*: *Index*, 270.

p. 78 / *At Breslau where she danced*: Bibliothèque Nationale.

p. 78 / (Footnote) *Craig wrote later*: *Index*, 270.

p. 99 / *read it to Topsy*: *Index*, 274.

p. 101 / *inspired by her dancing*:

I have just finished a book even now published entitled *The Art of the Theatre*, by Edward Gordon Craig.

This book seems to me to contain in little the bomb for an immense explosion of all things which exist as we know them in the theatre. An upheaval so general and so deadly at first it presents to our mind's eye the entire theatres of the world suddenly heaved sky high in the air together [with] pieces of the buildings, shreds of their scenes, tatters of their costumes and finally separate legs, arms, bodies— yea heads of their actors shooting through the air in one wild, chaotic bang! What if this bomb explodes, the last days of Pompei will but seem a scene of mild Sunday amusement in comparison with [the] last days of the theatre as threatened by the flaming torrent of lava from this new Vesuvius Theatre Destroyer. Oh! the comparison is very good— only, the lava of Vesuvius destroyed [and] covered with ashes thousands of feet deep, did it not, a beautiful city and the remains are still beautiful. But when the present great incubus, the present theatre, is destroyed, the ruins, poor ghastly ruins . . . will show us but the tell tale weak foundations of the one great ugly chaotic theatre fraud of today and we will scorn this poor weak remaining foundation and cart away the rubbish leaving clear space.

CLEAR SPACE.

Clear space. The enormous work of destruction is finished, the bomb has done its deadly work. The Vesuvius Theatre Destroyer has completed its ruinous mission. Theatre, scenes, costumes, actors, poets— Yes, laugh ye gods!—poets too! All in the air and clear space at last.

Also*—

Step up Mr. Thrower of deadly bombs, step up Mr. Vesuvius Theater Destroyer, step up Mr. Edward Gordon Craig, we have cleared away the last remaining tatters. Step up now and show us— *what's* to happen next.

At the beginning of Introduction:

This pamphlet is a sketch or part of a large book entitled *The Art of the Theatre*, in which I intend to write chapters on: the scene painter, the costume maker, the actor, the lights, the play, the author, the chorus, the dancer, the action, the gesture, the words, the word inflection, and all these things in their relation to the theatre and in their relation to each other and expressing themselves as one.

What the theatre should be:

The brain and heart of the nation. The reflection point of the nation's highest intellect. The constant mirror of its noblest strivings towards the highest beauty. What was the theatre once? A coming together of thought in its highest form. Action, music and dance. A meeting place of the Nine Muses where each bore an equal share of honour— an equal share— making up a perfect harmony, an absolute balance, presenting to the audience an entire whole— as well as the highest ideal possible of the development of [the] culture of mankind, where they saw the real man, a man who spoke, a man who danced, a man who sang, a man who spoke, danced, sang equally, and an entire production perfectly balanced between words, music, action and dance expressing by these equal means the complete gamut of man's possibilities. From the possibility of mere animal vivacity and power of springing movement upwards to the possibility of emotions, sentiments, and finally to the highest thoughts. In fact the theatre should be the

* This must be the German *also*, "therefore."

perfect expression of man's greatest in every channel, with each channel equal.

What has the theatre become?

The notebook containing this sketch is in the Irma Duncan Collection. A portion was published by Donald Oenslager in his introduction to Arnold Rood's catalogue of the Edward Gordon Craig memorial exhibition at The New York Public Library, 1967.

p. 101 / *harsh words from George Bernard Shaw*: Terry-Shaw, 70; also, an interview with George Bishop in *The Observer* of unascertained date. (Courtesy of Norman Marshall)

p. 103 / *Princess Henry VII of Reuss*: *Duncan Dancer*, 37–8.

p. 104 / *The subscription list mounted daily*: *ibid*.

p. 104 / *telegraphic replies*: HLH-LB.

p. 104 / *Most of the summer*: *Index*, 284–5.

p. 105 / *a contract between himself and Isadora*: Bibliothèque Nationale.

p. 106 / *$2,200 . . . in 1973*: Mr. Henry B. Thielbar; Ann S. Longfellow, Reference Department, Baker Library, Harvard University Graduate School of Business Administration.

p. 107 / *Caesar and Cleopatra*: correspondence in Texas.

p. 110 / (Footnote): The dancing by the children and Isadora at the private performance on July 20 so delighted everyone that it was decided, as a further fund-raising move, to give a public performance by the children alone. This took place in the Theater des Westens in Berlin the afternoon of Sunday, October 29. It, too, aroused enthusiasm. Irma quotes parts of a review from the (Berlin) *National Zeitung*:

> As the curtain rose a sweet little child skipped out onto the stage to a melody by Schumann in a delicate chiffon tunic. With bare feet she tripped lightly and daintily across the carpet . . . and soon there came a second, and then a third elfin figure until the stage was filled with about twenty similar shapes. The images they evoked were of enchanting gracefulness. They floated across and chased each other like iridescent butterflies with multicolored wings, bending, swaying, springing, and dancing like spirits from Oberon's court . . . At times they resembled allegorical figures representing Autumn and Winter, indicating with characteristic but simple gestures the disparate moods of nature.
>
> And again they appeared, this time as angels in long white gowns and wreaths of flowers in their hair striding gravely about. Then followed a very frolicsome dance . . . an animated swarm of colors and small shapes as if a storm wind had tossed the flowers in a meadow

together. [Irma says this was a "Blind-man's buff," choreographed by herself to a *Courante* by Corelli.] . . . Almost everything went along with admirable precision, but every now and then the set figures gave way and the little ones would skip about spontaneously, and this especially was delightful and interesting because it demonstrated conclusively how well they have learned to coordinate their movements . . ." [*Duncan Dancer*, 49]

Elizabeth's failure to "send a loge" to Craig for the October 29 performance was perhaps not accidental: for her, he continued to be a "Bogie Man," and relations between them were always strained. Irma, the chief source of information, portrays Elizabeth as something of a martinet.

The children were almost immediately taken on a tour of German cities, and from now on they were to appear frequently in public, both with and without Isadora. (*Duncan Dancer*, 51 sq.) By 1908 they had danced in twenty German cities, in Belgium and Holland, and in Warsaw and St. Petersburg. The story of the school and its subsequent transformations is told in detail by Irma Duncan in *Duncan Dancer*.

p. 111 / (Footnote): In her "Autobiography," Kathleen, Lady Kennet, tells of being introduced to Isadora by Rodin after Isadora had danced at his birthday party at Meudon in 1903. "Rodin took Isadora's and my hands in one of his and said, 'My children, you two artists should understand each other.' So began a long-lasting relationship of the most unusual order." Those of her remarks about Isadora which cover this brief period in 1905 when they were together in Holland combine information, affection, and rather severe feminine judgment:

As an artist I thought of the dancer as a resplendent deity; as a human being I thought of her as a disgracefully naughty child. As an artist I exulted in her; as a tiresome child I could not abandon her. "Come with me to Brussels," said she, and I went. "Come with me to Berlin," and I went. "Come with me to The Hague." At each place and many more she gave her grand performance. The greatest conductors led the finest orchestras for her; the houses were crowded out. At Liège one night the audience stood up in their seats and waved their hats and roared. I sat quietly on my seat, disposing of my preposterous tears before going round to see that my dancer had her fruit and milk and a shawl over her whilst she cooled off, before facing the wild enthusiasts who surged around the stage-door and yelled their delight.

No friends at all had we in these foreign towns. If pressmen came the dancer was self-conscious and austere, and since she talked nothing but American the interviews were brief. We got up early, ran in any park that was near, and did a few gymnastics. Whatever happened later, and terrible things did happen, at that time the dancer was a healthy, simple-living, hard-working artist, neither beautiful nor intelligent apart from her one great gift for expression. Moreover, she was not musical in the usual sense of the word, though her rhythm could rouse the greatest and the least to delirious rapture. She was open-handed, sweet-tempered, pliable, and easy-going. "Oh, what's the difference?" she would say, if I, who hated to see her put upon, wanted to stand out against over-charges. "What's the difference?" But she ate carefully, and drank nothing ever at this time but water or milk. She was making enormous sums of money. Whatever she may have thought of herself afterwards, at that time she was nothing but a frightened girl. [Kennet, 44]

p. 113 / (Footnote): *Duncan Dancer*, 51.

p. 119 / *Solodovnikov Theatre*: carbon copy of unsigned letter, HLH-LB.

p. 120 / *mine were of* The Mask: *Index*, 285.

CHAPTER FIVE

p. 121 / *nine in Stockholm alone*: Dansmuseet (The Dance Museum), Stockholm; Erik Näslund.

p. 121 / *He records*: *Index*, 286–7.

p. 122 / (Footnote) *Irma Duncan has written*: Irma Duncan Rogers, correspondence.

p. 122 / *As a sort of side-line*: *Up to Now*, 58–61.

p. 124 / *later on in this volume*: Shaw's account in *Up to Now*, 65–76, continues as follows:

The tour now began and we left for Nuremberg. What a contrast to Berlin! The romance of the Middle Ages pervaded the city. The castle, the cradle of the Hohenzollerns, filled me with a kind of romantic awe, built as it is into the solid rock and containing a well of fabulous depth. Even with the aid of a torch I could not see the bottom, and a pebble I dropped (by permission, I hasten to add) took nearly ten seconds before it splashed. This sounds incredible, but I do not think I am exaggerating. The cathedral and churches were what one had always dreamed they would be like. I remember the joy Craig felt in identifying the great door of the cathedral with one of the scenes in Irving's Lyceum production of *Faust*. Irving had journeyed specially to Nuremberg to get this scene painted. Nuremberg is the home of children's toys, and very delightful it was to see them on the booths in the cathedral square. Adjoining the cathedral, built on to it in fact, is the eating-house patronized long ago by Hans Sachs and the Meistersingers, and I ate a meal there of the tiny sausages so beloved by them. The place appeared untouched, and was certainly unspoilt.

Isadora Duncan's music was in dreadful chaos. The band-parts were the despair of my life. They were tattered and torn and very badly cued. As I have not a tidy mind it took me many days to reduce them to some kind of order. The first band rehearsal was a trying affair as I did not understand a word of German. However, one of the violinists happened to be an American and he translated for me. Fortunately the orchestra, the Nuremberg Philharmonic, was a really good one, having as conductor a brother of the composer Max Bruch. The test of an orchestra is its *pianissimo*, and Nuremberg's orchestra was as exquisite as any I have ever heard. The perennial squabble between stage and music desk as to what is *pianissimo*—the cause of endless friction at full rehearsals—therefore did not arise on this occasion. The night came; Isadora Duncan danced in her own divine manner, the music went well, and all was joy. Alas! never again did I have such an orchestra.

Our next town was Augsburg, which is architecturally even more enchanting than Nuremberg, but dull with the hopeless dullness of the provincial garrison town. I had here my first meeting with the German Army, the orchestra being composed of soldiers. They were most anxious to oblige, and I liked them, though their playing was, as might be expected, slightly heavy and mechanical. By this time I had learnt to count up to ten in German and so felt a little more confident. The honest, good-natured fellows settled down to it with a will, and, on the whole, didn't do so badly. After a few minutes one of the clarinets played a wrong note. I stopped and pointed out the mistake. The clarinettist bowed profusely and played the right note, looking at me, as I thought, rather nervously. I smiled my agreement, thinking he must be a little sensitive. All then went well until one of the violins came in a bar too soon. On the mistake being corrected, he also bowed and looked nervous. I put on my kindest expression and the rehearsal proceeded. There sounded a wrong note from the flute and this time the player positively blenched when I spoke. I was utterly mystified until, happening to turn round, I beheld behind me a huge and magnificent person in full military uniform. In his white gloved hand was a cane, which he was shaking in a very threatening manner at the offending flautist. It was the bandmaster. Engrossed in the rehearsal, I had not noticed him at my back. Every time I drew attention to the least mistake he had shaken his fist and glared at the wretched musician.

Five minutes before the evening performance all the orchestra lights suddenly failed and we were in complete darkness. My nice fellows never turned a hair. As if by magic, candles somehow materialized and at a muttered word from the first violinist knives were produced and each player cut his candle at a slope so that it would stand upright on the ledge of his desk. I never saw a contretemps more neatly met. All was ready in time and we had quite a good performance.

Our next halt was at gay, brilliant Munich, and here I had to conduct a really bad theatre orchestra. But there were compensations. One was the most wonderful military band in the great square on Sunday morning; a second that, as Nuremberg is the home of toys, so Munich is the home of lager beer; and after a visit to the Hof-Brau I felt more charitably disposed than before towards my scratchy fiddlers and coarse-toned wind players. Munich also seemed, less happily, to be the home of *l'art nouveau*, and the appalling original-at-all-costs look of the new houses was enough to give one a nightmare.

After a perfectly *schrecklich* band rehearsal I burst into Isadora's sitting-room to complain. I had got as far as 'Of all the putrid orchestras——' when I became aware of a dapper little elderly gentleman sitting on a sofa holding a book of Craig's theatrical designs which Isadora was explaining to him. It was the Grand Duke of Saxe-Meiningen . . .*

The next tour was in Holland and I had to go off in advance to engage orchestras and supervise the musical arrangements. I was very disappointed as I could now count up to fifteen in German and had to start all over again in Dutch. This sort of thing was always happening. As soon as we had been long enough in any country for me to learn to count up to ten with confidence I was moved on to another. I never got to twenty in any part of Europe.

. . . The following morning found me at Haarlem, where I had to rehearse my orchestra, which belonged to that city. It was a worse

---

* George II, Duke of Saxe-Meiningen (1826–1914), was a modern-minded stage director, admired by Craig and others of the avant-garde. From 1870 to 1890 he had supported and commanded his own renowned troupe, called the "Meininger," which was based at the Ducal Theatre in his own court city of Meiningen and toured European capitals.

orchestra than the one at the theatre in Munich. For one thing, the
rehearsal conditions were a farce. The players were seated in a room
that just held them comfortably—and no more. The din was, of course,
deafening and nothing came out clearly. It was impossible to tell
whether the players were sounding the right notes or not. Added to
this, every single one of them had a lighted cigar in his mouth, even
the wind players. The atmosphere may be more easily imagined than
described. I did my best with them, but the performances were rough
and heavy. It seemed to be our fate to have the Haarlem Orchestra
wherever we went in Holland. Finally things got so bad that one
night Isadora Duncan stopped and told the audience that she could
not go on. (This was naturally jolly for me!) The orchestra sat and
listened to her with Dutch phlegm. At the end of her speech she
relented and said she would try the dance again. But this I refused to
do, and we went on to the next item and somehow finished the
programme.

. . . Isadora Duncan was an enormous success in Amsterdam, despite
the Haarlem Orchestra. The extraordinary thing is that all countries
in Europe, England has welcomed her least. In St. Petersburg, Berlin,
Paris, Vienna, Munich, Copenhagen, Stockholm, Amsterdam, her name
was a household word among even the ordinary public. But in London
she was almost, judged by her own standard, a failure. Thrice she
danced in London. Once before she was known, the second time at
the height of her European fame, the last time just after the war. On
none of these occasions was the response what one would have expected. I am almost inclined to think that a possible reason for this is
that there was no sex appeal in Isadora's dancing. That in itself was new
and strange, and the English public does not like anything new or
strange.

. . . Craig and I spent one glorious afternoon skating on a large sheet
of water near Amsterdam. At that time he wore a voluminous Italian
cloak, and I a Bavarian one with a hood. The Dutch, who are nothing
if not conventional in their clothes, gazed at us with much wonder.
Eventually an elderly skater came up to us, raised his hat, bowed, and
said solemnly, 'Sirs, they do not understand you'. Having delivered
himself of this sentence he again bowed politely and skated off.

Isadora Duncan was booked for The Hague, so thither we all betook
ourselves, dogged by the Haarlem Orchestra. How I cursed them!
but there was no other available.

. . . Having learned to count up to ten in Dutch—a hard task, particularly the articulation of the word for seven—I was naturally pushed

off to Denmark. Copenhagen is a delightful city and I thoroughly enjoyed my visit there. The Town Hall chimes I always meant to use, but never did so until 1927 when they quite suddenly came to mind as I was composing a carol for *The Oxford Book of Carols*, and I based my tune upon them. I made a pilgrimage to the house of Hans Christian Andersen, loveliest of all writers of fairy tales. I was told that he disliked children, but I refuse to believe this.

Here again Isadora Duncan was a huge success, and the orchestra was at least better than the Haarlem.

We next went to Stockholm, where, as there is fortunately little difference between Danish and Swedish, my vocabulary served me equally well. Of all the cities I have visited, with perhaps the exception of Florence, Stockholm stands out in my memory as the most beautiful. When I arrived the ice was breaking up in the river and fiords, for spring was just about to begin. What a lovely spring that was! It was so warm that I used to lie out in the woods and bask.

We could not be in Stockholm without seeking out Strindberg. Of Craig's writings on the theatre he had said 'I find golden words in them'. After much difficulty, for no one seemed to know where he lived, we found him in a flat that might have come straight from the Earl's Court Road. An old woman opened the door just enough to say 'Nej'. Strindberg saw nobody. However, our names—or rather Craig's name—sufficed as passport and we were shown into a conventionally furnished drawing-room, which went oddly with our ideas of the writer. However, he came in and took us into his study, which made us feel better. August Strindberg was then about fifty, fine looking and magnificently built, with broad shoulders and a deep chest, and a mass of fair, greying hair. His eyes and his whole expression had an unutterable melancholy, amounting, one might almost say, to melancholia. One peculiarity of his was that he never smiled. He sometimes began to, but invariably checked himself. As he knew no English, and we no Swedish, the conversation had to be conducted in very broken German, eked out with pantomine. Besides being the dramatist of whom Ibsen had said 'Here is one that is greater than I', he was an admirable painter and passionately fond of music, being no mean pianist. He showed us some melodies that he was trying to arrange for a play, and I sat down to the piano and harmonized them, which pleased him very much. He and Craig did most of the talking and I chimed in with 'Ja wohl' now and again, the only German phrase I knew. The conversation was naturally mostly about the theatre. As we took our leave Strindberg said something which we took to mean that he was pleased to have seen us. We fell back upon the useful 'Ja wohl', Teddy Craig rounding it off with a masterly 'Danke sehr'.

Two days after this Craig and I were having lunch in a restaurant when a Swedish artist of our acquaintance who spoke English came up to us and said, 'Strindberg was very disappointed that you never came to dinner yesterday and so were the artists and musicians he had invited to meet you'. It seems that his last words to us as we left his flat were an invitation to dinner on the following evening and we, with our 'Ja wohls' and 'Danke sehrs', had of course given him the impression that we understood and accepted. We did our best to explain, and I only hope Strindberg understood. It was characteristic of him that he would not meet Isadora Duncan, saying, so our friend told her, that he was afraid of her.

p. 124 / *wrote to his third wife*: *Strindbergs brev till Harriet Bosse* [Strindberg's Letters to Harriet Bosse] (Stockholm, 1932), p. 227. (Dansmuseet, Stockholm; Erik Näslund.)

p. 124 / *Albert Engström*: *August Strindberg och jag* [August Strindberg and I] (Stockholm, 1923), pp. 39–40. (Dansmuseet, Stockholm; Erik Näslund.)

p. 125 / *Gothenburg*: *Up to Now*, 79.

p. 125 / *Verein . . . von Isadora Duncan*: The name is given in Isadora Duncan, *The Dance of the Future*, authorized edition (New York, The Bowles-Goldsmith Co., c. 1908); also in HLH-LB.

p. 126 / (Footnote) *A different story*: taped interview with Hedwiga Reicher by Howard L. Holtzman and Leon Bahr. HLH-LB.

p. 127 / *Craig once sought his advice*: Texas.

p. 129 / (Footnote) *The Book is the so-called "Isadora Mappe"*: Craig's original English "poem," one of the few existing copies of which is owned by Mr. Arnold Rood, is reproduced here with Mr. Rood's kind permission. Later, in the volume *Isadora Duncan*, edited by Paul Magriel (New York, Holt, 1947), there appeared an English version of Craig's lines, translated back from the German by George Amberg, who was apparently unable to find the original English. One of the drawings in the Insel-Verlag portfolio, included in the illustrations of the present work, was according to Edward A. Craig redrawn by Gordon Craig from a sketch made from the wings of the theater in Breslau.

INTRODUCTION

Much Noise, and a deep Unrest
∽ Sadness and Discord ∽

Is this in any way the final estimate of the whole?
⌇ The Reality?
Is it then so certain that Life is made up
of four Absurdities?
Is it not far more certain that Life is made up of
Four Beauties ⌇
⌇ of Calmness ⌇ Joy ⌇ Harmony ⌇
Rhythm ⌇ the truest Reality.
And what of the expression of all this ⌇ Art?
Must Pandemonium and Ugliness
ever stand for Strength?
⌇ Must Restlessness be made the Symbol of Life?
⌇ Must a noisy and discordant Sadness spread
itself over the Loveliness of all?
If these are questions, I am not one of the Questioners. ⌇
I have no doubt whatever ⌇
I see Calmness and Beauty both the Strong and the Sweet
advancing now with perfect ease ⌇
All makes way for this spirit ⌇
Nothing can hinder it.
Three marks of a pencil, or three hundred
It is ever the same Picture ⌇
A note sounded, or a fall of notes,
It is the same Song. ⌇
A step, or a hundred steps
It is the same Dance. ⌇
Something put down ⌇
a Record ⌇
Something uttered on that divine theme understood
so easily, and only with ease ⌇
that theme which commences
» *I AM HAPPY* . . . . «
and which ends in
» . . . . *it is Beautiful* «
This is the theme she dances ⌇
Not yet has she depicted a Gloom or a Sorrow unbearable ⌇
For ever it seems Sunlight with her ⌇
The little Shadows themselves are found out
and move away as she passes ⌇
This is the great power.
She comes of the lovely family ⌇

The great Companions ⌒
That Conquering Race which has held up the
World so that it might spin without difficulty.

⌒ The courageous Giants
⌒ the Preservers of Beauty
⌒ the Answerers of all Riddles.

p. 134 / (Footnote) *Reinhardt so admired*: Texas.

p. 134 / (Footnote) Theatre Collection, The New York Public Library.

p. 137 / (Footnote) *published in Dutch*: *Index*, 288.

p. 141 / (Footnote) *Craig had gone to London*: EAC, 214.

p. 144 / (Footnote) *Verkade*: *Index*, 215, 288–9.

p. 146 / *there came a letter from Isadora*: Kathleen's narrative is from Kennet, 61–5.

p. 150 / *actual entries in her diary*: Cambridge University Library, catalogued as "Kennet D/41."

p. 151 / *"I never imagined"*: EAC, correspondence.

p. 153 / (Footnote) *exhibition*: Texas.

p. 158 / (Footnote) *kings and queens*: EAC, correspondence.

p. 159 / *Irma*: *Duncan Dancer*, 61.

CHAPTER SIX

p. 161 / *rather a shy young man*: from Craig's article "On Signora Eleonora Duse," *The Dial*, Vol. LXXXIV, No. 5 (May 1928), pp. 361–71; reprinted in *Life and Letters*, Vol. I, No. 4 (September 1928), pp. 290–304. (Arnold Rood)

p. 161 / (Footnote): Craig wrote to Ellen Terry in 1895:

Dear Mother— I saw Miss Duse last night [in *Camille*]. She is very good for an actor or actress to see don't you think so.

I should like to hear her in English though. Can't you exchange tongues for a day; it would be interesting.

Her wonderful & godlike death. I could not applaud, I could not think of *Duse*, and could only shake with tears & keep as quiet as I could in my seat. It seemed as if there *there* in front of me was a glorious woman going away second by second & when she *went*:— one feels hopeless, everything else seemed to die too. No fall— no noise, not much speech, only that *good* look.

I can hardly think of anything else today.

I find myself sitting still to think of it.

Do you think you could get her to let me see it once *behind*, from the *corner*???? I should appreciate it more than I can say. I should like

to go every night— once more to enjoy it: then to study: I saw
Henry [Irving] today about the tour, & he helped me so kindly, but
for the life of me I couldn't help thinking of Camille & Armand half
the time I was there. No not half but now & then. *My love to you:
Ted.* [Texas]

To anticipate a little, Craig was to write to his mother again about
Duse and *Camille* from Florence, in 1906:

Duse said today— amongst a flood of other things equally courageous
& inspiring— "I have given all my love to 'Camille' when I was
young— *now* it is a past love— all is over— finished— it is the same
with plays as people, one does not love the same person and one cannot
always love the same play, but to *renew* love— that is the secret,
not to hang on to past & dead things— to sweep all past away & to
continually renew"— & not sadly all this but loving, intoxicated with
strength & the future. The words don't convey what was behind it
all— [Texas]

p. 161 / *Duse's daughter*: *Index*, 290–1.

p. 163 / *program note*: reprinted in Rose, 66.

p. 163 / *Rosmersholm, a house of shadows*: In its review of the Duse-
Craig *Rosmersholm* (9 December 1906), the Florentine journal *Il Mar-
zocco* said: "The scenery was by Gordon Craig, a young English painter
of great promise; with its symphonies of greens and blues, its exotic
flavor of slightly fantastic reality, it was well in tune with the Scandinavian ambience of *Rosmersholm*."

The Florentine English-language newspaper, *The Florence Herald*,
printed an interview with Craig on 4 December, headed "A Theatrical
Idealist." Readers were told that he was "closely related to Ellen Terry"
and were given the following resumé of his theatrical ideas:

. . . Mr. Gordon Craig is entirely opposed to the actor-manager
system, which he says prevents proper productions for several reasons
and, above all, because the actor-manager has his little jealousies and
is anxious to shine at all cost, even at that of making his comrades act
badly.

Mr. Gordon Craig wishes to raise the calling of theatrical managers
in public esteem. But first of all the manager must have mind and
training to enable him to grasp all the branches of his art. Especially
must he be able to design scenes, costumes and lighting, and direct
stage movements. He must put unity in what is now divided between
too many hands, often the cause of incongruities. "When this has been

obtained," says Mr. Gordon Craig, "the public will treat our occupation as important."

These and several other Florentine reviews of *Rosmersholm* are in The Theatre Collection of The New York Public Library.

p. 163 / *the Van Looys*: Texas.

p. 163 / *later letter to Shaw*: both letters in Texas, partially printed in EAC, 220, 221.

p. 171 / (Footnote) *Rambert*: Rambert, 36.

p. 178 / (Footnote) *One of Craig's notebooks*: UCLA.

p. 178 / (Footnote) *Mr. Lapidoth*: Texas.

p. 178 / (Footnote) *one of his notebooks*: UCLA.

p. 192 / *telegram that asked him to come to Nice*: Texas, dated Cap Martin, January 23, 1907. Translation in EAC, 222.

p. 192 / (Footnote) *Dear Duse*: Texas.

p. 193 / (Footnote) *in Rotterdam and the Hague*: Texas, EGC to De Nieuwe Muziekhandel, 4 January 1907.

p. 195 / *life of his father*: EAC, 222–3.

p. 197 / *in that lovely city*: Index, 292.

p. 197 / *Loeser and Craig met*: EAC, 229.

p. 199 / *there really was a "Pim"*: Irma Duncan says, " 'Pim' came with Isadora once to the small house near the church in Neuilly, where we children stayed in 1908. A pleasant-looking man with brown hair, brown eyes, smartly dressed all in brown, carrying a brown cane. We children promptly dubbed him *'der braune Mann.'* That was the only time I met him. In I.D.'s life he was only a passing fancy— Moment d'Amour." (Irma Duncan Rogers, correspondence)

p. 201 / (Footnote) *Craig, in an attempt to get Isadora dancing again*: HLH-LB.

p. 217 / "Blake's books" may refer to the lithographic facsimiles of seven of Blake's "Prophetic Books" in the third volume of the Ellis-Yeats *Works of Blake: Poetic, Symbolic, and Critical* (3 vols., London, 1893); or, more probably, to some of the individual facsimiles made by William Muir in the 1880s. Clearly the artists' interest in Blake was not a casual one. See note for p. 256.

p. 225 / *eight recitals in Stockholm*: Dansmuseet, Stockholm; Erik Näslund. Also Texas and HLH-LB.

CHAPTER SEVEN

p. 239 / (Footnote) *Irma Duncan says*: Irma Duncan Rogers, correspondence.

p. 242 / (Footnote) *Miss Kist*: Texas.

p. 253 / *Please answer my letter*: Texas.

p. 255 / (Footnote) *Mr. Loeser*: Charles Loeser was an early collector of Cézanne, and provisions in his will concerning some of his paintings by that master are perhaps of peripheral but intrinsic interest:

"My daughter Matilda Sofia shall be allowed to retain for her use and enjoyment throughout her life, or so long in her lifetime as she may wish to, my paintings by the great French master Cézanne. I give and bequeath, at the death of my said daughter . . . eight of these my paintings by Cézanne, and these the most valuable, to the President of the United States of America and his successors in office for the adornment of the White House at Washington. The President or his delegate shall choose these said eight paintings from among the number in my possession. These paintings should be placed in one or more rooms of the White House in which there are no other paintings. The bottom of the canvas should be at the height of about m: 1.70 from the floor. The pictures should be at a distance from one another, and so placed in relation to the furniture as to seem like apertures in the walls—windows displaying views of the outside. No ropes, or other means by which they are fixed or held in their places, should be left visible. Shown in this way and with due attention to the colour or colours on the walls and elsewhere in this room (or rooms), these pictures will be seen to possess a decorative value of the highest order. Should the President refuse this said gift and bequest, I in this event, with the same reservations as stated hereinabove, give and bequeath these said eight pictures to the United States of America, for the adornment of the building occupied by the Embassy of the U.S.A. in Paris. And should this last said offer meet with rejection I in this event order and direct that these eight pictures shall be sold at public auction in the City of New York and the money resulting from this sale shall be accounted for as belonging to the real residue and remainder of my possessions held or existing outside the Kingdom of Italy."

The eight Cézannes hung for many years in the American Embassy in Paris, & were later lent to the National Gallery of Art in Washington. In 1961 two of them finally entered the White House, chosen by Mrs. Kennedy. At present two are in the White House, two on display at the National Gallery, and four in storage at the National Gallery. [Courtesy National Gallery of Art. Mr. H. Lester Cooke, correspondence, April 1973]

p. 256 / *a different face*: David V. Erdman kindly offers the following observations on Isadora and Craig's quotations from Blake:

> Isadora's quotation from "The Shepherd" [on page 218] merely indicates familiarity with the well-known *Songs of Innocence and of Experience*. But the line she quotes here [page 256] is immediately followed by the line Craig quotes in response (in his letter of late December 1907 [page 282]), in what must have been their source, lines in Blake's letter of 16 August 1803. Blake, wincing under persecution and misunderstanding, was lamenting his uniqueness. Isadora and Gordon Craig, sharing the poem, share its application to themselves.

p. 262 / *I then decided*: Texas.

p. 263 / *She [had] come to Florence* and *we had parted*: Texas.

p. 264 / (Footnote) *I think that I*: private collection.

p. 264 / (Footnote) *Michael Carr was a painter*: EAC, 232–3.

p. 273 / *Mrs. William A. Bradley*: Mrs. Bradley's complete words are:

> Je ne crois pas que l'on puisse parler d'alcoolisme dans le cas d'Isadora. C'est après la perte de ses enfants, de son divorce avec Singer qu'elle s'est mise à chercher parfois dans la boisson le réconfort d'un vague oubli. Elle ne buvait pas lorsqu'elle était heureuse et qu'elle dansait. Ceci dit, elle aimait le champagne Goebler et en buvait lorsqu'elle en avait l'occasion, mais surtout pendant les dernières années alors qu'elle ne dansait plus, se sentait malheureuse et quelque peu délaissée. L'alcool était pour elle un remède agréable et elle le considérait comme tel en refusant par exemple d'en donner à un jeune pianiste accompagnateur, Yasha, qu'elle avait ramené de Russie—sous prétexte qu'il n'était pas malheureux et qu'il n'en avait pas besoin.
>
> Comme vous le savez, nous n'avons pas seulement vendu les Mémoires d'Isadora, mais mon mari les lui a fait écrire et a veillé à leur élaboration.
>
> Nous lui avions donné une secrétaire anglaise à laquelle elle dictait et qui remettait au clair les nombreuses pages qu'elle écrivait elle-même. Isadora était vite devenue pour nous une amie chère. [Mrs. William A. Bradley, correspondence]

p. 279 / *She was a strange* and *Our meeting first of all*: Texas.

p. 280 / *She was filled with enthusiasm*: Texas.

CHAPTER EIGHT

p. 284 / *Lykiardopoulos*: EAC, 252.

p. 285 / *During our talks about art*: Stanislavsky, 507.

p. 286 / *In his copy*: Bibliothèque Nationale.

p. 288 / *Isadora wrote to Stanislavski*: Stanislavski archives at the Moscow Art Theatre, as translated in Seroff, 115.

p. 288 / *on a picture post card*: Irma Duncan Collection. Ellen Terry and James Carew were "judicially separated" after two years. (Manvell, 311)

p. 295 / *I began to persuade*: Stanislavsky, 507.

p. 295 / *approximately $1,250 in 1973*: see note for page 105. EAC (272) says that Craig received, for *Hamlet*, a total of "only £1,500 plus expenses." The purchasing power of the £1,500 was approximately that of $35,700 today.

p. 295 / *The telegram arrived*: EAC, 245–6.

p. 296 / (Footnote) *an August 11 telegram*: Texas.

p. 303 / *her grandson Robert*: Robert Craig, conversation.

p. 303 / *Irma Duncan's memory*: *Duncan Dancer*, 80.

p. 303 / *another letter written by Isadora*: This letter was first printed in Manvell, 325–6.

p. 304 / (Footnote): Two letters written from New York in 1908 by the painter J. B. Yeats to his son W. B. Yeats in Ireland show Isadora from the points of view of Yeats and some of his American friends, including John Quinn, the lawyer and collector of modern art:

> *Grand Union Hotel, New York*
> *Nov. 11th, 1908*

. . . I met Mrs. Isadora (Duncan) privately and just missed seeing her dance in private. She is self-contained and regulates her life according to her own ideas, being, as such women are, free to do so. She said some daring things in a rather captivating way. People are much divided about her merits, the rival parties hating each other like the Capulets and the Montagues. The young girls are full of enthusiasm for her. Those a little older puzzled and somewhat shocked, the elder ladies furious. She herself wears a bonnet with a long veil and has a most demure expression.—

> *N.Y.*
> *Undated (1908)*

. . . Just at the time when I got your letter about Mrs. P. Campbell I was meeting Isadora Duncan. It seems to me that *great personal charm*

only belongs to people who are self-contained or when they are so.
They only can say and do the *spontaneous* and the *unsuspected*—everything Miss Duncan says is curiously interesting; it never becomes
'chatter', such as those things you quoted from Mrs. Campbell, but
which probably I should not have thought 'chatter' had I been under
the influence of Mrs. Campbell's physical beauty. An American lady
a few days ago described Miss Duncan as old, at least middle-aged, and
'homely' (American for ugly). I first met her in a restaurant and at once
understood her to be the oddest and most unexpected person in the
world. She forms her own plans and is quite indifferent to what people
think or say, for that reason she is never aggressive just as she makes no
effort to conciliate any one. I met her twice in private and since that I
saw her (from her own box) dancing in the biggest theatre, and on the
biggest stage in N. York—a figure dancing all alone on this immense
stage—and there again you felt the charm of the self-contained woman.
Several people said: Is it not like watching a kitten playing for itself?
We watched her as if we were each of us hidden in ambush. I don't
wonder that at first New York rejected her—she stood still, she lay
down, she walked about, she danced, she leaped, she disappeared, and
re-appeared—all in curious sympathy with a great piece of classical
music, and I did not sometimes know which I most enjoyed, her or the
music. America's great sculptor* was in the box and led the appreciation.
   Quinn says she dances like a cow &c. and has beefy limbs—he also says
that tho' he paid for a very expensive seat he only stayed half an hour.
Exactly! he did not stay long enough. The other day there was an
enormous house who were as still as if we were in church, except that
no one coughed. Genée the rival dancer whom Quinn likes so much has
the other *the lesser charm*, that she is eager for appreciation and popular
affection, and is indeed a delightful creature—*you wish her to succeed*,
in the other case you are dominated. [Yeats, 115–16]

p. 305 / *This time*: private collection.
p. 306 / *One night I looked at him*: My Life, 170–1.
p. 307 / *I love you*: as translated in Seroff, 117.
p. 310 / (Footnote) *Isadora's version*:

   That tournée in Russia was as successful as were the others, but it
was marked by an event that might have been tragic, though it turned
out rather comic. One afternoon Craig walked in to see me, and for a
short moment I was on the verge of believing that nothing mattered . . .
but just the joy of seeing him again.

* Perhaps Augustus St. Gaudens.

Craig was in high spirits, in the midst of creating his Hamlet for the Stanislavsky Art Theatre. All the actresses of the Stanislavsky troupe were in love with him. The actors were delighted with his beauty, geniality and extraordinary vitality. He would harangue them by the hour on the art of the theatre and they did their best to follow all his fantasies and imaginings.

When I saw him I felt again all the old charm and fascination, and things might have ended differently had it not been that I had with me a very pretty secretary. On the last evening, when we were just leaving for Kieff, I gave a little dinner to Stanislavsky, Craig, and the secretary. In the middle of the dinner Craig asked me if I meant to remain with him or not. As I could not answer, he flew into one of his old-time rages, lifted the secretary from her chair, carried her into the other room and locked the door. Stanislavsky was terribly shocked, and did his best to persuade Craig to open the door, but when we found that persuasion had no effect, we could do nothing but go to the station, where we found the train had left ten minutes before.

I returned with Stanislavsky to his apartment, and we tried to talk mournfully of modern art, and to avoid the subject of Craig, but I could see that Stanislavsky was distressed and shocked by Craig's behavior.

The next day I took the train to Kieff. There I was joined some days later by a rather pale and somewhat shaken secretary. When I asked her if she did not want to stay in Russia with Craig, she said emphatically that she did not, so we returned to Paris . . . [*My Life*, 235–6]

p. 312 / *even before meeting Singer*: Seroff, 176.

CHAPTER NINE

p. 313 / homme de goût: Oenslager.

p. 313 / *birth certificate*: Irma Duncan Collection.

p. 313 / *clashes of temperament*: The Collection of Donald Oenslager contains a letter from Isadora to Paris Singer which illustrates their difficulties:

68, Rue Chauveau, Neuilly*
[Probably summer, 1912]

Please if I really bore you as you say, if you are tired of me, or if there is anyone else that you would rather take to Greece please dear

* On the stationery of her Neuilly studio Isadora retained the device of flowers, designed by Craig.

tell me *now*— I am far too proud to care to stay with you if you do not want me— I love and adore you and I love little Patrick— the same, perhaps even more, when he cries as when he is amusing. Please tell me the *truth* if you do not care for me any longer— if there is anyone else— it would be much *kinder* to say so— I find it too humiliating to take everything from you and have you say that in return I only annoy you. If I am no longer any pleasure to you, tell me now. There is still time for me to cable to America and accept their offer. The idea that you may continue to see me from a sense of duty and not from love makes me quite sick & desperate. You know I never accepted anything from anyone before I met you— and I cannot *bear* the idea of taking things from you unless you love me. Answer me the *truth*—
     Isadora

p. 314 / *Le Théâtre du Beau*: The story of this project is drawn from documents in the collection of Donald Oenslager, which also contains several letters from Isadora to Singer and typescript variants of certain pages in *My Life*.

p. 316 / *calling card*: Texas.

p. 317 / *Elena Meo*: EAC, 282–3.

p. 317 / *Ellen Terry's birthday*: Rood, Exhibition, 46.

p. 318 / *newspapers*: e.g., *The New York Times*, April 20, 1913. (Museum of the City of New York)

p. 319 / *Isadora my dear*: addressed to Miss Isadora Duncan, 68 Rue Chauveau, Neuilly-sur-Seine, Paris, France. (Irma Duncan Collection)

p. 320 / *But Mother dear*: HLH-LB. Partially printed in EAC. Copy in Texas.

p. 322 / *Seroff*: Seroff, 193.

p. 322 / *Isadora dear*: addressed to Miss Isadora Duncan, Villa St. Stephanie [*sic*], Corfu, Greece. Printed in Seroff. (Irma Duncan Collection)

p. 324 / *Dear Miss Duncan*: letter in Irma Duncan Collection.

p. 329 / *I thought I would go*: Texas.

p. 330 / *By the way*: Texas.

p. 330 / *After her child died*: Texas.

p. 330 / *Never need she*: private collection.

p. 330 / *Edward A. Craig*: correspondence.

p. 330 / *Isadora was not maternal*: private collection.

p. 331 / *Irma Duncan's words*: Irma Duncan Rogers, correspondence.

p. 331 / *"Topsy & I: Murder"*: Texas.

p. 332 / *We emerged safely*: Robert Craig, conversation.

p. 332 / *I went over the Alps*: My Life, 290–1.

CHAPTER TEN

p. 339 / *It's the fashion*: letter written in Vence, 2-VIII-55. (Irma Duncan Collection)

p. 339 / *these accounts*: two biographies, those by MacDougall and Seroff, are in the Bibliography.

p. 340 / *So Dougie*: Vence, 20-V-55. (Irma Duncan Collection)

p. 340 / (Footnote) *Jean Cocteau*: letter to Glenway Wescott.

p. 347 / *a walk of a lifetime*: "Topsy & I: Murder." (Texas)

p. 347 / *Then came the terrible trial*: Book Topsy, 33. (Texas)

p. 347 / *I loved her*: Texas.

p. 347 / *We hurt each other*: private collection.

p. 348 / (Footnote) *Bellevue*: Seroff, 248.

p. 349 / *first French edition*: Arnold Rood kindly supplies the following information: "It was to appear in France in 1914 published by F. Riede et Cie. but didn't because of World War I. Possibly three proof copies exist. Date of translation is given as 1916 when it was published in Paris in 1920 by Editions de la Nouvelle Revue Française." The book was several times reissued in France—in 1942, 1943 and 1951.

p. 349 / (Footnote) *McCormick*: EAC, 294.

p. 350 / *You know she was as silly*: letter to Irma Duncan, Vence, 20-V-55. (Irma Duncan Collection)

p. 351 / *In a letter*: Herein Isadora also expresses dislike of some of Diaghilev's new ballets: "The Russian ballet are hopping madly about in Picasso pictures. Very silly— sort of Epileptic gymnastic with no strength or center. I often wonder to what domain of Insanity they will hop to next— If that is Art I prefer Aviation." The great vogue in Paris for Diaghilev's ballets is said to have diminished Isadora's public.

p. 351 / *The Foreword to* The Theatre Advancing: This was a specially printed edition of the foreword which Craig had written for the London edition of *The Theatre Advancing* (Constable, 1921). The tribute to Isadora is on pp. LXII–LXIII. The first (American) edition, without the foreword, but with a dash (*The Theatre—Advancing*), had been published in Boston in 1919. (Rood)

p. 352 / *through a friend*: Richard Wallace.

p. 352 / *I and Isadora strode along*: private collection.

p. 355 / *Topsy sur les Planches*: courtesy Mrs. William A. Bradley.